How organizations learn

Roger Miller

November 1996

> The 'learning organization' is a metaphor, with its roots in the vision of and the search for a strategy to promote individual self-development within a continuously self-transforming organization.
>
> (Ken Starkey, *Introduction*)

Organizational learning has emerged as a dominant theme in the 1990s. This book of readings brings together a collection of articles looking at the link between leadership and learning and the impact that organizational structure and management strategies have upon the learning process. Arguing that organizational learning is a vital key to efficiency, innovation and competitiveness, the articles look at the issues and challenges involved and discuss how the learning process can be made a reality.

The book is divided into three parts. Part I, *Strategy as a learning process*, examines the sources of learning and knowledge creation, linking learning to new models of organization, managerial work and strategy. Part II, *Learning, structure and process*, examines leading edge studies of organization structures and management processes that create learning with a particular focus on innovation as a crucial aspect of organizational effectiveness. Part III, *Leadership and the learning process*, looks at the link between leadership and learning. All of the chapters reinforce the concept that learning and knowledge are vital strategic resources, crucial to competitive advantage.

Edited by Ken Starkey, who also provides summaries of the key themes raised in each section, and presenting articles from leading writers in the field, including Senge and Peters, this volume will be seen as a state-of-the art summary of the debates in this area.

Ken Starkey is Professor of Strategic Management at the School of Management and Finance, University of Nottingham.

How organizations learn

Edited by Ken Starkey

(1996)

INTERNATIONAL THOMSON BUSINESS PRESS
I(T)P An International Thomson Publishing Company

London • Bonn • Boston • Johannesburg • Madrid • Melbourne • Mexico City • New York • Paris
Singapore • Tokyo • Toronto • Albany, NY • Belmont, CA • Cincinnati, OH • Detroit, MI

How organizations learn

© 1996 Ken Starkey

First published 1996 by International Thomson Business Press

I(T)P A division of International Thomson Publishing Inc.
The ITP logo is a trademark under licence

British Library Cataloguing in Publication Data
A catalogue record for this book is available from the British Library

Library of Congress Cataloguing in Publication Data
A catalogue record for this book has been requested

First printed 1996
Typeset in the UK in Palatino by LaserScript, Mitcham, Surrey
Printed in the UK

ISBN 0–415–12609–6
ISBN 0–415–12610–X (pbk)

International Thomson
Business Press
Berkshire House
168–173 High Holborn
London WC1V 7AA
UK

International Thomson
Business Press
20 Park Plaza
14th Floor
Boston MA 02116
USA

Contents

Figures

Tables

Introduction

Nothing succeeds like success but, alas, nothing fails like success! This paradox captures the managerial uncertainties of our time. Success breeds both success and a complacency that blinds us to the need for change. The key to lasting success is to bridge the gap between working on the continuous improvement of what the firm currently does well and innovating for the future. Innovation frequently challenges our existing mind-sets. This joint challenge – efficiency and innovation – requires unceasing learning. Learning is the creation of useful meaning, individual or shared. Learning generates knowledge which serves to reduce uncertainty. This book – which gathers together key readings that help us to understand and manage the challenge of organizational learning – argues that learning and knowledge are major strategic resources, crucial to competitive advantage.

An emphasis upon learning requires that we critically examine our assumptions about organization and strategy. Until recently, the Western view of management has been based upon a top-down view that has bred conservatism. Management was seen as a science. Frederick Taylor's 'scientific management' provided a dominant image of organization (Morgan, 1986). Information was 'out there', to be gathered and processed rationally in search of the 'one best' answer. This view was challenged, but not demolished, by writers such as Henry Mintzberg (1973) who showed that successful managerial work was based upon skills that it was hard to codify and upon intuitions that were hard to make explicit. Mintzberg's work focused our attention upon the actual nature of managerial work, in particular that of top management. The 1980s saw a plethora of studies extolling the virtues of leadership, most notably Peters and Waterman's (1982) best-selling *In Search of Excellence*. The lure of the powerful charismatic leader was strong at a time when new competition from Japan had demonstrated the vulnerability of Western firms.

Hubris was at hand and new models of world class manufacturing arrived from the Far East to change our view of the world. To the champions of leadership, it was the heroic efforts of charismatic supermen (and the occasional superwoman) that were crucial to the regeneration of Western industry. But the emphasis upon this form of leadership reinforces the top-down image of organizations as no more, or less, than the reflection of heroic leaders, dependent for their success upon the vitality of the founding vision. The 1990s are producing a sea change in the Western thinking about management. This change is coalescing around the concept of the 'learning organization'. The new clothes of the 1980s heroic view of leadership have been found to be transparent (Sonnenfeld, 1988).

This should not surprise us. In 1961, the psychiatrist W.R. Bion synthesized the findings of the work of the London Tavistock Institute for Human Relations into a book whose main theme is the nature of authority and leadership. Bion analyses what he describes as the basic assumptions of group members about authority. People expect leadership. Human relations are characterized by a basic dependency need. In situations where leadership is withheld, group members regress into infantile behaviour. But dependency upon the leader is itself infantile to the extent that individuals refuse to take responsibility for the creation of conditions that impinge upon their well-being, 'real work' in Bion's sense.

The emphasis upon an elite few as the fount of all knowledge is a source of some amusement to Japanese commentators. Their view of business success is more democratic, based upon the contributions of a whole range of 'little brains' as opposed to a limited, and finite, number of 'big brains'. Womack et al. (1991), in what Business Week described as the 'best current book on the changes reshaping manufacturing', demonstrate that the Japanese model of 'lean production' results in a better, more cost-efficient product, higher productivity and greater customer loyalty. The hallmarks of lean production are teamwork, communication and the efficient use of resources. Workers are given responsibility for the control of their own work. Lean production is premised upon worker and managers learning a broader set of skills than they do in the West and in applying these creatively in a team setting rather than in a rigid hierarchy with the leader at the apex.

The 'learning organization' is metaphor, with its roots in the vision of and the search for a strategy to promote individual self-development within a continuously self-transforming organization. Learning is associated with the capacity for continuous transformation, based upon individual and organizational development. The subject of individual learning has received much attention in psychology but organizational learning, which draws upon the integration of the sum of individuals' learning to create a whole that is greater than the sum of its parts, is far less understood. In the learning organization human resource development strategy is central to strategic management. Excellent organizations, we increasingly realize, depend upon the commitment of their people in a context where cost constraints require that the human resource is utilized to its fullest capability. Strategy formation is quintessentially a learning process. The learning company is 'design-led', 'as befits an "information age" in which ideas provide the engines of the new industrial order' (Pedler *et al.*, 1989: 7).

This book aims to contribute to the debate about leadership and the learning organization by bringing together a variety of readings that enable us to understand the potential synergy between leading and learning and how organization structure and management process impact upon learning. Its context is the changing nature of organization and strategy in an era of globalization of business, more intelligent competition, increasingly demanding customers, major technological change and growing cultural diversity. The book is divided into three parts. Part I, 'Strategy as a learning process', examines the sources of learning and knowledge creation, linking learning to new models of organization, managerial work and strategy. In particular, it suggests that learning (or its absence) directs the logic of organization development and provides a sense of fundamental purpose for successful organizations. Part II, 'Learning, structure and process', examines leading edge studies of organization structures and management processes that create learning. In particular, it focuses upon innovation as a crucial aspect of organizational effectiveness – with particular reference to product development – and analyses how management development can open up new potential for corporate transformation. Part III, 'Leadership and the learning process', makes explicit the link between leadership and learning. Learning, it suggests, is the key to management innovation. The quality of leadership, embodied in the top management team process, determines the organization's ability to learn.

REFERENCES

Bion, W.R. (1961) *Experiences in Groups*, London, Tavistock.
Mintzberg, H. (1973) *The Nature of Managerial Work*, New York, Harper & Row.
Morgan, G. (1986) *Images of Organization*, Beverly Hills, Sage.
Pedler, M., Boydell, T. and Burgoyne, J. (1989) 'Towards the learning company', *Management Education and Development*, 20, 1, 1–8.
Peters, T. and Waterman Jr, R.H. (1982) *In Search of Excellence*, New York, Harper & Row.
Sonnenfeld, J. (1988) *The Hero's Farewell*, New York and Oxford, Oxford University Press.
Womack, J.P., Jones, D.T. and Roos, D. (1991) *The Machine that Changed the World*, London and New York, Rawson Associates/Macmillan.

Part I
Strategy as a learning process

Introduction

Part I starts with a challenge to the reader. In 'The knowledge-creating company', Ikujiro Nonaka argues that the only reliable source of competitive advantage is knowledge. Successful strategy is integrally linked to knowledge creation. The future belongs to those organizations which can create new forms of knowledge and can translate this knowledge into action via new technological knowledge embodied in products and processes. But the knowledge he is describing lies not outside the organization, to be discovered and processed. It is latent in the organization itself, in its memory and in its potential. The key to unlocking this source of competitive advantage is to create a sense of identity between employee and organization and to tap into the commitment that is thus generated.

Nonaka uses empirical examples of managers in action to articulate an image of strategy as learning in practice. Articulation – the conversion of tacit knowledge into the explicit – is a crucial category in his model. The explicit can be used as the vehicle for the socialization of new recruits into the reality of your business. But the process does not stop with making the tacit explicit. Accepted and articulated ways of doing things, standard operating procedures, and the mental models upon which they rest, are constantly challenged to create new metaphors (such as Honda's challenge to its product development teams 'Let's gamble') that lead to new ways of thinking about products. In the Honda case, the outcome was a totally new car concept, simultaneously 'short' and 'tall'. This concept contradicted the existing dominant logic of car design with its acceptable parameters set as 'long and low'. Challenges require new forms of language to disrupt conventional thinking. The very notion of metaphor depends upon constructive conflict, the attempt to hold together two ideas that seem at odds with each other but that, considered together, lead to new possibilities of thought.

Nonaka's metaphor of management as chaos recalls the philosopher Nietzsche's comment that the thinker needs to contemplate and tolerate chaos to bring forth a new thought equivalent to a 'dancing star'. He emphasizes the importance of information being freely available to all employees, the very antithesis of top-down management with its drip-feed of information on a 'need to know' basis. In knowledge-rich organizations, to continue the liquid metaphor, employees are 'immersed' in/'deluged with' information. There are abundant opportunities to replenish their own information-creation capacities. The role of management is to provide employees with a conceptual framework that helps them make sense of such information. Senior managers probe the defences of their employees, looking for ways to stimulate their hunger for new learning.

Top managers do not provide answers. The answers lie in the minds of front-line employees. No one is more expert in the realities of a company's business than they are. Top managers challenge them with questions in an open-ended dialogue: What are we trying to learn? What do we need to know? Where should we be going? And, perhaps the most profound and challenging, who are we? While front-line employees deal with what is ('real work'), senior managers address the issue of what ought to be. Senior managers are romantics, in search of the ideal, not the hard-headed pragmatists who prosper in Western companies. They develop the ideals of the organization. Middle managers then have to interpret these ideals and translate them into practice. They manage the conflict that necessarily arises when individuals, as they must do if they are to survive, challenge the status quo.

In the next chapter in Part I, 'Beyond the rational model', Tom Peters and Robert Waterman critically address our over-reliance upon the notion of management as an analytical activity, arguing that business education, encapsulated in the Master of Business Administration (MBA) degree, has damaged our ability to think strategically. The preoccupation with rational thinking, they argue, needs to be balanced by a new concern with 'vision'. The analytic tools of strategy formulation need to be viewed in the light of the problems of strategy implementation. As one (in)famous *Fortune* survey of the early 1980s highlighted, only a very small proportion of strategic plans ever work in practice, a finding that is elaborated in Henry Mintzberg's (1993) recent critique of strategic planning. Indeed, Mintzberg heralds the demise, the 'fall' of planning as a strategy input.

Peters and Waterman's critique does not imply that management should be or is irrational (although, even under a veneer of apparent reason, it frequently is). What the authors highlight is how much the rational approach to management leaves out of the equation governing successful management practice. Facts, they argue, are important. But over-complex, inflexible analysis is wrong-headed. Planning at the expense of action ('paralysis by analysis') cannot work because real work implies the translation of thought into practice. Peters and Waterman also suggest that, alongside reason, we have to incorporate love into the management process – love of what we produce and a passion for our work. What is lost in the obsession with specialization, standardization, efficiency, productivity and quantification is the concern for getting things done, for moving an organization forward. Top management's role is to set the parameters for this moving forward, for future direction, to focus attention on what is important, to steer a consistent course through myriad unpredictabilities and distractions. Planning is, at best, a tool to aid the management process, a focus for dialogue about future alternatives. It should not be an end in itself.

Peters and Waterman orientate their critique of management orthodoxy around an argument for a paradigm shift. The notion of paradigm draws upon the seminal work of the philosopher of science, Thomas Kuhn (1970). Kuhn argues that scientific enterprise is distinguished at any one point in time by what he terms a 'dominant paradigm'. This paradigm is the foundation stone of conventional wisdom and 'normal' science. Scientists share a set of common beliefs about the world. At epochal turning points in the history of science these paradigms are challenged by new knowledge. The champions of this new knowledge – if they survive the outrage of their peers and the wider community – create a new sense of the future. For example, there was a crucial shift in astronomy when the Copernican view of the universe (with the sun at its centre) replaced the Ptolemaic view that the earth was the universe's centre.

We are witnessing a major paradigm shift in our thinking about management with the focus moving from a 'hard', 'scientific', content-oriented approach to a processual 'softer', more people-focused view. In Kuhnian terms, the 'normal science' of management has been found wanting. It no longer encompasses the rules of what Abernathy and his Harvard colleagues (Abernathy et al., 1981) call the new competition. What is needed is a world-view that seeks to accommodate the new global business environment. The dominant paradigm promulgates the virtues of size/scale, cost/efficiency, conformism/groupthink, abstraction/heartlessness, decision-making/planning, control/structure, discipline/punishment, overcomplexity/inflexibility. The new paradigm emphasizes quality/ value/service, faith/creativity, experimentation/fluidity, communication/ informality, values/culture, adaptation/change. Peters and Waterman champion an aesthetic, intuitive design process, where the concept of design encompasses product and process, organization struc- ture and restructuring, and guiding values.

In the next chapter, 'Beyond the cowboy and the corpocrat', Rosabeth Moss Kanter challenges us to reconsider both the sources of competitive advantage and our image of leadership in a business context that is simultaneously Olympic Games and *Alice in Wonderland*. In the croquet game in Wonderland everything changes its shape with bewildering rapidity and the rules of the game change without notice. Kanter suggests, like Peters and Waterman, that the old corporate forms and processes are obsolete. She suggests four new management principles: focus, speed, cooperation and flexibility. Of these, the primary guiding principle is to focus upon one's core business competence as the basis of synergy between different businesses.

The role of leadership in this context is to ensure that people reflect upon and discover what they do best and work to do it better. Successful companies of the future will tend to be less diversified than traditional corporations. Managements are exhorted to become 'lean' not 'mean', to avoid a macho (usually male) style of management that encourages damaging internal competition. This view does not deny the importance of competition. Rather, it points out the possible dysfunctions of competition that is construed as a zero-sum game, the survival only of the fittest. Management has to combine internal competition with commitment to overarching goals of survival and shared prosperity. The focus on core competence also leads to new modes of alliance formation, for example with contracting out of non-core activities, but again in relationships of cooperation and a spirit of mutual benefit with suppliers. Cooperative behaviour requires unprecedented degrees of information-sharing, both internal and external, and a communication process to support this. A core value of the new corporation championed by Kanter is innovation.

Kanter describes the new form of organization for the future as 'inside-out', with a simultaneous loosening of internal relationships through strategies such as spinning off, and a tightening of formerly loose relations with other entities such as suppliers. Others have talked of emerging forms of organization in terms of 'flexible specialization' (Piore and Sabel, 1984), small specialized firms focused upon core skills/competences and using flexible forms of contracting to buy in services supplement this core. Miles and Snow (1986) talk of network organizations, core firms at the nexus of a dynamic array of relationships, elements of which are activated as necessitated by particular projects. These new forms of organization are entrepreneurial rather than bureaucratic. Their competitive advantage is dependent upon the ability to exploit opportunities on an *ad hoc* basis. Indeed, they recall elements of what Mintzberg terms the 'adhocracy' (1979). The bureaucracy – Mintzberg calls it 'the machine bureaucracy' to emphasize its mechanical, routine aspects – only functions well in environments with known routines, uniformly provided. Bureaucracy fails in dynamic, unpredictable situations.

We are living through the unfolding of major changes that affect individual lives and social systems. Kanter contrasts post-entrepreneurial organizations with old-style 'corpocracies'.

Corpocracy	*Post-entrepreneurial organization*
position-centred	person-centred
status or rank is critical	authority derives from expertise
repetition-oriented	creation-oriented
rules-oriented	results-oriented
pay for status	pay for contribution
formal structures	fluid relationships
restrict the flow of information	expansion of information
seek ownership and control	seek leverage and experimentation
stability-based	renewal-oriented
order, uniformity, repetition	creativity and deal-making

At the individual level, successful careers now depend upon the ability to adapt to the new post-entrepreneurial corporate environment. Adaptation is contingent upon the individual's skill in recreating him/herself through continuous learning. The majority can no longer expect life-time careers and need to think of their working lives as a sequence of working projects, probably with increasing number of employers. This creates the social dilemma of the tension between the organization's new need for flexibility and the individual desire for security.

There is also a broader societal issue of who is responsible for whose learning? Individuals will have to take more responsibility for life-time learning but this learning is likely to be less company-specific and company-led. A burning issue is: what institutions will step into the vacuum that the dwindling of long-term relationships between organizations and individuals creates? The other side of the coin here is the dilemma experienced by those 'fortunate' enough to remain in secure employment. As the numbers in this group dwindle, the pressures these individuals experience increases. Work overload, the pressures to perform in organizations that are increasingly complex in terms of the learning and knowledge they require to remain competitive, create growing tensions between work and personal life. Families face either the pressures of adapting to a world with less work and far greater uncertainty of supply *or* of increasing work demands.

Kanter suggests a new kind of leadership to guide us through the new corporate (or post-corporate) landscape which combines the skills of organization man/corpocrat (discipline) and those of the maverick/cowboy (entrepreneurial zeal). The new leaders must learn to operate without the support of bureaucracy and hierarchy. They must know how to compete *and* cooperate. High ethical standards are required, in situations of increasing ethical ambiguity. Managers must combine self-confidence with humility, they must live like athletes, constantly training, upgrading their skills, loving learning. From their learning they must create a new vision of corporate life and communicate the values upon which successful strategy will depend.

One can think of managers as the architects of organization, encouraging the creation and diffusion of new knowledge and nurturing those ideas that hold the greatest capacity for organizational renewal. The building material of organizational architecture is the process of human interconnection. 'Whether an organization is a "new construction" or a "renovation," it must be brought into being through a complex process of human interaction that involves hundreds and often thousands of people' (Nadler *et al.*, 1992: 13). New information technologies function as 'structural material', analogous to concrete or steel in physical constructions, and make new previously unthinkable architectures, such as network organizations, realizable. Leaders can be thought of as 'master builders', highly skilled individuals who combine the knowledge of architect, building contractor and construction manager.

Janson (1991: 84) defines architecture as 'the art of shaping space and human needs and aspirations'. Organizations, like architecture, provide spaces (physical and psychic) which provide the context for the achievement of aspirations. Their 'layout', including, crucially, managerial mental maps, guide and facilitate or hinder and frustrate this achievement. If they are to endure, new designs should be ahead of their time when they are planned, otherwise they will not be in keeping with future times (Rasmussen, 1991). Architecture is a social rather than a solitary act. Sometimes paintings are achieved by a team of artists, the master artist and his/her apprentices, but usually they are produced by a single artist wrestling with his/her materials and personal vision. Architecture is the outcome of a large number of people working together to achieve the vision of the architect. The architecture analogy recalls Peter Drucker's story of the three labourers on a building site, told to illustrate the importance of a sense of mission in organizations. When asked what they were doing, one said that he was breaking stones. Another said he was earning a living. A third told the questioning passer-by that he was helping to build a cathedral!

Kanter's chapter recalls Philip Selznick's pioneering work on leadership (Selznick, 1957) in which he makes a crucial distinction between administrative management and institutional leadership, a distinction that echoes through later work, such as Kotter's (1990), which contrasts leaders and managers. To 'institutionalize', according to Selznick, means to infuse organizations with values. Values form the basis of commitment so that organizations cease to be merely technical devices, composed of tasks, procedures and technologies. For the committed member, organizations are a valued necessity and belonging to one is a crucial part of self-identity. Organizations can be 'engineered'. Institutions are the 'receptacles of group idealism'.

It is the institutional element that Peter Vaill examines in the next chapter, 'The purposing of high-performing systems'. Vaill develops

Selznick's argument that high performance depends upon a sense of purpose and the systems' view of organization as responsive and adaptive organisms. Successful organizations are social systems imbued with the art of the long view (Schwartz, 1991). Vaill's purpose is to substantiate his claim that the definition and clarification of purposes is a fundamental part of strategic management and a key feature that explains the effectiveness of high-performing systems (HPSs). HPSs are characterized by high levels of commitment and motivation and by strong clear leadership. Purpose serves as the basis for cooperation (Barnard, 1938).

In many organizations top management fails to confront the issue of basic purpose, yet a crucial top management responsibility is to engender purpose. Effective leadership transforms doubt into purpose, thus creating the psychological basis for cooperative action. Purpose is encapsulated in shared pictures composed of perceptions of environmental demands, the needs and expectations of organizational members, evolving technologies and organization structures that both divide responsibilities and condition communication. In conditions of extreme environmental turbulence 'paradigm leadership' is vital. As the ground on which we base our beliefs moves, so should the basic paradigms and images we use to organize experience.

'Purposing' describes the process by which leaders induce clarity, consensus and commitment regarding the organization's basic purposes out of an ongoing stream of 'proposings'. Purposing is about the establishment, clarification and modification of purposes. Leaders inculcate belief, transform doubts and embody purpose. People become clear why the system exists and their roles in it. Purposing concerns the articulation of the grounds for basic strategic decisions. For example, a clear sense of purpose allows one to forgo options. It forms the basis for communication and discipline. It allows people to see how their organization differs from others. Leaders are felt, themselves, to be committed to the organization for the long term. They are not merely 'tourists', passing through (see Starkey, Chapter 20 in Part III).

Purpose thrives on myths and stories. HPS leadership relies upon the integration of time, feeling and focus. Leaders are focused, in the myriad calls upon their time and attention, upon a limited number of key issues and variables. Vaill's advice to leaders is: 'Seek to do what is right and what is needed (Focus). Commit your energy to it (Time). Invest your whole psyche in it (Feeling).' The problem of over-absorption is that strength of feeling can blind a leader to the changing needs of an organization as its environment evolves. This problem becomes more acute, the more turbulent the environment. Systems can 'drift' into irrelevance. Core competences can become core rigidities (Dougherty, 1992). In these circumstances, top management has become myopic and has lost its ability to see that the meanings it has built up and the purposes it has fostered have become maladaptive. They have lost their ability to learn and fail to perceive the need to refocus. This situation is examined by Chris Argyris in the next chapter, 'Skilled incompetence'.

Skilled incompetence occurs when managers use practised routine behaviour (skill) to produce unintended consequences (incompetence). Managers fail to create the vision and the strategy they intend. Between desire and reality falls the shadow. Managers fall into a skills trap by failing to test their own assumptions. The exercise of skill precludes problem resolution and strategy realization. This form of incompetence occurs when managers do not talk to each other. Organizational defensive routines – policies and acts designed to avoid the necessary pain of confronting the roots of failure – drive out interpersonal exchanges. Attitudes, assumptions and actions create self-fulfilling prophecies and 'self-sealing' processes. These are projected onto others who are blamed for the impasse faced by the organization.

To surmount this stalemate, people must be willing to air their hidden agendas, to face their own blindspots and to learn new skills. Managers have to confront their own defensiveness. Argyris recommends various practical methods for facilitating this self-questioning process. People have to be taught how to step back from the hurly-burly of the day-to-day to create time for reflection and reflexiveness in their interactions with others. They need to create a moratorium on substantive issues to improve their management process by learning new skills of self-inquiry. Paradoxically, the solution to the problem of skilled incompetence is 'unlearning'.

The next chapter, by Arie de Geus, 'Planning as learning', describes how one of the world's most successful companies, Shell, came to view planning as a process of learning. According to de Geus, companies survive because they create a harmonious relationship with their business environment through a cycle of learning – about survival when times are tough, and about self-development in less turbulent times. Long-term survival depends upon effective and continuous learning and the ability to translate learning into action and change. Strategic learning depends upon the sharing of information and quality of the learning experience through which management teams change their mental models of the company and its industry context, including market dynamics and the moves of competitors. De Geus identifies one of the most important themes of this book, that the learning level of management teams is frequently the Achilles' heel of organizational learning, particularly when the guiding principle of organization is functional specialization.

The speed of learning and change depends upon organizational factors such as culture and structure. Underlying de Geus's argument is the basic premise that the learning process is a crucial source of competitive advantage. Indeed, he argues that the ability to learn faster than competitors may be the only sustainable source of competitive advantage. The critical management task, if you accept this premise, is to accelerate learning. A successful learning experience confirms or leads to the reshaping of managers' mental models of their business. Models structure our experience of 'reality'. Learning is a multi-stage process composed of cycles of information collection, communication, absorption, digestion, confirmation and action. De Geus focuses upon the role of the planning team in the learning process. Planners in Shell act as facilitators, catalysts and accelerators of the learning process. Learning needs to be translated into real work by those who have the power to act. In Shell this means the operating company management teams.

Spurs to learning include changing existing rules or suspending them. Rules constitute the 'glue' of organization. Planning is conceptualized as a playful challenge to existing ways of doing things. Play is synonymous with meaningful work. In the play of planning we create new ways of understanding the world and of working. Computer simulation can be a useful form of play. Information technology can be used to create increasingly sophisticated 'microworlds', alternative 'virtual' realities. Through interaction in virtual space we can discover what we need to know, what we need to learn. The planner can act as an internal consultant or external consultants can be used to make explicit and to challenge the status quo.

The final chapter in Part I, C.K. Prahalad and Richard Bettis's 'The dominant logic: A new linkage between diversity and performance', addresses the issue of the link between managerial knowledge and strategic action. This is analysed from the perspective of strategy content and also in terms of the conditions that create logics of managerial thought. The starting point of the chapter is the vexed relationship between diversity and performance. The authors argue that there is a dominant logic (a dominant general management logic) that provides the linkage between strategy (diversification) and performance. This dominant logic consists of managers' mental maps developed through years of experience of a firm's core business. Industries too have dominant logics in the sense described by Grinyer and Spender (1979) as industry recipes – managers' mental maps of the rules of competition in particular industries. Diversification into different business arenas requires different mental maps based upon learning the new rules of competition in these industries.

Most important to strategic success – competitive advantage – are the mental maps of top management, the dominant coalition in organizations (Hambrick and Mason, 1984). Managers approach events not like newborn babies for whom everything is confusion. Managers' mental maps dictate what they expect. They process events through existing knowledge systems or schemas, beliefs, theories and propositions based upon previous learning. Interpretation is based upon expectations of the patterning of events by the dynamics of particular industries. (In a later article, Prahalad examines how Japanese firms gain competitive advantage by ignoring the existing rules of competition in the creative destruction of new rules – Hamel and Prahalad, 1989.) Schemas allow managers to optimize their use of time by providing the search rules that lead to timely decisions. Schemas are defined as general mental structures that 'store' the shared and dominant general management logic of firms and industries. This logic informs critical decisions such as resource allocation across the value chain. The dominant logic is both a knowledge structure and a set of management processes elicited by the appropriate stimuli. As such, it both enables and constrains action.

How these logics are created and sustained can be analysed from a variety of learning perspectives. Behavioural psychology suggests operant conditioning. Behaviour that was effective in the past persists into the present and the future because it has been rewarded. However, these behaviours may be inappropriate for new businesses or in changing environments. This view of learning suggests that it takes time to learn new behaviours and for a new dominant logic to emerge. The psychology of pattern-recognition is also useful here. The best chess players make their decisions by comparing events in the game they are playing with patterns from previous games. They ask themselves 'What worked before?', adapting their strategy to an emergent pattern of events rather than applying a 'grand' strategy from the start. But the effectiveness of this strategy depends upon a fixed set of rules. In the 'game' of business, the pattern-recognition that managers have built up through experience ceases to be useful when the rules of the game change. Similarly, cognitive psychology suggests that decisions display distinct cognitive biases.

Applying these principles to management, when managers are faced by uncertain and complex environments they often rely upon a limited number of heuristic principles, based upon a dominant logic, thus simplifying the decision process. In new circumstances such as diversification, uncertainty increases but the same heuristics tend to be applied, with negative results. In times of change, top managers must learn how to revise or discard dominant logics. The problems of Western firms in mature industries such as steel and automobiles in the face of new competition indicates how difficult and lengthy this process can be. Changes in business variety in the direction of greater complexity, either through major structural changes in an industry with new competition operating according to new rules – such as just-in-time management and network principles of organization – or through the acquisition of a new business, present a major challenge to the existing dominant logic. The ability of a firm to cope with strategic variety depends upon the range of skills of its top management team and its ability to develop new logics of action as the business context requires. Recent emphasis on the importance of strategic focus – for example Peters and Waterman's 'back to basics' injunction, suggests that we over-elaborate our range of activity at our peril.

Prahalad and Bettis agree with de Geus's view that the ability of a firm and its top management team to learn is a critical aspect of the capability to manage strategically. The limited research evidence available in this area suggests that crisis is the main trigger to a change in dominant logic. Changes in top management personnel may also have the same effect but here there is less evidence available. Existing and entrenched logics may resist efforts of new managers to change them. Unlearning must take place to open up psychic space for the drawing of new mental maps but, ironically, the greater past success the more difficult the unlearning process!

REFERENCES

Abernathy, W., Clark, K.B. and Kantrow, A.M. (1981) 'The new industrial competition', *Harvard Business Review*, September–October, 69–77.

Barnard, C.I. (1938) *The Functions of the Executive*, Cambridge, Mass., Harvard University Press.

Dougherty, S. (1992) 'A practice-centered model of organizational renewal through product innovation', *Strategic Management Journal*, 13, Special Issue, Summer.

Grinyer, P.H. and Spender, J.-C. (1979) 'Recipes, crises, and adaptation in mature businesses', *International Studies of Management and Organization*, 9, 113–133.

Hambrick, D.C. and Mason, P.A. (1984) 'Upper echelons: The organization as a reflection of its top managers', *Academy of Management Review*, 9, 193–206.

Hamel, G. and Prahalad, C.K. (1989) 'Strategic intent', *Harvard Business Review*, May–June, 63–76.

Janson, F.W. (1991) *History of Art*, New York, Abrams.

Kotter, J.P. (1990) 'What leaders really do', *Harvard Business Review*, May–June, 103–111.

Kuhn, T. S. (1970) *The Structure of Scientific Revolutions*, Chicago, University of Chicago Press.

Miles, R.E. and Snow, C.C. (1986) 'Organizations: new concepts for new forms', *California Management Review*, 27, 62–73.

Mintzberg, H. (1979) *The Structuring of Organizations*, Englewood Cliffs, NJ, Prentice-Hall.

Mintzberg, H. (1993) *The Rise and Fall of Strategic Planning*, New York, Prentice-Hall.

Nadler, D., Gerstein, M.S. and Shaw, R.B. (1992) *Organizational Architecture*, San Francisco, Jossey-Bass.

Piore, M. and Sabel, C. (1984) *The Second Industrial Divide*, New York, Basic Books.

Rasmussen, S.E. (1991) *Experiencing Architecture*, Cambridge, Mass., MIT Press.

Schwartz, P. (1991) *The Art of the Long View*, London, Century Business.

Selznick, P. (1957) *Leadership in Administration*, New York, Harper & Row.

Chapter 1

The knowledge-creating company

Ikujiro Nonaka

In an economy where the only certainty is uncertainty, the one sure source of lasting competitive advantage is knowledge. When markets shift, technologies proliferate, competitors multiply, and products become obsolete almost overnight, successful companies are those that consistently create new knowledge, disseminate it widely throughout the organization, and quickly embody it in new technologies and products. These activities define the 'knowledge-creating' company, whose sole business is continuous innovation.

And yet, despite all the talk about 'brainpower' and 'intellectual capital', few managers grasp the true nature of the knowledge-creating company – let alone know how to manage it. The reason: they misunderstand what knowledge is and what companies must do to exploit it.

Deeply ingrained in the traditions of Western management, from Frederick Taylor to Herbert Simon, is a view of the organization as a machine for 'information processing'. According to this view, the only useful knowledge is formal and systematic – hard (read: quantifiable) data, codified procedures, universal principles. And the key metrics for measuring the value of new knowledge are similarly hard and quantifiable – increased efficiency, lower costs, improved return on investment.

But there is another way to think about knowledge and its role in business organizations. It is found most commonly at highly successful Japanese competitors like Honda, Canon, Matsushita, NEC, Sharp and Kao. These companies have become famous for their ability to respond quickly to customers, create new markets, rapidly develop new products, and dominate emergent technologies. The secret of their success is their unique approach to managing the creation of new knowledge.

To Western managers, the Japanese approach often seems odd or even incomprehensible. Consider the following examples:

- How is the slogan 'Theory of Automobile Evolution' a meaningful design concept for a new car? And yet, this phrase led to the creation of the Honda City, Honda's innovative urban car.

- Why is a beer can a useful analogy for a personal copier? Just such an analogy caused a fundamental breakthrough in the design of Canon's revolutionary mini-copier, a product that created the personal copier market and has led Canon's successful migration from its stagnating camera business to the more lucrative field of office automation.
- What possible concrete sense of direction can a made-up word such as 'optoelectronics' provide a company's product-development engineers? Under this rubric, however, Sharp has developed a reputation for creating 'first products' that define new technologies and markets, making Sharp a major player in businesses ranging from color televisions to liquid crystal displays to customized integrated circuits.

In each of these cases, cryptic slogans that to a Western manager sound just plain silly – appropriate for an advertising campaign perhaps but certainly not for running a company – are in fact highly effective tools for creating new knowledge. Managers everywhere recognize the serendipitous quality of innovation. Executives at these Japanese companies are *managing* that serendipity to the benefit of the company, its employees, and its customers.

The centerpiece of the Japanese approach is the recognition that creating new knowledge is not simply a matter of 'processing' objective information. Rather, it depends on tapping the tacit and often highly subjective insights, intuitions, and hunches of individual employees and making those insights available for testing and use by the company as a whole. The key to the process is personal commitment, the employees' sense of identity with the enterprise and its mission. Mobilizing that commitment and embodying tacit knowledge in actual technologies and products require managers who are as comfortable with images and symbols – slogans such as Theory of Automobile Evolution, analogies like that between a personal copier and a beer can, metaphors such as 'optoelectronics' – as they are with hard numbers measuring market share, productivity, or ROI.

The more holistic approach to knowledge at many Japanese companies is also founded on another fundamental insight. A company is not a machine but a living organism. Much like an individual, it can have a collective sense of identity and fundamental purpose. This is the organizational equivalent of self-knowledge – a shared understanding of what the company stands for, where it is going, what kind of world it wants to live in, and most important, how to make that world a reality.

In this respect, the knowledge-creating company is as much about ideals as it is about ideas. And that fact fuels innovation. The essence of innovation is to re-create the world according to a particular vision or ideal. To create new knowledge means quite literally to re-create the company and everyone in it in a nonstop process of personal and organizational self-renewal. In the knowledge-creating company, inventing new knowledge is not a specialized activity – the province of the R&D department or marketing or strategic planning. It is a way of behaving, indeed a way of being, in which everyone is a knowledge worker – that is to say, an entrepreneur.

The reasons why Japanese companies seem especially good at this kind of continuous innovation and self-renewal are complicated. But the key lesson for managers is quite simple: much as manufacturers around the world have learned from Japanese manufacturing techniques, any company that wants to compete on knowledge must also learn from Japanese techniques of knowledge creation. The experiences of the Japanese companies discussed below suggest a fresh way to think about managerial roles and responsibilities, organization design, and business practices in the knowledge-creating company. It is an approach that puts knowledge creation exactly where it belongs: at the very center of a company's human resources strategy.

THE SPIRAL OF KNOWLEDGE

New knowledge always begins with the individual. A brilliant researcher has an insight that leads to a new patent. A middle-manager's intuitive sense of market trends becomes the catalyst for an important new product concept. A shop-floor worker draws on years of experience to come up with a new process innovation. In each case, an individual's personal knowledge is transformed into organizational knowledge valuable to the company as a whole.

Making personal knowledge available to others is the central activity of the knowledge-creating company. It takes place continuously and at all levels of the organization. And as the following example suggests, sometimes it can take unexpected forms.

In 1985, product developers at the Osaka-based Matsushita Electric Company were hard at work on a new home bread-making machine. But they were having trouble getting the machine to knead dough correctly. Despite their efforts, the crust of the bread was overcooked while the inside was hardly done at all. Employees exhaustively analyzed the problem. They even compared X-rays of dough kneaded by the machine and dough kneaded by professional bakers. But they were unable to obtain any meaningful data.

Finally, software developer Ikuko Tanaka proposed a creative solution. The Osaka International Hotel had a reputation for baking the best bread in Osaka. Why not use it as a model? Tanaka trained with the hotel's head baker to study his kneading technique. She observed that the baker had a distinctive way of stretching the dough. After a year of trial and error, working closely with the project's engineers, Tanaka came up with product specifications – including the addition of special ribs inside the machine – that successfully reproduced the baker's stretching technique and the quality of the bread she had learned to make at the hotel. The result: Matsushita's unique 'twist dough' method and a product that in its first year set a record for sales of a new kitchen appliance.

Ikuko Tanaka's innovation illustrates a movement between two very different types of knowledge. The end point of that movement is 'explicit' knowledge: the product specifications for the bread-making machine. Explicit knowledge is formal and systematic. For this reason, it can be easily communicated and shared, in product specifications or a scientific formula or a computer program.

But the starting point of Tanaka's innovation is another kind of knowledge that is not so easily expressible: 'tacit' knowledge like that possessed by the chief baker at the Osaka International Hotel. Tacit knowledge is highly personal. It is hard to formalize and, therefore, difficult to communicate to others. Or in the words of the philosopher Michael Polanyi, 'We can know more than we can tell.' Tacit knowledge is also deeply rooted in action and in an individual's commitment to a specific context – a craft or profession, a particular technology or product market, or the activities of a work group or team.

Tacit knowledge consists partly of technical skills – the kind of informal, hard-to-pin-down skills captured in the term 'know-how'. A master craftsman after years of experience develops a wealth of expertise 'at his fingertips'. But he is often unable to articulate the scientific or technical principles behind what he knows.

At the same time, tacit knowledge has an important cognitive dimension. It consists of mental models, beliefs, and perspectives so ingrained that we take them for granted and therefore cannot easily articulate them. For this very reason, these implicit models profoundly shape how we perceive the world around us.

The distinction between tacit and explicit knowledge suggests four basic patterns for creating knowledge in any organization:

1 *From tacit to tacit.* Sometimes, one individual shares tacit knowledge directly with another. For example, when Ikuko Tanaka apprentices herself to the head baker at the Osaka International Hotel, she learns his tacit skills through observation, imitation, and practice. They become part of her own tacit knowledge base. Put another way, she is 'socialized' into the craft.

But on its own, socialization is a rather limited form of knowledge creation. True, the apprentice learns the master's skills. But neither the apprentice nor the master gains any systematic insight into their craft knowledge. Because their knowledge never becomes explicit, it cannot easily be leveraged by the organization as a whole.

2 *From explicit to explicit.* An individual can also combine discrete pieces
of explicit knowledge into a new whole. For example, when a
comptroller of a company collects information from throughout the
organization and puts it together in a financial report, that report is
new knowledge in the sense that it synthesizes information from many
different sources. But this combination does not really extend the
company's existing knowledge base either.

But when tacit and explicit knowledge interact, as in the Matsushita
example, something powerful happens. It is precisely this exchange
between tacit and explicit knowledge that Japanese companies are
especially good at developing.

3 *From tacit to explicit.* When Ikuko Tanaka is able to articulate the foundations of her tacit knowledge of bread-making, she converts it into
explicit knowledge, thus allowing it to be shared with her project-
development team. Another example might be the comptroller who,
instead of merely compiling a conventional financial plan for his company, develops an innovative new approach to budgetary control
based on his own tacit knowledge developed over years in the job.

4 *From explicit to tacit.* What's more, as new explicit knowledge is shared
throughout an organization, other employees begin to internalize it –
that is, they use it to broaden, extend, and reframe their own tacit
knowledge. The comptroller's proposal causes a revision of the company's financial control system. Other employees use the innovation
and eventually come to take it for granted as part of the background of
tools and resources necessary to do their jobs.

In the knowledge-creating company, all four of these patterns exist in
dynamic interaction, a kind of spiral of knowledge. Think back to
Matsushita's Ikuko Tanaka:

1 First, she learns the tacit secrets of the Osaka International Hotel baker
(socialization).
2 Next, she translates these secrets into explicit knowledge that she can
communicate to her team members and others at Matsushita
(articulation).
3 The team then standardizes this knowledge, putting it together into a
manual or workbook and embodying it in a product (combination).
4 Finally, through the experience of creating a new product, Tanaka and
her team members enrich their own tacit knowledge base (internalization). In particular, they come to understand in an extremely intuitive
way that products like the home bread-making machine can provide
genuine quality. That is, the machine must make bread that is as good
as that of a professional baker.

This starts the spiral of knowledge all over again, but this time at a higher level. The new tacit insight about genuine quality developed in designing the home bread-making machine is informally conveyed to other Matsushita employees. They use it to formulate equivalent quality standards for other new Matsushita products – whether kitchen appliances, audio-visual equipment, or white goods. In this way, the organization's knowledge base grows ever broader.

Articulation (converting tacit knowledge into explicit knowledge) and internalization (using that explicit knowledge to extend one's own tacit knowledge base) are the critical steps in this spiral of knowledge. The reason is that both require the active involvement of the self – that is, personal commitment. Ikuko Tanaka's decision to apprentice herself to a master baker is one example of this commitment. Similarly, when the comptroller articulates his tacit knowledge and embodies it in a new innovation, his personal identity is directly involved in a way it is not when he merely 'crunches' the numbers of a conventional financial plan.

Indeed, because tacit knowledge includes mental models and beliefs in addition to know-how, moving from the tacit to the explicit is really a process of articulating one's vision of the world – what it is and what it ought to be. When employees invent new knowledge, they are also reinventing themselves, the company, and even the world.

When managers grasp this, they realize that the appropriate tools for managing the knowledge-creating company look very different from those found at most Western companies.

FROM METAPHOR TO MODEL

To convert tacit knowledge into explicit knowledge means finding a way to express the inexpressible. Unfortunately, one of the most powerful management tools for doing so is also among the most frequently over-looked: the store of figurative language and symbolism that managers can draw from to articulate their intuitions and insights. At Japanese companies, this evocative and sometimes extremely poetic language figures especially prominently in product development.

In 1978, top management at Honda inaugurated the development of a new-concept car with the slogan, 'Let's gamble'. The phrase expressed senior executives' conviction that Honda's Civic and the Accord models were becoming too familiar. Managers also realized that along with a new postwar generation entering the car market, a new generation of young product designers was coming of age with unconventional ideas about what made a good car.

The business decision that followed from the 'Let's gamble' slogan was to form a new-product development team of young engineers and designers (the average age was 27). Top management charged the team with two – and only two – instructions: first, to come up with a product concept fundamentally different from anything the company had ever done before; and second, to make a car that was inexpensive but not cheap.

This mission might sound vague, but in fact it provided the team with an extremely clear sense of direction. For instance, in the early days of the project, some team members proposed designing a smaller and cheaper version of the Honda Civic – a safe and technologically feasible option. But the team quickly decided this approach contradicted the entire rationale of its mission. The only alternative was to invent something totally new.

Project team leader Hiroo Watanabe coined another slogan to express his sense of the team's ambitious challenge: 'Theory of Automobile Evolution'. The phrase described an ideal. In effect, it posed the question: If the automobile were an organism, how should it evolve? As team members argued and discussed what Watanabe's slogan might possibly mean, they came up with an answer in the form of yet another slogan: 'man-maximum, machine-minimum'. This captured the team's belief that the ideal car should somehow transcend the traditional human–machine relationship. But that required challenging what Watanabe called 'the reasoning of Detroit', which had sacrificed comfort for appearance.

The 'evolutionary' trend the team articulated eventually came to be embodied in the image of a sphere – a car simultaneously 'short' (in length) and 'tall' (in height). Such a car, they reasoned, would be lighter and cheaper, but also more comfortable and more solid than traditional cars. A sphere provided the most room for the passenger while taking up the least amount of space on the road. What's more, the shape minimized the space taken up by the engine and other mechanical systems. This gave birth to a product concept the team called 'Tall Boy', which eventually led to the Honda City, the company's distinctive urban car.

The Tall Boy concept totally contradicted the conventional wisdom about automobile design at the time, which emphasized long, low sedans. But the City's revolutionary styling and engineering were prophetic. The car inaugurated a whole new approach to design in the Japanese auto industry based on the man-maximum, machine-minimum concept, which has led to the new generation of 'tall and short' cars now quite prevalent in Japan.

The story of the Honda City suggests how Japanese companies use figurative language at all levels of the company and in all phases of the product development process. It also begins to suggest the different kinds of figurative language and the distinctive role each plays.

One kind of figurative language that is especially important is metaphor. By 'metaphor', I don't just mean a grammatical structure or allegorical expression. Rather, metaphor is a distinctive method of perception. It is a way for individuals grounded in different contexts and with different experiences to understand something intuitively through the use of imagination and symbols without the need for analysis or generalization.

Through metaphors, people put together what they know in new ways and begin to express what they know but cannot yet say. As such, metaphor is highly effective in fostering direct commitment to the creative process in the early stages of knowledge creation.

Metaphor accomplishes this by merging two different and distinct areas of experience into a single, inclusive image or symbol – what linguistic philosopher Max Black has aptly described as 'two ideas in one phrase'. By establishing a connection between two things that seem only distantly related, metaphors set up a discrepancy or conflict. Often, metaphoric images have multiple meanings, appear logically contradictory or even irrational. But far from being a weakness, this is in fact an enormous strength. For it is the very conflict that metaphors embody that jump-starts the creative process. As employees try to define more clearly the insight that the metaphor expresses, they work to reconcile the conflicting meanings. That is the first step in making the tacit explicit.

Consider the example of Hiroo Watanabe's slogan, 'Theory of Automobile Evolution'. Like any good metaphor, it combines two ideas one wouldn't normally think of together – the automobile, which is a machine, and the theory of evolution, which refers to living organisms. And yet, this discrepancy is a fruitful platform for speculation about the characteristics of the ideal car.

But while metaphor triggers the knowledge-creation process, it alone is not enough to complete it. The next step is analogy. Whereas metaphor is mostly driven by intuition and links images that at first glance seem remote from each other, analogy is a more structured process of reconciling contradictions and making distinctions. Put another way, by clarifying how the two ideas in one phrase actually are alike and not alike, the contradictions incorporated into metaphors are harmonized by analogy. In this respect, analogy is an intermediate step between pure imagination and logical thinking.

Probably the best example of analogy comes from the development of Canon's revolutionary mini-copier. Canon designers knew that for the first personal copier to be successful, it had to be reliable. To ensure reliability, they proposed to make the product's photosensitive copier drum – which is the source of 90 per cent of all maintenance problems – disposable. To be disposable, however, the drum would have to be easy and cheap to make. How to manufacture a throwaway drum?

The breakthrough came one day when task-force leader Hiroshi Tanaka sent out for some beer. As the team discussed design problems over their drinks, Tanaka held one of the beer cans and wondered aloud, 'How much does it cost to manufacture this can?' The question led the team to speculate whether the same process for making an aluminium beer can could be applied to the manufacture of an aluminium copier drum. By exploring how the drum actually is and is not like a beer can, the mini-copier development team was able to come up with the process technology that could manufacture an aluminium copier drum at the appropriate low cost.

Finally, the last step in the knowledge-creation process is to create an actual model. A model is far more immediately conceivable than a metaphor or an analogy. In the model, contradictions get resolved and concepts become transferable through consistent and systematic logic. The quality standards for the bread at the Osaka International Hotel led Matsushita to develop the right product specifications for its home bread-making machine. The image of a sphere leads Honda to its Tall Boy product concept.

Of course, terms like 'metaphor', 'analogy' and 'model' are ideal types. In reality, they are often hard to distinguish from each other: the same phrase or image can embody more than one of the three functions. Still, the three terms capture the process by which organizations convert tacit knowledge into explicit knowledge: first, by linking contradictory things and ideas through metaphor; then, by resolving these contradictions through analogy; and finally, by crystallizing the created concepts and embodying them in a model, which makes the knowledge available to the rest of the company.

FROM CHAOS TO CONCEPT: MANAGING THE KNOWLEDGE-CREATING COMPANY

Understanding knowledge creation as a process of making tacit knowledge explicit – a matter of metaphors, analogies, and models – has direct implications for how a company designs its organization and defines managerial roles and responsibilities within it. This is the 'how' of the knowledge-creating company, the structures and practices that translate a company's vision into innovative technologies and products.

The fundamental principle of organizational design at the Japanese companies I have studied is redundancy – the conscious overlapping of company information, business activities, and managerial responsibilities. To Western managers, the term 'redundancy', with its connotations of unnecessary duplication and waste, may sound unappealing. And yet, building a redundant organization is the first step in managing the knowledge-creating company.

Redundancy is important because it encourages frequent dialogue and communication. This helps create a 'common cognitive ground' among employees and thus facilitates the transfer of tacit knowledge. Since members of the organization share overlapping information, they can sense what others are struggling to articulate. Redundancy also spreads new explicit knowledge through the organization so it can be internalized by employees.

The organizational logic of redundancy helps explain why Japanese companies manage product development as an overlapping process where different functional divisions work together in a shared division of labor. At Canon, redundant product development goes one step further. The company organizes product-development teams according to 'the principle of internal competition'. A team is divided into competing groups that develop different approaches to the same project and then argue over the advantages and disadvantages of their proposals. This encourages the team to look at a project from a variety of perspectives. Under the guidance of a team leader, the team eventually develops a common understanding of the 'best' approach.

In one sense, such internal competition is wasteful. Why have two or more groups of employees pursuing the same product-development project? But when responsibilities are shared, information proliferates, and the organization's ability to create and implement concepts is accelerated.

At Canon, for example, inventing the mini-copier's low-cost disposable drum resulted in new technologies that facilitated miniaturization, weight reduction, and automated assembly. These technologies were then quickly applied to other office automation products such as microfilm readers, laser printers, word processors, and typewriters. This was an important factor in diversifying Canon from cameras to office automation and in securing a competitive edge in the laser printer industry. By 1987 – only five years after the mini-copier was introduced – a full 74 per cent of Canon's revenues came from its business machines division.

Another way to build redundancy is through strategic rotation, especially between different areas of technology and between functions such as R&D and marketing. Rotation helps employees understand the business from a multiplicity of perspectives. This makes organizational knowledge more 'fluid' and easier to put into practice. At Kao Corporate, a leading Japanese consumer-products manufacturer, researchers often 'retire' from the R&D department by the age of 40 in order to transfer to other departments such as marketing, sales, or production. And all employees are expected to hold at least three different jobs in any given ten-year period.

Free access to company information also helps build redundancy. When information differentials exist, members of an organization can no longer interact on equal terms, which hinders the search for different interpretations of new knowledge. Thus Kao's top management does not allow any discrimination in access to information among employees. All company information (with the exception of personal data) is stored in a single integrated database, open to any employee regardless of position.

As these examples suggest, no one department or group of experts has the exclusive responsibility for creating new knowledge, in the knowledge-creating company. Senior managers, middle managers, and frontline employees all play a part. Indeed, the value of any one person's contribution is determined less by his or her location in the organizational hierarchy than by the importance of the information he or she provides to the entire knowledge-creating system.

But this is not to say that there is no differentiation among roles and responsibilities in the knowledge-creating company. In fact, creating new knowledge is the product of a dynamic interaction among three roles.

Frontline employees are immersed in the day-to-day details of particular technologies, products, or markets. No one is more expert in the realities of a company's business than they are. But while these employees are deluged with highly specific information, they often find it extremely difficult to turn that information into useful knowledge. For one thing, signals from the marketplace can be vague and ambiguous. For another, employees can become so caught up in their own narrow perspective that they lose sight of the broader context.

What's more, even when employees *do* develop meaningful ideas and insights, it can still be difficult to communicate the import of that information to others. People don't just passively receive new knowledge, they actively interpret it to fit their own situation and perspective. Thus what makes sense in one context can change or even lose its meaning when communicated to people in a different context. As a result, there is a continual shift in meaning as new knowledge is diffused in an organization.

The confusion created by the inevitable discrepancies in meaning that occur in any organization might seem like a problem. In fact, it can be a rich source of new knowledge – *if* a company knows how to manage it. The key to doing so is continuously challenging employees to reexamine what they take for granted. Such reflection is always necessary in the knowledge-creating company, but it is especially essential during times of crisis or breakdown, when a company's traditional categories of knowledge no longer work. At such moments, ambiguity can prove extremely useful as a source of alternative meanings, a fresh way to think about things, a new sense of direction. In this respect, new knowledge is born in chaos.

The main job of managers in the knowledge-creating company is to orient this chaos toward purposeful knowledge creation. Managers do this by providing employees with a conceptual framework that helps them make sense of their own experience. This takes place at the senior management level at the top of the company and at the middle management level on company teams.

Senior managers give voice to a company's future by articulating metaphors, symbols, and concepts that orient the knowledge-creating activities of employees. They do this by asking the questions: What are we trying to learn? What do we need to know? Where should we be going? Who are we? If the job of frontline employees is to know 'what is', then the job of senior executives is to know 'what ought to be'. Or in the words of Hiroshi Honma, senior researcher at Honda: 'Senior managers are romantics who go in quest of the ideal.'

At some of the Japanese companies I have studied, CEOs talk about this role in terms of their responsibility for articulating the company's 'conceptual umbrella': the grand concepts that in highly universal and abstract terms identify the common features linking seemingly disparate activities or businesses into a coherent whole. Sharp's dedication to opto-electronics is a good example.

In 1973, Sharp invented the first low-power electronic calculator by combining two key technologies – liquid crystal displays (LCDs) and complementary metal oxide semiconductors (CMOSs). Company technologists coined the term 'optoelectronics' to describe this merging of microelectronics with optical technologies. The company's senior managers then took up the word and magnified its impact far beyond the R&D and engineering departments in the company.

Optoelectronics represents an image of the world that Sharp wants to live in. It is one of the key concepts articulating what the company ought to be. As such, it has become an overarching guide for the company's strategic development. Under this rubric, Sharp has moved beyond its original success in calculators to become a market leader in a broad range of products based on LCD and semiconductor technologies, including the Electronic Organizer pocket notebook, LCD projection systems, as well as customized integrated circuits such as masked ROMs, ASICs, and CCDs (charge-coupled devices, which convert light into electronic signals).

Other Japanese companies have similar umbrella concepts. At NEC, top management has categorized the company's knowledge base in terms of a few key technologies and then developed the metaphor 'C&C' (for 'computers and communications'). At Kao, the umbrella concept is 'surface active science', referring to techniques for coating the surface area of materials. This phrase has guided the company's diversification into products ranging from soap detergents to cosmetics to floppy disks – all natural derivatives of Kao's core knowledge base.

Another way top management provides employees with a sense of direction is by setting the standards for justifying the value of the knowledge that is constantly being developed by the organization's members. Deciding which efforts to support and develop is a highly strategic task.

In most companies, the ultimate test for measuring the value of new knowledge is economic – increased efficiency, lower costs, improved ROI. But in the knowledge-creating company, other more qualitative factors are equally important. Does the idea embody the company's vision? Is it an expression of top management's aspirations and strategic goals? Does it have the potential to build the company's organizational knowledge network?

The decision by Mazda to pursue the development of the rotary engine is a classic example of this more qualitative kind of justification. In 1974, the product-development team working on the engine was facing heavy pressure within the company to abandon the project. The rotary engine was a 'gas guzzler', critics complained. It would never succeed in the marketplace.

Kenichi Yamamoto, head of the development team (and currently Mazda's chairman), argued that to stop the project would mean giving up on the company's dream of revolutionizing the combustion engine. 'Let's think this way,' Yamamoto proposed. 'We are making history, and it is our fate to deal with this challenge.' The decision to continue led to Mazda's successful rotary-engine sports car, the Savanna RX-7.

Seen from the perspective of traditional management, Yamamoto's argument about the company's 'fate' sounds crazy. But in the context of the knowledge-creating company, it makes perfect sense. Yamamoto appealed to the fundamental aspirations of the company – what he termed 'dedication to uncompromised value' – and to the strategy of technological leadership that senior executives had articulated. He showed how the rotary-engine project enacted the organization's commitment to its vision. Similarly, continuing the project reinforced the individual commitment of team members to that vision and to the organization.

Umbrella concepts and qualitative criteria for justification are crucial to giving a company's knowledge-creating activities a sense of direction. And yet, it is important to emphasize that a company's vision needs also to be open-ended, susceptible to a variety of different and even conflicting interpretations. At first glance, this may seem contradictory. After all, shouldn't a company's vision be unambiguous, coherent, and clear? If a vision is *too* unambiguous, however, it becomes more akin to an order or an instruction. And orders do not foster the high degree of personal commitment on which effective knowledge creation depends.

A more equivocal vision gives employees and work groups the freedom and autonomy to set their own goals. This is important because while the ideals of senior management are important, on their own they are not enough. The best that top management can do is to clear away any obstacles and prepare the ground for self-organizing groups or teams. Then, it is up to the teams to figure out what the ideals of the top mean in reality. Thus at Honda, a slogan as vague as 'Let's gamble' and an extremely broad mission gave the Honda City product-development team a strong sense of its own identify, which led to a revolutionary new product.

Teams play a central role in the knowledge-creating company because they provide a shared context where individuals can interact with each other and engage in constant dialogue and discussion. They pool their information and examine it from various angles. Eventually, they integrate their diverse individual perspectives into a new collective perspective.

This dialogue can – indeed, should – involve considerable conflict and disagreement. It is precisely such conflict that pushes employees to question existing premises and make sense of their experience in a new way. 'When people's rhythms are out of sync, quarrels occur and it's hard to bring people together', acknowledges a deputy manager for advanced technology development at Canon. 'Yet if a group's rhythms are completely in unison from the beginning, it's also difficult to achieve good results.'

As team leaders, middle managers are at the intersection of the vertical and horizontal flows of information in the company. They serve as a bridge between the visionary ideals of the top and the often chaotic market reality of those on the front line of the business. By creating middle-level business and product concepts, middle managers mediate between 'what is' and 'what should be'. They make reality according to the company's vision.

Thus at Honda, top management's decision to try something completely new took concrete form at the level of Hiroo Watanabe's product-development team in the Tall Boy product concept. At Canon, the company aspiration, 'Making an excellent company through transcending the camera business', became a reality when Hiroshi Tanaka's task force developed the 'Easy Maintenance' product concept, which eventually gave birth to the personal copier. And at Matsushita, the company's grand concept, 'Human Electronics', came to life through the efforts of Ikuko Tanaka and others who developed the middle-range concept, 'Easy Rich', and embodied it in the automatic bread-making machine.

In each of these cases, middle managers synthesized the tacit knowledge of both frontline employees and senior executives, made it explicit, and incorporated it into new technologies and products. In this respect, they are the true 'knowledge engineers' of the knowledge-creating company.

Chapter 2

Beyond the rational model

Thomas J. Peters and Robert H. Waterman, Jr

Professionalism in management is regularly equated with hard-headed rationality. The numerative, rationalist approach to management dominates the business schools. It teaches us that well-trained professional managers can manage anything. It seeks detached, analytical justification for all decisions.

It doesn't, however, tell us what the excellent companies have apparently learned. It doesn't teach us to love the customers. It doesn't instruct our leaders in the rock-bottom importance of making the average Joe a hero and a consistent winner. It doesn't show how strongly workers can identify with the work they do if we give them a little say-so. It doesn't tell us why self-generated quality control is so much more effective than inspector-generated quality control. It doesn't tell us to nourish product champions like the first buds in springtime. It doesn't command that we overspend on quality, overkill on customer service, and make products that last and work. The rational approach to management misses a lot.

True, courses in strategy are starting to recognize and address the problem of implementation. Courses in manufacturing policy (although overwhelmingly quantitative) are at least edging back into the curriculum. But the 'technical jocks', as an ex-plant manager colleague calls them, are still a dominant force in American business thinking. Finance departments are still as strong as ever in the business schools. Talented teachers and gifted students in sales management and manufacturing – the core disciplines of most businesses – are still as scarce (and as refreshing) as rain in the desert.

A QUESTION OF BALANCE

We are not against quantitative analysis *per se*. The best of the consumer marketers, such as Procter and Gamble (P & G), Chesebrough-Pond's and Ore-Ida, do crisp to-the-point analysis that is the envy and bedevilment of their competitors. Actually, the companies that we have called excellent are among the best at getting the numbers, analyzing them and solving problems with them. Show us a company without a good fact base – a good quantitative picture of its customers, markets and competitors – and we will show you one in which priorities are set through the most byzantine of political maneuvering.

What we are against is wrong-headed analysis, analysis that is too complex to be useful and too unwieldy to be flexible, analysis that strives to be precise (especially at the wrong time) about the inherently un-knowable – such as detailed market forecasts when end use of a new product is still hazy (remember, most early estimates supposed that the market for computers was 50 to 100 units) – and especially analysis done to line operators by control-oriented, hands-off staffs. Texas Industries' (TI) Patrick Haggerty insisted that 'those who implement the plans must make the plans'; his renowned strategic planning system was overseen by only three staffers, all temporary, all ex-line officers headed that way again.

We are also against situations in which action stops while planning takes over – the all-too-frequently observed 'paralysis through analysis' syndrome. We have watched too many line managers who simply want to get on with their job but are deflated by central staffs that can always find a way to 'prove' something won't work, although they have no way of quantifying why it might work. The central staff plays safe by taking a negative view; and as it gains power, it stamps all verve, life and initiative out of the company.

Above all, we deplore the unfortunate abuse of the term 'rational'. It means sensible, logical, reasonable – a conclusion flowing from a correct statement of the problem. But the word 'rational' has come to have a very narrow definition in business analysis: to wit, the 'right' answer minus all of that messy human stuff, such as good strategies that do not allow for persistent old habits, implementation barriers, and simple human inconsistencies.

Take economies of scale. If maximum process efficiency could be reached if all suppliers produced flawless supplies and produced them on time, if absenteeism were absent, and if sloppy human interaction didn't get in the way, then all big plants would outproduce all small ones. But, as one researcher has pointed out in a rare quantification of part of the problem, whereas unionized shops with 10 to 25 employees average 15 lost-time days from labor disputes per 1,000 employees per year, facilities with 1,000 or more employees lost on average 2,000 days, or a multiple of 133. Take also innovation. A researcher concluded recently that research effectiveness was inversely related to group size: assemble more than seven people and research effectiveness goes down.

As advocates of sound analysis, we wouldn't deny for a moment that the management techniques of the last 25 years have actually been necessary. The best companies on our list combine a tablespoon of sound analysis with a pint of love for the product. Before the rise of the analytical model, the seat-of-the-pants technique was all there was. And it was wholly inadequate for dealing with a complex world. Hence, learning to segment markets, to factor in the time value of many, and to do sound cash-flow projection have long since become vital steps to business survival. The trouble arose when those techniques became the pint, and love of the product the tablespoon. The analytical tools are there to assist – and they can do so admirably – but they still can't make or sell products.

Underlying the whole problem may be a missing perspective: the lack of any feeling for the whole on the part of the so-called professional manager. H. Edward Wrapp of the University of Chicago puts it thus:

> The system is producing a horde of managers with demonstrable talents, but talents that are not in the mainstream of the enterprise. Professional managers are willing to study, analyze and define the problem. They are steeped in specialization, standardization, efficiency, productivity and quantification. They are highly rational and analytical. They insist on objective goals. . . . In some organizations, they can succeed if they are simply good at making presentations to the board of directors or writing strategies or plans. The tragedy is that these talents mask real deficiencies in overall management capabilities. These talented performers run for cover when grubby operating decisions must be made and often fail miserably when they are charged with earning a profit, getting things done and moving an organization forward.[1]

The reason behind the absence of focus on product or people in so many American companies, it would seem, is the simple presence of a focus on something else. That something else is overreliance on analysis from corporate ivory towers and overreliance on financial sleight of hand, the tools that would appear to eliminate risk but also, unfortunately, eliminate action.

'A lot of companies overdo it,' says Wrapp. 'They find planning more interesting than getting out a saleable product. . . . Planning is a welcome respite from operating problems. It is intellectually more rewarding, and does not carry the pressures that operations entail. . . . Formal long-range planning almost always leads to overemphasis on technique.' Fletcher Byrom of Koppers offers a suggestion. 'As a regimen,' he says, 'as a discipline for a group of people, planning is very valuable. My position is go ahead and plan, but once you've done your planning, put it on the shelf. Don't be bound by it. Don't use it as a major input into the decision-making process. Use it mainly to recognize change as it takes place.'

The problem, of course, is not that companies plan but that the planning becomes an end in itself. The plan becomes the truth and data that don't fit the preconceived plan (e.g. real customer response to a pre-test market action) are denigrated or blithely ignored. Gamesmanship replaces pragmatic action. ('Have you polled the corporate staffs yet about the estimate?' was a common query in one corporate operating committee that we observed.)

NO YEN FOR ZEN

The recent deterioration of US business performance relative to Japan and other international competitors has led thoughtful executives, business reporters and academics to search for root causes in the heartland of American management practice. Not surprisingly, the brunt of the attack has been directed at our recent dependence on over-analysis and narrow rationality. Unfortunately, it has been seen as an assault on rationality and logical thought *per se*, as if the solution were to move Ford board meetings to the local Zen centre. But that – it hardly needs saying – is not what we have in mind.

What we mean by the fall of the rational model is really what Thomas Kuhn, in his landmark book *The Structure of Scientific Revolutions*, calls a paradigm shift.[2] Kuhn argues that scientists in any field and in any time possess a set of shared beliefs about the world, and for that time the set constitutes the dominant paradigm.

What he terms 'normal science' proceeds nicely under this set of shared beliefs. Experiments are carried out strictly within the boundaries of those beliefs and small steps toward progress are made. An old but excellent example is the Ptolemaic view (which held until the sixteenth century) that the earth was at the center of the universe, and the moon, sun, planets and stars were embedded in concentric spheres around it. Elaborate mathematical formulas and models were developed that would accurately predict astronomical events based on the Ptolemaic paradigm. Not until Copernicus and Kepler found that the formula worked more easily when the sun replaced the earth as the center of it all did an instance of paradigm shift begin.

After a paradigm shift begins, progress is fast though fraught with tension. New discoveries pour in to support the new belief system (e.g. those of Kepler and Galileo). And scientific revolution occurs. Other familiar examples of paradigm shift and ensuing revolution in science include the shift to relativity in physics, and to plate tectonics in geology. The important point in each instance is that the old 'rationality' is eventually replaced with a new, different, and more useful one.

ANTIQUATED AXIOMS

We are urging something of this kind in business. The old rationality, in our opinion, has ceased to be a useful discipline. Judging from the actions of managers who seem to operate under this paradigm, some of its shared beliefs include the following:

Big is better because you can always get economies of scale. When in doubt, consolidate things: eliminate overlap, duplication and waste. Incidentally, as you get big, make sure everything is carefully and formally coordinated.

Low-cost producers are the only sure-fire winners. Customer utility functions lead them to focus on cost in the final analysis. Survivors always make it cheaper.

Analyze everything. We've learned that we can avoid big dumb decisions through good market research, discounted cash-flow analysis and good budgeting. If a little is good, then more must be better, so apply things like discounted cash flow to risky investments like research and development. Use budgeting as a model for long-range planning. Make forecasts. Set hard numerical targets on the basis of those forecasts.

Get rid of the disturbers of the peace – i.e. fanatical product champions. After all, we've got a plan. We want one new product development activity to produce the needed breakthrough and we'll put 500 engineers on it if necessary, because we've got a better idea.

The manager's job is decision making. Make the right calls. Make the tough calls. Balance the portfolio. Buy into the attractive industries. Implementation, or execution, is of secondary importance. Replace the whole management team if you have to get implementation right.

Control everything. A manager's job is to keep things tidy and under control. Specify the organization structure in detail. Write long job descriptions. Develop complicated matrix organizations to ensure that every possible contingency is accounted for. Issue orders. Make black and white decisions. Treat people as factors of production.

Get the incentives right and productivity will follow. If we give people big, straightforward monetary incentives to do right and work smart, the productivity problem will go away. Over-reward the top performers. Weed out the 30–40 percent dead wood who don't want to work.

Inspect in order to control quality. Quality is like everything else; order it done. Triple the quality control department if necessary (forget that the QC force per unit of production in Japanese auto companies is just a third as big as in the United States). Have it report to the president. That will show the workers that you mean business.

A business is a business is a business. If you can read the financial statements, you can manage anything. The people, the products and the services are simply those resources you have to align to get financial results.

Top executives are smarter than the market. Carefully manage the cosmetics of the income statement and balance sheet, and you will look good to outsiders. Above all, don't let quarterly earnings stop growing.

It's all over if we stop growing. When we run out of opportunity in our industry, buy into industries we don't understand. At least we can then continue growing.

But though it may seem to drive the engine of business today, the conventional business rationality simply does not explain most of what makes the excellent companies work. Why not? What are its shortcomings?

1 *For one, the numerative, analytical component has an in-built conservative bias. Cost reduction becomes priority number one and revenue enhancement takes a back seat.* This leads to obsession with cost, not quality and value; to patching up old products rather than fooling with untidy new product or business development; and to fixing productivity through investment rather than revitalization of the workforce. A buried weakness in the analytic approach to business decision making is that people analyze what can be most readily analyzed, and more or less ignore the rest.

As Harvard's John Steinbruner observes: 'If quantitative precision is demanded, it is gained, in the current state of things, only by so reducing the scope of what is analysed that most of the important problems remain external to the analysis.'[3] This leads to fixation on the cost side of the equation. The numbers are 'hardest' there. The fix, moreover, is mechanical and easy to picture – buy a new machine to replace 19 jobs, reduce paperwork by 25 percent, close down two lines and speed up the remaining one.

Numerative analysis leads simultaneously to another unintended devaluation of the revenue side. Analysis has no way of valuing the extra oomph, the overkill, added by an IBM or Frito-Lay sales force.

In fact, according to a recent observer, every time the analysts got their hands on Frito's '99.5 percent service level' (an 'unreasonable' level of service in a so-called commodity business) their eyes began to gleam and they proceeded to show how much could be saved if only Frito would reduce its commitment to service. The analysts are 'right'; Frito would immediately save money. But the analysts cannot possibly demonstrate the impact of a timely degree of service unreliability on the heroic 10,000-person sales force – to say nothing of the Frito's retailers – and, therefore, on eventual market share loss or margin decline.

Viewed analytically, the over-commitment to reliability by Caterpillar ('Forty-eight-hour parts service anywhere in the world – or Cat pays') or Maytag ('Ten years' trouble-free operation') makes no sense. Analytically, purposeful duplication of effort by IBM and 3M on product development, or cannibalization of one P & G brand by another P & G brand is, well, just that, duplication. Delta's family feeling, IBM's respect for the individual, and McDonald's and Disney's fetish for cleanliness makes no sense quantitatively.

2 *The exclusively analytic approach run wild leads to an abstract, heartless philosophy.* Our obsession with body counts in Vietnam and our failure to understand the persistence and long time horizon of the Eastern mind culminated in America's most catastrophic misallocation of resources – human, moral and material. But Defense Secretary Robert McNamara's fascination with numbers was just a sign of the times. One of his fellow whiz kids at Ford, Roy Ash, fell victim to the same affliction. Says *Fortune* of his Litton misadventures: 'Utterly abstract in his view of business [Ash] enjoyed to the hilt exercising his sharp mind in analysing the most sophisticated accounting techniques. His brilliance led him to think in the most regal of ways: building new cities: creating a shipyard that would roll off the most technically advanced vessels the way Detroit builds automobiles.'[4] Sadly, *Fortune*'s analysis speaks not only of Ash's Litton failure but also of the similar disaster that undid AM International 10 years later.

3 *To be narrowly rational is often to be negative.* Peter Drucker gives a good description of the baleful influence of management's analytic bias: '"Professional" management today sees itself often in the role of a judge who says "yes" or "no" to ideas as they come up. . . . A top management that believes its job is to sit in judgement will inevitably veto the new idea. It is always "impractical".'[5] John Steinbruner makes a similar point commenting on the role of staffs in general: 'It is inherently easier to develop a negative argument than to advance a constructive one.' Says George Gilder in *Wealth and Poverty*: 'Creative thought requires an act of faith.' He dissects example after example in support of his point, going back to the laying out of railroads, insisting that 'when they were built they could hardly be justified in economic terms'.[6]

4 *Today's version of rationality does not value experimentation and abhors mistakes.* The conservatism that leads to inaction and years-long 'study groups' frequently confronts businessmen with precisely what they were trying to avoid – having to make, eventually, one big bet. Giant product development groups analyze and analyze until years have gone by and they've designed themselves into one home-run product, with every bell and whistle attractive to every segment. Meanwhile, less risk-averse competitors, each a hotbed of experimentation, have

proceeded 'irrationally' and chaotically, and introduced 10 more new products each during the same period. Advancement takes place only when we do something: try an early prototype on a customer or two, run a quick and dirty test market, stick a jury-rig device on an operating production line, test a new sales promotion on 50,000 subscribers.

Experimentation is the fundamental tool of science: if we experiment successfully, by definition, we will make many mistakes. Yet the dominant culture in most big companies demands punishment for a mistake, no matter how useful, small, invisible.

5 *Anti-experimentation leads inevitably to over-complexity and inflexibility.* The 'home-run product' mentality is nowhere more evident than in the pursuit of the 'superweapon' in defense. Says a senior Pentagon analyst: 'Our strategy of pursuing ever-increasing technical complexity and sophistication has made high-technology solutions and combat readiness mutually exclusive.' Caution and paralysis-induced-by-analysis lead to an anti-experimentation bias. That, in turn, ironically leads to an ultimately risky 'big bet' mentality. And to produce the resulting superproducts, hopelessly complicated and ultimately unworkable management structures are required.

The IBM 360 is one of the grand product success stories in American business history, yet its development was sloppy. Along the way, chairman Thomas Watson, Sr. asked vice-president Frank Carey to 'design a system to ensure us against a repeat of this kind of problem'. Carey did what he was told. Years later, when he became chairman himself, one of his first acts was to get rid of the laborious product development structure he had created for Watson. 'Mr Watson was right,' he conceded. 'It [the product development structure] will prevent a repeat of the 360 development turmoil. Unfortunately, it will also ensure that we don't ever invent another product like the 360.'

The excellent companies' response to complexity is fluidity, the administrative version of experimentation. Reorganizations take place all the time. 'If you've got a problem, put the resources on it and get it fixed,' says one Digital Equipment executive. Adds Koppers' Fletcher Byrom: 'Over-organization produces a rigidity that is intolerable in an era of rapidly accelerating change.' And Hewlett-Packard's (HP) David Packard notes: ' You've got to avoid having too rigid organization . . . I've often thought that after you get organized, you ought to throw the chart away.'

6 *The rationalist approach does not celebrate informality.* Analyze, plan, tell, specify and check up are the verbs of the rational process. Interact, test, try, fail, stay in touch, learn, shift direction, adapt, modify and see are some of the verbs of the informal managing processes. We hear the latter much more often in our interviews with top performers. Intel puts in extra conference rooms, simply to increase the likelihood of

informal problem solving among different disciplines. 3M sponsors clubs of all sorts specifically to enhance interaction. HP and Digital overspend on their own air and ground transportation systems just so people will visit one another. Product after product flows from Patrick Haggerty's bedrock principles of 'tight coupling' at TI. It means people talk, solve problems and fix things, rather than posture, debate and delay.

Unfortunately, management by edict feels more comfortable to most American managers. They shake their heads in disbelief at 3M, Digital, HP, Bloomingdale's, or even IBM, companies whose core processes seem out of control. After all, who in his right mind would establish 'management by wandering around' (MBWA) as a pillar of philosophy, as HP does? It turns out that the informal control through regular, casual communication is actually much tighter than rule by numbers, which can be avoided or evaded. But you'd have a hard time selling that idea outside the excellent companies.

7 *The rational model causes us to denigrate the importance of values.* While it is true that the excellent companies have superb analytic skills, we believe that their major decisions are shaped more by their values than by their dexterity with numbers. The top performers create a broad, uplifting, shared culture, a coherent framework within which charged-up people search for appropriate adaptations. Their ability to extract extraordinary contributions from very large numbers of people turns on the ability to create a sense of highly valued purpose. Such purpose invariably emanates from love of product, providing top-quality services, and honoring innovation and contribution from all. Such high purpose is inherently at odds with 30 quarterly MBO objectives, 25 measures of cost containment, 100 demeaning rules for production-line workers, or an ever-changing, analytically derived strategy that stresses cost this year, innovation next, and heaven knows what the year after.

8 *There is little place in the rationalist world for internal competition.* A company is not supposed to compete with itself. But throughout the excellent companies research, we saw example after example of that phenomenon. Moreover, we saw peer pressure – rather than orders from the boss – as the main motivator. General Motors pioneered the idea of internal competition 60 years ago: 3M, P & G, IBM, HP, Bloomingdale's and Tupperware are its masters today. Division overlap, product-line duplication, multiple new-product development teams, and vast flows of information to spur productivity comparison – and improvements – are the watchwords. Why is it that so many have missed the message?

Again, the analyze-the-analyzable bias is ultimately fatal. It is true that costs of product-line duplication and non-uniformity of manufacturing procedures can be measured precisely. But the incremental revenue benefits from a steady flow of new products developed by zealous champions and the increment of productivity gains that comes from continuous innovation by competing shop-floor teams are much harder, if not impossible, to get a handle on.

MISPLACED EMPHASIS

Perhaps the most important failing of the narrow view of rationality is not that it is wrong *per se*, but that it has led to a dramatic imbalance in the way we think about managing. Stanford's Harold Leavitt has a wonderful way of explaining this point. He views the managing process as an interactive flow of three variables: pathfinding, decision making and implementation. The problem with the rational model is that it addresses only the middle element – decision making.

Obviously, the three processes are interconnected, and emphasis on any one trait to the exclusion of the other two is dangerous. The business ranks are full of would-be-pathfinders-artists who can't get anything done. Likewise, implementers abound – compromising salesmen who have no vision. And, as we have argued, those who overemphasize decision making are legion. The point is that business management has at least as much to do with pathfinding and implementation as it does with decision making. The processes are inherently different, but they can complement and reinforce one another.

Pathfinding is essentially an aesthetic, intuitive process, a design process. There is an infinity of alternatives that can be posed for design problems, whether we are talking about architectural design or the guiding values for business. From the infinity, there are plenty of bad ideas, and here the rational approach is helpful in sorting out the chaff. One is usually left with a large remaining set of good design ideas, however, and no amount of analysis will choose among them, for the final decision is essentially one of taste.

Implementation is also greatly idiosyncratic. As Leavitt points out, 'People like their own children a lot, and typically aren't that interested in other people's babies.' As consultants, we repeatedly find that it does the client no good for us to 'analytically prove' that option A is the best – and to stop at that point. At that phase in the consulting process, option A is our baby, not theirs, and no amount of analytical brilliance is going to get otherwise uncommitted people to buy it. They have to get into the problem and understand it – and then own it for themselves.

Rationality is important. A quality analysis will help to point a business in the right direction for pathfinding and will weed out the dumb options. But if America is to regain its competitive position in the world, or even hold what it has, we have to cure ourselves of overreliance on the rational model.

NOTES

1 *Dun's Review*, September 1980, p. 82.
2 University of Chicago Press, 1970, 2nd edn.
3 *The Cybernetic Theory of Decision*, Princeton University Press, 1974, p. 328.
4 'A rejuvenated Litton is once again off to the races.' *Fortune*, October 8, 1979, p. 160.
5 *The Age of Discontinuity*, New York, Harper & Row, 1969, pp. 56–57.
6 New York, Basic Books, 1981.

Chapter 3

Beyond the cowboy and the corpocrat

Rosabeth Moss Kanter

Slowly but surely, America is waking up to the emerging economic realities. Across the business landscape, companies in many different industries, of many different ages and sizes, are reshaping into contenders in the global corporate Olympics. The motivation for adopting new forms is mixed. Companies are as much pushed by their need to reduce costs and manage constrained resources as they are pulled by the lure of entrepreneurial opportunities as barriers to worldwide business activity fall away. The changes are implemented poorly in some cases and well in others. For people, the new business forms are accompanied by insecurity and overload at the same time that they generate more exciting and involving workplaces and give more people more chances to operate like entrepreneurs, even from within the corporate fold.

But despite the unsolved problems, slowly but surely, America is learning how to compete in the corporate Olympics. Rapid change in the business environment makes the Olympic contest sometimes resemble the croquet game in Alice in Wonderland. . . . In that kind of game, every element is in motion – technology, suppliers, customers, employees, corporate structure, industry structure, government regulation – and none can be counted on to remain stable for very long. It is impossible to win games like that by using the old corporate forms: elaborate hierarchies and slow decision-making processes; in-house rivalries and adversarial relationships with stakeholders; risk-averse systems that crush new ideas not directly related to the mainstream business: and rewards geared to climbing the ladder from position to position rather than to accomplishment or contribution.

But even though that game is fraught with uncertainty and lack of control, there is a way to win it. A contest that puts a premium on responsiveness and teamwork can be won by employing four F's: Focused, Fast, Friendly, and Flexible.

For corporations to get in shape for Olympic competition, then, they must evolve flatter, more focused organizations stressing synergies; entrepreneurial enclaves pushing newstream businesses for the future;

and strategic alliances or stakeholder partnerships stretching capacity by combining the strength of several organizations. Together, these strategies constitute the strategic, business action agenda.

SYNERGIES

The first major component of post-entrepreneurial strategy is to seek that combination of businesses, array of internal services, and structure for organizing them that promotes synergies – a whole that multiplies the value of the parts. Olympic contenders need leaner, more cooperative, more integrated organizations. Compared to the traditional corporation, post-entrepreneurial companies have fewer layers of management and smaller corporate staffs; they minimize the interveners that delay action. A key concept guiding the post-entrepreneurial corporation is focus: ensuring that people at all levels are able to concentrate on contributing what they do best, in a company itself fully focused on maximizing its core business competence.

Driven by an imperative to make sure that all activities 'add value,' post-entrepreneurial companies decentralize some functions, putting them close to the business unit those functions support; they contract out for some services, turning to suppliers that are specialists in that area and reducing the need for the company to manage activities largely unrelated to their core business competence; and they convert some service departments into 'businesses' that compete with external suppliers to sell their wares both inside and outside the company. Such organizational changes allow post-entrepreneurial companies to do more with less, because their staffs are smaller, their fixed costs are lower, resources are available closer to the site of business action, and all departments are more clearly focused on their contributions to the business.

To move from simply adding value to multiplying it, the post-entrepreneurial company also builds the connections between its various products or businesses, encouraging such cooperative efforts as cross-selling, product links in the marketplace, exchange of technological or market information, resource sharing to apply one unit's competence to another's problem, or letting each division serve as the 'lead' for particular innovations. This means that the typical post-entrepreneurial company is less diversified than the traditional corporation, tending to add only those businesses that build on existing competence or can extend it.

But the search for synergies is sometimes forgotten in a corporation's rush to restructure. Many cut costs without considering the consequences. They work on the 'use less' side of the equation but not the 'achieve more' side. Or they acquire new businesses because theoretically there is a 'fit,' but then foster rivalries that interfere with getting benefits from that strategic fit. Reshaping an organization to create more value runs the risk of subtracting value rather than adding it. The issue is how to restructure thoughtfully instead of downsizing mindlessly. There are two principal problems: poor management of the transition itself and setting up contests that produce 'winners' and 'losers.'

First, top management typically overestimates the degree of cooperation it will get and underestimates the transition costs. Among the by-products of significant restructuring are discontinuity, disorder, and distraction – all of which tend to reduce productivity. People can lose energy, projects can lose key resources, and initiative can grind to a halt. Faith in leaders can be diminished, and power differences are made uncomfortably visible, showing many people that they lack control over their own fate. But even if some of these transition problems are temporary, a more permanent residue can be left: an undermining of commitment to the future. 'Shall I write the list of our locations in pencil?' one manager asked.

The second danger is inducing the 'mean' along with the 'lean' – a cowboy style of management that encourages groups to shoot it out with one another in internal competitions. Such in-house rivalries can stem from any situation that promotes battles over scarce resources among groups with a reason to be antagonistic to one another – for example, the conquerors and the vanquished after an acquisition, parallel start-ups with the goal of only one survivor, or creeping market boundaries that cause divisions of the same company to seek one another's customers. But in-house competition undermines goal achievement, leading groups to emphasize defeating their rivals instead of strong task performance. It can drive out innovation and can lower standards.

The management challenge is to retain value and increase it by handling transitions so that they reinforce commitment and build the cooperation that brings synergies. This means, first of all, managing with an eye on the past and the future as well as the present: in any major change, minimizing the losses people have to face while allowing grieving about the past; providing positive visions of the future; and reducing the uncertainty of the present by active communication. After a transition, it means actively organizing to motivate the search for synergies: championing the cause from the top, providing forums to help managers identify opportunities outside their own areas, offering incentives and rewards for teamwork, making resources available for joint projects, and promoting relationships and communication to help people know one another and share information across diverse areas – to perceive that their fate is shared and that they can help one another.

The post-entrepreneurial emphasis on synergies decreases the 'vertical' dimension of organization, reducing elaborate corporate hierarchies and large central staffs, and increases the 'horizontal' dimension – the direct cooperation between peers across divisions and departments.

ALLIANCES

The second major component of post-entrepreneurial strategy involves developing close working relationships with other organizations, extending the company's reach without increasing its size. Strategic alliances and partnerships are a potent way to do more with less. They permit the company to remain lean, controlling costs while gaining access to more capacity than what is owned or employed directly. The traditional corporation was stuck with the limitations of do-it-oneself-or-don't-do-it-at-all mentalities. Partnerships are a flexible alternative acquisition, with a more modest investment and the ability to remain independent. The leaner organization that contracts out for services depends on the suppliers of those services and therefore benefits from close cooperation with them. Furthermore, in a rapidly changing business environment, alliances with other organizations on whom one company depends are a powerful way to ensure that all change in the same direction, thereby reducing uncertainty. The traditional corporation's mistrust of outsiders and desire for control made it impossible to plan jointly with customers or suppliers. Post-entrepreneurial companies find a number of benefits in coalitions with other companies: information access, windows on technology, speed of action, and mutual accommodation to innovation that creates faster payback. Post-entrepreneurial companies pool resources or link their systems to create even greater joint capacity in a variety of ways. There are groups of companies contributing to consortia that provide a special service for all of them, joint ventures to pursue particular business opportunities, and partnerships between a company and its suppliers, customers, or even unions. . . .

The management challenge is to select only those relationships that are sufficiently important that they will be entered into with full commitment and with a willingness to invest the resources and make the internal changes that successful external partnerships entail – the sharing of information, the linking of systems, and the establishment of agreements for governing the partnership. The 'six I's' of successful alliances – Importance, Investment, Interdependence, Integration, Information, Institutionalization – make it possible for the post-entrepreneurial corporation to use partnerships to do more with less. But they also require major shifts away from bureaucracy and hierarchy.

NEWSTREAMS

The third major post-entrepreneurial strategy is to actively promote newstreams – a flow of new business possibilities within the firm. To do more with less in the demanding context of the global Olympics means being able to capture and develop opportunities as they arise, to ensure that good ideas don't slip away and that new ventures are ready to join the mainstream business or lead the company in new directions. Thus, post-entrepreneurial companies extend the domain for invention well beyond the R&D department, and the domain for new venture formation well beyond the acquisition department. They are unlike traditional corporations in giving more people, at more levels, the chance to develop and lead newstream projects.

While post-entrepreneurial companies want a climate for innovation in which every employee feels that innovation is part of his or her job, they do not just depend on the lucky break of an innovation's spontaneously arising in some corner of the company and making its way to a leader's attention. Instead, they create official channels to speed the flow of new ideas: for example, special funds to support new ideas without eating into mainstream business budgets; canters for creativity to speed the application of new ideas; incentives to find and nurture employee-led projects; incubators to grow new ventures; or investments in new technology ventures outside that can be linked to established businesses inside. The managers who preside over newstream channels may simply act as scouts to find ideas already under development, or they may more actively coach potential project developers and inspire them to come forward.

But simply establishing newstream channels does not automatically assure that newstream projects will be successful. Just as with the other two post-entrepreneurial strategies, success depends on the effectiveness and appropriateness with which the strategy is implemented; it requires a management sensibility not part of the traditional repertoire. The very existence of newstreams generates tensions and dilemmas because the requirements for nurturing a new venture conflict with management systems geared for running mainstream businesses or at least better tolerated by the mainstream.

For one thing, 'planning' for a newstream means placing bets rather than being able to predict a relatively assured set of results from a known line of business. Newstreams are not yet routinized; they are characterized instead by unexpected events, which makes scheduling difficult. Newstreams are uncertain in a number of respects; their course is bumpy, and they rock boats because they are controversial. Newstream projects are intense; they absorb more mental and emotional energy than established activities, generate new knowledge at a rapid rate, require excellent communication among those with fragments of knowledge, and are thus more dependent on teamwork and more vulnerable to turnover. Finally, newstreams benefit from autonomy – perhaps places of their own for the projects, removed from the mainstream and allowing experimentation, but certainly to be added to all the other things corporations are attempting to do. They represent a fundamentally different set of organizing principles from bureaucracy, a different way of conducting corporate life. These values and practices are often present as a matter of course in new ventures, but now they are increasingly finding their place in established corporations as well. Whereas bureaucratic management is inherently preservation-seeking, entrepreneurial management is inherently opportunity-seeking. The major concern of bureaucracy is to administer a known routine uniformly, guided by past experiences, whereas the major concern of an entrepreneurial organization is to exploit opportunity wherever it occurs and however it can be done, regardless of what the organization has done in the past. The post-entrepreneurial organization brings entrepreneurial principles to the established corporation.[1]

All of these developments represent a dramatic new corporate ideal, one very different from the old-style corpocracy:

> Bureaucracy tends to be position-centred, in that authority derives from position, and status or rank is critical. Post-entrepreneurial organizations tend to be more person-centred, with authority deriving from expertise or from relationships.

> Bureaucratic management is repetition-oriented, seeking efficiency through doing the same thing over and over again. Post-entrepreneurial management is creation-oriented, seeking innovation as well as efficiency.

> Bureaucratic management is rules-oriented, defining procedures and rewarding adherence to them. Post-entrepreneurial management is results-oriented, rewarding outcomes.

> Bureaucracies tend to pay for status, in the sense that pay is position-based, positions are arrayed in a hierarchy, and greater rewards come from attaining higher positions. Post-entrepreneurial organizations tend to pay for contribution, for the value the person or team has added, regardless of formal position.

> Bureaucracies operate through formal structures designed to channel and restrict the flow of information. Post-entrepreneurial organizations find opportunities through the expansion of information, through the ability to maximize all possible communication link – with coalition partners inside and outside the organization.

> Bureaucracies assign specific mandates and territories, to circumscribe the action arena. In post-entrepreneurial organizations, charters and home territories are only the starting point for the creation of new modes of action; furthermore, opportunities come from the ability to make relationships across territories.

Bureaucracies seek ownership and control. Post-entrepreneurial organizations seek leverage and experimentation.

Thus, to use an overworked expression, the dominant business paradigm is changing. Three principles emerge from observing the new organizational strategies in practice, intertwined post-entrepreneurial principles that create the flexibility required to meet the strategic challenge of doing more with less:

Minimize obligations and maximize options. Keep fixed costs low and as often as possible use 'variable' or 'contingent' means to achieve corporate goals.

Find leverage through influence and combination. Derive power from access and involvement, rather than from full control or total ownership.

Encourage 'churn.' Keep things moving. Encourage continuous regrouping of people and functions and products to produce unexpected, creative new combinations. Redefine turnover as positive (a source of renewal) rather than negative.

In this context, each of the popular management buzzwords and fads of the last decade seems a way station on the road to a more comprehensive rethinking of corporate strategy and organizational form. For example, participative management and employee involvement, 'intrapreneurship' and 'quality circles' have each found their niche and reached their logical limits in many companies. Advocates have rightly praised these corporate innovations for their benefits: usually local increases in productivity, quality, or innovation. Skeptics have rightly condemned them for being faddish, superficial, quick fixes with fragmented implementation. Still, in retrospect, each has been important in moving corporations toward challenging the old managerial assumptions, loosening their structures, and experimenting with new practices. One offshoot of many of these programs is the weakening of hierarchy and the reduction of levels of organization as employees are given more opportunities to influence decisions and exercise control.

Alongside the pro-people corporate policies popular in the last decade, however, are a number of other business maneuvers often characterized as antipeople: financial manipulation and a takeover binge leading to involuntary restructuring and job displacement. Ironically, these manipulations also tend to create leaner, less hierarchical organizations, as acquirers seek to reduce costs by eliminating corporate staffs and unnecessary layers of management or divesting business units that can function alone, thereby giving them entrepreneurial independence. But when done for financial speculation rather than to enhance long-term capacity, this strategy can subtract value rather than add it.[2]

The post-entrepreneurial principles I have identified clearly have both an upside and a downside. At their best, they increase opportunity, giving people the chance to develop their ideas, pursue exciting projects, and be compensated directly for their contributions. At their best, they encourage collaboration across functions, across business units, and even across corporations. The business benefits from the use of these principles are lower fixed costs and increased entrepreneurial reach.

But at their worst, the same strategies can lead to displacement instead of empowerment, rivalries instead of teamwork, and short-term asset-shuffling and one-night stands with the latest attractive deal instead of long-term commitments to build capacity. The same strategies executed unwisely and without concern for the organizational and human consequences will not produce continuing business benefits – especially if people withhold effort and commitment for fear of being displaced or to hedge their own bets against change.

It is not the strategies themselves but their execution that make the difference in whether the consequences for people are expanded entrepreneurial opportunity or anxiety, insecurity, and loss of motivation to produce.

LIFE IN A POST-ENTREPRENEURIAL WORLD: THE HUMAN CONSEQUENCES

We are witnessing a crumbling of hierarchy, a gradual replacement of the bureaucratic emphasis on order, uniformity, and repetition with an entrepreneurial emphasis on creativity and deal-making. But at the same time, we are also watching new societal dilemmas arise in the wake of this change.

The post-entrepreneurial revolution changes not only the organization and management of the corporation, but also the lives people lead in the business world. There are more contingencies, more uncertainties. The very rigidity of the traditional corporate bureaucracy also provided a measure of security; if people had to 'know their place,' at least that place was relatively stable and unchanging from day to day and year to year. But today, companies must either move away from bureaucratic guarantees to post-entrepreneurial flexibility or they stagnate, thereby cancelling by default any commitments they have made.

Post-entrepreneurial strategies hold out the promise of more satisfaction and rewards for people, but more of those benefits are contingent on what the individual – and the team – does and not on what the corporation automatically provides. The three forms of contribution-based pay – profit-sharing and gain-sharing, performance bonuses, and a share of venture returns – give people the power to grow their own earnings and distribute the corporation's rewards more fairly to those who deserve them, and they do not force people to wait in line for promotions as the only way to make progress. The excitement of projects in which people are empowered to act on their own ideas makes work more satisfying and more absorbing, increasing the sense of accomplishment. The opportunity to be essentially in business for oneself, inside or outside the large corporation, puts more control in the hands of smaller groups. And because these consequences of the shift to post-entrepreneurial strategies are more motivating for people, the corporation should reap benefits, too, in increased productivity.

The post-entrepreneurial revolution has a dramatic impact on people's careers – the sequence of jobs that constitutes their life's work – and this illustrates both the potential and the problems that ensue. The three major strategies that give flexibility to the corporation (corporate restructuring, which eliminates some jobs altogether or shuffles employers; greater comfort with alliances, which increases reliance on suppliers outside the firm rather than on employees inside; and the encouragement of newstream ventures) also shift the center of career action from promotion up a ladder to *ad hoc* projects. The bureaucratic career is disappearing; the corporate ladder is losing rungs and stability. The traditional corporation is in such turmoil that it can no longer carry the weight of people's hopes and dreams, or society's expectation of permanence to which a variety of welfare benefits and pension funds are tied.

Success in a post-entrepreneurial career combines the knowledge base and search for reputation of the professional with the entrepreneur's ability to move from project to project, creating new value. People's careers are more dependent on their own resources and less dependent on the fate of a particular company. This means that some people who know only bureaucratic ropes are cut adrift. It means that incomes are likely to fluctuate rather than increase in an orderly fashion every year. It means more risk and uncertainty. It does not necessarily mean lower productivity, for professional standards and concern for reputation may be sufficient incentives and also the best guarantee of continuity of employment even with the same corporation. No longer counting on the corporation to provide security and stature requires people to build those resources in themselves, which ultimately could result in more resourceful people.

But these benefits do not accrue as yet to everyone, because not all companies have as yet moved fast enough or far enough to the post-entrepreneurial style. Some companies try to go halfway and flub it, and others have not changed at all. Furthermore, because most American social policy is still geared to the assumption that the traditional corporation is alive and well, there are problems emerging in the wake of the post-entrepreneurial revolution that are not yet well understood or well handled. Some people joyously leap off the corporate ladder into post-entrepreneurial careers, but others are shoved off callously, without a safety net or help in getting back on their feet. Some people are absorbed in more exciting work, but others are working harder just to pick up the slack when companies cut staff and get wage concessions yet still expect the same amount of work to be done.

The first major problem that must be addressed in the post-entrepreneurial world is the tensions between corporate flexibility and individual security. Businesses want and need the flexibility to restructure, to change shape, and to pursue newstreams, while employees want the security of knowing there is a place for them. Yet even that is too simple. Fewer and fewer people are really counting on a permanent career in one company any more; but still, they want to have a measure of control over their careers, instead of being cast adrift without the resources to begin again, and they want to feel that they are making progress with each career step. Income security has not been a cornerstone of recent American social and business policy; but employment security has been central – for example a key element for unions that know that wage rates cannot continue to rise without limit, and therefore shift to job security as a bargaining principle. Job security has also been an implicit part of the employment contract for managers and professionals in large corporations. It was this security that apparently produced commitment and loyalty, the ability to plan for the long term, and the desire of both employer and employee to invest in each other's success. The post-entrepreneurial strategies make that guarantee of long-term employment more difficult to sustain even if it were still desired.

In the post-entrepreneurial world, the best source of security for people is a guarantee not of a specific job or a specific employer, but of their employability. Employability security means offering people the chance to grow in skills and accomplishments so that their value to any employer is enhanced – the present one or a future one or themselves as independent entrepreneurs. In the future companies will invest in people not because they are stuck with them for life but because employability security produces better performance from more highly skilled people.

Workplace overload is a second significant problem, one that spills over into personal and family life. People are working long hours because leaner organizations put pressure on the remaining staff to do more work, because there are more exciting opportunities to pursue projects that bring great rewards, and because post-entrepreneurial strategies increase complexity and the need for communication. The absorption with work goes up when people can earn performance bonuses, share in productivity gains, get funding for newstream ventures, develop joint ventures with other divisions, or work more closely with partners outside the company. Flexible organizations that innovate, that seek synergies, have more changes to keep up with, and they are more complex. As more people are empowered, more people can initiate activities that create work for still others; the slate of activities is continually expanding. It becomes difficult to set limits, difficult to determine how much work is 'enough.'

It is not hard work or long hours *per se* that pose the problem; after all, if companies are going to win in the corporate Olympics they need this kind of Olympic effort. But not all the overload is necessary; some reflects frenzy and chaos rather than crisp focus. More significantly, this work style tends to turn the workplace into the prime site for absorbing relationships, a center of emotional life for single people (and sometimes for married ones as well). It eats into personal life and exaggerates the conflict between work and family.

In some cases, workplace overload could be reduced through better management: by delegating authority along with responsibility minimizing the number of simultaneous changes, and emphasizing simplicity over complexity. That helps some. But businesses must also make space for personal life. It is a matter not simply of making arrangements to ensure that children are cared for (although consider it a given that more child care must be made available), but also of providing time for families to be together, uninterrupted by work. Nor is it realistic, in the post-entrepreneurial era, to expect many people or companies to tolerate reduced hours every day or every week. Instead, time-out should be organized around the longer cycles of post-entrepreneurial work rhythms, the rhythms of projects. Periods of intense work should be matched by periods of relaxation and renewal. Rewards should come at the ends of projects, not on a calendar that is the same for everybody regardless of the work they do; and these moments of reward should mark a clear ending of one intense effort and a pause for personal life before beginning the next.

IN SEARCH OF THE POST-ENTREPRENEURLAL HERO: INDIVIDUAL SKILLS FOR SUCCESS

If the post-entrepreneurial corporation requires a different kind of work system and career system, it also requires a very different set of individual skills. We need a new image of the hero in business – the kind of leader who can manage the balancing act and guide us to victory in the corporate Olympics.

Our archetypal images of business leadership have themselves derived from the two poles that define today's corporate balancing act. We could choose between the conservative resource preserver (what Howard Stevenson and David Gumpert called the 'trustee') and the insurgent entrepreneur (Stevenson and Gumpert's 'promoter').[3] In popular lore, the former was reflected in images of the 'organization man' or 'corpocrat,' while the latter was described as a 'maverick' or 'cowboy,' each character occupying one end of the conserve-or-build spectrum.

The corpocrat has long been the target of well-deserved criticism, and the corpocratic style is gradually disappearing from progressive businesses. But despite glorification of the maverick in the 1980s entrepreneurial revival, the cowboy is also too extreme to be entirely satisfactory as a leadership image – just as John Sculley found at Apple Computers. It is easy to see the weakness in both styles when cowboys and corpocrats clash. From Steve Jobs's problems at Apple to Ross Perot's clash with General Motors after GM purchased his company, EDS, these are the typical sources of tension:

The cowboy lives in a world of immediate action; the corporation manager wants review and deliberation. What the cowboy views as time-wasting, rear-covering conservatism the corporation manager may see as the consensus-building necessary to implement decisions that many people control.

The cowboy wants to seize every opportunity, betting big – but if he loses he's wiped out. The corporation manager makes complex resource-allocation decisions balancing the protection of past investments with the pursuit of new opportunities; after all, the corporation is the trustee of other people's assets.

The cowboy strains limits, but the corporation manager has to establish limits to guide the actions of multitudes of people efficiently. The cowboy breaks rules and gets away with it, but the corporation manager thrives on controls and the uniform application of rules. There are few worse morale-plungers in a corporation than the realization that some are more equal than others.

The cowboy motivates by personal loyalty, surrounded as he is by just a few trusted cronies who love the work the way he does. The cowboy's direct control means that he can manage through impulse and whim, 'shooting from the hip.' But the corporation manager has to make complex and longer-term agreements that make him out of place, and he or she seeks an impersonal commitment to the philosophy of go-anywhere-do-anything regardless of personal ties or feelings about the job.

The cowboy rejects fancy 'citified' trappings, living simply at work – just one of the folks, regardless of wealth. But the corporation displays symbols of affluence to make people believe in its importance; it establishes gradations of privilege and perquisites to motivate people to seek the highest ranks.

The large corporate manager's suspicion of the cowboy, then, is not necessarily a politically motivated bias against mavericks who fight oppressive authority or speak unpleasant truths. It comes from a recognition that the cowboy personifies a challenge to the very premises on which a large corporation operates. Allow too many cowboys, and the foundations of hierarchy begin to crumble – but so does the basis for cooperation and discipline.

Without the bold impulses of take-action entrepreneurs and their constant questioning of the rules, we would miss one of the most potent sources of business revitalization and development. But without the discipline and coordination of conventional management, we could find waste instead of growth, unnecessary risk instead of revitalization. Just as Kodak and Pacific Telesis needed more cowboys, Apple and Digital needed more corporate discipline and cooperation.

Today's corporate balancing act requires a different style from either extreme, a post-entrepreneurial style better suited to playing in the corporate Olympics. Our new heroic model should be the athlete who can manage the amazing feat of doing more with less, who can juggle the need to both conserve resources and pursue growth opportunities. This new kind of business hero avoids the excesses of both the corpocrat and the cowboy. Where the former rigidly conserves and protects, the latter relentlessly speculates and promotes. But the business athlete has the strength to balance somewhere in the middle, taking the best of the corpocrat's discipline and the cowboy's entrepreneurial zeal. Again the four F's come to mind: Focused, Fast, Friendly, and Flexible. Business athletes need to be intense, lean and limber, able to stretch, good at teamwork, and in shape all the time.

There are seven skills and sensibilities that must be cultivated if managers and professionals are to become true business athletes.

First, they must learn to operate without the might of the hierarchy behind them. The crutch of authority must be thrown away and replaced by their own personal ability to make relationships, use influence, and work with others to achieve results. Business athletes stand and run on their own two feet, rather than being propelled automatically by the power of their position, just as a member of any athletic team is revered not for wearing the uniform but for his or her own performance. The traditional corporate hierarchy is rapidly crumbling, and title or formal position count for less anyway, in a world of negotiations involving internal collaborations or strategic alliances or the formation of new ventures. In strategic partnerships, for example, there is no room for faceless bureaucrats sending impersonal memos. Partners become more exposed and available to one another as people, as the Grotech joint venture participants and the Pacific Bell managers began to realize. Or in newstream ventures, the manager has little more to offer to potential members of the venture team than the excitement of trying because of the power of his or her vision. In many ways, business athletes have to count on their use of self, not their use of organizational status, to achieve results.

Second, business athletes must know how to 'compete' in a way that enhances rather than undercuts cooperation. They must be oriented to achieving the highest standard of excellence rather than to wiping out the competition. In the new game, today's competitors may find themselves on the same team tomorrow, and competitors in one sphere may also be collaborators in another. Even America's trade adversaries are potential partners, and it would be a mistake for the conduct of temporary competition to undermine the ability to cooperate later. Thus, business athletes must be skilful collaborators. Whether companies are seeking synergies through internal collaboration across business units or seeking leverage through strategic alliances and partnerships, the lesson is clear. Successful managers in the corporate Olympics must not only be good negotiators, seeking the best deal for 'their' unit, but also understand when and how to share resources, to combine forces, to do things that benefit another group – in the interests of superior overall performance. This relationship orientation means knowing how to assess and value what is good for all parties in the long run, not simply analyzing the 'fairness' of a single transaction.[4]

Third, and related, business athletes must operate with the highest ethical standards. While business ethics have always been important from a social and moral point of view, they also become a pragmatic requirement in the corporate Olympics. The doing more with less strategies place an even greater premium on trust than did the adversarial–protective business practices of the traditional corporation.

Business collaborations, joint ventures, labor–management partnerships, and other stakeholder alliances all involve the element of trust – a commitment of strategic information or key resources to the partners. But the partners have to rely on one another not to violate or misuse their trust. Even newstream ventures involve a high degree of trust, in the willingness to commit corporate resources to untried and uncertain activities with a minimum of monitoring. The trust required for all of these new business strategies is built and reinforced by a mutual understanding that each party to the relationship will behave ethically, taking the needs, interests, and concerns of all others into account.

A fourth asset for business athletes is to have a dose of humility sprinkled on their basic self-confidence, a humility that says that there are always new things to learn. Just as other kinds of athletes must be willing to learn, willing to accept the guidance of coaches, constantly in training, and always alert to the possibility of an improvement in their techniques, so must business athletes be willing to learn. A learning attitude is a clear necessity for swimming in newstreams, for exploring uncharted waters, but it is also a necessity for seeking synergies and for discovering the benefits of strategic alliances, many of which form so that partners can learn from one another.

I have seen this attitude emerge in companies and people that used to be closed in every sense. At Apple Computers in 1985, for example, I was often told that 'we have nothing to learn from anyone else'; but by 1988, Apple was actively creating strategic alliances for learning, and a major effort to reshape the finance function began with visits to other companies. Of course, to learn from others, people must – literally – learn to speak their language, whether Japanese, Spanish, or computer-ese.

Fifth, business athletes must develop a process focus – a respect for the process of implementation as well as the substance of what is implemented. They need to be aware that how things are done is every bit as important as what is done. My case studies and comparative data make it clear that execution may matter more than strategy. Whether restructuring builds synergies or leaves dead bodies in its path, whether alliances and partnerships indeed stretch capacity or simply stretch relationships to the breaking point, whether newstream investments lead to effective projects that produce results or to nothing – all this relies not only on the quality of the big strategic idea behind it but also on the concern for excellence of implementation.

Both Eastern Airlines and Western Airlines, for example, faced the same do-more-with-less pressures in the early 1980s, both made the bold strategic move of seeking wage concessions from employees in exchange for an announced 'business partnership,' and both were later acquired by other airlines. Yet the contrast in how they implemented their strategies could not be more striking. Eastern botched it by showing poor faith and not quite taking the steps that would make the employee partnership work, and since a hostile acquisition by Texas Air (resisted by management and sought by demoralized employee leaders), Eastern has been hurt financially by public displays of employee discontent, including claims of safety problems. Western, in contrast . . . managed the same strategic move by a careful attention to process and netted a more valuable company that merged smoothly with Delta to the benefit of employees, shareholders, and customers.

Sixth, business athletes must be multifaceted and ambidextrous, able to work across functions and business units to find synergies that multiply value, able to form alliances when opportune but to cut ties when necessary, able to swim equally effectively in the mainstream and in newstreams. There is no room for narrow or rigid people in the new business environment. Each component of the new business strategies that I have described relies heavily on the ability to form teams, to make connections, and to integrate functions. Business athletes must bring their own professional or functional skill to the team, but also must know how to connect it to the skills brought by others.

Seventh, business athletes must gain satisfaction from results and be willing to stake their own rewards on them. The accomplishment itself is really the only standard for the business athlete. With post-entrepreneurial

pay-for-performance a growing reality, and with the middle management hierarchy dismantled, the measure of success must, in any case,
shift from status to contribution, from attainment of a position to attainment of results. Promotion cannot be a reward at a time when there are
fewer layers of management and employment security is being under-
mined or redefined. At the same time, the shift toward doing-more-with-
less strategies opens up new kinds of opportunities for achievement and
rewards – whether via participation on the frontiers of partnerships,
where more power and responsibility fall upon partner representatives,
or via involvement in newstream ventures that turn ordinary employees
into entrepreneurs.

These seven managerial skills also point toward the individual skills
required to manage a career at a time when climbing the corporate ladder
has been replaced by hopping from opportunity to opportunity:

A belief in self rather than in the power of a position alone.

The ability to collaborate and become connected with new teams in
various ways.

Commitment to the intrinsic excitement of achievement in a particular
project that can show results.

The willingness to keep learning.

All of these attributes constitute an investment in one's own human
capital rather than a reliance on accumulating organizational capital.
Ultimately, this new loyalty to project rather than to employer can be
better for the company, too, because it produces results-oriented, entre-
preneurially inclined employees who are dedicated to their activities
instead of being dedicated to corporate politics and position enhancement.
And certainly it is better attuned to the workplace realities of the emerging business strategies.

NOTES

1 Pat Choate and J. K. Linger, *The High-Flex Society: Shaping America's Economic Future* (New York: Knopf, 1987); Michael J. Piore and Charles F. Sable, *The Second Industrial Divide: Possibilities for Prosperity* (New York: Basic Books, 1984); Raymond E. Miles and Charles C. Snow, 'Organizations: A New Con-cept for New Forms,' *California Management Review*, vol. 28, no. 3 (Spring 1986), pp. 62–73.
2 Corporate raiders looking for quick financial gains represent one abuse that US policy may already be moving to prevent – by disallowing tax deductions associated with hostile takeover costs, by placing limits on deductions for debt service when takeovers are involved, by barring 'greenmail' payments designed to make a raider go away, or by protecting employee pension funds against their use to finance a takeover bid. But even if hostile takeovers are

reduced in number or frequency, the buying and selling of corporate assets by corporations is likely to continue. Ensuring that these have positive rather than negative consequences for the companies involved, the shareholders, employees, and the American economy is a harder task, because managerial skill is involved. Allied Corporation embarked on a major restructuring in the early 1980s (changing its name in the process), buying many companies for financial reasons; though 'synergy' was often invoked as an ideal, it was hard to find in practice. Over time, Allied sold many of the assets it had acquired. A few years ago the company spun off a group of losing companies as the Henley Group, under the leadership of an executive whose goals were long-term investment and revitalization. The 'losers' are now outperforming the parent company.

3 Howard Stevenson and David Gumpert, 'The Heart of Entrepreneurship,' *Harvard Business Review*, vol. 64 (March–April 1985), pp. 84–94.

4 This attitude is related to the new feminist view of morality as encompassing not just analytic 'justice' or 'rightness' in the abstract but also maintenance of relationships.

Chapter 4

The purposing of high-performing systems

Peter B. Vaill

What brought my thinking about purposing of high-performing systems to a head was the front page of the *Washington Post* for October 29, 1980, which carried the following headlines:

POLAND'S TRADE UNIONS SET A DEADLINE FOR NEW STRIKE
THE WAR AND PEACE DEBATE – CARTER AND REAGAN TRADE SALVOS
'LANDMARK' FCC RULING ALLOWS AT & T TO ENTER COMPUTER FIELD
1 MAN CONVICTED IN MIAMI RIOTING
KHOMEINI SILENT ON HOSTAGES IN SPEECH
FORD LOSS 2ND HIGHEST IN US HISTORY
ARISTOTLE AND MACHIAVELLI GET ROCKVILLE TEACHER IN TROUBLE
LOTTERY COMPANY STARTS $80,000 BLITZ IN DISTRICT
SAUDIS SEVER TIES WITH LIBYA, CITE QADDAFI ATTACKS
IRAN CRISIS FINALLY FORCES ITSELF ON VANCE [FIFTH OF A SERIES ON 'THE FALL OF THE SHAH']

These headlines, plus a two-column, eight-inch-high picture of the planet Saturn as photographed by the *Voyager 1* spacecraft, stimulated my thinking about this page as a kind of collage.

Saturn! The picture was thrilling to me.

Already jostling my self-image was the story of the Rockville teacher who had been ordered to stop teaching the *Poetics* and *The Prince* because they were considered too difficult for his 10th-grade students, the story of Lech Walesa and his union, Solidarity, challenging the power politics in a totalitarian state, and the stories of two great American corporations whose fortunes and names, in another value system, have as much meaning for me as Saturn: the one losing big, the other winning big – or so it seemed. The politicians' voices provided a counterpoint in the collage. Do these guys know anything? asked a part of me.

As I reflected on what had become for me much more than just another day's front page, I felt the *Post* editors had posed a kind of global conundrum: 'Here is the nature of the world,' they may have been saying, 'the present and future. You figure it out.' This chapter is my attempt to be responsive, to say something new about the conundrum.

Two broad streams of thought that I had been pursuing for some nine years also affected my reflections. The first is the study of 'high-performing systems', a phrase I use to refer to human systems that perform at levels of excellence far beyond those of comparable systems. The second focus was on what is called, in the literature, 'strategic planning'. My initial inquiries into this field had depended heavily on other people's concepts and other people's data, but by the fall of 1980 I had developed my own perspectives, theories, and ways of talking about the subject.

My particular angle of vision showed me excellence written all over that front page: the achievements of *Voyager*, the struggles of Solidarity, the lonely classics teacher, the FCC attempting to peer competently into the murky bank of its regulatory responsibility, the single-mindedness of Qaddafi and of a Washington lottery chieftain – even the crafted vacuity of the Presidential debates. The page is testimony to the personal energy and purposefulness of men and women. My high-performing systems research helped me see how excellence and the drive to achieve it were manifesting themselves in these stories. My interests in strategic planning permitted me to see decisions that affected the survival and development of whole organizations and of the worlds in which they exist. I could also see efforts to recover from strategic blunders of the past – in, for example, the stories about Ford, Miami, the Shah, and the Polish government. Today's news often occurs because someone did something or failed to do something at the strategic level months or even years ago.

This chapter will not try to explain these particular trends and events, but it does develop a way of thinking about leadership in high-performing systems that applies, I think, to large-scale movements like these as well as to more mundane management situations. *The thesis of this chapter is that the definition and clarification of purposes is both a fundamental step in effective strategic management, and a prominent feature of every high-performing system I have ever investigated.* This is the kernel I take from the *Post*'s collage: It showed us the ebb and flow, the basic interaction, of purposes. We have to understand this process. It is the basis of the theory developed below.

WHAT IS A HIGH-PERFORMING SYSTEM?

Because the theory of leadership developed here derives from my studies of high-performing systems, it is necessary at the outset to describe these systems. This section describes criteria by which I identify high-performing systems, and the next gives eight broad findings about high-performing system characteristics.

A variety of sources provided the data on which my ideas have been developed since the original formulation of the idea of a high-performing system in 1978. The bibliography at the end of this chapter is only a partial list of those sources. In addition, I have had the benefit of a number of unpublished case studies passed along to me by friends and students. These include studies of a top college marching band and a Coast Guard cutter that went from a bottom to a top rating in six months; several studies of hospital emergency rooms and shock-trauma units; various accounts of military units, both in battle and behind the lines; a study of a highly successful drug rehabilitation agency; a study of one of Washington's most successful stockbrokerages; various accounts of the formation of successful small businesses; and a very large number of singular observations of excellence in one type of human system or another.

An 'excellent human system' – a high-performing system – presents one at the outset with a profound conceptual problem: How does one define *excellent*? Your 'high-performing system' might be my 'case of the compulsive pursuit of a socially useless objective'. Or vice versa. There is no real escape from this problem because the way that we define *performance* and *excellence* depend on values. As working rules of thumb, I have treated as high-performing systems those organizations or groups that meet one or more of the following criteria:

1 They are performing excellently against a known external standard. The clearest example is a team that does more of something, such as manufacturing automobiles, in a given time period, or does a set amount faster than it is usually done or than it is done by the team's competitors.
2 They are performing excellently against what is assumed to be their potential level of performance.
3 They are performing excellently in relation to where they were at some earlier point in time. (This is a developmental criterion.)
4 They are judged by informed observers to be doing substantially better qualitatively than other comparable systems.
5 They are doing whatever they do with significantly less resources than it is assumed are needed to do what they do.
6 They are perceived as exemplars of the way to do whatever they do, and thus they become a source of ideas and inspiration for others. (This is a style criterion.)
7 They are perceived to fulfil at a high level the ideals for the culture within which they exist – that is, they have 'nobility'.
8 They are the only organizations that have been able to do what they do at all, even though it might seem that what they do is not that difficult or mysterious a thing.

One of the delightful things about searching for high-performing systems is that one discovers a very large number of human systems that meet several of these criteria. Even though the behavioral sciences don't acknowledge it, excellence is alive and well. Some such organizations are famous, glamorous, or 'trendy', but others are very humble and insignificant, even drab. The criteria lead one to discover many varieties of beauty in human relationships and many forms of striving that a 'tighter' set of criteria would overlook. Whether doing serious social research or just living in the world, these criteria will introduce one to extraordinary human phenomena.

THE CHARACTERISTICS OF HIGH-PERFORMING SYSTEMS

Here is what I have found out about high-performing systems (HPSs):

1 HPSs are clear on their broad purposes and on nearer-term objectives for fulfilling these purposes. They know why they exist and what they are trying to do. Members have pictures in their heads that are strikingly congruent.
2 Commitment to these purposes is never perfunctory – although it is often expressed laconically. Motivation, as usually conceived, is always high. More important than energy level, however, is energy focus. Motivation is 'peculiar' in the literal sense of that word: 'Belonging exclusively to one person or group; special; distinctive; different.' Credit for suggesting the term 'peculiar' here goes to Deborah D. Vaill, thus ending what had been a frustrating search for the right term. (Outsiders find motivation peculiar, too, in the more usual sense of 'weird, eccentric'.) Energy is invested in particulars – in specific methods, tools, idea systems, arrangements, and styles.

   In most HPSs, there is some sense of their operation, analogous to a feeling of rhythm. One of the important 'peculiarities' of motivation is the way members express their energy and commitment through getting into a 'groove' of some kind.
3 Teamwork in HPSs is focused on the task. Social psychology's favorite distinction between 'task functions' and 'group maintenance functions' tends to dissolve. Members will have discovered those aspects of system operations that require integrated actions and will have developed behaviors and attitudes that fulfil these requirements.

   Coupled with the previous proposition about the focus of motivation, this means that there is usually a strong conservatism evident in the HPS. There are firm beliefs in a 'right organizational form', and a noticeable amount of effort is devoted to attaining and maintaining this form. Theoretically, 'form follows function', but once members have found a form that works they cling to it.

4 Leadership in HPSs is strong and clear. It is not ambivalent. There is no question of the need for initiative or of its appropriate source (although it may not always be the same person). Leadership style varies widely from HPS to HPS, but is remarkably consistent within a given HPS. Leadership style is never conflicted: it does not swing between cool and warm, close and distant, or demanding and *laissez-faire*. Leaders are reliable and predictable.

5 HPSs are fertile sources of inventions and new methods within the scope of the task they have defined and within the form they have chosen. HPSs are relatively conservative about new methods and inventions that take them outside the task boundaries and structural forms they have traditionally practiced: they 'do not tamper with a good thing'.

6 HPSs are clearly bounded from their environments and a considerable amount of energy, particularly on the part of leaders, is usually devoted to maintain these boundaries. Bounding occurs in terms of firm, even if unofficial, membership rules, methods (technologies) employed, times and time durations in which the system is 'on', and the spaces the system occupies when it is operating. There is a strong consciousness that 'we are different'. These ongoing bounding efforts are among the ways in which this consciousness displays itself most clearly.

7 Proposition (6) leads to another consistent finding – that is, HPSs are often seen as 'a problem' by entities in their environment – even those entities that have a great deal of power over them. HPSs avoid external control. They scrounge resources from the environment nonapologetically. They produce what they want by their standards, not what someone else wants. Thus they often frustrate environmental entities, especially in bureaucratic settings. One can note continual annoyance, even fury with HPSs. People decide, 'They've got to be broken up.' This is especially true when an HPS is a subunit of a larger organization. The HPS is thus a paradox: it fulfills the larger system's desires for high performance but the price is a relatively unmanageable subunit.

8 Above all, HPSs are systems that have 'gelled', even though the phenomenon is very difficult to talk about. Neither mechanical nor organic metaphors are usually adequate for describing the 'fit' of the system's various elements and practices.

Frequently the elements of an HPS, when examined one at a time, do not seem to qualify for membership; HPSs are often composed of castoffs and rejects.

Beyond its concrete existence, the phenomenon of the HPS poses social science with a profound conceptual challenge – namely, that of learning to talk about intense human interdependency in terms more descriptively accurate than those provided by either physics or biology.

These propositions are what used to be called 'clinical uniformities' that were made on the basis of intensive study of individual cases. The propositions can be illustrated and certainly debated, but they are difficult to prove unequivocally. Each of these propositions, furthermore, could be discussed at much greater length. Each contains many unitary observations of, to me, great fascination. In the rest of this chapter, however, I am going to restrict myself to the implications of propositions 1 and 4.

THE ROLE OF CLARITY OF PURPOSES

Many writers on large-system leadership have stressed the importance of purposes. A fundamental remark is the following by Chester Barnard:

> an objective purpose that can serve as the basis for a cooperative system is one that is *believed* by the contributors (or potential contributors) to it to be the determined purpose of the organization. The *inculcation of belief* in the real existence of a common purpose is an essential executive function. (Emphasis added)

This observation captures, albeit awkwardly, the problematic character of purposes. They are not given; they do not exist independent of members' perceptions and values or of the 'pictures in their heads', as I called purposes above. Yet the implication of Barnard's remark is that the relativity of purposes – that they *do* depend on perceptions – is not something that should be prominent in members' minds as they go about the organization's work. 'Why are we doing this? Why are we doing it this way?' are questions we would prefer not to have people asking whenever they feel like it. Can an organization act and at the same time be questioning the grounds of its action – doubting, as it were? Such a dual awareness is an attractive notion to those who philosophize about the consciousness of the truly civilized person, but one may question the idea's extension to the collective level. Systemic doubt is quite another matter.

The political scientist, Norton Long, put the matter of the leader/s role with respect to doubts and second thoughts quite trenchantly some years ago in an extraordinary essay in which he said:

> In the everyday routine of life, the problematic nature of reality is made up of a multiplicity of potentially applicable norms cutting in different directions, a fragmentary state of information, an absence of any relevant substantial amount of scientific knowledge, and a pressure of time flooding by constraining decision on the most precarious definition of the situation. . . . The reduction of the political problem (that is, of effective action) to a scientific problem is a natural result of the confusion of propositions of value and propositions of fact. It is also a

result of the human desire to escape the sheer anguish of creative decision. *Leadership is concerned with the transformation of doubts into the psychological grounds of cooperative common action.* (Emphasis added)

Twenty-five years ago, Philip Selznick in his landmark book, *Leadership in Administration*, proposed the 'definition of institutional mission and role' and the 'institutional embodiment of purpose' as being two essential functions of his 'institutional leader'.

In these three sets of ideas, there is a quality of 'ongoingness' that has often been overlooked. In my own experiences with management groups, I frequently encounter an impatience, even an exasperation, with discussions of basic purposes. It is as if leaders would rather believe either that these matters are understood once and for all by organization members, or that the ongoingness occurs by a kind of osmosis – but that, in any case, they the leaders have no responsibility to creatively revivify purposes.

This impatience may be justified in a stable world. A pervasive sense of purpose in an organization endures, after all, in relation to other forces, and as long as these are stable and predictable, purposes will probably continue to mean what they have always meant. But, as we all know, these other forces are themselves in motion. Most important among these forces in my opinion are the following four categories:

1 *Environmental demands and opportunities.* The more heterogeneous and dynamic these are, the more they present the organization with an ongoing need to interpret and reinterpret what is going on. It can take nothing for granted. The changing equivocality of environmental signals must constantly be removed.
2 *Organization members' needs, expectations, abilities and values.* These constitute the changing world brought into the organization. By the nature of organization itself they must literally be 'incorporated', and in the process it is frequently necessary to renegotiate the meaning of the organization's purpose.
3 *The technologies the organization employs in pursuit of its purposes.* These entail learning time to exploit their productive and economic potential. If the organization is constantly 'upgrading' its technologies, it may never reach a smooth flow of habituated actions, a flow on which the economics of efficiency and profitable action are based.
4 *The phenomenon of reorganization itself.* This is less often noted than the previous three. Many more structural alternatives exist for the modern large system than existed 25 years ago, and many organizations are continually experimenting with new forms. The impact of these changes on role relationships, chains of command, felt senses of accountability, and so forth, is not as thoroughly discussed as it should be, particularly the impact of all this flux on purposes.

In other words, the extent to which members can come to share pictures in their heads about the organization's basic purposes depends on some degree of stability in (1) environmental demands, (2) members' own expectations and needs, (3) the technologies they are operating, and (4) the structures through which they are bound together. *Beyond some un-known threshold, too much change in this system of factors breaks down the shared sense of what the organization is, why it exists, and what its basic purposes are.*

This is the key implication of F. E. Emery and E. L. Trist's famous remark that in their Type IV – Turbulent Field, 'the ground itself is moving'. The moving-ground metaphor refers to the most basic para-digms and images that we use to organize experience. It is one thing for the objectives and techniques that flow from a paradigm to be rapidly changing, but when the paradigm itself is undergoing substantial revision, there is no longer a firm basis for any proposal.

Emery and Trist were aware of the leadership problems this situation creates, but they did not deal with the question at any length. They suggest that Douglas McGregor's Theory Y seems to hold promise, which was a plausible expectation in the early 1960s but is, I think, considered to be quite insufficient today. They speculate prophetically about the ability of matrix structures to absorb large amounts of ambiguity. They are convinced that the articulation of overarching values is a crucial step. They seem to be saying that even if *things* cannot be stabilized, conscious-ness might be – through the development of broadly shared values. *Paradigm* leadership is needed; that is the apparent thrust of their argument.

Others, of course, were issuing similar calls in the 1960s when the first pains of the collapsing paradigm were felt. ('This is the age when things have not turned out as we thought they would', said David Matthews on being sworn in as Secretary of Health, Education and Welfare in the early 1970s.) But even now, a decade later, I think the question of leadership under conditions of extreme turbulence is no nearer to a working solution than it was when first articulated 20 or 30 years ago.

So we must ask, more urgently than ever, what becomes of the 'in-culcation of belief' (Barnard), the 'embodiment of purpose' (Selznick), and the 'transformation of doubts' (Long)? What does this behavior look like in the first place? Under increasingly turbulent conditions, how does it change? Who among the leaders of the world's organizations, of what-ever kind, is doing this work well?

First of all, the behavior we are talking about needs a name. I propose the word *purposing* to refer to *that continuous stream of actions by an organiz-ation's formal leadership that has the effect of inducing clarity, consensus, and commitment regarding the organization's basic purposes.* I decided on the term *purposing* as a result of investigating the etymology of the word *purpose* and discovering that it and the word *propose* derive from the same Latin root, *proponere*. In other words, through the filters of Old and Middle French and English our thinking has come to divide an idea that was originally more unified: that there is *both* an ongoing stream of proposing and the results of the process – purposes. We need the new word, *purposing*, to remind ourselves that there is a special class of proposing that needs to occur in organizations – proposing that has to do with the establishment, clarification, and modification of purposes. This, I propose, we call purposing.

THE FUNCTIONS OF PURPOSING

With the idea of purposing in hand, it is possible to begin to indicate some of the forms it takes in organizations. In general, my argument is that high-performing systems are, among other things, systems in which we can observe the phenomenon of purposing working well. People are not mixed up about why the system exists or about what their role in it is. Of course leaders do not refer to what they do as purposing; nevertheless, they inculcate belief, transform doubts, and embody purpose.

From high-performing systems as well as from other settings, I have identified the following seven functions of purposing:

1 *Purposing occurs in relation to the expectations of those who own or charter the system.* This does not mean that leaders merely preach conformity to these expectations, but rather that the content of what they talk about and do is seen to have these key outside forces as reference points.

2 *Purposing is seen in the articulation of the grounds for basic strategic decisions.* These decisions may be of many different kinds: to add a particular person to the system, to change its posture toward systems with which it competes, to adopt new technology, to fundamentally alter its internal structure, and so forth. The point is that such decisions are not made or explained in isolation from basic purposes.

3 *Purposing is seen in leaders' accounts of the meaning of the system's daily activity.* The hours people put in, the skills they practice to acquire, the sacrifices they make, the pains they take, and the pains they experience – all these can be interpreted in terms of the system's basic purposes, and in high-performing systems it is a very noticeable phenomenon.

4 *Purposing is evident in decisions NOT to do things.* Examples include the decision not to offer proposed new products, enter new territories, add available new technology, or hire or retain particular people. The phrases, 'It's not us', or 'It wouldn't be right for us', and so forth, are frequently heard in high-performing systems, as Thomas J. Peters mentioned in his study of America's best-managed companies.

Attractive-options-forgone is one of the most powerful forms of purposing. It communicates and inculcates discipline.

5 *Purposing differentiates the organization from other superficially similar
organizations.* Members of every organization are conscious of what
other systems somewhat like their own are doing. A key process by
which they come to identify with their own organization is to be
helped to see how it is not quite like any other. Warren G. Bennis called
this process 'identity' several years ago. It is a phenomenon that needs
to be much more widely understood.

6 *Purposing is the expression of what the leadership wants.* In the social
science literature, preoccupation with what the boss wants is often
treated as a kind of neurotic dependency reaction. But it is possible to
be curious and concerned in a healthy way about what the boss wants.

It is important to distinguish between wanting something for the
system and wanting something for oneself. The leadership of many
large systems today is 'just passing through', 'getting a ticket
punched', 'on a fast track'. Self-aggrandizement and self-promotion
are often these leaders' basic motives. The worst thing in the world,
some of them seem to feel, is actually to become entangled in the
system.

I have never found a high-performing system whose leadership was
perceived by members as on a fast track to something else. To be
perceived as wanting something for the system is crucial. And it cannot be faked.

7 *Purposing in some sense entails the mythologizing of oneself and the
organization.* When Selznick speaks of the institutional embodiment of
purpose, one aspect of the process is to let oneself come to embody the
organization. Perhaps people find it easier to identify with a complex
social system. This means that the leadership becomes a kind of vessel
or vehicle.

In the way leaders talk and act, in the preferences they express, in their
passions and tantrums, meanings echo for members. Harrison Owen, a
long-time observer of the large system machinations in Washington DC,
speaks of the leader needing to become the center of a 'myth-modification
process' – as an articulator of the new 'likely stories', as Owen calls them,
that can become the basis for future action.

To be willing to become a mythic figure is perhaps the true expression
of the 'loneliness of command'. The loneliness derives from the felt
discrepancy between what one is feeling and how one knows a con-
templated action will be received by members and the organization's
public. The search, agonized as it may be, is for courses of action that are
responsive to the ownership (No. 1), substantively sound (No. 2), not
merely demagogic or exploitative (No. 3), consistent with the system's

evolving identity (Nos. 4 and 5), and honest expressions of one's own values (No. 6).

No wonder it is so difficult; no wonder it is rare – although it is not as rare as some might think.

In high-performing systems, men and women are finding ways to conduct purposing in terms of the characteristics I have just discussed. This is why high-performing systems are such powerful and instructive exemplars. The final section of this chapter is concerned with synthesizing many of these remarks into a simple statement of what leaders of high-performing systems actually do.

THE PURPOSING OF HIGH-PERFORMING SYSTEMS

I believe that three characteristics appear 100 percent of the time in the actions of leaders of high-performing systems. I think these three characteristics and their interrelationships have profound implications for the world of organizations and organizational leaders, not because they are such esoteric or mysterious factors, but because they are so well known they are apparently easily overlooked.

- Leaders of high-performing systems put in extraordinary amounts of *time*.
- Leaders of high-performing systems have very strong *feelings* about the attainment of the system's purposes.
- Leaders of high-performing systems *focus* on key issues and variables.

I have come to call this the *Time–Feeling–Focus theory* of high-performing systems leadership. There are, of course, many nuances, subtleties, and local specialities connected with the leadership of any high-performing system, but over and over again, Time, Feeling and Focus appear – no matter what else appears. They may not be totally sufficient in themselves, but they are necessary to the leadership of HPSs. In the following section, I say a few more words about each, following which I will describe what happens in human systems when one or two of the three are absent. I then conclude with some comments about the interrelationships of leader and system development, and about the question of leadership style.

Time

Leaders of high-performing systems work very hard. That is basic. They put in many hours. Their consciousness is dominated by the system's issues and events. They see the rest of life, often, in terms of the system's jargon, technology, and culture. Their awareness of the system does not respect the clock, and hence they can be seen scribbling notes to themselves or others, making phone calls, and replaying and debriefing system events at all kinds of odd times – evenings, weekends, vacation periods, the wee hours. Their consciousness does not respect place either: they work in the office, at home, in airport-boarding areas, in the back seats of taxicabs, or anywhere else they happen to be. At halftimes and intermissions, they duck out to call the office. They are often perceived by system members and others as living, eating, sleeping, breathing the system.

The hours they put in are matters of frequent comment by those around them. Stories accumulate about the amounts of time they put in and about their nonstop work habits. Curiously, the quality of what they accomplish in all these hours is commented on much less frequently – not because the quality is thought to be mediocre or low, but because it is apparently felt to be a natural result of all those many hours of extra-ordinary effort.

It is of great importance that these leaders put in large amounts of both microtime and macrotime. Microtime is the hour-to-hour, day-to-day kind of investment. Less frequently noted is macrotime – that is, leaders of high-performing systems tend to stay in their jobs for many years; they do not simply 'pass through'. They make a large commitment of both microtime and macrotime.

Sometimes the high-performing system is a rather temporary system – that is, it is not intended to last indefinitely. In such a case, macrotime is the willingness to 'commit for the duration'.

Feeling

'An executive ought to want something,' says my colleague, Professor David Brown. In this rather simple assertion, which emerges from his studies of large-system leadership, he has neatly captured a second element that is always present in the attitudes and behaviors I see in leaders of high-performing systems: they care deeply about the system. This includes its purposes, its structure and conduct, its history, its future security and, although this is sometimes expressed in a way that would make a psychologist shudder, they care about the people in the system.

For the leader of a high-performing system, constant energetic purposing is a natural expression of Feeling – that is, of his or her own deep values and beliefs. Purposing is not a style or function that is adopted for some occasion. Feeling furthermore sustains the person through many hours of labor discussed under time. Involvement with the system is the person's life, which is why, from his or her frame of reference, the amount of time put in is a natural thing to do.

Macrotime often plays a key role in the development and expression of feeling. With many large systems, it is not immediately clear what makes them special. A leader 'cycling through' on an 18-to-24-month assignment may never experience the system much more deeply than its immediate issues permit. Many, many executives bring high achievement motivation to their jobs. In macrotime this motivation becomes invested in the system's culture and this culture comes to be seen as something valuable for its own sake rather than as a vehicle for the leader's ambition, development, and next assignment.

Motivation in high-performing systems, I said, has 'peculiarity'. In leaders this peculiarity can be seen in the way they have integrated their innate energies and ambitions with the system's needs and opportunities. Selznick's 'institutional embodiment of purpose', therefore, is not a one-way phenomenon. In high-performing systems there is a two-way embodiment in Feeling of leader-in-system and system-in-leader. When a person becomes 'Mr . . . (whatever the activity or industry is)' or 'the First Lady of . . . (the activity or industry)', the two-way embodiment is complete.

Through Feeling, leaders of high-performing systems tend to take themselves and their systems quite seriously. They often become the targets of worldly-wise cynics and satirists. For example, such leaders' total absorption makes them vulnerable to interpretations of their behavior that are askance to the values and beliefs they hold. Some years ago in the *Harvard Business Review*, Seymour Tilles compared the strategy used by the founder of Lestoil to beat Procter & Gamble with Hadrian's strategy. The *New Yorker* quoted a key paragraph from that article in one of its famous column footings with the editorial remark: 'Every age has its heroes.'

More seriously, the very strength of Feeling can sometimes blind a leader to what the system needs as the environment changes. They sometimes cannot see that the meanings they have built up about the system may be becoming manipulative, that they have to rethink what the system is and what it can be in the new conditions. All organizations go through this process and high-performing systems are not immune. The conservatism about new methods and the boundaries that separate them from the environment are in a continuous tension with the dynamic environment. Where a system drifts into irrelevance over time, it is usually the result of a combination of very strong Feeling on the part of leaders and members and insufficient wisdom about the next element discussed – Focus.

Focus

Management literature frequently discusses what it is that the boss ought to be working on. Chester Barnard's original essay was devoted to this question. Situational theory has been answering this question in recent years: 'The boss ought to be working on whatever the system needs at the moment.'

Leaders of high-performing systems have solved this problem. Behind attention to detail, which is possible because of Time, one can note persistent factors that they focus on. In one system attention may be focused on recruitment, in another on the securing of stable funding, in another on the buffering of the system from the environment, and in another on the hands-on involvement in the system's basic activity. There seems to be no fixed formula, no short list of variables that are always important. But I am saying there always is some short list of priorities that leaders have clearly in mind – that is, in Focus.

Furthermore, one can note leaders actively communicating their judgements about what is important to members. They help bring focus to others' behavior as well as their own. This function is of extreme importance because in any organization, at any moment, there are many things that need attention. These factors do not exist as abstract impersonal matters, but rather are actively voiced by various organization members. The organization is a texture of proposing, as I said earlier. Leaders of high-performing systems are not distracted by this cacophony. They know which few things are important, and in their statements and actions they make these priorities known. Members also learn what is important in macrotime, and, therefore, in high-performing systems the cacophony of proposing is less chaotic and centrifugal than in other systems – although it is rarely absent entirely. Focus is really focusing in dynamic terms: it is an ongoing process of choosing what to emphasize and what to leave alone.

Strategic planning and strategic management, as they are discussed in the literature, are primarily the study of Focus. What are the key variables? In Thomas J. Peters's survey of America's best-managed companies, excellent companies are found to have 'simultaneous loose–tight controls' – that is, they have picked out key variables and developed tight controls over these and are willing to use relatively loose controls over the rest. Such an approach at one and the same time communicates what is important and a desire to allow as much freedom and latitude as possible.

Without Time and Feeling, strategic planning, as discussed in the bulk of the current literature, is an empty technical exercise. For example, one of the most common problems in strategic management is the length of view that top managers take. It tends to be too short. Their term of office does not extend far enough into the future. They will not be around when the fruits (or poisons) of their decisions appear. This is why the concept of macrotime is so important. Focus constitutes the *what* of executive leadership, but it cannot carry by itself the *why* or the *when* or the *how*. The *why* resides primarily in what I am calling Feeling. The *when*, in Time. The *how*, as I shall develop below, is not as important – in high-performing systems at least – as writers on leadership have made it.

VARIATIONS ON TIME–FEELING–FOCUS

I have said that these three elements are always present in the actions of leaders of high-performing systems. It is instructive to pause and comment on situations in which one or two or all three are absent. Some very familiar patterns emerge.

1 *Time with no Feeling or Focus.* The phenomena associated with workaholism and Type A behavior are inherent in this situation and the next. The investment of large chunks of time without a positive feeling that the activity is important and without a focus on key issues has the quality of compulsiveness. There are extreme forms that are, indeed, neurotic, because with this pattern we are talking about a person who works very hard without knowing exactly what to work on or why. Attention to detail and the investment of time alone is not characteristic of HPS leaders.

2 *Time and Feeling without Focus.* The leader who cares deeply and is willing to work very hard, but for whom everything seems to be of equal importance, is a somewhat tragic figure. In large and complex organizations this mix of factors can be an actual killer. Managers who speak of having to run harder and harder just to stay in the same place may be stuck in this pattern. The person who has time and feeling without focus needs help in understanding the system and in managing her or his own time. It is to this person that we say, 'You need to step back and really think about what is important.' Sadly, though, the person caught in the grip of this mix misinterprets the advice. He or she thinks the advice is, 'Put in less time; don't feel so strongly.' Of course, the person can't do it – doesn't even want to do it. Time and Feeling are deep expressions of the person's history and character and are not easily modified. How such a person learns to focus without cutting back on Time or Feeling is a major challenge to students of executive development.

3 *Time and Focus without Feeling.* This is, I am afraid, characteristic of a large number of the young people we see today in our professional schools of management. I quickly add that the cultures of the schools themselves tend to reward this pattern lavishly, so even a young person not initially disposed toward this pattern will feel enormous pressure to adopt it.

   Time and Focus without Feeling says, 'Don't get too involved. Look at the facts. Make a decision and move on to the next thing. Be willing to work hard because there is no free lunch, but don't get your identity too wrapped up in what you are doing. Build your track record; get your tickets punched; do quality at each milestone on the fast track. Somewhere out in your future – in your forties, perhaps – you'll have accumulated the "clout" to do what you want to do and be the person you want to be. (You'll have earned the right to Feeling.)' Unfortunately for too many, the forties do not bring this opportunity; instead they bring a set of work habits and personal financial circumstances that seem to require continuation of the same patterns.

It is important to say that with Time and Focus without Feeling, the pattern is not dysfunctional *per se*. It is just never found in leaders of high-performing systems. Some occupations, for example, require that Feeling be detached from the immediate system in favor of adherence to standards and procedures that are independent of the immediate system – that is, they derive from another system of which the person is a member. There is no question that this displacement of Feeling from an immediate system to some broader professional system is socially important. Law, medicine, and accounting are examples. The possibility of a 'high-performing relationship' with an immediate client is sometimes a secondary consideration compared with adhering to professional standards.

4 *Feeling without Time or Focus.* This condition is usually labelled as idealism or cynicism. It is possible to care very deeply about various organizations in society without actually devoting much time to them or really understanding what is involved in operating them effectively (Focus). Without the commitment of energy expressed in Time and the thought and practicality expressed in Focus, the Feeling-driven person issues calls to arms or fulminates. Again, this is a social role that is historically of great importance, but it is not found in HPS leaders.

5 *Feeling and Focus without Time.* Three very well-known social roles frequently manifest this pattern. The staff person who does very good work but who goes home at five o'clock is one example. The astute social commentator is a second. The third are those engaged in one of America's fastest growing industries – namely, consulting. A good consultant has his or her efforts focused on the right variables and cares that the client organization does better. But consultants are not continuously present. They phase in and out. They are often not there when the system needs them most. Their function is not to sustain the system but to get it started, to get it pointed in the right direction. So once again, it is not that Feeling and Focus without Time are bad or dysfunctional *per se*, but rather that this mix is not found in HPS leaders.

6 *Focus without Time or Feeling.* This describes a person who is working on the right things but who is not putting in more hours than absolutely necessary and for whom there is no very deep personal meaning in the activity. This mix is never found in HPS leadership. Actually, this pattern describes an 'employee' whose focus actually comes from someone else who has defined the task carefully. Such person just works the expected hours at the expected energy level. Focus without Time or Feeling is just a job.

7 *Absence of Time, Feeling and Focus.* So far I have described situations in which one or two of the three elements are strongly present. What about the situations in which none of them is present to any significant degree? This chapter is not concerned with diagnosing pervasive organizational or societal ills. My high-performing systems research, however, causes me constantly to wonder: to what extent have we drifted into a broad social condition where one can be a member or even a leader of an organization without Time or Feeling or Focus as I have defined them? It is a sobering exercise to reflect on all the social forces today that work against the investment of Time, the flowering of Feeling and the attainment of Focus.

RELATION OF TIME, FEELING AND FOCUS TO SYSTEM DEVELOPMENT

The three factors seem to be interrelated and interdependent, although they do not exist in direct causal relationships one to another. In retrospect, however, one can see in the actions and attitudes of HPS leaders how investments of Time tend to deepen Feeling; how the development of Feeling leads to putting in more Time; how Focus is both expressive *of* Time and Feeling and leads *to* further investments of Time and new patterns of Feeling. I emphasize that these relationships are noticed in retrospect. One cannot say, prospectively, that putting in Time, for example, will automatically deepen Feeling and make more likely the discovery of the key variables captured in the idea of Focus.

That strength in one factor does not automatically cause development in the other two suggests that there are some additional forces present in the development of HPS leaders that are relatively absent in the development of leaders of other systems. Such forces lie in the system itself; the system's developing strength and success somehow make more likely the discovery of the key things to Focus on, the willingness to put in Time, and the development of ever-stronger Feeling about the system and its purposes.

There is a good deal of anecdotal evidence to support this idea. For example, most of us have, at one time or another, experienced success in some organizational effort that seems to trigger a collection of improvements in the system in a sometimes startling fashion. Effort gets more efficient; morale jumps; members' confidence in each other increases apace; and leadership improves in a variety of ways, including the three factors I have been discussing. Sometimes such systems get on a 'streak' where, for a period at least, they just seem to do everything right. A process like this, I am suggesting, little-understood as it is, could be quite a significant influence on the development of the system's leadership. We know, of course, that 'Nothing succeeds like success.'

A second kind of evidence to suggest that the evolving success of the system has a powerful developmental effect on the leadership comes from the way members of high-performing systems talk about the early formative period of the system. Consistently they come out with such statements as, 'We had no idea things would turn out like this.' 'In the early years, we hardly knew what we were doing.' 'We were really groping.' 'We just did what we thought we were supposed to do.' And so forth. I have never found an HPS member who claims that the high achievements of the system are merely the logical results of a preexisting plan, although the notion of 'having a dream and seeking to realize it' is very common. Nor do I have data from members or leaders of high-performing systems to suggest that the leaders knew all along what they were doing. In a high-performing system, omniscient strategies are usually not attributed to the leadership.

So, in summary, my current thinking is that the grasp of Time, Feeling and Focus by the leader develops and coexists with the system's life and achievements.

This, however, is not a particularly satisfying way to talk about leadership in high-performing systems. More tempting is the assertion that 'Leaders cause higher performing systems.' That certainly is the thrust of much of the writing on management and leadership – that if the individual somehow does something to his or her attitude, knowledge, or style, major system improvements will occur. Social scientists have implicitly been promising this to practitioners for years. Marginal improvements do seem to occur in some cases, but I have no evidence that the breakthrough to a high-performing condition as I have defined it will occur.

I said earlier that high-performing systems have 'gelled' in a way that cannot be easily discussed in our current language system of mechanical and organic metaphors. That finding is relevant to this question of the relationship between the leader's attitude and behavior and the development of the system. One reason I think the Time–Feeling–Focus model has promise is that it is simple. It does not overcategorize and overspecify what it is we are trying to understand. Similarly, the eight broad generalizations about high-performing systems given at the beginning of this chapter are deliberately phrased in as commonsense a way as possible. I am trying to keep our attention on the experience of members and leaders in these settings.

I have discussed the Time–Feeling–Focus approach to this point as a way of understanding leaders' behavior. The scheme is also very useful for understanding members' behavior and for understanding the system as a whole. With due regard for the different roles they play and scopes of responsibility they carry, Time–Feeling–Focus can be used to evaluate anyone in the high-performing system.

It is not just the leader but the system as a whole that can be seen functioning at all sorts of odd times and in odd places. Members come in on evenings and weekends. The culture of the system blends into the cultures of their families. These are manifestations of the Time factor. Congruence of Feeling, as I have said several times, is a distinguishing characteristic of a high-performing system. What I called the peculiarity of motivation is shared and intensely valued among members. Focus as an inter-member phenomenon is one of the most striking features of a high-performing system as contrasted with other human systems. In a high-performing system, people actually agree, without having to go through tortuous processes of negotiation and conflict management, on what the key factors are.

Perhaps a high-performing system is not an objective entity at all. The criteria by which its success is measured are subjective. The meanings it transmits to members and observers in its environment are intensely personal and subjective. It is full of all kinds of events and processes that social science has tended to ignore. Statements like these, of course, could be made about all social systems. They are all objects of consciousness in the first instance and as such should not be reduced to simple machine models, cause–effect models, or other superficially attractive metaphors. I think phenomenology has the most interesting things to say about these issues, but an exploration of these things is beyond the scope of this chapter. Suffice it to say, for the moment, that I regard a high-performing system as a frame on which members' consciousnesses interact. The interesting thing about leaders' consciousness is that it seems to be described by the Time–Feeling–Focus scheme.

THE QUESTION OF STYLE

The Time–Feeling–Focus idea leads to the final observation that a leader's style does not seem to determine the level of the system's performance. Therefore, what I've learned about high-performing systems seems to differ radically from the views that have been expressed in the management literature over the last 25 years – that is, that managerial and leadership styles have a definite effect on the organization's performance. Perhaps the problem lies in the fact that most research in this area has been carried out in low-performing systems. Thus researchers have frequently concluded that the *way* the leader or manager was working – his or her style – was having a significantly negative effect on performance. They have extrapolated from this conclusion to the idea that a change in style will repair the damage that is being done to motivation, morale, communication, trust and problem solving. I need not review further the thousands of pages on the subject of warm vs. cool, participative vs. autocratic, demanding vs. accepting styles, and so forth. My main point is that, for the most part, all this interest in style is beside the point *in high-performing systems*.

I have seen every style I can conceive of in the leadership of high-performing systems. There are tyrants whose almost maniacal commitment to achieving the system's purposes makes one think that they'd be locked up if they were not in charge of an organization that was the best of its kind. There are warm, laid-back father figures who hardly seem to be doing anything at all, until one looks a little more closely. There are technocrats devoted to computerized representations of the system, and dreamers who seem to care nothing about the operational data. Some of these leaders are educated to the highest levels, and others never finished high school. Owing to the Focus factor, they all possess expertise in what the system does, but some express this expertise constantly, and others don't. Some seem clearly to be 'Type As' on the way to exhaustion or an early grave, but most are in good health and have noticeably strong constitutions. Some are rah-rah optimists and others are dour critics who express their love for the system by enumerating its imperfections. Leaders of high-performing systems are all over the style map.

What the theory described in this chapter says to the would-be leader is: 'Seek constantly to do what is right and what is needed in the system (Focus). Do it in terms of your energy (Time). Put your whole psyche into it (Feeling).' This is the normative lesson I derive from studying HPS leaders. It is a very simple prescription, and in its simplicity is somewhat at variance with the fine and precise distinctions in the literature. But it is these three factors, always understood in combination rather than one at a time, that my results suggest.

CONCLUSION

In high-performing systems, as I have defined them, one can note their constant purposing by the system leadership. Purposing occurs through the investment of large amounts of micro- and macrotime, the experience and expression of very strong Feeling about the attainment of purposes and the importance of the system, and the attainment of understanding of the key variables for system success (Focus). All leaders of high-performing systems have integrated these three factors at a very high level of intensity and clarity.

The number of social scientists who are trying to understand excellence in human systems is very small. Pathology is more accessible and, for some, more fun. The question of what it takes to govern and lead a high-performing system and the question of how we are going to develop more men and women who are equipped to do so await the increased attention that I believe high-performing systems deserve. This chapter has been an effort to stimulate such attention.

SELECTED BIBLIOGRAPHY

The literature on high-performing systems is quite scattered. The author's original statement appears as a chapter titled 'Toward a Behavioral Description of High Performing Systems' in Morgan McCall and Michael Lombard's (eds) *Leadership: Where Else Can We Go?* (Duke University Press, 1976). A classic statement concerning large business organizations is Thomas J. Peters's 'Putting Excellence into Management' (*Business Week*, July 21, 1980). What are called 'institutional histories' can sometimes be very useful, for example Ray Kroc's *Grinding It Out: The Making of McDonalds* (Regnery, 1977) or Melvin T. Copeland's *And Mark an Era: The History of Harvard Business School* (Little, Brown, 1958). 'Project histories' like Norman Mailer's extraordinary account of the Apollo Moon program, *Of a Fire on the Moon* (Little, Brown, 1970), or John Hunt's *The Ascent of Everest* (Hodder & Stoughton, 1953), also contain many valuable insights.

The idea of 'purposing' is implicit in most discussions of the key functions of top managers. Chester Barnard's classic, *The Functions of the Executive* (Harvard University Press, 1939) makes the point over and over. Philip Selznick is less well known among businessmen, but he is considered to have made one of the more profound statements about top executive functions in his *Leadership in Administration* (Harper & Row, 1957). Norton Long is a political scientist who developed fundamental new insights some years ago in a remarkable essay, 'The Political Act as an Act of Will' (*Sociology*, July, 1963). Clearly Warren Bennis has been one of the most important contributors to our understanding of what top leaders do. One of his better statements is in *The Temporary Society*, co-authored with Philip Slater (Harper & Row, 1968).

There is a developing literature that can be called 'phenomenological' in the sense that it deals with the way organizations and organizational process actually present themselves to human consciousness – that is, how we 'make sense' of the social world we live in. Useful laymen's introductions to the field of phenomenology are Richard Zaner's *The Way of Phenomenology* (Bobbs-Merrill Pegasus Books, 1970) and Ernest Keen's *A Primer of Phenomenological Psychology* (Holt, Rinehart & Winston, 1975). Jerry Harvey of George Washington University has been probing our experience of the social world for years. One of his lesser known but more useful commentaries is 'Eight Myths OD Consultants Believe in . . . and Die by!' (*OD Practitioner*, February, 1975). The 'phenomenology of the environment', so to speak, is powerfully discussed in F. E. Emery and E. L. Trist's classic, 'The Casual Texture of Organizational Environments' (*Human Relations*, February, 1965), and Karl Weick's 'organizing model' as described in *The Social Psychology of Organizing* (Addison-Wesley, 1979, 2nd edn). For the serious student of phenomenological approaches to organizational life, Peter Berger and Thomas Luckman's *The Social Construction of Reality* (Anchor Books, 1967) is indispensable.

ACKNOWLEDGEMENT

Many, many people have contributed over the years to my understanding of high-performing systems. But no one has been more important than my colleague at George Washington University, Professor Jerry B. Harvey. His intellect and wit and continuous support, and his unfeigned delight in the ideas that fall out of the HPS focus, are simply of incalculable value to me.

Chapter 5

Skilled incompetence

Chris Argyris

The ability to get along with others is always an asset, right? Wrong. By adeptly avoiding conflict with coworkers, some executives eventually wreak organizational havoc. And it's their very adeptness that's the problem. The explanation for this lies in what I call skilled incompetence, whereby managers use practiced routine behavior (skill) to produce what they do not intend (incompetence). We can see this happen when managers talk to each other in ways that are seemingly candid and straightforward. What we don't see so clearly is how managers' skills can become institutionalized and create disastrous side effects in their organizations. Consider this familiar situation:

The entrepreneur-CEO of a fast-growing medium-sized company brought together his bright, dedicated, hardworking top managers to devise a new strategic plan. The company had grown at about 45 per cent per year, but fearing that it was heading into deep administrative trouble, the CEO had started to rethink his strategy. He decided he wanted to restructure his organization along more rational, less *ad hoc*, lines. As he saw it, the company was split between the sales-oriented people who sell off-the-shelf products and the people producing custom services who are oriented toward professionals. And each group was suspicious of the other. He wanted the whole group to decide what kind of company it was going to run.

His immediate subordinates agreed that they must develop a vision and make some strategic decisions. They held several long meetings to do this. Although the meetings were pleasant enough and no one seemed to be making life difficult for anyone else, they concluded with no agreements or decisions. 'We end up compiling lists of issues but not deciding,' said one vice-president. Another added, 'And it gets pretty discouraging when this happens every time we meet.' A third worried aloud, 'If you think we are discouraged, how do you think the people below us feel who watch us repeatedly fail?'

This is a group of executives who are at the top, who respect each other, who are highly committed, and who agree that developing a vision and strategy is critical. Yet whenever they meet, they fail to create the vision and the strategy they desire. What is going on here? Are the managers really so incompetent? If so, why?

WHAT CAUSES INCOMPETENCE

At first, the executives in the previous example believed that they couldn't formulate and implement a good strategic plan because they lacked sound financial data. So they asked the financial vice-president to reorganize and reissue the data. Everyone agreed he did a superb job.

But the financial executive reported to me, 'Our problem is *not* the absence of financial data. I can flood them with data. We lack vision of what kind of company we want to be and a strategy. Once we produce those, I can supply the necessary data.' The other executives reluctantly agreed.

After several more meetings in which nothing got done, a second explanation emerged. It had to do with the personalities of the individuals and the way they work with each other. The CEO explained, 'This is a group of lovable guys with very strong egos. They are competitive, bright, candid and dedicated. But when we meet, we seem to go in circles, we are not prepared to give in a bit and make the necessary compromises.'

Is this explanation valid? Should the top managers become less competitive? I'm not sure. Some management groups are not good at problem solving and decision making precisely because the participants have weak egos and are uncomfortable with competition.

If personality were really the problem, the cure would be psychotherapy. And it's simply not true that to be more effective, executives need years on the couch. Besides, pinpointing personality as the issue hides the real culprit.

THE CULPRIT IS SKILL

Let's begin by asking whether counterproductive behavior is also natural and routine. Does everyone seem to be acting sincerely? Do things go wrong even though the managers are not being destructively manipulative and political?

For the executive group, the answer to these questions is yes. Their motives were decent, and they were at their personal best. Their actions were spontaneous, automatic and unrehearsed. They acted in milliseconds; they were skilled communicators.

How can skilful actions be counterproductive? When we're skilful we usually produce what we intend. So, in a sense, did the executives. In this case, the skilled behavior – the spontaneous and automatic responses – was meant to avoid upset and conflict at the meetings. The unintended by-products are what cause trouble. Because the executives don't say what they really mean or test the assumptions they really hold, their skills inhibit a resolution of the important intellectual issues embedded in developing the strategy. Thus the meetings end with only lists and no decisions.

This patter of failure is not only typical of this group of managers. It happens to people in all kinds of organizations regardless of age, gender, educational background, wealth, or position in the hierarchy. Let me illustrate with another example that involves the entire organizational culture at the upper levels. Here we'll begin to see how people's tendency to avoid conflict, to duck the tough issues, becomes institutionalized and leads to a culture that can't tolerate straight talk.

WHERE THE SKILFUL THRIVE

The top management of a large, decentralized corporation was having difficulty finding out what some of its division presidents were up to. Time and time again the CEO would send memos to the presidents asking for information, and time and time again they'd send next to nothing in return. But other people at headquarters accepted this situation as normal. When asked why they got so little direct communication from their division heads, they'd respond, 'That's the way we do things around here.'

Here is an organization that isn't talking to itself. The patterns that managers set up among themselves have become institutionalized, and what were once characteristic personal exchanges have now become organizational defensive routines. Before I go on to describe what these routines look like, let's look at how this situation arose.

Built into decentralization is the age-old tug between autonomy and control: superiors want no surprises, subordinates want to be left alone. The subordinates push for autonomy; they assert that by leaving them alone, top management will show its trust from a distance. The superiors, on the other hand, try to keep control through information systems. The subordinates see the control devices as confirming their suspicions – their superiors don't trust them.

Many executives I have observed handle this tension by pretending that the tension is not there. They act as if everyone were in accord and trust that no one will point out disagreements and thereby rock the boat. At the same time, however, they do feel the tension and can't help but soft-pedal their talk. They send mixed messages. (See Figure 5.1.)

The CEO in this example kept saying to his division presidents, 'I mean it – you run the show down there.' The division presidents, wanting to prove their mettle, believed him until an important issue came up. When it did the CEO, concerned about the situation and forgetting that he wanted his division chiefs to be innovative, would make phone calls and send memos seeking information.

DEFENSIVE ROUTINES EMERGE

One of the most powerful ways people deal with potential embarrass-ment is to create 'organizational defensive routines'. I define these as any

---

How does a manager send mixed messages?
It takes skill. Here are four rules:

1
Design a clearly ambiguous message. For example, 'Be innovative and take risks, but be careful' is a message that says in effect, 'Go, but go just so far' without specifying how far far is. The ambiguity and imprecision cover the speaker who can't know ahead of time what is too far.

The receiver, on the other hand, clearly understands the ambiguity and imprecision. Moreover, he or she knows that a request for more precision would likely be interpreted as a sign of immaturity or inexperience. And the receivers may also need an out some day and may want to keep the message imprecise and ambiguous. Receivers don't want 'far' defined any more clearly than the senders do.

2
Ignore any inconsistencies in the message. When people send mixed messages, they usually do it spontaneously and with no sign that the message is mixed. Indeed, if they did appear to hesitate, they would defeat their purpose of maintaining control. Even worse, they might appear weak.

3
Make the ambiguity and inconsistency in the message undiscussable. The whole point of sending a mixed message is to avoid dealing with a situation straight on. The sender does not want the message's mixedness exposed. An executive is not about to send a mixed message and then ask, 'Do you find my message inconsistent and ambiguous?' The executive also renders the message undiscussable by the very natural way of sending it. To challenge the innocence of the sender is to imply that the sender is dupli-citous – not a likely thing for a subordinate to do.

4
Make the undiscussability also undiscussable. One of the best ways to do this is to send the mixed message in a setting that is not conducive to open inquiry, such as a large meeting or a group where people of unequal organizational status are present. No one wants to launder linen in public. While they are sending mixed messages during a meeting, people rarely reflect on their actions or talk about how the organizational culture, including the meeting, makes discussing the undiscussable difficult.

Figure 5.1 **Four easy steps to chaos**

action or policy designed to avoid surprise, embarrassment, or threat. But they also prevent learning and thereby prevent organizations from investigating or eliminating the underlying problems.

Defensive routines are systemic in that most people within the company adhere to them. People leave the organization and new ones arrive, yet the defensive routines remain intact.

To see the impact of the defensive routines and the range of their effects, let's return to the division heads who are directed by mixed messages. They feel a lack of trust and are suspicious of their boss's intentions but they must, nonetheless, find ways to live with the mixed messages. So they 'explain' the messages to themselves and to their subordinates. These explanations often sound like this:

> 'Corporate never *really* means decentralization.'
> 'Corporate is willing to trust divisions when the going is smooth, but not when it's rough.'
> 'Corporate is more concerned about the stock market than about us.'

Of course, the managers rarely test their hypotheses about corporation motives with top executives. If discussing mixed messages among themselves would be uncomfortable, then public testing of the validity of these explanations would be embarrassing.

But now the division heads are in a double bind. On the one hand, if they go along unquestioningly, they may lose their autonomy and their subordinates will see them as having little influence with corporation. On the other hand, if the division executives do not comply with orders from above, headquarters will think they are recalcitrant, and if noncompliance continues, disloyal.

Top management is in a similar predicament. It senses that division managements have suspicions about headquarters' motives and are covering them up. If headquarters makes its impression known, though, the division heads may get upset. If the top does not say anything, the division presidents could infer full agreement when there is none. Usually, in the name of keeping up good relations, the top covers up its predicament.

Soon, people in the divisions learn to live with their binds by generating further explanations. For example, they may eventually conclude that openness is a strategy that top management has devised intentionally to cover up its unwillingness to be influenced.

Since this conclusion is based on the assumption that people at the top are covering up, managers won't test it either. Since neither headquarters nor division executives discuss or resolve the attributions or the frustrations, both may eventually stop communicating regularly and openly. Once in place, the climate of mistrust makes it more likely that the issues become undiscussable.

Now both headquarters and division managers have attitudes,

assumptions and actions that create self-fulfilling and self-sealing processes that each sees the other as creating.

Under these conditions, it is not surprising to find that superiors and subordinates hold both good and bad feelings about each other. For example, they may say about each other: 'They are bright and well intentioned but they have a narrow, parochial view'; or 'They are interested in the company's financial health but they do not understand how they are harming earnings in the long run'; or 'They are interested in people but they pay too little attention to the company's development.'

My experience is that people cannot build on their appreciation of others without first overcoming their suspicions. But to overcome what they don't like, people must be able to discuss it. And this requirement violates the undiscussability rule embedded in the organizational defensive routines.

Is there any organization that does not have these hang-ups and problems? Some people suggest that getting back to basics will open lines of communication. But the proffered panacea does not go far enough; it does not deal with the underlying patterns. Problems won't be solved by simply correcting one isolated instance of poor performance.

When CEOs I have observed declared war against organizational barriers to candor and demanded that people get back to basics, most often they implemented the new ideas with the old skills. People changed whatever they could and learned to cover their asses even more skilfully. The freedom to question and to confront is crucial, but it is inadequate. To overcome skilled incompetence, people have to learn new skills – to ask the questions behind the questions.

Defensive routines exist. They are undiscussable. They proliferate and grow underground. And the social pollution is hard to identify until something occurs that blows things open. Often that something is a glaring error whose results cannot be hidden. The 1986 space shuttle disaster is an example. Only after the accident occurred were the mixed messages and defensive routines used during the decision to launch exposed. The disaster made it legitimate for outsiders to require insiders to discuss the undiscussable. (By the way, writing a tighter set of controls and requiring better communication won't solve the problem. Tighter controls will only enlarge the book of rules that William Rogers, chairman of the president's committee to investigate the *Challenger* disaster, acknowledged can be a cure worse than the illness. He pointed out that in his Navy years, when the players went by the book, things only got worse.)

Managers do not have the choice to ignore the organizational problems that these self-sealing loops create. They may be able to get away with it today, but they're creating a legacy for those who will come after them.

HOW TO BECOME UNSKILLED

The top management group I described at the beginning of this chapter decided to learn new skills by examining the defenses they created in their own meetings.

First, they arranged a two-day session away from the office for which they wrote a short case beforehand. The purpose of these cases was twofold. First, they allowed the executives to develop a collage of problems they thought were critical. Not surprisingly, in this particular group at least half wrote on issues related to the product versus custom service conflict. Second, the cases provided a kind of window into the prevailing rules and routines the executives used. The form of the case was as follows:

1 In one paragraph describe a key organizational problem as you see it.
2 In attacking the problem, assume you could talk to whomever you wish. Describe, in a paragraph or so, the strategy you would use in this meeting.
3 Next split your page into two columns. On the right-hand side, write how you would begin the meeting: what you would actually say. Then write what you believe the other(s) would say. Then write your response to their response. Continue writing this scenario for two or so double-spaced typewritten pages.
4 In the left-hand column write any of your ideas or feelings that you would not communicate for whatever reason.

The executives reported that they became engrossed in writing the cases. Some said that the very writing of their case was an eye-opener. Moreover, once the stories were distributed, the reactions were jocular. They enjoyed them: 'Great, Joe does this all the time'; 'Oh, there's a familiar one'; 'All salespeople and no listeners'; 'Oh my God, this is us.'

What is the advantage of using the cases? Crafted and written by the executives themselves, they become vivid examples of skilled incompetence. They illustrate the skill with which each executive sought to avoid upsetting the other while trying to change the other's mind. The cases also illustrate their incompetence. By their own analysis, what they did upset the others, created suspicion, and made it less likely that their views would prevail.

The cases are also very important learning devices. During a meeting, it is difficult to slow down behavior produced in milliseconds, to reflect on it, and to change it. For one thing, it's hard to pay attention to interpersonal actions and to substantive issues at the same time.

A collage from several cases appears in Figure 5.2. It was written by executives who believed the company should place a greater emphasis on custom service.

The cases written by individuals who supported the product strategy did not differ much. They too were trying to persuade, sell or cajole their fellow officers. Their left-hand columns were similar.

In analyzing their left-hand columns, the executives found that each side blamed the other for the difficulties, and they used the same reasons. For example, each side said:

> 'If you insist on your position, you'll harm the morale I've built.'
> 'Don't hand me that line. You know what I'm talking about.'
> 'Why don't you take off your blinders and wear a company hat?'
> 'It upsets me when I think of how they think.'
> 'I'm really trying hard, but I'm beginning to feel this is hopeless.'

These cases effectively illustrate the influence of skilled incompetence. In crafting the cases, the executives were trying not to upset the others and at the same time were trying to change their minds. This process requires skill. Yet the skill they used in the cases has the unintended side effects I talked about. In the cases, the others became upset and dug in their heels without changing their minds.

Here's a real problem. These executives and all the others I've studied to date can't prevent the counterproductive consequences until and unless they learn new skills. Nor will it work to bypass the skilled incompetence by focusing on the business problems, such as, in this case, developing a business strategy.

THE ANSWER IS LEARNING

The crucial step is for executives to begin to revise how they'd tackle their case. At their two-day seminar each manager selected an episode he wished to redesign so that it would not have the unhappy result it currently produced.

In rewriting their cases, the managers realized that they would have to slow things down. They could not produce a new conversation in the milliseconds in which they were accustomed to speak. This troubled them a bit because they were impatient to learn. They had to keep reminding themselves that learning new skills meant they had to slow down.

Each manager took a different manager's case and crafted a new conversation to help the writer of the episode. After five minutes or so, they showed their designs to the writer. In the process of discussing these new versions, the writer learned a lot about how to redesign his words. And, as they discovered the bugs in their suggestions and the way they made them, the designers also learned a lot.

The dialogues were constructive, cooperative, and helpful. Typical comments were:

'If you want to reach me, try it the way Joe just said.'

'I realize your intentions are good, but those words push my button.'

'I understand what you're trying to say, but it doesn't work for me. How about trying it this way?'

'I'm surprised at how much my new phrases contain the old messages. This will take time.'

Practice is important. Most people require as much practice to overcome skilled incompetence as to play a not-so-decent game of tennis. But it doesn't need to happen all at once. Once managers are committed to change, the practice can occur in actual business meetings where executives set aside some time to reflect on their actions and to correct them.

Thoughts and feelings	Actual conversation
He's not going to like this topic, but we have to discuss it. I doubt that he will take a company perspective, but I should be positive.	*I:* Hi, Bill. I appreciate having the opportunity to talk with you about this custom service versus product problem. I'm sure that both of us want to resolve it in the best interests of the company.
	Bill: I'm always glad to talk about it, as you well know.
I better go slow. Let me ease in.	*I:* There are a rising number of situations where our clients are asking for custom service and rejecting the off-the-shelf products. I worry that your salespeople will pay an increasingly peripheral role in the future.
	Bill: I don't understand. Tell me more.
Like hell you don't understand. I wish there was a way I could be more gentle.	*I:* Bill, I'm sure you are aware of the changes [*I explain*].
	Bill: No I don't see it that way. My salespeople are the key to the future.
There he goes, thinking like a salesman and not a corporate officer.	*I:* Well, let's explore that a bit.

Figure 5.2 Case of the custom-service advocate

But how does unlearning skilled incompetence lead to fewer organizational snafus? The first step is to make sure executives are aware of defensive routines that surround the organizational problems that they are trying to solve. One way to do this is to observe them in the making. For example, during a meeting the top line and corporate staff were having problems working effectively. They identified at least four causes:

The organization's management philosophy and policies are inadequate.
Corporation staff roles overlap and lead to confusion.
Staff lacks clear-cut authority when dealing with line.
Staff has inadequate contact with top line officers.

The CEO appointed two task forces to come up with solutions. Several months later, the entire group met for a day and hammered out a solution that was acceptable to all.

This story has two features that I would highlight. First, the staff–line problems are typical. Second, the story has a happy ending. The organization got to the root of its problems.

But there is a question that must be answered in order to get at the organizational defensive routines. Why did all the managers – both upper and lower – adhere to, implement, and maintain inadequate policies and confusing roles in the first place?

Why open this can of worms if we have already solved the problem? Because defensive routines prevent executives from making honest decisions. Managers who are skilled communicators may also be good at covering up real problems. If we don't work hard at reducing defensive routines, they will thrive – ready to undermine this solution and cover up other conflicts.

There is great skill in knowing how to conceal one's skill.

(La Rochefoucauld)

Chapter 6

Planning as learning

Arie P. de Geus

Some years ago, the planning group at Shell surveyed 30 companies that had been in business for more than 75 years. What impressed us most was their ability to live in harmony with the business environment, to switch from a survival mode when times were turbulent to a self-development mode when the pace of change was slow. And this pattern rang a familiar bell because Shell's history is similarly replete with switches from expansion to self-preservation and back again to growth.

Early in our history, for example, there was a burst of prosperity in the Far East and we dominated the market for kerosene in tins and 'oil for the lamps of China.' Survival became the keynote, however, when Rockefeller's Standard Oil snatched market share by cutting price. In fact, it was the survival instinct that led in 1907 to the joining of Royal Dutch Petroleum and the Shell Transport and Trading Company – separate businesses until then and competitors in the Far East. This, in turn, paved the way for Shell's expansion into the United States in 1911 with a new product, Sumatran gasoline – also a reaction to Standard Oil's activities.

Outcomes like these don't happen automatically. On the contrary, they depend on the ability of a company's senior managers to absorb what is going on in the business environment and to act on that information with appropriate business moves. In other words, they depend on learning. Or, more precisely, on institutional learning, which is the process whereby management teams change their shared mental models of their company, their markets, and their competitors. For this reason, we think of planning as learning and of corporate planning as institutional learning.

Institutional learning is much more difficult than individual learning. The high level of thinking among individual managers in most companies is admirable. And yet, the level of thinking that goes on in the management teams of most companies is considerably below the individual managers' capacities. In institutional learning situations, the learning level of the team is often the lowest common denominator, especially with teams that think of themselves as machines with mechanistic, specialized parts: the production manager looks at production, the distribution manager looks at distribution, the marketing manager looks at marketing.

Because high-level, effective, and continuous institutional learning and ensuing corporate changes are the prerequisites for corporate success, we at Shell* have asked ourselves two questions. How does a company learn and adapt? And, what is planning's role in corporate learning?

My answer to the first question, 'how does a company learn and adapt?', is that many do not or, at least, not very quickly. A full one-third of the Fortune 500 industrials listed in 1970 had vanished by 1983. And W. Stewart Howe has pointed out in his 1986 book *Corporate Strategy* that for every successful turn-around there are two ailing companies that fail to recover. Yet some companies obviously do learn and can adapt. In fact, our survey identified several that were still vigorous at 200, 300, and even 700 years of age. What made the difference? Why are some companies better able to adapt?

Sociologists and psychologists tell us it is pain that makes people and living systems change. And certainly corporations have their share of painful crises, the recent spate of takeovers and takeover threats conspicuously among them. But crisis management – pain management – is a dangerous way to manage for change.

Once in a crisis, everyone in the organization feels the pain. The need for change is clear. The problem is that you usually have little time and few options. The deeper into the crisis you are, the fewer options remain. Crisis management, by necessity, becomes autocratic management.

The positive characteristic of a crisis is that the decisions are quick. The other side of that coin is that the implementation is rarely good; many companies fail to survive.

The challenge, therefore, is to recognize and react to environmental change before the pain of a crisis. Not surprisingly, this is what the long-lived companies in our study were so well able to do.

All these companies had a striking capacity to institutionalize change. They never stood still. Moreover, they seemed to recognize that they had internal strengths that could be developed as environmental conditions changed. Thus, Booker McConnell, founded in 1906 as a sugar company, developed shipping on the back of its primary resource. British American Tobacco recognized that marketing cigarettes was no different from marketing perfume. Mitsubishi, founded in 1870 as a marine and trading company, acquired coal mines to secure access to ships' bunkers, built shipyards to repair imported ships, and developed a bank from the exchange business it had begun to finance shippers.

Changes like these grow out of a company's knowledge of itself and its environment. All managers have such knowledge and they develop it further all the time, since every living person – and system – is continuously engaged in learning. In fact, the normal decision process in corporations is a learning process, because people change their own mental models and build up a joint model as they talk. The problem is that the speed of that process is slow – too slow for a world in which the ability to learn faster than competitors may be the only sustainable competitive advantage.

Some five years ago, we had a good example of the time it takes for a message to be heard. One way in which we in Shell trigger institutional learning is through scenarios.[1] A certain set of scenarios gave our planners a clear signal that the oil industry, which had always been highly integrated, was no longer. That contradicted all our existing models. High integration means that you are more or less in control of all the facets of your industry, so you can start optimizing. Optimization was the driving managerial model in Shell. What these scenarios essentially were saying was that we had to look for other management methods.

The first reaction from the organization was at best polite. There were few questions and no discussion. Some managers reacted critically: the scenarios were 'basic theory that everyone already knew'; they had 'little relevance to the realities of today's business.' The message had been listened to but it had not yet been heard.

After a hiatus of some three months, people began asking lots of questions; a discussion started. The intervening months had provided time for the message to settle and for management's mental models to develop a few new hooks. Absorption, phase one of the learning process, had taken place.

During the next nine months, we moved through the other phases of the learning process. Operating executives at Shell incorporated this new information into their mental models of the business. They drew conclusions from the revised models and tested them against experience. Then, finally, they acted on the basis of the altered model. Hearing, digestion, confirmation, action: each step took time, its own sweet time.

In my experience this time span is typical. It will likely take 12 to 18 months from the moment a signal is received until it is acted on. The issue is not whether a company will learn, therefore, but whether it will learn fast and early. The critical question becomes, 'Can we accelerate institutional learning?'

I am more and more persuaded that the answer to this question is yes. But before explaining why, I want to emphasize an important point about learning and the planner's role. The only relevant learning in a company is the learning done by those people who have the power to act (at Shell, the operating company management teams). So the real purpose of effective planning is not to make plans but to change the microcosm, the mental models that these decision makers carry in their heads. And this is what we at Shell and others elsewhere try to do.

In this role as facilitators, catalyst, and accelerator of the corporate learning process, planners are apt to fall into several traps. One is that we sometimes start with a mental model that is unrecognizable to our audience. Another is that we take too many steps at once. The third, and most serious, is that too often we communicate our information by teaching. This is a natural trap to fall into because it's what we've been conditioned to all our lives. But teaching, as John Holt points out, is actually one of the least efficient ways to convey knowledge.[2] At best, 40 per cent of what is taught is received; in most situations, it is only about 25 per cent.

It was a shock to learn how inefficient teaching is. Yet some reflection on our own experience drove the point home. After all, we had spent nearly 15 man-years preparing a set of scenarios which we then transmitted in a condensed version in 2.5 hours. Could we really have believed that our audience would understand all we were talking about?

Teaching has another disadvantage as well, especially in a business setting. Teachers must be given authority by their students based on the teachers' presumed superior understanding. When a planner presents the results of many man-years of looking at the environment to a management team, she is usually given the benefit of the doubt: the planner probably knows more about the environment than the management team she is talking to. But when the same planner walks into a boardroom to start teaching about the strategy of the company, her authority disappears. When you cannot be granted authority, you can no longer teach.

Fortified with this understanding of planning and its role, we looked for ways to accelerate institutional learning. Curiously enough, we learned in two cases that changing the rules, or suspending them, could be a spur to learning. Rules in a corporation are extremely important. Nobody likes them but everybody obeys them because they are recognized as the glue of the organization. And yet, we have all known extraordinary managers who got their organizations out of a rut by changing the rules. Intuitively they changed the organization and the way it looked at matters, and so, as a consequence, accelerated learning.

Several years ago one of our work groups introduced, out of the blue, a new rule into the corporate rain dance: 'Thou shalt plan strategically in the first half of the calendar year.' (We already had a so-called business planning cycle that dealt with capital budgets in the second half of the calendar year.)

The work group was wise enough not to be too specific about what it had in mind. Some operating companies called up and asked what was meant by 'strategic planning.' But the answer they got – that ideas were more important than numbers – was vague. Other companies just started to hold strategic planning meetings in the spring.

In the first year the results of this new game were scanty, mostly a rehash of the previous year's business plans. But in the second year the plans were fresher and each year the quality of thinking that went into strategic planning improved. So we asked ourselves whether, by having changed the rules of the game – because that's what the planning system is, one of the rules of the corporate game – we had accelerated institutional learning. And our answer was yes. We changed the rules and the corporation played by the new rules that evolved in the process.

A similar thing happened when we tried suspending the rules. In 1984 we had a scenario that talked about $15 a barrel oil. (Bear in mind that in 1984 the price of a barrel of oil was $28 and $15 was the end of the world to oil people.) We thought it important that, as early in 1985 as possible, senior managers throughout Shell start learning about a world of $15 oil. But the response to this scenario was essentially, 'If you want us to think about this world, first tell us when the price is going to fall, how far it will fall, and how long the drop will last.'

A deadlock ensued which we broke by writing a case study with a preface that was really a license to play. 'We don't know the future,' it said. 'But neither do you. And though none of us knows whether the price is going to fall, we can agree that it would be pretty serious if it did. So we have written a case showing one of many possible ways by which the price of oil could fall.' We then described a case in which the price plummeted at the end of 1985 and concluded by saying: 'And now it is April 1986 and you are staring at a price of $16 a barrel. Will you please meet and give your views on these three questions: What do you think your government will do? What do you think your competition will do? And what, if anything, will you do?'

Since at that point the price was still $28 and rising, the case was only a game. But that game started off serious work throughout Shell, not on answering the question 'What will happen?' but rather exploring the question 'What will we do if it happens?' The acceleration of the institutional learning process had been set in motion.

As it turned out, the price of oil was still $27 in early January of 1986. But on February 1 it was $17 and in April it was $10. The fact that Shell had already visited the world of $15 oil helped a great deal in that panicky spring of 1986.

By now, we knew we were on to something: games could significantly accelerate institutional learning. That's not so strange when you think of it. Some of the most difficult and complex tasks in our lives were learned by playing: cycling, tennis, playing an instrument. We did it, we experimented, we played. But how were we going to make it OK to play?

Few managers were able to say, 'I don't mind a little mistake. Go ahead, experiment', especially with a crisis looming. We didn't feel we could go to executives who run some of the biggest companies in the world and say, 'Come on, let's have a little game.' And in any case, board meetings have agendas, are fixed to end at a certain time, and require certain action to be taken. Still, within these constraints, we have found ways to learn by playing.

One characteristic of play, as the Tavistock Institute in London has shown, is the presence of a transitional object. For the person playing, the transitional object is a representation of the real world. A child who is playing with a doll learns a great deal about the real world at a very fast pace.

Successful consultants let themselves be treated as transitional objects. The process begins when the consultant says something like this to a management team: 'We know from experience that many good strategies are largely implicit. If you let us interview people at various levels in your organization, we'll see whether we can get your strategy out on paper. Then we'll come back and check whether we've understood it.'

Some weeks later the consultant goes back to the team and says: 'Well, we've looked at your strategy and we've played it through a number of likely possibilities, and here is what we think will be the outcome. Do you like it?' The management team will almost certainly say no. So the consultant will say: 'All right, let's see how we can change it. Let's go back to your original model and see what was built in there that produced this result.' This process is likely to go through a number of iterations, during which the team's original model will change considerably. Those changes constitute the learning that is taking place among the team's members.

Like consultants, computer models can be used to play back and forth management's view of its market, the environment, or the competition. The starting point, however, must be the mental model that the audience has at the moment. If a planner walks into the room with a model on his computer that he has made up himself, the chances are slim that his audience will recognize this particular microworld. If the target group is a management team, the starting model must be the sum of their individual models. How can this be done?

One way is to involve team members in the development of a new common model and leave their individual models implicit. Alternatively, one can bring the individual models out in the open through interviews and make them explicit. In both approaches, computers can serve as transitional objects in which to store the common models that get built.

To most planners, one all-important aspect of these microworlds is counterintuitive: the probability that they have little relation to the real world. God seems to have told model builders that a model should have predictive qualities and that therefore it should represent the real world. In building microworlds, however, this is totally irrelevant. What we want to capture are the models that exist in the minds of the audience. Almost certainly, these will not represent the real world. None of us has a model that actually captures the real world, because no complex reality can be represented analytically and a model is an analytical way of representing reality. Moreover, for the purpose of learning, it is not the reality that matters but the team's model of reality, which will change as members' understanding of their world improves.

But why go to all this trouble? Why not rely on the natural learning process that occurs whenever a management team meets? For us at Shell, there are three compelling reasons. First, although the models in the human mind are complex, most people can deal with only three or four variables at a time and do so through only one or two time iterations.

Look, for instance, at current discussions about the price of oil. Nine out of ten people draw on a price-elasticity model of the market: the price has come down, therefore demand will go up and supply will eventually fall. *Ergo*, they will conclude, at some time in the future the price of oil must rise. Now we all know that what goes up must come down. But our minds, in thinking through this complex model, work through too few iterations, and we stop at the point where the price goes up. If we computerize the model of the person who stops thinking at the moment the price rises, however, the model will almost certainly show the price falling after its rise. Yet this knowledge would be counterintuitive to the very person (or persons) who built the model.

The second reason for putting mental models into computers is that in working with dynamic models, people discover that in complex systems (like markets or companies) cause and effect are separated in time and place. To many people such insight is also counterintuitive. Most of us, particularly if we are engaged in the process of planning, focus on the effect we want to create and then look for the most immediate cause to create that effect. The use of dynamic models helps us discover other trigger points, separated in time and place from the desired effect.

Lastly, by using computer models we learn what constitutes relevant information. For only when we start playing with these microworlds do we find out what information we really need to know.

When people play with models this way, they are actually creating a new language among themselves that expresses the knowledge they have acquired. And here we come to the most important aspect of institutional learning, whether it be achieved through teaching or through play as we have defined it: the institutional learning process is a process of language development. As the implicit knowledge of each learner becomes explicit, his or her mental model becomes a building block of the institutional model. How much and how fast this model changes will depend on the culture and structure of the organization. Teams that have to cope with rigid procedures and information systems will learn more slowly than those with flexible, open communication channels. Autocratic institutions will learn faster or not at all – the ability of one or a few leaders being a risky institutional bet.

Human beings aren't the only ones whose learning ability is directly related to their ability to convey information. As a species, birds have great potential to learn, but there are important differences among them. Titmice (blue tits), for example, move in flocks and mix freely, while robins live in well-defined parts of the garden and for the most part communicate antagonistically across the borders of their territories. Virtually all the titmice in the UK quickly learned how to pierce the seals of milk bottles left at doorsteps. But robins as a group will never learn to do this (though individual birds may) because their capacity for institutional learning is low; one bird's knowledge does not spread.[3] The same phenomenon occurs in management teams that work by mandate. The best learning takes place in teams that accept that the whole is larger than the sum of the parts, that there is a good that transcends the individual.

What about managers who find themselves in a robin culture? Clearly, their chances of accelerating institutional learning are reduced. Nevertheless, they can take a significant step toward opening up communication and thus the learning process by keeping one fact in mind: institutional learning begins with the calibration of existing mental models.

We are continuing to explore other ways to improve and speed up our institutional learning process. Our exploration into learning through play via a transitional object (a consultant or a computer) looks promising enough at this point to push on in that direction. And while we are navigating in poorly charted waters, we are not out there alone.[4]

Our exploration into this area is not a luxury. We understand that the only competitive advantage the company of the future will have is its managers' ability to learn faster than their competitors. So the companies that succeed will be those that continually nudge their managers toward revising their views of the world. The challenges for the planner are considerable. So are the rewards.

NOTES

* I use the collective expression 'Shell' for convenience when referring to the companies of the Royal Dutch/Shell Group in general, or when no purpose is served by identifying the particular Shell company or companies.
1 Pierre Wack wrote about our system in 'Scenarios: Uncharted Waters Ahead', *Harvard Business Review*, September–October 1985, p.72 and in 'Scenarios: Shooting the Rapids', *Harvard Business Review*, November–December 1985, p. 139.
2 John Holt, *How Children Learn*, rev. edn (New York: Delacorte, 1983) and John Holt, *How Children Fail*, rev. edn (New York: Delacorte, 1982).
3 Jeff S. Wyles, Joseph G. Kunkel, and Allan C. Wilson, 'Birds, Behaviour and Anatomical Evolution', *Proceedings of the National Academy of Sciences, USA*, July 1983.
4 Through MIT's Program in Systems Thinking and the New Management Style, a group of senior executives are looking at this and other issues.

Chapter 7

The dominant logic
A new linkage between diversity and performance

C.K. Prahalad and Richard Bettis

For the past 35 years product-market diversification of large firms has continued at a rapid pace. Today, over two-thirds of the firms in the USA Fortune 500 are highly diversified and similar patterns of diversification exist in Western Europe and Japan (Rumelt, 1974; Pavan, 1972; Thanheiser, 1972; Pooley, 1972; Channon, 1973; Suzuki, 1980). As a consequence, interest in the relationship between corporate diversification and financial performance has grown among practitioners, academics, and public policy makers.

Accompanying this interest has been a spate of research on the patterns of diversification and the determinants of performance in diversified firms by the academic community. Concurrently, consulting firms have been actively promoting a variety of approaches for managing diversified firms. The results of these efforts have been mixed, at best. There is, as yet, no overall theory that links diversification with performance and the linkage, if any, remains elusive.

The purpose of this chapter is to propose a crucial linkage, which has largely been ignored in the literature on the relationship between diversification and performance; and to show how this approach can add significantly to our managerial understanding of performance in the diversified firms.

This linkage is referred to as the 'dominant general management logic' (or dominant logic) and consists of the mental maps developed through experience in the core business and sometimes applied inappropriately in other business.

A BRIEF REVIEW OF RESEARCH ON DIVERSITY AND PERFORMANCE

The purpose of this section is to review briefly the major academic research streams and consulting framework relevant to the relationship between diversity and performance. These represent alternative approaches to research in this area. While significant literature exists in support of each of the streams of research outlined below, we will reference and discuss only the seminal works in each area.

The strategy of diversification

Pioneering work by Chandler (1962) and Ansoff (1965) established the motivations for diversification and the general nature of the diversified firm. Wrigley (1970) refined and extended Chandler's study by investigating the various options open to a diversifying firm. Building on the work of Chandler, Wrigley and others, Rumelt (1974, 1977) investigated the relationships among diversification strategy, organizational structure, and economic performance. Rumelt used four major and nine minor categories to characterize the diversification strategy of firms. The major categories were single business, dominant business, related business and unrelated business. These categories provide a spectrum of diversification strategies – from firms that remained essentially undiversified to firms that diversified significantly into unrelated areas. Using statistical methods, Rumelt was able to relate diversification strategy to performance. The related diversification strategies – related-constrained and related-linked (e.g. General Foods and General Electric) – were found to outperform the other diversification strategies on the average (relatedness was defined in terms of products, markets, and technology). The related-constrained was found to be the highest performing on the average. (In related-constrained firms most component businesses are related to each other, whereas in related-linked firms only one-to-one relationships are required.) By contrast, the unrelated conglomerate strategy was found to be one of the lowest performing on the average.

In 1982 Nathanson and Cassano conducted a statistical study of diversity and performance using a sample of 206 firms over the years 1973–78. They developed a two-dimensional typology (market diversity and product diversity) for capturing diversification strategy that refines Rumelt's categories. They found returns remained relatively steady as market diversity increased. However, they also found that size plays an important moderating role on the relationships. For both the market and product diversity, smaller firms did well relative to larger firms in categories marked by no diversification and in categories of extremely high diversification. Larger firms did significantly better than smaller firms in the in-between categories – those characterized by intermediate levels of diversification.

In both these studies linking diversification and performance (Rumelt and Nathanson/Cassano) the key point to note is that *choosing the generic strategy of diversification (how much and what kind of relatedness)* is the key to achieving performance.

Economic characteristics of individual businesses

Porter (1980), among others, established that the characteristics of the various industries in which a firm participates, and the position of the firm's businesses in these industries, impacts overall on firm performance.

Two studies have in fact empirically validated these influences for diversified firms. The widely discussed PIMS program of the Marketing Science Institute (see Schoeffler *et al.*, 1974, for an introduction) has shown that variables such as market share and relative product quality directly influence the profitability of constituent businesses in large diversified firms. More recently, Montgomery (1979) has examined the performance differences in diversified firms using the market structure variables of industrial organization economics. Montgomery found that diversified firms with higher levels of performance tended to have well-positioned businesses in industries with 'favourable' market structures.

In summary, for both studies (PIMS and Montgomery) *the structure of the industries in which the firm completes and the competitive position of the firm's businesses within these industries are the key determinants of performance.*

Portfolio concepts

What are here called 'portfolio concepts' go by various names such as portfolio grids, SBU concepts, and SBU matrices. Although there are numerous slight variations among the approaches used by various consultant groups and firms, they all rely on a matrix or grid with two axes. The matrix classifies businesses by product-market attractiveness, or some variant of it, along one axis and by competitive position or some variant of it along the other axis. Typically these matrices are divided into either four or nine boxes. (For a thorough discussion see Hofer and Schendel, 1978.) The position (box) that each business occupies represents its strategic position and determines the role that the business should play in the corporate portfolio. This role involves varying degrees of cash generation or cash usage. Studies by Bettis (1979) and Haspeslagh (1982) suggest that managers use these concepts to varying degrees – as a tool or as dogma – in managing a diversified portfolio of businesses.

For each variant of the portfolio concept the key points are: (1) the strategic position of each business determines its cash flow characteristics; and (2) it is the 'balance' of these cash flow characteristics of the collection of businesses that determines the overall performance of the diversified firm.

Et cetera

In addition to the streams of research discussed above, a number of studies focusing on performance in large firms, by researchers concerned with organizational theory and human motivation, have appeared recently. Representative of this line of research are Peters and Waterman (1982), Deal and Kennedy (1982), Pascale and Athos (1981), and Ouchi (1981). While these studies do not consider the problems of managing diversity explicitly, they often do make some implicit recommendations on the issue, but the nature of the recommendations varies widely. (For example, Peters and Waterman suggest that 'excellent firms' confine their operations to businesses they know or 'they stick to the knitting'.)

The three streams of research lead to somewhat different conclusions. To summarize, the linkage between diversity and performance would appear to be a function of:

1 the generic diversification strategy (how much and what kind of relatedness), or
2 the profit potential of the industries in which the individual businesses are positioned and the actual competitive position of the businesses in each industry, or
3 the cash flow characteristics of the various businesses and the internal cash flow balance for the total firm.

Undoubtedly all three perspectives provide partial answers to the question. Just how partial these answers are becomes more obvious when you consider that Rumelt (1974) was able to explain less than 20 percent of the variance in performance, while Montgomery could explain only about 38 percent of the variance in performance. These results suggest that further conceptual development could enhance our understanding of diversity and performance.

The importance of 'quality of management'

Bettis *et al.* (1978) have argued that, if we move away from the traditional research preoccupation with central tendencies, but focus on outliers – the very high and very poor performers – we may learn more about the elusive linkage between diversity and performance. By studying just 12 firms, six of which were high performers and six low performers, across the three generic categories of dominant, related, and unrelated diversifiers (with a sample of four firms each, two in high- and two in low-performance categories), they concluded that the quality of management was as critical in explaining performance as any other factor. (It should be noted that their definition of quality was somewhat ambiguous.) The study was not based on the large sample (and it could not be by design, as their concern was with outliers), and the conclusions were tentative. (In a much larger study, Bettis and Mahajan were able to show that the high-performance attributes usually attributed to related diversification were not recognized in the overwhelming majority of related diversifiers.)

The real departure in the academic perspective on diversity and performance indicated by the study was the concern with very good and very poor performances in the same generic diversifi- cation category – or a desire to study outliers – and the inclusion of the concept of the 'quality of management' as a major variable linking diversity and performance.

Top management in a diversified firm a distinct skill?

Two in-depth clinical studies suggest that the skills that constitute the 'quality of management' in a single-business firm are distinct from a diversified firm; and that as firms diversify, top managers have to acquire those skills. Rajan Das (1981) studied one firm's attempt to diversify out of the core business (tobacco) and how it had to learn the process of general management in the new businesses into which it ventured. The conclusion was that it was not the quality of the business – its competitive structure – or the pattern on diversification *per se* that determined early failures and successes later, but the evolution of the top management and its ability to acquire new skills and recognize that its approach to managing a diversified firm must be different from the way it had managed the single-business firm. The study by Miles (1982) of tobacco companies in the USA and their attempts to diversify away from tobacco, also leads to a similar conclusion. The firms had to learn as much about general management in the diversified firm, as a distinct process and skill, as about the characteristics of the new businesses. Both these studies indicate that the work of top management in diversified firms is a distinct skill and can contribute to the success or failure of any one of the businesses within the firm or the firm as a whole.

The management of a diversified firm

Studies of the work of top management and the process by which they manage a diversified firm are not numerous. Bower (1972a) demonstrated that top managers influence the strategic choices made by unit-level managers by orchestrating the organizational context – the formal structure and systems. In other words, the tools of top management were administrative in character. He labelled the term 'metamanagement' (Bower, 1972b) to describe the job of top managers in diversified firms. Hamermesh (1977) outlined the process by which top managers intervene in a divisional profit crisis. Prahalad and Doz (1981) outlined, in detail, how top managers can use administrative tools to shift the strategic direction of a business. This line of research established the broad scope of the work of top management, but more importantly how that influences the strategic choices made by lower-level managers at the business-unit level, thereby impacting on the overall performance. There exists a logical, though only partially empirically verified, link between the quality of management – or the quality of the processes by which top managers influence the business-level managers in their work – and the performance of the firm.

The two questions that we posed ourselves based on the literature were:

1 If top managers in single-business firms had to learn the process of managing a diversified portfolio, should top managers in diversified firms go through a similar learning process when they add new businesses? Is the task of top management in the diversified firm dependent on, or at least partially influenced by, the underlying strategic characteristics of the businesses?
2 If the tools available to top managers in diversified firms to influence the strategic direction of businesses are essentially administrative as regards the organizational context, does it follow that the substance of businesses is irrelevant? In other words, can the same conceptual organizational context management capabilities suffice if the mix of businesses changes?

THE ELUSIVE LINKAGE

It is important before proceeding to differentiate at least two distinct levels of general management in a diversified firm – that at the SBU (strategic business unit) or business level and the corporate management team. Often, in diversified firms, there tends to be an intermediate level of general management, called group or sector executives, between business level and corporate management. Our focus will be on the corporate management team, and its relationships with business- and group-level managers, as it pertains to managing the totality of the firm.

Given this focus on corporate management, the conceptual framework linking diversity and performance proposed in this chapter is based on the following premises:

1 Top management of a (diversified) firm should not be viewed 'as a faceless abstraction', but as a 'collection of key individuals' (i.e. a dominant coalition) who have significant influence on the way the firm is managed. This collection of individuals, to a large extent, influences the style and process of top management, and as a result the key resource allocation choices (Donaldson and Lorsch, 1983).

Few organizational events are approached by these managers (or any managers) as being totally unique and requiring systematic study. Instead, they are processed through pre-existing knowledge systems. Known as schemas (see Norman, 1976, for a discussion of schemas), these systems represent beliefs, theories and propositions that have developed over time based on the manager's personal experiences. At a broader unit of analysis, Huff (1982) implied the possibility that organizations' actions can be characterized as schemas. An organizational schema is primarily a product of managers' interpretations of experiences while operating within certain firms and industries.

Schemas permit managers to categorize an event, assess its consequences, and consider appropriate actions (including doing nothing), and to do so rapidly and often efficiently. Without schemas a manager, and ultimately the organizations with which he/she is associated, would become paralysed by the need to analyze 'scientifically' an enormous number of ambiguous and uncertain situations. In other words, managers must be able to scan environments selectively so that timely decisions can be made (Hambrick, 1982). The selection of environmental elements to be scanned is likely to be affected by a manager's schema.

Unfortunately, schemas are not infallible guides to the organization and its environments. In fact, some are relatively inaccurate representations of the world, particularly as conditions change. Furthermore, events often are not labelled accurately, and sometimes are processed through inaccurate and/or incomplete knowledge structures.

For the purpose of this research it is important to understand what managers' schemas actually represent. Kiesler and Sproul (1982) offer the following concise description: 'Managers operate on mental representations of the world and those representations are likely to be of historical environments rather than of current ones' (p. 557). (Furthermore, as Weick, 1979, discusses, it is the schema concept that provides the vehicle for his concept of the social construction (or enactment) of a firm's environment.)

For the present purposes the schema concept is introduced as a general mental structure that can store a shared dominant general management logic. (The specific nature and content of this 'logic' is discussed below.)

2 The strategic characteristics of businesses in a diversified firm, determined by the underlying competitive structure, technologies, and customers of specific businesses, vary. The differences in strategic characteristics of the businesses in the portfolio of the firm, a measure of *strategic variety*, impact the ability of a top management group to manage. This premise implies that complexity of the top management process is a function of the strategic variety, not just the number of distinct businesses or the size of those businesses. For example, the management of a very large, primarily one-industry firm (e.g. General Motors), or the management of a diversified firm in strategically similar businesses (e.g. Procter and Gamble), is a lot simpler than

managing a diversified firm in strategically dissimilar industries (e.g. General Electric).

3 Strategically similar businesses can be managed using a single dominant general management logic. A dominant general management logic is defined as the way in which managers conceptualize the business and make critical resource allocation decisions – be it in technologies, product development, distribution, advertising, or in human resource management. These tasks are performed by managing the infrastructure of administrative compensation, career management, and organization structure. If the businesses in a diversified firm are strategically similar, one dominant general management logic would suffice. However, diversified firms with strategic variety impose the need for multiple dominant logic.

The dominant logic is stored via schemas and hence can be thought of as a structure. However, some of what is stored is process knowledge (e.g. what kind of process should be used in a particular kind of resource alleviation decision or how new technologies should be evaluated). Hence, more broadly the dominant logic can be considered as both a knowledge structure and a set of elicited management processes. (The actual content of this knowledge structure and how this context is established is discussed below.)

4 The ability of top management group (a group of key individuals) to manage a diversified firm is limited by the dominant general management logic(s) that they are used to. In other words, the repertoire of tools that top managers use to identify, define, and make strategic decisions, and their view of the world (mind sets), is determined by their experiences. Typically, the dominant top management logic in a diversified firm tends to be influenced by the largest business or the 'core business' which was the historical basis for the firm's growth (e.g. semiconductors at Texas Instruments, public switching and telephones at GTE). The characteristics of the core business, often the source of top managers in diversified firms, tend to cause managers to define problems in certain ways and develop familiarity with, and facility in the use of, those administrative tools that are particularly useful in accomplishing the critical tasks of the core business (Figure 7.1).

The sources of dominant logic

Dominant logic, as we have defined it here, is a mind set or a world view or conceptualization of the business and the administrative tools to accomplish goals and make decisions in that business. It is stored as a shared cognitive map (or set of schemas) among the dominant coalition. It is expressed as a learned, problem-solving behaviour. As such, in order to

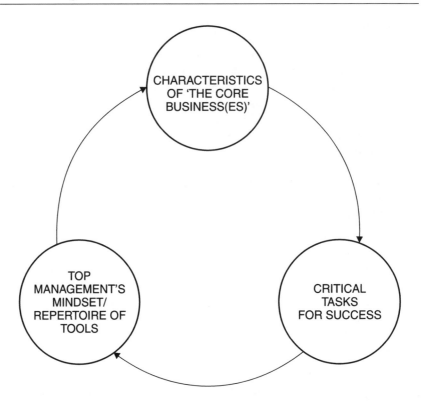

Figure 7.1 **Dominant general management logic evolves due to . . .**

understand dominant logic, we first need to examine the research streams that deal with the development of cognitive maps and the associated problem-solving behaviour. We identified four streams of research – operant conditioning, paradigms, cognitive biases, and artificial intelligence – to highlight the process by which a dominant logic evolves (i.e. how the cognitive map originates and changes) and the difficulties in changing it or adding new logic to one's repertoire. The relationships of these fours streams to problem-solving behaviour are shown in Figure 7.2.

Operant conditioning

Skinner (1953), in his seminal work on operant conditioning, argued that behaviour was a function of its consequences. Behaviour could be understood by considering the contingencies that were administered by the environment in response to certain behaviour. Behaviour was administered by the environment in response to certain behaviours. Behaviour

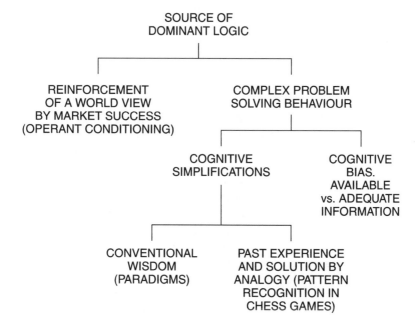

Figure 7.2 **Conceptual foundations of dominant logic**

that was reinforced was emitted more frequently in the future. By contrast, behaviour that was ignored or punished (negative reinforcement) was likely to diminish over time. A dominant logic can be seen as resulting from the reinforcement that results from doing the 'right things' with respect to a set of businesses. In other words, when top managers effectively perform the tasks that are critical for success in the core business they are positively reinforced by economic success. This reinforcement results in their focusing effort on the behaviours that led to success. Hence they develop a particular mind set and repertoire of tools and preferred processes. This in turn determines the approaches that they are likely to use in resource allocation, control over operations, and the approach to intervention in a crisis. If the firm acquires or develops a business for which the critical tasks for success are substantially different from those in the core business, because of operant conditioning the behaviour of top managers and the approaches they use to mange the new business are likely to remain those that were appropriate for the core business even though they may be inappropriate in the new business. In other words it is difficult for a top management group to be effective in managing a new business by learning and using a new dominant logic in a short time. The problems faced by American Can (e.g. Pickwick

International), and Exxon (e.g. office systems), in managing acquisitions of businesses totally different from their core businesses, in the early stages, are an illustration of the power of operant conditioning on the dominant logic used by top management.

The power of paradigms

The concept of dominant logic also derives direct support from Kuhn's (1970) work on scientific paradigms and Allison's (1971) work on the importance of alternate paradigms in the context of analysing government actions during the Cuban missile crisis.

Kuhn, a historian of science, argued that a particular science at any point in time can be characterized by a set of 'shared beliefs' or 'conventional wisdom' about the world that constitutes what he called the 'dominant paradigm'. What Kuhn calls 'normal science' is carried out efficiently under this set of shared beliefs. In a sense, Kuhn's 'paradigm' is simply a way of defining and managing the world and a basis for action in that world. Kuhn points out how difficult it is to shift dominant paradigms, and illustrates this with several examples such as the shift from the Ptolemaic view of the universe (earth-centred) to the Copernican view of the universe (sun-centred) in astronomy. The analogy from science to a business firm is simple and direct. The dominant paradigm and the dominant logic are conceptually similar but employed in different fields. Allison used paradigmatic analysis to show how the adoption of a particular paradigm powerfully affects our evaluation of events. He characterized a paradigm as 'a systematic statement of the basic assumptions, concepts and propositions employed by a school of analysis'. Different paradigms resulted in dramatically different analyses of his chosen example: the Cuban missile crisis. The parallel between Allison's use of the word paradigm and our use of dominant logic is obvious.

The pattern-recognition process

As part of the development of 'intelligent' computer programs there have been numerous efforts to develop chess-playing programs (see Newell and Simon, 1972, for a review). Inevitably such research has required intense studies of how chess experts make decisions in a chess game. In particular, the decision-making and problem-solving process used by grand masters and masters has been compared to that of lesser players (de Groot, 1965). These studies have shown that the better players could remember more 'patterns' of previous games than the lesser players. Simon (1979) estimated that class A players could remember about 1,300 familiar patterns while masters or grand masters remember about 50,000. This 'vocabulary' of previous games lets players make effective decisions by comparison with earlier games. In other words, chess players decide on the basis of experience or 'what worked before', not on the basis of some best strategy or optimizing procedure. Now consider a situation where the design of the gameboard or rules of chess are changed. The stored 'vocabulary' of games is no longer as useful in this new game. Similarly, when the economic gameboard or rules are changed either by structural changes in existing businesses or by a diversification move, the vocabulary of economic moves stored through experience in the core business may no longer be as useful. In other words, solutions based on 'past experience' or solution by 'analogy' may be inappropriate.

Cognitive biases

A final area from which research results are suggestive of the concept of a dominant top management logic is cognitive psychology. The psychology of cognitive biases is the study of how people in making decisions sometimes make systematic (and often severe) errors (see Tversky and Kahneman, 1974, for an introduction and survey). When dealing with uncertain and complex tasks people often rely on a limited number of heuristic principles which greatly simplify the decision process. In general these heuristics are useful, but on some occasions they can result in significant errors.

For present purposes the most interesting of these heuristic principles is what is called the availability heuristic (see Tversky and Kahneman, 1974, for a thorough discussion). Basically, the availability heuristic leads people to make decisions by using information that can easily be brought to mind (i.e. information that is 'available'). This often leads to severe and systematic errors. This field of research also suggests that decision-makers do not necessarily use analytical approaches to evaluate the information content of available data or search for 'adequate information' (Nisbett and Ross, 1980). For example, Tversky and Kahneman (1974) point out that one may assess the risk of heart attack among middle-aged people by recalling such occurrences among one's acquaintances even if it can be shown that it is an inappropriate basis for drawing such a conclusion. Obviously, for top managers, knowledge of the core business and the business they are most familiar with will be a significant source of available information. They tend to apply it to other businesses where it may or may not be appropriate (Das, 1981). Research on cognitive processes suggests that the mind set and repertoire of tools that constitute the dominant logic are likely to be inappropriately applied by managers confronted with a 'different' business, and that there is significant 'learning' that precedes change in those biases. The difficulty of operating in diverse businesses which require multiple dominant logic is obvious.

STRATEGIC VARIETY AND THE DOMINANT LOGIC

The premises outlined above help us develop a framework for assessing the linkage between diversity and performance. Essentially they relate strategic variety amongst businesses in the firm, and changes in it, with the appropriateness of the dominant general management logic(s) that top managers in that firm use. We will examine in the rest of the chapter the problems that diversified firms face in relating strategic variety and the dominant general management logic(s).

Strategic variety

Strategic variety in a diversified firm depends on the characteristics of the mix of business the firm is engaged in. During the past decade top managers have tended to reduce the strategic variety (not necessarily the number of district businesses) in the portfolio of the firm. This is accomplished, often, by divesting businesses that do not 'fit' – those that increase strategic variety. Many of the businesses divested are profitable (e.g. Sperry's sale of Vickers to concentrate on information technology, ITT's sale of its bakery division). Divesting businesses to get more 'focus' to the portfolio results from an implicit recognition that the demands on top management of strategic variety can be significant. Not all diversified firms have been proactive in reducing strategic variety. Some have been forced to divest businesses, after years of poor profit performance and an inability on their part to turn around the 'sick businesses'.

An alternative to the approach outlined above – reducing strategic variety by restricting the mix of businesses in the firm to those whose strategic characteristics are similar – is followed by firms like General Electric, Textron, or 3M. Typically, businesses with similar strategic characteristics tend to be grouped together into 'sectors' for management purposes. As a result there is little strategic variety within a sector, but across sectors there can be significant differences. This approach reduces the strategic variety that top managers have to deal with by creating an intermediate level of general management. These group- or sector-level executives tend to manage the strategic direction of specific businesses within the sector. Conceptually, this arrangement explicitly recognizes the need to contain strategic variety for effective management. However, in practice, the role of sector executives and their relationship both with business-level managers and with the top management of the firm can become unclear if top management of the firm attempts to directly influence the conduct of any one business or a group of businesses.

Changing strategic variety

So far we have considered how firms can contain strategic variety in a diversified firm, at a given point in time. But over time, even with an unchanging mix of businesses, the strategic variety can change. For example, the strategic characteristics of businesses can change due to changes in the structure of industries. The toy industry was changed, in a relatively short period of time, by the availability of inexpensive microprocessors. The combination of telecommunication and computers and deregulation is changing the financial services industry. Globalization has changed the nature of competition in several industries such as TV, hi-fi, autos, steel, machine tools, etc. As a result, even firms which do not ostensibly change the mix of businesses will have to cope with increasing strategic variety, as the underlying structural characteristics of businesses change. Top managers, as a result, must possess the ability to revise the dominant logic they used to manage those businesses. The inability of top managers both to identify changing structural characteristics of businesses and to accept the need for change in dominant logic(s), may provide at least a partial explanation for the difficulties traditional businesses like steel, machine tools, and autos have faced during the past five years in the US.

An addition of a new business, either through internal development or acquisition, can also change the strategic variety within the firm. If the new business is distinctly different (e.g. General Motors' acquisition of EDS, or General Electric's acquisition of Utah International) the strategic variety it adds is easily recognized. In such acquisitions, top managers also recognize that hasty attempts to impose the dominant logic of the firm on the acquired business may be dysfunctional. Often the acquired firm is 'left alone', at least for a time.

When a new business is created through internal development it is harder to recognize the different structural characteristics of that business compared to those in the current mix of businesses; more so if the new business is technologically not dissimilar to existing businesses. For example, the experience of the calculator, digital watch, and personal computer businesses at Texas Instruments illustrates the point. The dominant logic which worked so well for TI in the semiconductor business, when applied to the new business, led to failure. A dramatic contrast is the early recognition at IBM that the personal computer business was structurally quite distinct. This recognition resulted in the creation of an independent business unit for managing that business. It was not subject to the dominant logic of the mainframe business. As the PC business evolves, and as it takes on the characteristics of the mainframe business, at least in some applications and with some customer segments, IBM may reimpose the dominant logic of mainframes on that business. To summarize, strategic variety in a diversified firm can change due to:

- changes in the structural characteristics of the existing mix of businesses, or
- changes in the mix of businesses caused by acquisitions or internal development.

In either case, top managers must explicitly examine the implications of changes in strategic variety. In other words, major structural changes in an industry have the same effect on the strategic variety of a firm as acquiring a new business.

The task of top management is to constantly re-examine its portfolio to ascertain if there are perceptible changes in the strategic variety as well as explicitly to assess the impact of new businesses on dominant logic(s) in the firm. The task of top management under various combinations of 'sources of strategic variety' and 'top management orientation' give us six possible combinations, as shown in Table 7.1. In a firm with a single dominant logic, if the nature of the core business changes significantly, then top managers will have to revise the dominant logic (A). If a new business is added, and is strategically similar (B), no change in dominant logic is needed. If, however, the new business is dissimilar, top managers have to create the capacity within the firm to cope with multiple dominant logic (C). In a firm operating with multiple dominant logic, if the nature of a significant business changes, then top managers may have to revise the dominant logic applied to that business or regroup it under a different 'sector' or 'group' (D). If the new business is strategically similar to one of the 'groups' or 'sectors' within the firm, then top managers may assign it to the appropriate sector (E). If the new business is dissimilar to the existing businesses, then top managers have to add variety to the dominant logic within the firm (F).

CONCLUSIONS

The concept of dominant general management logic and the role of top managers in understanding and managing the logic(s) are important aspects to be considered in the research on diversity and performance. There are several implications of including these concepts in the study of diversity and performance. Some are dealt with in the following sections.

Limits to diversity

We have argued that the 'real diversity' in a managerial sense in a firm does not arise from the variety in technologies or markets or by the number of distinct businesses *per se*, but from the strategic variety among businesses requiring a variety in the dominant logic used by top management. Further, the variety of dominant logic that top management can

Table 7.1 **Nature of top management tasks in diversified firms**

| | *Sources of strategic variety* | | |
| | | *Addition of a new business* | |
Top management orientation	Significant structural changes in core business	Similar to existing business	Dissimilar from existing business
Single dominant logic	(A) Revise the dominant logic	(B) No change required	(C) Create the capacity for multiple dominant logic(s)
	(D) Revise the dominant logic applied to that business or regroup it under another sector	(E) Assign business to appropriate 'sector'	(F) Add to the variety of dominant logic(s)

handle depends on the composition of the team, and their experiences, as well as their attitude toward learning. These factors suggest that we ought to recognize that the limit to the diversity of businesses within a firm is determined by the strategic variety, and that the strategic variety that a firm can cope with is dependent on the composition of a top management team.

Undoubtedly, organization structure can help cope with increased strategic variety. One basic aspect of decentralization is to make decisions at the level where the proper expertise is available. In other words, the cognitive map is more likely to fit the strategic imperatives of the business. However, not all decision making can be decentralized. For example, resource allocation decisions among a firm's portfolio of businesses must be made. Furthermore, plans, strategies, and budgets must be reviewed at the corporate level and managerial performance must be assessed. Hence organizational structure, although useful, is limited. It can attenuate the intensity of strategic variety that corporate level management must deal with, but it cannot substitute for the need to handle strategic variety at the corporate level.

An alternative or supplementary approach is to reduce the strategic variety in the businesses of the firm – what has come to be known as 'focus' in the portfolio. An interesting variant on this is to impose a single strategic approach on each business. For example as Porter *et al.* (1983) discuss, Emerson Electric has a uniform goal across businesses of being the low-cost producer in each of its markets. Such an approach reduces strategic variety but may impose an inappropriate logic on a particular business. Interestingly, Emerson usually seeks to divest businesses that cannot meet this goal.

Ultimately many firms exceed the limits of organizational structure in attenuating the intensity of strategic variety and/or cannot reduce or limit strategic variety adequately. These firms face the reality of having to deal intensively with strategic variety at the corporate level and the necessity of developing multiple dominant logic if performance is to be sustained.

The bottom line is that each top management team at a given point in time has an inbuilt limit to the extent of diversity it can manage. Organizational structure and focus in the portfolio can help extend this limit but they cannot eliminate it.

Diversity and performance: the hidden costs

A high level of performance in a diversified firm requires the ability to 'respond fast' to competitor moves, as well as 'respond appropriately'. One of the implications of our thesis, so far, is that top managers are less likely to 'respond appropriately' to situations where the dominant logic is different, as well as not respond quickly enough, as they may be unable to interpret the meaning of information regarding unfamiliar businesses. The 'hidden costs' associated with diversifying into non-familiar businesses are shown schematically in Figure 7.3. These 'hidden costs' are not explicitly recognized when the overall business climate is very favourable. Problems surface when the newly acquired businesses (which are strategically dissimilar) encounter competitive problems or are faced with a profit crisis. Top managers find themselves unable to respond to the crisis under those circumstances (Hamermesh, 1977).

Changing or adding dominant logic

The process of adding dominant logic is, given the previous discussion, obviously an important aspect in the management of diversified firms. Also, as the argument so far suggests, the process of changing dominant logic is important to any firm that encounters rapid change in the structure of the industries in which it competes. These issues revolve around the ability of the firm or its dominant coalition to learn. Fortunately, there is a small but growing literature on organizational learning (see Hedberg, 1981, for an introduction and survey). This literature suggests ways in which organizations can change or add dominant logic.

First, let us consider the situation involved in changing the dominant logic of a (single-logic) firm. The explicit assumption here is that the

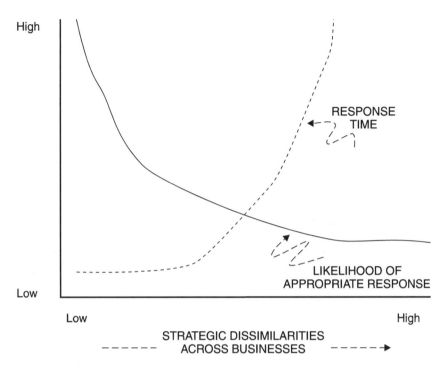

High

RESPONSE
TIME

LIKELIHOOD OF
APPROPRIATE RESPONSE

Low

Low   High

STRATEGIC DISSIMILARITIES
ACROSS BUSINESSES

Figure 7.3 **Diversity and performance**

structure of the core industry the firm competes in is or has changed significantly.

In general it appears that changes in the ways organizations solve significant new problems (i.e. change dominant logics) are triggered by substantial problems or crises (see March and Simon, 1958; Downs, 1967; Terreberrey, 1968; Cyert and March, 1963; Starbuck, 1976; Hedberg, 1973; Hedberg *et al.*, 1976). Hedberg (1981) also suggests that opportunities or changes in key executives may also trigger learning, but here the evidence is small by comparison. (Key executive changes are often made in response to crises.) It would appear that in the overwhelming number of instances a crisis is needed to precipitate change (e.g. 'Why fix it if it is not broke?'). Not only must there be a crisis but as Nystrom *et al.* (1976) propose and illustrate, the initial response to the crisis is likely to be inappropriate. In other words the initial response is likely to draw on the now inappropriate but still current dominant logic. This, of course, provokes a deepening of the crisis and a search for other solutions. Survival is likely to become dependent on finding a new logic.

Given that the opportunity for learning has been elicited by a crisis (or other event) the organizational learning literature (e.g. Hedberg, 1981) suggests that unlearning must occur to make way for new mental maps. Unlearning is simply the process by which firms eliminate old logics and behaviours and make room for new ones. Interestingly, the more successful organizations have been, the more difficult unlearning becomes (Argyris and Schon, 1978; Starbuck and Hedberg, 1977).

Given that these two preconditions, a precipitating crisis and a start of unlearning, have occurred, the stage is set for the kind of learning that can result in a new dominant logic. However, as Michael (1973) and Hedberg (1981) have observed, little is known about how organizations' cognitive structures are changed. Hence, the discussion here must be largely speculative. Hedberg (1981) makes four general suggestions: (1) making organizations more experimental; (2) regulating organizations' sensitivity to environmental changes to an optimal level (neither too low nor too high); (3) redesigning organizations' inner and outer environments; and (4) achieving a dynamic balance between stabilizing and destabilizing influences. Beyond these general areas the current authors suggest: (1) structuring the top management team to include individuals with significantly different experience bases; (2) encouraging top managers to enrich their experience bases through sabbaticals and educational experiences; (3) rehearsing as a management team for a broad range of future industry scenarios; (4) separating economic evaluation from manager evaluation so that executives can be rewarded for experimenting even when projects fail; and (5) legitimizing dissent. Furthermore, in an interesting article about managerial responses to changing environments, Kiesler and Sproul (1982) suggest developing schemas that incorporate the expectation of change as a fundamental component. Unfortunately, again the 'how to' remains largely undefined.

The discussion in this section so far has considered changing dominant logics, not adding new ones. Adding new logics implies retaining the old one and not unlearning it, but developing the ability to deal simultaneously with other logics. This generally falls beyond what has been studied in the organizational learning literature. Diversification is often not triggered by a crisis, and unlearning as described above is not desirable. It appears that what must occur is some kind of meta-learning in which the dominant coalition learns to simultaneously conceptualize different types of businesses. Perhaps some sort of meta-logic evolves that specifies the necessity of, and rules for, picking between partially contradictory mental maps. Further research here is obviously needed.

The meaning of 'relatedness'

The concept of related or conglomerate diversification was typically based on an analysis of the technological and market characteristics. The view presented here suggests that we may have to develop a concept of relatedness based on the 'strategic similarities' of businesses and the cognitive composition of the top management team. Relatedness may be as much a cognitive concept as it is an economic and technical concept.

Future research

The concept of a dominant logic presents opportunities to deepen our understanding of the management of diversification and the relationships between diversity and performance. A first necessary step is to move beyond the purely conceptual stage to measurement of the construct, or, in other words, to being able to specify just what a particular dominant logic actually is. The authors have had experience in trying to construct the dominant logic of a firm by in-depth interviewing of the top management team, and believe that useful results and insights can be achieved. However, such an approach, though useful as a consulting framework, lacks the rigour necessary to establishing general results. Furthermore, quantification is complicated by the cognitive nature of the dominant logic.

Decision-makers' descriptions of their own policies are often inaccurate (Hoffman, 1960; Slovic, 1969; Balke et al., 1973). Similarly, stated policies and intentions often vary from what is actually used. Argyris and Schon (1974) describe this as the difference between 'espoused theories' and 'theories in use' that actually govern behaviour. These researchers suggest that a person's theory in use cannot be obtained simply by asking for it. Creative questionnaires and analysis procedures, however, can be developed that elicit the true nature of the dominant logic. For example, the policy-capturing methodology (Slovic and Liechtenstein, 1971; Slovic et al., 1977) would seem to be a powerful approach to measuring a firm's dominant logic.

Another approach to establishing a firm's dominant logic could be through the use of historical analysis. As previous arguments have discussed, the dominant logic is developed as a result of the experiences of the key executives. Hence, delving into the industry and firm experience of these key individuals would seem to be a fruitful approach, especially when coupled with in-depth interviews of the individuals and their immediate subordinates.

A second important area for future research is the previously mentioned process of learning to use multiple dominant logics. The organizational learning literature deals primarily with changing cognitive maps. It does not deal with the process of learning to use multiple, partially contradictory maps. Some firms have obviously been able to solve this problem. Longitudinal clinical investigation is necessary to determine how.

REFERENCES

Allison, Graham J. (1971) *Essence of Decision: Explaining the Cuban Missile Crisis.* Little, Brown, Boston, MA.

Ansoff, H. Igor (1965) *Corporate Strategy.* McGraw-Hill, New York.

Argyris, C. and D. A. Schon (1974) *Theory in Practice: Increasing Professional Effectiveness.* Jossey-Bass, San Francisco, CA.

Argyris, C. and D. Schon (1978) *Organizational Learning.* Addison-Wesley, Reading, MA.

Balke, W. M., K. R. Hammond and G. D. Meyer (1973) 'An alternative approach to labor–management negotiations', *Administrative Science Quarterly*, 18, 1973, pp. 311–327.

Bettis, R. A. (1979) 'Strategic portfolio management in the multibusiness firm: implementing the portfolio concept'. Unpublished doctoral dissertation, University of Michigan.

Bettis, R. A. and V. Mahajan (1985) 'Risk/return performance of diversified firms', *Management Science*, 31, pp. 785–799.

Bettis, R. A., W. K. Hall and C. K. Prahalad (1978) 'Diversity and performance in the multibusiness firm', *National Proceedings of the American Institute for Decision Sciences*, pp. 210–212.

Bower, J. L. (1972a) *Managing the Resource Allocation Process.* Irwin, Homewood, IL.

Bower, J. L. (1972b) 'Metamanagement: a technology and a philosophy'. Paper presented at the Winter meeting of AAAS, 20 November.

Chandler, Alfred D. (1962) *Strategy and Structure.* MIT Press, Cambridge, MA.

Channon, Derek (1973) *The Strategy and Structure of British Enterprise.* Graduate School of Business Administration, Harvard University, Boston.

Cyert, R. and J. March (1963) *A Behavioral Theory of the Firm.* Prentice-Hall, Englewood Cliffs, NJ.

Das, Rajan (1981) *Managing Diversification: The General Management Perspective.* Macmillan India, New Delhi.

Deal, Terrence E. and Allan A. Kennedy (1982) *Corporate Cultures.* Addison-Wesley, Reading, MA.

de Groot, A. D. (1965) *Thought and Choice in Chess.* Mouton, The Hague.

Donaldson, G. and Jay Lorsch (1983) *Decision Making at the Top.* Basic Books, New York.

Downs, A. (1967) *Inside Bureaucracy.* Little, Brown, Boston, MA.

Hambrick, D. C. (1982) 'Environmental scanning and organizational strategy', *Strategic Management Journal*, 3, pp. 159–174.

Hamermesh, R. G. (1977) 'Responding to the divisional profit crisis'. Unpublished doctoral dissertation, Harvard Business School.

Haspeslagh, P. (1982) 'Portfolio planning: uses and limits', *Harvard Business Review*, January–February, pp. 58–73.

Hedberg, B. (1973) 'Organizational stagnation and choice of strategy'. Working paper, International Institute of Management, Berlin.

Hedberg, B. (1981) 'How organizations learn and unlearn'. In Nystron, P. and W. Starbuck (eds), *Handbook of Organizational Design.* Oxford University Press, Oxford.

Hedberg, B., P. Nystrom and W. Starbuck (1976) 'Camping on seesaws: prescriptions for a self-designing organization', *Administrative Science Quarterly*, 21, pp. 41–65.

Hofer, Charles W. and Dan Schendel (1978) *Strategy Formulation: Analytical Concepts.* West, St Paul, MN.

Hoffman, P. (1960) 'The paramorphic representation of clinical judgment', *Psychological Bulletin*, 47, pp. 116–131.

Huff, A. S. (1982) 'Industry influence on strategy reformulation', *Strategic Management Journal*, 3, pp. 119–131.

Kiesler, S. and L. Sproul (1982) 'Managerial response to changing environments: perspectives and problem sensing from social cognition', *Administrative Science Quarterly*, 37, pp. 548–570.

Kuhn, Thomas S. (1970) *The Structure of Scientific Revolutions*, 2nd edn. University of Chicago Press, Chicago, IL.

March, J. and H. Simon (1958) *Organizations*. Wiley, New York.

Michael, Donald N. (1973) *On Learning to Plan and Planning to Learn*. Jossey-Bass, San Francisco, CA.

Miles, R. H. (1982) *Coffin Nails and Corporate Strategies*. Prentice-Hall, Englewood Cliffs, NJ.

Montgomery, Cynthia (1979) 'Diversification, market structure and firm performance: an extension of Rumelt's model', PhD dissertation, Purdue University.

Nathanson, Daniel and James Cassano (1982) 'Organization, diversity, and performance', *Wharton Magazine*, Summer, pp. 19–26.

Newell, A. and Herbert Simon (1972) *Human Problem Solving*. Prentice-Hall, Englewood Cliffs, NJ.

Nisbett, R. and L. Ross (1980) *Human Inference: Strategies and Shortcomings of Social Judgement*. Prentice-Hall, Englewood Cliffs, NJ.

Norman, D. (1976) *Memory and Attention*, 2nd edn. Wiley, New York.

Nystrom, P., B. Hedberg and W. Starbuck (1976) 'Interacting processes as organizational designs'. In Kilman, R., L. Pondy and D. Slevin (eds), *The Management of Organization Design*. Elsevier, New York.

Ouchi, William G. (1981) *Theory Z*. Addison-Wesley, Reading, MA.

Pascale, Richard J. and Anthony G. Athos (1981) *The Art of Japanese Management*. Simon & Schuster, New York.

Pavan, R. J. (1972) 'Strategy and structure of Italian enterprise'. Unpublished doctoral dissertation, Harvard Business School.

Peters, Thomas J. and Robert H. Waterman, Jr (1982) *In Search of Excellence*. Harper & Row, New York.

Pooley, G. (1972) 'Strategy and structure of French enterprise'. Unpublished doctoral dissertation, Harvard Business School.

Porter, M. (1980) *Competitive Strategy*. The Free Press, New York.

Porter, M. D. Collis, J. DeBelina, J. Elsasser, J. Hornthal and R. Shearer (1983) 'The chain saw industry in 1974'. In Porter, M. (ed.) *Cases in Competitive Strategy*. The Free Press, New York.

Prahalad, C. K. and Y. Doz (1981) 'An approach to strategic control in MNCs', *Sloan Management Review*, Summer, pp. 5–13.

Rumelt, Richard (1974) *Strategy, Structure, and Economic Performance*. Division of Research, Graduate School of Business Administration, Harvard University.

Rumelt, Richard P. (1977) *Diversity and profitability*, Paper NGL–51, Managerial Studies Center, Graduate School of Management, University of California, Los Angeles.

Scholeffler, Sidney, Robert D. Buzzell and Donald F. Heany (1974) 'Impact of strategic planning on profit performance', *Harvard Business Review*, March–April, pp. 137–145.

Simon, Herbert A. (1979) 'Information processing models of cognition', *Annual Review of Psychology*, 30, pp. 363–396

Skinner, B. F. (1953) *Science and Human Behaviour*. Macmillan, New York.

Slovic, P. (1969) 'Analysing the expert judge: a descriptive study of stockbrokers' decision processes', *Journal of Applied Psychology*, 53, pp. 255–263.

Slovic, P. and S. Liechtenstein (1971) 'Comparison of Bayesian and regression approaches to the study of information processing in judgement', *Organisational Behaviour and Human Performance*, 6, pp. 649–744.

Slovic, P., B. Fishcoff and S. Liechtenstein (1977) 'Behavioural decision theory'. In Rosenzweig, R. and L.W. Porter (eds), *Annual Review of Psychology*, Annual Review, Palo Alto, CA, pp. 1–39.

Starbuck, W. (1976) 'Organisations and their environments'. In Dunnette, M. (ed) *Handbook of Industrial and Organisational Psychology*. Rand McNally, Chicago, IL.

Starbuck, W. and B. Hedberg (1977) 'Saving an organization from a stagnating environment'. In Thorelli, H. (ed.) *Strategy + Structure = Performance*. Indiana University Press, Bloomington, IN.

Suzuki, Y. (1980) 'The strategy and structure of top 100 Japanese industrial enterprises 1950–1970', *Strategic Management Journal*, 3, pp. 265–291.

Terreberrey, S. (1968) 'The evolution of organizational environments', *Administrative Science Quarterly*, 12, pp. 590–613.

Thanheiser, H. (1972) 'Strategy and structure of German enterprise'. Unpublished doctoral dissertation, Harvard Business School.

Tversky, Amos and Daniel Kahneman (1974) 'Judgement under uncertainty: heuristics and biases', *Science*, 185, pp. 1124–1131.

Weick, K. (1979) *The Social Psychology of Organizing*, 2nd edn. Addison-Wesley, Reading, MA.

Wrigley, Leonard (1970) 'Divisional autonomy and diversification'. DBA dissertation, Harvard University.

Part II

Learning, structure and process

Introduction

Prahalad and Bettis ended the final chapter of Part I with an analysis of how organizations change their cognitive structures, the thought and thinking structures that underpin behaviour and develop new mental maps. Little is known about this important issue although a variety of methods have been suggested for changing these structures. These include optimizing sensitivity to business environments, reconstituting top management teams to include individuals with different backgrounds (thus, in theory, bringing a range of mental maps to the top management decision process while legitimizing the expression of 'dissident views), top management development to enable managers to rethink, and developing skills of scenario planning. Part II addresses issues of organization structure and process and, in particular, how structure and process can be managed to encourage innovation.

Organization structure is traditionally associated with issues of specialization, divided responsibilities, coordination and bureaucratization. The roots of modern thinking about these issues lie in the work of the sociologist Max Weber. Weber analysed history as a process of increasing rationalization. Modernity is characterized by formal rationality, the shaping of organizations, institutions and society at large by rules and structures. Individuals are not free to pursue their own means. The role of management is to ensure that actions conform to existing rule structures which guide/constrain/control behaviour. The notion of constraint is encapsulated in Weber's notion of bureaucracy as an iron cage. Ritzer (1993) develops this notion in his argument that society is now subject to a process of 'McDonaldization'. He suggests that the iron cage is tightening its grip upon our thought processes and our behaviours through the increasing ubiquity of a 'fast-food' model of work and social organization.

The process of rationalization has four basic principles – efficiency, calculability, predictability and increasing control through the use of technology. Bureaucracy is appropriate in stable and simple environments where a strategy of mass production – the predictable manufacture/

delivery of large quantities of the same standardized product/service – is viable because demand is stable and markets homogeneous. In such an environment firms will compete on cost not on product differentiation through quality and customization. The bureaucratic approach loses (some of) its justification when demand changes and becomes more complex and markets fragment. In such conditions customization is the order of the day and competitive advantage is dependent upon innovatory capacity, the ability to respond to and to shape fast-changing and varied consumer demand. In such a context it is more useful to think of the firm in terms of learning processes rather than organizational structures. In conditions of rapid technological change, organizational learning is crucial. We need a unified view of working, learning and organization in which learning is viewed as an expression of a 'community' of shared and developing practices (Brown and Duguid, 1991). The notion of community suggests the integration of effort across organizational structures. In mass production effort is segmented across occupational and organizational boundaries.

Sustainable innovation is increasingly the holy grail of management. According to the opening chapter of Part II, Michael Tushman and David Nadler's 'Organizing for innovation', the management of innovation and change is *the* most vital of management tasks. Innovation, the authors argue, is the outcome of management that is strategic and leadership that is visionary. Innovation can become an organizational 'way of life' through the skilful management of people, structures, values and learning.

What characterizes innovative organizations? The answer is: they are highly effective at learning, self-critical and committed to continuous improvement. They are also effective at synthesizing marketing knowledge with product development and manufacturing know-how. Those organizations that have a reputation for innovation have won that reputation through radical, discontinuous product or process innovation. For example, Sony is associated with a stream of revolutionary consumer products such as the Walkman. Pilkington pioneered the float-glass manufacturing process, thus making previous process technologies obsolete. Radical innovation challenges dominant design and the dominant logic of thinking about product and process.

One of the problems of growth is that the success of a particular product or service and the increase in the volume of its provision requires the elaboration of structures based upon existing knowledge. The tendency is for behaviours that are currently successful to persist beyond the moment when adaptation to a new environment is necessary. Old habits prevail but prove increasingly dysfunctional. This is organizational 'momentum' (Miller, 1990). Successful vision becomes tunnel vision, competence becomes complacency. The sensitivity to external opportunities and threats and the sense of internal possibilities dwindle. A major problem of innovation, then, can be the trap of success, although a small number of organizations – such as 3M and Citibank – do seem able to remain innovative over long periods of time. One would have included IBM in this group until recently and it is struggling to recapture its former glory. Another small number of firms – such as Xerox – lose their innovative edge but manage to recapture it.

Tushman and Nadler identify a number of parameters of the innovative organization. Individual expertise is combined with team problem-solving skills so that the whole is greater than the sum of its parts. The leadership task is to build a top team with the requisite functional expertise and the learning and problem-solving capacities to sense and to solve tomorrow's dilemmas. Formal organization must allow for linking between different functions and encourage collaboration throughout the organization. People are incentivized to transcend purely functional expertise by developing a collaborative frame of mind. An optimal level of job diversity is sought through the career-planning system. Core values play a crucial role in focusing and motivating behaviour. It is leadership's task to infuse the organization with value and to serve as a role model of the behaviours required by innovation. Innovative leadership is envisioning, energizing and enabling. Innovation requires periods of diversity in which these values provide a stable touchstone for self-evaluation. Innovation is inherently disruptive so conflict must be viewed as valuable and constructive.

Tushman and Nadler stress informality in their vision of the innovation process. For Jay Galbraith, in the next chapter, 'Designing the innovating organization', the design of the innovating organization is a task of conscious design and innovation requires a form of organization specifically designed for that purpose. The building blocks of any organization – structures, processes, rewards and people – need a special configuration (Mintzberg, 1979) if innovation is to result. Innovating organizations differ from operating organizations, designed to produce efficiently known product and services. But if innovation is to be effective, a transition process is needed to transfer ideas from the innovating organization to the operating organization.

Galbraith compares structure, processes, reward systems and people management in operating and innovating organizations. In the latter, people self-select for key roles that focus upon the getting and blending of ideas rather than upon the implementation of plans that are realized through rules handed down from the top. Programmes are more important than a precise division of labour. The opportunity and autonomy to pursue self-realization motivates as much as the compensation package. Successful innovators have deep knowledge of the structures of their industry and the ability to extend these. They are not true believers, totally imbued with their industry's 'religion'. Rather, they are sceptics, knowledgeable about the issues but not totally convinced that the one best way for the industry yet exists. They are generalists, not specialists, creating insights that challenge current orthodoxy, for example about appropriate product lines. They need a broad experience of career development to develop the generalist's perspective. They are comfortable with long time-frames and view control as based upon people and ideas, not numbers and budget targets.

Top management must orchestrate a process (innovation) that is 'destructive' of previous investments and career plans. It must also find a means of legitimizing the challenge to the status quo. Creative destruction requires innovative approaches to integration across functional and divisional divides. Innovation depends upon the simultaneous coupling of knowledge from a variety of sources rather than its linear sequential processing. (Galbraith's argument here recalls current debates about simultaneous engineering – for example, Clark and Fujimoto, 1991.) Like Galbraith, Ralph Kilmann, in the next chapter, 'Designing collateral organizations', advocates a formal, purposeful approach to organizational design as a means of coping with ill-defined problems. Innovation, by definition, starts out as lacking in definition. We cannot know the problem that something we have yet to discover will be capable of resolving. Indeed, Kilmann suggests that the basic problem is defining what the problem is. Once one can do this, one can begin analysing the problem, seeking relevant information, creating new knowledge and implementing solutions.

According to Galbraith, innovation requires forms of organization specifically designed for that purpose but one neglects the transition process that is required to transfer ideas from the innovating organization to the operating organization at one's peril. Kilmann's argument extends Galbraith's in its analysis of how ideas, created in collateral organizations, can be assimilated into the operating organization through a process of problem sensing, problem definition, problem solving and solution implementation. Operational design deals with production. Collateral design deals with ill-defined, long-term and system-wide problems. Strategy is concerned with the long-term health of the business and, as such, has to deal with an ill-defined and difficult-to-conceive future. Strategy is implemented through operational management.

The collateral organization can be seen as a means of resolving strategic issues. It constitutes a parallel structure to the operational structure with overlapping membership. The design of parallel and overlapping membership increases the likelihood of transfer of knowledge from collateral to operational. The parallel structure overcomes the problem of using a separate staff group for problem resolution (for example, a planning group for strategic analysis). Such groups are remote from the source of the problem and lack the authority to implement their own plans. Collateral organizations are composed of groups from a number of departments, thus bringing a wide range of experience and knowledge to their task. They differ from task forces and project teams which are more suitable for well-defined problems because they function according to clear rules of design, for example, in their composition. They also differ from matrix structures because they contain members, senior managers, with the authority to implement their ideas in the operational structure.

Kilmann suggests a number of rules for designing collateral organizations that include the identification of people with the necessary skills and knowledge, the 'clustering' of tasks in ways that maximize interdependencies within subunits, and optimizing ways of coordinating subunits and the flow of learning between the collateral and the operational units. Particularly difficult to manage are 'reciprocal-interdependent' tasks which require ongoing interactions between different collateral groups who need to adjust to each other's discoveries. Kilmann also suggests that firms should consider knowledge networks available outside the firm, such as the use of external consultants. One needs as broad a conception as possible of what constitutes an adequate pool of human resources for the mission in question, even if this means redefining the boundaries of the organization.

Collateral innovating organization manages a complex flow of problems, people, information and knowledge. It is very demanding. Above all it requires creativity in forging links between those parts of the organization that have significant potential for knowledge creation. One weakness of Kilmann's argument is that, towards the end of his chapter, he reverts to what some will see as an over-rational (and probably over-optimistic) approach to setting objectives in his argument that organizations need to be clear about the 'final outcomes or objectives', then work backwards to organization design. This assumes a degree of foresight/ wishful thinking in situations such as strategic 'planning' where problems cannot be clearly prioritized and the final outcomes are not clear. In such a context, strategy is more emergent than pre-determined (Mintzberg, 1993).

In the next chapter, 'Intelligent technology, intelligent workers: a new pedagogy for the high-tech workplace', Gloria Schuck examines the implication of managing as if workers had brains in the context of the ways in which new technologies change skills needs. Schuck builds upon the pioneering work of Zuboff (1989) and her important distinction between the use of information technology to automate or to 'informate'. To informate requires a work environment which enhances thinking and problem-solving by involving workers in the redefinition of the work process in search of cost and quality improvements. In such an environment, workers are expected to use the new information possibilities to generate business insights and innovations of their own.

In the 'informated' workplace we need a new approach to teaching and training. The old distinction between 'teacher' and 'learner' is no longer useful because the new environment is quintessentially one of uncertainty. These work environments require the development/liberation of higher order cognitive skills, the intellective skill needed to make new meaning out of the data generated by new information technology, as an antidote towards the conventional way of acting in a programmed way. Two important conditions must apply to make such a learning context feasible. Discipline needs to be allied with play but play that is not just 'playing by the rules'. People have to use play to discover/invent new rules. Just as children use play to recreate ostensibly familiar objects in a new way (Holt, 1970), so adult play can liberate the imagination and create a new sense of meaning.

Learning is a social experience, built upon interaction and dialogue with significant others in a context where people are willing to share their ideas with others. The best solutions often occur when different points of view are integrated into this dialogue. Traditional training methods only teach people what to think. A new pedagogy is necessary to give workers the knowledge to think for themselves, rather than the old training which gives information only on a 'need to know' basis. If people cannot learn how to learn, they run the risk of becoming 'walking encyclopedias' of outdated information. What is needed is a work environment of inquiry – people questioning the continuing viability of what they thought they knew.

The learning process in organizations requires the creative destruction of barriers to learning and the broadening of access to new sources of knowledge and experience. In many companies this requires a new culture of learning. People have to feel free to ask questions. They must not feel threatened by their ignorance. In some companies the three words 'I don't know' are anathema. They can ruin careers. But the fear of this form of expression stifles growth. If we are not comfortable revealing our ignorance we cannot overcome it. This requires a new mode of management. The manager must encourage people to ask questions and create an atmosphere of intellectual play by improving the mediation of learning. The manager seeks to leverage the knowledge that the people at the point of production often have but that is doomed to remain latent and untapped. What is required is the searching examination of existing roles and reward systems. Workers and managers need to become partners in creating meaning.

In the next chapter, 'Product development in Ford of Europe: undoing the past/learning the future', Ken Starkey and Alan McKinlay chart the problems of organizational self-renewal in a study of the evolution of the management of product development in Ford of Europe. Ford is one of the world's most successful companies but the 1980s found it with major problems of maintaining market share in an automobile market where the rules of competition were constantly changing, not least with the advent of more efficient, higher quality and more innovative competition from Japan. Changes in product development at Ford required a major assault on the traditional functional mind-set of the company. This assault was led by the product development group who were increasingly aware that functional organization structure slowed down product development and compromised the integrity of product design and its implementation.

Ford benchmarked its product development processes against the Japanese, in particular Mazda in which Ford holds a significant minority ownership stake. Mazda differs from Ford in the way it is able to integrate functional activity across organizational divides. From Mazda and other of its competitors Ford learned the possible benefits of a matrix approach to product development. However, organizational politics intervened and old attitudes prevailed in resistance to the new initiatives. It was exceedingly difficult to generate a sense of a common ownership of the problems facing the company. The reflex reaction was to blame other groups and to deny one's own involvement in the need for change. However, over time, but perhaps not quickly enough, attitudes did change and by the end of the 1980s it became generally accepted that something drastic was necessary if Ford of Europe was to improve its product development effectiveness.

The goal was clear – 'best product/ best process/ first time'. What now occurred was convergence around a form of organization – simultaneous engineering – that would make this happen. The broad mass of the company finally accepted that survival was at stake and that a quantum leap in organization process, rather than superficial structural reorganization, was necessary. The effectiveness of simultaneous engineering depends upon a new valuing of communication, cooperation and skill and a new sense of common purpose as a customer-driven organization. Managers and employees have had to learn a new sense of the importance of interdependence, based upon a team culture, that builds upon the virtues of the old sense of Ford discipline. For the first time at Ford, the notion of learning became a prime value.

A crucial aspect of the Ford case is the importance of developing new managerial attitudes and behaviours. This organization and management development issue provides the focus of the last two chapters in Part II. In 'Developing the forgotten army: learning and the top manager', Bill Braddick and David Casey address the important issue of senior management development. In many organizations, once they reach senior positions, managers are deemed to be fully formed. They have been developed by their previous experiences and learning and are now considered, at least implicitly, either to possess all the knowledge they need or to be quite capable of self-development. Here lies one of the black holes of organizational learning. Organizations lack an explicit strategy for developing their senior managers. Yet, as Braddick and Casey argue, the need for management development for this group has never been more pressing. This group must learn to think and act more strategically.

Braddick and Casey highlight what should be a core concern in top management development – the need to replace functional thinking by strategic thinking. Successful top management is about team work and managing through structures and process. It is about 'unlearning' old habits, both skills and knowledge, and learning through reflection upon experience rather than through theoretical discussion. It is about confronting skilled incompetence. The authors propose the action learning set as a viable learning experience that has structural and processual elements. Learning sets work by exposing you to others with different frames of reference. They help individuals break the bars of the prison of their existing frames in a supportive context. Facilitators ease the task process and supply the much needed maintenance process, dealing with the feelings of people going through the pain of change. Problems are reframed in radically different ways. For example, 'How do I pacify this irate group of customers?' might be reframed as 'Who's managing this company – me or my customers?' Participants learn by doing, by active experimentation, by reflection and by building new models to help structure their thinking processes. Top managers can find in this experience an antidote to the often deep isolation that they experience as a result of their position and of their subordinates' expectations.

One has to decide how to structure learning sets in terms of their participants' aspirations and experience so that the sets serve the needs of both the organization and its members. Here one has to clearly decide the purpose of the set – is it an 'action' set, task oriented, geared to particular projects and with clear goals, or is it a 'reflective' set (some would prefer the term 'reflexive') orientated to the personal development of the participants, with unclear goals? Crucial to the learning process is 'reframing', stepping outside the frame of reference that has heretofore structured thinking. One has to recognize the barriers to learning, the tendency to persist in learnt behaviours, the lure of utopias which are forever unattainable, the implacable momentum in change initiatives that only reinforces the status quo.

Innovation and change can be construed as radically altering the 'genetic code' of the corporation. In the next chapter, 'GE's Crotonville: a staging ground for corporate revolution', Noel Tichy examines General Electric's efforts to break its old genetic code under the leadership of CEO Jack Welch. According to Tichy, corporate 'revolution' requires a new breed of leader to redesign the 'social architecture' of the organization. This should be an ongoing process based upon the creation of new forms of 'design teams', better communication and cultural integration. Welch sees his greatest mistake as having been too cautious in dismantling GE's bureaucratic structures built upon years of thinking of the company in terms of discrete business units. GE needs to be liberated from this 'old way' of management based upon hierarchical bureaucracy and reshaped as a non-hierarchical, flexible, adaptive organization.

At GE the redesign process has been spearheaded by Crotonville, GE's Management Development Institute. Under Welch, Crotonville reports direct to executive management and not to employee relations staff. The old textbooks were 'symbolically burned'. Management development initiatives are carefully constructed to link closely to new thinking about career development and succession planning. Course membership is devised to cut through the old chain of command and to forge a direct link to top management. The learning process is validated by top managerial commitment and participation in courses. Top management demonstrates ownership and responsibility for the overall design and architecture, delivery and integration of the development process with individual and organizational needs. Top management exposes itself to the same rigorous self-examination and self-criticism that it expects of others.

It is a central part of Tichy's argument, based upon his own experience as manager of Crotonville, that investment in development is often under-leveraged by most large corporations because there is little or no visible personal commitment to the process by top management. Such commitment is a measure of leadership in the learning organization. Approximately 8,000 managers a year went through the programmes and the goal was both individual development and organizational development through new team skills and problem-solving approaches to stimulate fundamental change. Executives come to Crotonville at key transition points in their careers ('moments of opportunity'). The focus is on learning from experience and from reflection upon that experience. Crucial here is that the company develop a framework that provides guidelines that integrate on-the-job development with the development that takes place during formal learning periods. We return to the crucial issue of top management development in Part III.

REFERENCES

Brown, J.S. and Duguid, P. (1991) 'Organizational learning and communities-of-practice: toward a unified view of working, learning and innovation', *Organization Science*, 2, 1, 40–57.

Clark, K. and Fujimoto, T. (1991) *Product Development Performance*, Cambridge, Mass., Harvard Business School Press.

Holt, J. (1970) *How Children Learn*, Harmondsworth, Pelican.

Miller, D. (1990) *The Icarus Paradox*, New York, HarperBusiness.

Mintzberg, H. (1979) *The Structuring of Organizations*, Englewood Cliffs, NJ, Prentice-Hall.

Mintzberg, H. (1993) *The Rise and Fall of Strategic Planning*, Englewood Cliffs, NJ, Prentice-Hall.
Ritzer, G. (1993) *The McDonaldization of Society*, Newbury Park, CA, Pine Forge Press.
Zuboff, S. (1989) *In the Age of the Smart Machine*, London, Heinemann.

Chapter 8

Organizing for innovation

Michael Tushman and David Nadler

In today's business environment, there is no executive task more vital and demanding than the sustained management of innovation and change. It sometimes seems that every aspect of business is in a state of flux – technology, government regulation, global competition. These rapid changes in the marketplace make it increasingly difficult, and essential, for business to think in terms of the future, to constantly anticipate tomorrow's definition of value – the right mix of quality, service, product characteristics, and price. To compete in this ever-changing environment, companies must create new products, services, and processes; to dominate, they must adopt innovation as a way of corporate life.

Sustained innovation is both important and tremendously difficult. Consider these brief examples: for more than 30 years General Radio dominated the market for electronic-test-equipment. While new competitors took advantage of computers, systems technology, and innovative approaches to working with customers, General Radio remained committed to the technologies and marketing practices that it knew best. During the 1960s, market share and profits declined. It took a complete transformation of the organization, driven by mostly new managers, to bring about product, market, and production innovations.

Technicon Corporation created the automated clinical diagnostic instrument industry. Technicon initially prospered by successfully producing a number of product innovations based on their expertise in hydraulics technologies. While Technicon led with product innovation, other firms entered the market leading with process innovation (i.e. cost and quality) and with a broadened view of the clinical market. Technicon's response to the external threat was increased reliance on its old winning formula. Market share and relative performance declined. It was not until Technicon was acquired by Revlon that the organization was able to successfully develop product, process and market innovation.

Biogen is known world-wide as an organization doing excellent basic research in genetic engineering. While science flourishes at Biogen, marketing and product development have been ignored. Nobel laureate Walter

Gilbert no longer runs Biogen. A new management team has been brought in to create the conditions for enhanced product, market and process innovation.

The common theme is obvious: in all three cases, once highly innovative organizations became trapped by their own success. These examples are not unique. In one industry after another, the same factors that create a successful innovative company often plant the seeds of complacency and failure as competitive conditions change.

Nevertheless, many exceptional firms have demonstrated that sustained innovation, though difficult, is certainly attainable. Large corporations (such as IBM, 3M, Citicorp, American Airlines, GE, Merck, and Philip Morris) as well as smaller firms (such as Rolm, Wang, Charles River Breeding Labs, Federal Express, and Dunkin' Donuts) have been highly innovative over long periods. They have simultaneously managed the dual challenges of innovating for the markets of both the present and the future.

What are the organizational factors which enhance innovation? The most innovative organizations are highly effective learning systems. Organizations that can be self-critical – and can learn to keep improving on today's work while aggressively preparing for tomorrow's – will be more successful than those organizations that evolve toward greater stability and complacency. Sustained innovation, somewhat paradoxically, requires both stability and change: stability permits scale economies and incremental learning, while change and experimentation are necessary for advances in products, processes, and technologies.

TYPES OF INNOVATION

Innovation is the creation of any product, service, or process which is new to a business unit. While innovation is often associated with major product or process advances (e.g. xerography, transistors, float-glass), the vast majority of successful innovations are based on the cumulative effect of incremental change in products and processes, or the creative combination of existing techniques, ideas, or methods. Innovation is not just R&D; just as important are marketing, sales, and production. Effective innovation requires the synthesis of market needs with technological possibility and manufacturing capabilities.

At the most basic level, there are two kinds of innovation: product innovation, or changes in the product a company makes or the service it provides; and process innovation, a change in the way a product is made or the service provided. Within each of these two categories, there are three degrees of innovation – incremental, synthetic, and discontinuous (see Figure 8.1). Some illustrations help clarify these differences.

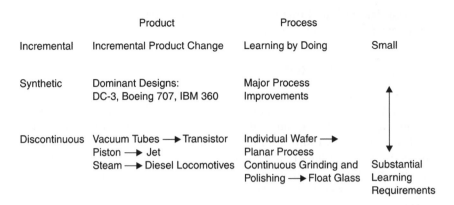

Figure 8.1 **Types of innovation**

PRODUCT INNOVATION

Most product innovations are incremental changes. They provide added features, new versions or extensions to an otherwise standard product line. Obviously, such innovations occur all the time, and large numbers of incremental innovations related to customer requirements can add up to a significant competitive advantage.

A second type of product innovation, synthetic, involves the combination of existing ideas or technologies in creative ways to develop significantly new products. For example, the DC–3 incorporated existing airplane innovations which, together, resulted in a single airplane which combined speed, efficiency, and size. Similarly, the 707 and 747 and Merrill Lynch's Cash Management Account were important synthetic product innovations which dominated their respective industries. These product innovations didn't require any new technology. Rather, each represented a creative combination of existing technology which, when linked with marketing and production skill, resulted in a product which set the standard in its product class – until the next major product innovation came along.

The third category, discontinuous product innovations, involves the development or application of significant new technologies or ideas. Examples include the shift from piston airplanes to jets, the change from steam to diesel locomotives, or the move from core to semiconductor memory. These major innovations required new skills, processes, and systems throughout the organization. Each required wholesale changes in those firms moving from old to new product technologies.

As innovation moves from incremental to discontinuous, there are higher risks and greater uncertainty. It becomes increasingly important for organizations to function as effective learning systems, benefiting from both failure and success.

PROCESS INNOVATION

Process innovations change the way products and services are made or delivered. Process innovation may be invisible to the user except through changes in the cost or quality of the product. As in product innovation, most process innovations are incremental improvements which result in lowered costs, higher quality, or both. Learning curve efficiencies and learning-by-doing produce small process innovations that incrementally improve upon existing production processes.

Synthetic process innovations involve sharp increases in size, volume, or capacity of well-known production processes. For example, the rotary kiln in cement manufacturing or Owens' process in glassware production were significant innovations, but they were basically larger, faster, and more efficient versions of well-known existing processes.

Discontinuous process innovations are totally new ways of producing products or services. For example, the float-glass process in glass manufacturing, planar processes in semiconductors, and the use of robots in auto plants are fundamentally different ways of making established products. Major process innovations reduce costs and increase the quality of the product or service, but they require new skills, new ways of organizing, and, frequently, new ways of managing. As with product innovation, the greater the degree of process change, the greater the uncertainty and the greater the required organizational learning.

THE STRATEGIC ROLE OF PRODUCT AND PROCESS INNOVATION

Both product and process innovation are important, yet their relative importance changes over time. Studies in multiple industries find predictable patterns in the amount and degree of innovation over the product life cycle (see Figure 8.2). In the introductory stage, there is a substantial amount of product innovation as several forms of the same product compete for dominance. For example, during the early stages of the automobile industry, at least four automobile types (internal combustion, battery, wood, and steam-powered) competed for the relatively small market. This period of product competition leads to the emergence of a dominant design, representing industry standardization in the product's basic configuration and characteristics: for example the DC–3, IBM 360, Smith Model 5 typewriter, the Fordson tractor, VHS design in video cassette recorders, all represent dominant designs which shaped the evolution of their respective product classes for years.

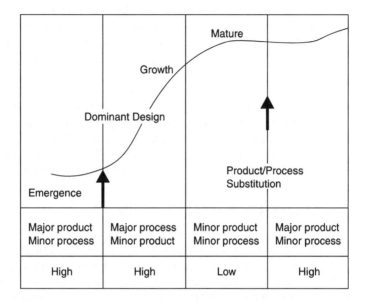

			Mature
		Growth	
Dominant Design			
Emergence			Product/Process Substitution

Dominant Innovation Types	Major product Minor process	Major process Minor product	Minor product Minor process	Major product Minor process
Learning Requirement	High	High	Low	High

Figure 8.2 **Types of innovation over product life cycle**

In the next stage, major product variation gives way to competition based on price, quality, and segmentation – in other words, process innovation rather than product innovation. Thus, major process innovation, combined with incremental product innovation, allows firms to enhance the product and open the market to a more diverse customer base. In the mid-1970s, for example, personal computers were sold mainly to customers with substantial computer expertise; standardization of the Apple and IBM PCs permitted the development of customized software and services for small businesses, homes, and schools.

During the mature stage of a product life cycle, this pattern of incremental product and major process innovation continues until the product and its associated production processes are so intertwined that only incremental product and process innovation are possible. This period can be very profitable, since small changes in the product or processes can lead to significantly decreased costs or higher quality. The mature phase of product life cycle, with its emphasis on incremental innovation, lasts until some external shock such as deregulation, technological change, or foreign competition triggers a new wave of major product innovation. For example, Ford's Model T was enormously profitable until fully enclosed cars were made possible by advances in steel. Thus, product innovation initiated by General Motors forced Ford to reinitiate major product and, in turn, major process innovations.

Consequently, innovation is a complex and uncertain endeavor which shifts over time and requires the close collaboration of R&D, marketing, sales, and production. Effective organizations create conditions that allow today's work to be done well while simultaneously generating tomorrow's innovations. The challenge is to optimize today's work while producing the uncertainty and chaos so essential to tomorrow's innovation. Only those organizations which can manage stability and, at the same time, nurture the capacity to experiment and learn will be able to master both product and process innovation. Those organizations that get stuck in a single mode of operation will be incapable of producing different kinds of innovation as product life cycles evolve.

ORGANIZING FOR TODAY'S WORK

This formula for innovation-managing for today while building the infrastructure for tomorrow involves a basic dilemma: building the systems and processes for the short run often undercuts the innovative process.

The general manager has two basic tasks. The first task is strategy formulation: making fundamental decisions about markets, products, and competitive basis in the context of a larger environment, a set of resources, and organizational history. The second task is organizing. This involves creating, building, and maintaining the organization – a mechanism which transforms strategy into output.

One way of thinking about organizing is that there are four major components to any organization:

Task: the basic work to be done
Individuals: the members of the organization
Organizational arrangements: the formal structures and processes created to get individuals to perform tasks
Informal organization: the unwritten, constantly evolving arrangements – including 'culture' – which define how things get done.

In the short to medium term, organizational effectiveness is greatest when two conditions are met. First, the four components are designed and managed so that they are congruent; in other words, they fit well together. Second, the pattern of congruence of the four components matches the basic requirements of the strategy (see Figure 8.3).[1]

When strategy fits environmental conditions, congruence is associated with organizational effectiveness. Since organizations are never totally congruent, part of management's job is to initiate incremental changes to fine-tune the organization. Incremental change is relatively easy to implement and builds increasing consistency among strategy, structure, people, and processes. Increasing congruence, however, can be a double-edged sword. As organizations grow and become more successful, they develop

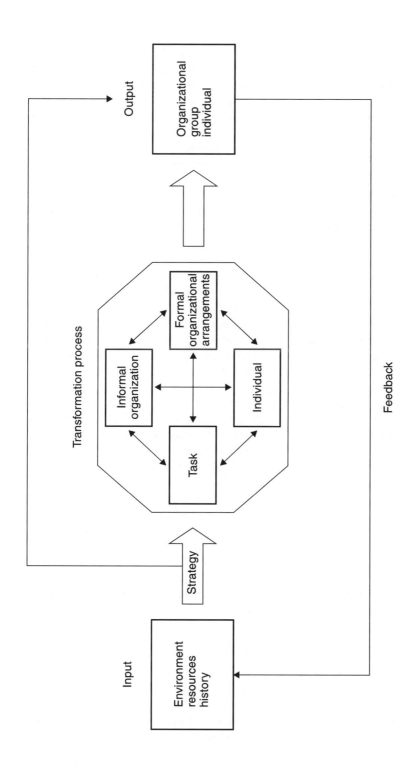

Figure 8.3 A congruence model of organizational behavior

internal pressures for stability. Organizational structures and systems become so interlinked that they allow only compatible changes. Further, over time, employees develop habits; patterned behaviors begin to take on values (e.g. 'service is our number one goal') and employees develop a sense of competence in knowing how to get work done within the system. These reinforcing norms, values, and patterns of behavior contribute to increased organizational stability and, over time, to a sense of organizational history epitomized by common stories, heroes, and standards.

This organizational momentum is profoundly functional as long as the organization's strategy is appropriate. At Technicon, Biogen, and General Radio, the culture, structure and systems, and associated internal momentum were critical to each organization's success. However, when a new strategy is called for, this momentum cuts the other way. The organizational history – which can be a source of tradition, precedent, and pride – can also be an obstacle to alert problem solving and organizational learning. When faced with an environmental threat, highly inertial organizations either may not register the threat due to organizational complacency and / or stunted external vigilance (e.g. the automobile or steel industries) or if the threat is recognized, the response, very often, is more rigid conformity to the status quo and an increased commitment to keep doing 'what we do best.' For example, when faced with a technological threat, dominant firms frequently have responded with even greater reliance on the obsolete technology (e.g. telegraph / telephone; vacuum tube / transistor; core memory / semiconductor memory). A paradoxical result of long periods of success may be increased organizational complacency and a stunted ability to learn.

To summarize, long periods of success can easily result in organizational complacency and tunnel vision: the longer the success lasts, the greater the internal forces for stability, and the less the system is able to learn and innovate. This pattern is accentuated in business units that dominate a product class (for example Polaroid or Caterpillar), in historically regulated organizations (AT&T, GTE, or financial service firms), or in organizations that have traditionally been shielded from competition (universities, not-for-profit organizations, and government agencies).

ORGANIZING FOR TOMORROW'S WORK

Successful organizations innovate for today as well as for tomorrow. Managing this duality is an immensely difficult task. Each company described in our previous examples was a once-innovative firm which had become trapped by its own success. Put in the context of our organizational model, congruence and internal consistency, taken to extremes, diminished learning and discouraged major innovation. But firms such as 3M, Lilly, IBM, and Citibank manage to produce for the short run while keeping close to customers, competitors, technologies, and internal competence. This sensitivity to external opportunities and internal possibilities provides the stimulus for organizational learning and sustained innovation.

The most innovative organizations are effective learning systems; they maximize both their ability to acquire information about customers, competitors and technology, and their ability to process that information. They gather diverse input and involve multiple actors in processing these data. While costly, chaotic, and potentially disruptive, this process of generating ideas and solving problems provides the foundation for tomorrow's innovation.

What are the key elements of designing for tomorrow's work? Research on innovative organizations has begun to shed some light on this question.[2] Using our organizational model, we can identify some approaches and practices related to the major components (Individual, Organization Arrangements, and Informal Organization) that can be used to manage a new Task, preparing for tomorrow's work (see Figure 8.4).

Individuals

Because innovation requires multiple disciplines and in-depth expertise, management's challenge is to hire, train, and develop a set of individuals with diverse skills and abilities, and the capacity to innovate. But in-depth and diverse expertise is not sufficient. Because organizational learning and innovation is a group and intergroup phenomenon, individual contributors rarely produce the creative ideas or solutions required for complex or discontinuous innovation. Thus, strong individual specialization must be bolstered by skills in problem solving, communication, conflict resolution, and team building. Those skills which broaden an individual's ability to communicate with other professionals and to appreciate multiple perspectives can be developed in the organization through recruitment, training, and socialization practices. For example, IBM managers must spend 40 hours per year on managerial education. This program, which gathers individuals from different disciplines and/or divisions for up to three weeks, continually reinforces the importance of communication, collaboration, and problem solving.

The general manager has to build a top team to help provide direction, energy, and enthusiasm for the organization. These are the role models who create the conditions for learning and innovation throughout the organization. This senior team needs skills and abilities which match environmental demands; it requires individuals who are respected for their disciplinary competence, and who are well linked to external sources of information and expertise. This senior team not only manages for

**Informal
Organization**

- Core values
- Norms
- Communications
  networks
- Critical roles
- Conflict
  resolution
- Problem-solving
  processes

Tasks

**Organization
Arrangements**

- Linking
  mechanisms
- Designs for
  venturing
- Incentives
- Joint evaluation
- Job
  rotation/design
- Education

Individual

- Diverse expertise
- Problem-solving
  skills
- Team-building
  skills

Figure 8.4 **Critical factors in managing innovation**

today, but is alert to external opportunities and threats. As competitive conditions change, so too must composition of the executive team.

Group problem-solving skills are particularly important if the senior team is to take advantage of its collective expertise to develop and communicate its vision of organizational objectives and core values. This executive team needs to develop internal processes that work against both the complacency so common in dominant organizations and the 'group-think' (i.e. stunted problem solving) that often accompanies crisis conditions. The tasks of the general manager are to build a top team that has the required functional expertise and to develop the group's problem-solving processes so that it can effectively manage both today's work and tomorrow's innovation.

Formal organizational arrangements

Formal organizational arrangements provide structures, systems, and procedures which direct and motivate behavior. Consequently, these arrangements exert an important influence on organizational learning and innovation. Formal organizational arrangements include these key elements:

Formal linking mechanisms

The choice of basic organization form (e.g. product, market, functional, geographic) focuses resources on critical strategic contingencies. No single organization form is inherently more conducive to innovation than the next: each can either stimulate or retard innovation. Whatever the basic form chosen, organizations must develop formal internal linking mechanisms, which are important vehicles for creativity and innovation. These links – bridges connecting disparate functions – encourage collaboration and problem solving throughout the organization. For example:

Teams, committees, or task forces bring together individuals from diverse areas to work on common opportunities or problems. At Lilly Research, for example, where the laboratory was organized by disciplines, research teams organized by therapeutic area pooled the expertise of scientists and managers from different disciplines. At Xerox, an innovation board brought a diverse group of marketing, production, and R&D executives together to evaluate and provide early funding for corporate ventures.

Project managers play a formal linking role which brings a general management perspective deep in the organization. A project manager works to achieve integration and coordination for new product and/or process development

Formal meetings provide a regularly scheduled setting for individuals from different areas to share information and trade ideas. These meetings have the added benefit of building informal relationships which further facilitate cross-organization problem solving and collaboration. For example, NCR has 'show and tell' meetings in which R&D, marketing, and manufacturing individuals unveil their latest ideas. At Union Carbide's product fairs, the various divisions present new products and ideas to each other. At Tetra-Pak, cross-functional teams regularly visit customers and then return to generate new product/process ideas.

Organization designs for venturing and entrepreneurship

Linking mechanisms are most effective when the nature of required learning and innovation is relatively small. When major innovation is required, working across the existing organizational structure may not be effective. A series of organization forms, all outside the core organization, can stimulate major corporate innovation. These major innovation forms include venture capital, joint ventures, licensing, acquisition, internal venturing, and independent business units. Some of these forms are much more closely tied to the core organization than others; venture capital, for example, is the most distant form of venturing in that it only provides a window on new technologies and markets, while internal venturing builds on in-house expertise.

The more dissimilar the required technology or markets, the greater the required organizational learning and the greater the use of the more independent venture forms. When both required technology and markets are unfamiliar, the most appropriate vehicles might be licensing, joint ventures, or venture capital. On the other hand, when organizations want to take advantage of internal expertise yet still produce major innovation, corporate venturing or independent business units may be most effective.

Independent business units or corporate venture units are separated from the core organization. These units are small and made up of individuals from all important disciplines and functions. These teams tend to be self-selected, and operate as independent ventures. Their business plans may be evaluated by a board of directors made up of corporate executives who have some interest in the venture; they act as venture capitalists, providing funding and overall review. The venture teams are not evaluated by traditional corporate yardsticks (e.g. profit, ROA), but on the basis of criteria more relevant to ventures – growth in sales or market share, for example. Similarly, the entrepreneur's compensation is pegged to performance against long-term targets and may involve stock or paper ownership in the new venture. The basic idea is to build in risk/return relationships that are similar to those encountered by outside entrepreneurs.

Corporate ventures are vehicles to marshal dedicated resources for major new products and/or process development. These entrepreneurial units can move rapidly and get quick feedback from the market. Corporate venturing and independent business units are important vehicles for organizational learning. These high-risk/high-return organizational experiments may fail nine times out of ten. Yet, they are relatively low-cost ventures and, when they fail, provide new information about technologies and markets. Further, these successes can be highly profitable and strategically important for the firm in the long run (e.g. IBM's PC business or Dupont's Nylon venture in the 1930s). Those ventures that succeed are either folded into existing divisions (e.g. IBM's PC independent business unit) or set up as distinct divisions. IBM, 3M, Dupont, Tektronix, and Control Data, among others, have had considerable success with venture units.

Incentives

Incentives and rewards have a major impact on individual and group behavior. Organizations get what they reward. If organizations only measure and reward short-term performance, or if everyone is rewarded equally, then innovation suffers. To encourage innovation, organizations must base rewards on actual performance and make innovation an important dimension of individual and group performance. Bonuses, stock options, salaries, and promotions can be linked to innovation and new product/process development. For example, at Biogen, as long as scientists are evaluated solely on the quality of their pure science and marketing people strictly on the basis of sales, the firm will never enjoy sustained innovation and collaboration from these critical groups.

Management can bolster formal incentives with special recognition and rewards for particularly innovative employees. For example, the Watson awards at IBM or innovation prizes at H-P and 3M provide special status to innovative individuals and teams. At Intel, highly innovative teams may go to trade shows where their products are introduced. Formal and informal rewards are an important managerial lever to stimulate innovation. Innovative individuals and groups can clearly see the benefits of innovation; non-innovators can just as easily see the consequences of clinging to the status quo.

Joint evaluation, staffing, and appraisal

As innovation necessarily involves individuals from different disciplines and departments, management can use joint problem-solving teams to maximize ownership and coupling between areas. Together, such teams can develop priorities, direction, and emphasis on new products and processes. These teams can then sell their innovations to their more local colleagues and greatly improve internal technology or product transfer. Further, these problem-solving teams can evaluate their successes and failures. Such joint evaluation helps the organizations learn and reduces finger-pointing and the 'not-invented-here' syndrome which together reduce learning and innovation. The most innovative organizations create these joint problem-solving teams early in the product development cycle; thus, problem solving comes to be perceived as part of the normal process, rather than a bureaucratic intrusion. For example, at Pharmacia, joint problem solving and evaluation have been institutionalized throughout the corporation and are given much credit for this firm's extraordinary innovation record.

Job design, job rotation, and careers

Innovation depends on motivated employees who are willing to experiment and be creative. The design of jobs, job rotation, and career paths all have important effects on the creativity of managers and their employees. Jobs with substantial autonomy, variety, and individual involvement offer intrinsic motivation to perform well. Jobs with low involvement and autonomy cannot capture an employee's enthusiasm; motivation comes only from extrinsic factors (e.g. pay). Larger jobs involve more of the individual and create greater internal drive for learning innovation. Career paths also play an important role: individuals who spend an entire career in a single functional or product area will be more narrowly focused and less innovative than their colleagues with broader career experiences. Employees with experience in multiple areas and functions will have a more balanced view of the organization's strengths and weaknesses and a broader set of contacts from whom they can learn. Similarly, within many R&D organizations, scientists and engineers have the opportunity of pursuing either managerial or technical career tracks. Such dual ladders, when effectively implemented, can encourage innovation and specialization along both tracks. Though an organizational structure that discourages job diversity can inhibit innovation, it is also true that a human resource system that produces too many promotions, and too quickly, can have the same effect. Firms that lead employees to expect a promotion every two years encourage short time frames. Innovation and change take time; individuals must expect to stay in jobs long enough to influence both short- and long-term performance indicators. Thus, career-planning systems must find the right balance between the complacency bred by narrow career mobility, and the short-run mentality of job-hopping.

Education

Education programs are also an influential tool in effecting innovation. Education and training programs expose managers from different areas of a firm to the other disciplines and functions in the organization, to the nature and importance of innovation and change, and to skills in communication, problem solving, and conflict resolution. IBM, Control Data, GTE, and PepsiCo all have programs in managing innovation that involve cross-sections of the corporations in joint work on innovation-related problems.

Quite apart from their substance, these educational programs provide a relaxed setting in which individuals meet and get to know a range of different individuals from throughout the organization. These informal contacts provide a valuable informal infrastructure which nurtures both individual and organizational learning and innovation. IBM's three-week innovation program, for example, provides substantial content on innovation and change; but, even more importantly, it provides an opportunity for 50 managers from around the corporation to become much better acquainted with each other and their respective areas. IBM is not alone; the most innovative firms invest substantially in the training and education of their managers.

Informal organization

Innovation is disruptive and complex work which requires close collaboration between actors who are usually quite separate. A competent set of individuals and the correct formal organization are not enough to deal with the complexities and uncertainties inherent in innovative work. The informal organization must bolster and complement the formal system. While formal organization arrangements facilitate corporate learning and innovation, individual creativity springs from a healthy informal organization. Several dimensions of the informal organization are particularly important in managing innovation.

Core values

Core values provide the basic normative foundation of a business unit. Core values are beliefs about what is good or bad, right or wrong in a particular firm. For example, IBM core values are the importance of individuals, service, and excellence; Tandem's are quality, personal excellence, and teamwork. A clear set of core values helps focus and motivate behavior. The most innovative firms have clear core values that provide focus in a sea of diversity, and a common objective on which disparate professionals and divisions can agree.

Some examples of core values that facilitate innovation:

developing technology that meets users' needs
individual autonomy and organizational identification
risk taking and tolerance of failure
informality in problem solving
disciplinary and organizational effectiveness
high performance standards for short and long run
an emphasis on human resources and the importance of individual
    growth and development

As these examples suggest, core values in highly innovative firms emphasize the duality so important to the innovation process. Also, core values in innovative firms are broad enough to be meaningful across a diverse organization. Thus IBM's trilogy of service, individuals, and excellence is broad enough to fit a highly decentralized organization, yet is also pointed enough to guide and focus behavior. Though any organization can publicly espouse a set of core values, most innovative organizations have effectively infused their value system throughout the company.

Norms

While core values (for example service or excellence) have no clear behavioral referents, norms do; they elaborate and specify the meaning of core values in a particular firm. Norms are expected behaviors: if they are violated, the individual or group is informally censured. For example, norms help specify dress codes, language, work standards and hours, decision-making processes, boss–subordinate relations, inter-unit communication, conflict resolution processes, and the degree of risk taking and playfulness in the organization. In general, highly innovative organizations have norms that stress informality in behavior, dress, and boss–subordinate relations; high work standards and individual/group performance expectations; flexibility in decision making, problem solving, and conflict resolution patterns; and strong informal linkages within and outside the organization. This informality, high work standard, and exposure to multiple sources of information facilitate collaboration, learning, and innovation. Less innovative firms, on the other hand, have norms which emphasize formality, standardization, and operating 'by the book.'

Rewarding risk

Highly innovative organizations deftly manage the subtleties of reward and punishment. Paradoxically, they provide highly visible rewards for success but often downplay the punishment for failure. This approach may seem contradictory, but many companies have made it work. In essence, they make decisions regarding promotions, job assignments, and careers with an eye toward strengthening the informal system's support for innovation and risk taking. The cornerstone of this approach is that those who perform well, and in particular the successful innovators, receive rapid promotion or successively more challenging assignments. It becomes clear to others in the organization that outstanding performance is the surest path to success.

At the other extreme there is little tolerance for those whose performance falls short of the organization's standards. Those who perform poorly are encouraged to leave and, if necessary, are forced out. We have just described a highly performance-oriented organization culture which is not unique. But some very innovative organizations take the added step of creating conditions that tolerate failure and sometimes even support it. They apply this approach to employees with an established record of performance, when their failure is the result of risk taking or experimentation, rather than incompetence or dereliction.

This attitude emboldens potential innovators: they see the likely prospect of tangible rewards for success and relatively few risks if they try something new and fail. As the belief spreads throughout the organization, the entire environment becomes increasingly innovative. An organization that has worked hard to nurture this culture is Citibank – one of the USA's most innovative corporations – where many senior executives have tried new things and 'failed.' Failure often results in assignment to the 'penalty box,' or a job with less responsibility. But after spending time in a 'penalty box' assignment, people can return to a position comparable to – or even more responsible than – their 'pre-failure' job.

Innovation occurs when organizations function as effective learning systems, and learning comes through experimentation and failure. Truly innovative organizations are those where people can take risks, reap the rewards of success, and survive constructive failures.

Communication networks

Informal communication networks are vital to innovation. For new products and processes, direct feedback and problem solving is much more effective than formal bureaucratic procedures. The most innovative organizations have diverse informal communication networks; people know who to call. And the calls generally solve problems, if the participants share a common set of core values and language. These informal networks are important both within the organization as well as between the organization and customers, vendors, suppliers, and external professional sources. Direct contact is an effective way of keeping close to customers, competitors, and technology.

Critical roles

Several informal roles are critical in the innovation process.

Idea generators are those key individuals who creatively link diverse ideas. These individuals see new approaches to linking technologies to markets, products with new processes, etc. Without idea generators, organizations have very few breakthroughs.

Champions or internal entrepreneurs take creative ideas (which they may or may not have generated) and bring the ideas to life. These individuals have the aggressiveness, energy, and risk-taking personalities to actively champion their causes. Without internal entrepreneurs, organizations may have many ideas but few tangible innovations.

Gatekeepers or boundary spanners link their more local colleagues to external information sources. They acquire, translate, and distribute external information within the organization or steer their colleagues to the right sources. Without gatekeepers, organizations are deaf to the outside sources of information so vital to innovation.

Sponsors, coaches, or mentors are senior managers who provide informal support, access to resources, and protection as new products or ventures emerge. Without sponsors and mentors, new products and processes get smothered by organizational constraints. Each of these roles is critical; if any fails to emerge informally, innovation suffers. Formalizing these roles seems to make them disappear. While these roles cannot be formalized, they can be diagnosed, developed, and nurtured. Management can develop each role through job rotation and design, formal and informal rewards, educational programs, and personal encouragement.

Conflict resolution and problem-solving practices

Innovation is an inherently disruptive phenomenon; it creates conflict among various parts of the organization, each with its own perceptions and priorities. For innovation to succeed, the informal organization must value conflict and provide constructive ways to resolve it. IBM's contention management system engenders such conflict, while relying on its deeply embedded norms and values to deal with it at low levels in the organization. At Pharmacia, a shared problem-solving framework is used to diagnose the causes of conflict and to adjudicate it in ways that benefit the company.

Clearly the informal organization is critical to innovation. Informal processes can encourage risk taking, experimentation, and learning. Management must shape different informal processes in different parts of the organization (e.g. R&D vs. production), while providing informal linkages between these areas.[3] In the most innovative organizations, the informal organization allows individuals to be creative and learn, and promotes creative problem solving both within and outside the organization. While formal organization arrangements are relatively more important in high-volume, low-innovative settings, the informal organization is more important for tasks that require learning and innovation; the greater the required learning, the greater the importance of the informal organization.

EXECUTIVE LEADERSHIP AND INNOVATION

Beyond making choices concerning strategy, structure, individuals, and the informal organization, leaders also face the crucial, personal task of infusing their organizations with a set of values and a sense of enthusiasm that will support innovative behavior. Without a clearly committed executive team which consistently emphasizes the importance of innovation, organizations inevitably become slaves of the status quo. At the first, middle, and senior managerial levels, the management team must send a clear and consistent set of messages about the importance of short-term management and long-term innovation.

Several aspects of executive leadership behavior can help (or hinder) innovation.

The executive team can develop and communicate a clear image of the organization's strategy and core values and the role of innovation in meeting the organization's strategy. If objectives are unclear and the role of innovation ambiguous, individuals and groups will focus on the status quo. The executive team must clearly and consistently articulate the importance of innovation and reinforce the necessary behavior.

The executive team can be a role model for subordinates. Executive behavior, actions, and statements send important messages to subordinates about the importance of learning and innovation. Inconsistent signals about the importance of innovation confuse subordinates; if faced with ambiguity, they will stick to the safest course, the status quo. For example, though the CEO of a large advertising agency talked a lot about creativity and innovation, his actions spoke eloquently about the importance of safe, non-controversial ad campaigns. Innovation and creativity floundered. On the other hand, Jack Welch's obsession with innovation at GE sends clear messages about the importance of new product and process innovation.

The executive team can use formal and informal rewards to reinforce innovation. Innovative individuals and groups must receive recognition, attention, and support as well as formal rewards from the executive team. If mediocrity is rewarded, or if everyone is equally rewarded by the executive team, then excellence will disappear. The management team must use all the formal and informal rewards at its disposal to consistently reinforce behavior consistent with strategy and core values.

Organizational history has an important impact on today's innovation. Key crises, events, prior executives, organizational myths, and heroes all shape and constrain current behavior. Highly stable organizations may have no tradition or precedent that fosters innovation. For example, both AT&T and General Radio had proud 75-year histories which glorified the role of engineers and minimized the relevance of marketing. For these organizations to be innovative, management must create new heroes, new visions, and new histories.

Executive leadership can seize upon innovative aspects of an organization's history and build new stories, myths, and heroes consistent with current competitive conditions. For example, management's challenge at Xerox is to take advantage of a proud history of innovation while trying to build a new tradition that emphasizes quality and technology transfer.

The senior executive (that is, CEO, general manager, functional manager, etc.) cannot manage the organization alone. As stated earlier, senior executives must build executive teams with appropriate technical, social, and conceptual skills to accomplish diverse tasks. As the required innovation changes, so too must the nature of the executive team. Executive succession and promotion are powerful tools in innovation management. At General Radio the move to marketing and process innovation was driven by a new management team made up of both old-line General Radio engineers and new executives skilled in marketing and manufacturing.

The senior executive must also develop effective problem-solving processes in the top team. The team must be alert to external opportunities and threats, and possess the internal dynamics to deal effectively with uncertainty. Once the decisions are made, the executive team must implement these decisions with a single voice. Publicized dissension within the top team can bury innovation in organizational politics.

Managing innovation requires visionary executives who provide clear direction for their organizations and infuse that direction with energy and value. Observation and research indicate that such executives frequently display three types of behavior: first, they work actively on envisioning or articulating a credible yet exciting vision of the future. Second, they personally work on energizing the organization by demonstrating their own excitement, optimism, and enthusiasm. Third, they put effort into enabling required behaviors by providing resources, rewarding desired behaviors, building supportive organizational structures and processes, and by building an effective senior team.

SUMMARY

Organizations cannot stand still. In ever more global markets, effective performance depends more and more on the successful management of innovation. Organizations can gain competitive advantage only by managing effectively for today while simultaneously creating innovation for tomorrow. But, as we have seen, success often breeds stagnation; in dominant companies, the challenge is to rekindle the innovative spirit that led to past success.

The challenge for executives is to build congruent organizations both for today's work and tomorrow's innovation. Organizations need to have sufficient internal diversity in strategies, structures, people, and processes to facilitate different kinds of innovation and to enhance organization learning.

There is perhaps no more pressing managerial problem than the sustained management of innovation. There is nothing mysterious about innovation: it doesn't just happen. Rather, it is the calculated outcome of strategic management and visionary leadership that provide the people, structures, values, and learning opportunities to make it an organizational way of life.

NOTES

1 For an in-depth discussion of this congruence approach to organizational effectiveness, see P.A. Nadler and M.L. Tushman, 'A Congruence Model for Diagnosing Organizational Behavior,' *Organization Dynamics* (1980).
2 See W. Abernathy, *The Productivity Dilemma* (Baltimore, MD: Johns Hopkins University Press, 1979); T. Allen, *Managing the Flow of Technology* (Cambridge, MA: MIT Press, 1983); R. M. Kanter, *The Change Masters* (New York: Simon & Schuster, 1984); P. R. Lawrence and D. Dyer, *Renewing American Industry* (New York: The Free Press, 1983); P. A. Nadler and M. L. Tushman, *Strategic Organization Design* (Homewood, IL: Scott, Foresman, 1986); M. L. Tushman and W. Moore, *Readings in the Management of Innovation* (Marshfield, MA: Pitman Publishing, 1982).
3 For a detailed discussion of shaping informal processes, see Nadler and Tushman, *Strategic Organization Design*.

Chapter 9

Designing the innovating organization

Jay R. Galbraith

Innovation is in. New workable, marketable ideas are being sought and promoted these days as never before in the effort to restore US leadership in technology, in productivity growth, and in the ability to compete in the world marketplace. Innovative methods for conserving energy and adapting to new energy sources are also in demand.

The popular press uses words like revitalization to capture the essence of the issue. The primary culprit of our undoing, up until now, has been management's short-run earnings focus. However, even some patient managers with long-term views are finding that they cannot buy innovation. They cannot exhort their operating organizations to be more innovative and creative. Patience, money, and a supportive leadership are not enough. It takes more than these things to achieve innovation.

It is my contention that innovation requires an organization specifically designed for that purpose – that is, such an organization's structure, processes, rewards, and people must be combined in a special way to create an innovating organization, one that is designed to do something for the first time. The point to be emphasized here is that the innovating organization's components are completely different from and often contrary to those of existing organizations, which are generally operating organizations. The latter are designed to efficiently process the millionth loan, produce the millionth automobile, or serve the millionth client. An organization that is designed to do something well for the millionth time is not good at doing something for the first time. Therefore, organizations that want to innovate or revitalize themselves need two organizations, an operating organization and an innovating organization. In addition, if the ideas produced by the innovating organization are to be implemented by the operating organization, they need a transition process to transfer ideas from the innovating organization to the operating organization.

This chapter will describe the components of an organization geared to producing innovative ideas. Specifically, in the next section I describe a case history that illustrates the components required for successful innovation. Then I will explore the lessons to be learned from this case history by describing the role structure, the key processes, the reward systems, and the people practices that characterize an innovating organization.

THE INNOVATING PROCESS

Before I describe the typical process by which innovations occur in organizations, we must understand what we are discussing. What is innovation? How do we distinguish between invention and innovation? Invention is the creation of a new idea. Innovation is the process of applying a new idea to create a new process or product. Invention occurs more frequently than innovation. In addition, the kind of innovation in which we are interested here is the kind that becomes necessary to implement a new idea that is not consistent with the current concept of the organization's business. Many new ideas that are consistent with an organization's current business concept are routinely generated in some companies. Those are not our current concern; here we are concerned with implementing inventions that are good ideas but do not quite fit into the organization's current mold. Industry has a poor track record with this type of innovation. Most major technological changes come from outside an industry. The mechanical typewriter people did not invent the electronic typewriter; vacuum tube companies did not introduce the transistor, and so on. Our objective is to describe an organization that will increase the odds that such non-routine innovations can be made. The following case history of a non-routine innovation presents a number of lessons that illustrate how we can design an innovating organization.

THE CASE HISTORY

The organization in question is a venture that was started in the early 1970s. While working for one of our fairly innovative electronics firms, a group of engineers developed a new electronics product. However, they were in a division that did not have the charter for their product. The ensuing political battle caused the engineers to leave and form their own company. They successfully found venture capital and introduced their new product. Initial acceptance was good, and within several years their company was growing rapidly and had become the industry leader.

However, in the early 1970s Intel invented the microprocessor, and by the mid-to-late 1970s, this innovation had spread through the electronics industries. Manufacturers of previously 'dumb' products now had the capability of incorporating intelligence into their product lines. A competitor who understood computers and software introduced just such a product into our new venture firm's market, and it met with high acceptance. The firm's president responded by hiring someone who knew something about microcomputers and some software people and instructing the engineering department to respond to the need for a competing product.

The president spent most of his time raising capital to finance the venture's growth. But when he suddenly realized that the engineers had not made much progress, he instructed them to get a product out quickly. They did, but it was a half-hearted effort. The new product incorporated a microprocessor but was less than the second-generation product that was called for.

Even though the president developed markets in Europe and Singapore, he noticed that the competitor continued to grow faster than his company and had started to steal a share of his company's market. When the competitor became the industry leader, the president decided to take charge of the product development effort. However, he found that the hardware proponents and software proponents in the engineering department were locked in a political battle. Each group felt that its 'magic' was the more powerful. Unfortunately, the lead engineer (who was a co-founder of the firm) was a hardware proponent, and the hardware establishment prevailed. However, they then clashed head-on with the marketing department, which agreed with the software proponents. The conflict resulted in studies and presentations, but no new product. So here was a young, small (1,200 people) entrepreneurial firm that could not innovate even though the president wanted innovation and provided resources to produce it. The lesson is that more was needed.

As the president became more deeply involved in the problem, he received a call from his New England sales manager, who wanted him to meet a field engineer who had modified the company's product and programmed it in a way that met customer demands. The sales manager suggested, 'We may have something here.'

Indeed, the president was impressed with what he saw. When the engineer had wanted to use the company's product to track his own inventory, he wrote to company headquarters for programming instructions. The response had been: It's against company policy to send instructional materials to field engineers. Undaunted, the engineer bought a home computer and taught himself to program. He then modified the product in the field and programmed it to solve his problem. When the sales manager happened to see what had been done, he recognized its significance and immediately called the president.

The field engineer accompanied the president back to headquarters and presented his work to the engineers who had been working on the second-generation product for so long. They brushed off his efforts as idiosyncratic, and the field engineer was thanked and returned to the field.

A couple of weeks later the sales manager called the president again. He said that the company would lose this talented guy if something wasn't done. Besides, he thought that the field engineer, not engineering, was right. While he was considering what to do with this ingenious engineer, who on his own had produced more than the entire engineering department, the president received a request from the European sales manager to have the engineer assigned to him.

The European sales manager had heard about the field engineer when he visited headquarters, and had sought him out and listened to his story. The sales manager knew that a French bank wanted the type of application that the field engineer had created for himself; a successful application would be worth an order for several hundred machines. The president gave the go-ahead and sent the field engineer to Europe. The engineering department persisted in their view that the program wouldn't work. Three months later, the field engineer successfully developed the application, and the bank signed the order.

When the field engineer returned, the president assigned him to a trusted marketing manager who was told to protect him and get a product out. The engineers were told to support the manager and reluctantly did so. Soon they created some applications software and a printed circuit board that could easily be installed in all existing machines in the field. The addition of this board and the software temporarily saved the company and made its current product slightly superior to that of the competitor.

Elated, the president congratulated the young field engineer and gave him a good staff position working on special assignments to develop software. Then problems arose. When the president tried to get the personnel department to give the engineer a special cash award, they were reluctant. 'After all,' they said, 'other people worked on the effort, too. It will set a precedent.' And so it went. The finance department wanted to withhold $500 from the engineer's pay because he had received a $1,000 advance for his European trip, but had turned in vouchers for only $500.

The engineer didn't help himself very much either; he was hard to get along with and refused to accept supervision from anyone except the European sales manager. When the president arranged to have him permanently transferred to Europe on three occasions, the engineer changed his mind about going at the last minute. The president is still wondering what to do with him.

There are a number of lessons about the needs of an innovative organization in this not uncommon story. The next section elaborates on these lessons.

THE INNOVATING ORGANIZATION

Before we can draw upon the case history's lessons, it is important to note that the basic components of the innovating organization are no different from those of an operating organization. That is, both include a task, a structure, processes, reward systems, and people as shown in Figure 9.1.

Figure 9.2 compares the design parameters of the operating organization's components with those of the innovating organization's components.

This figure shows that each component must fit with each of the other components and with the task. A basic premise of this chapter is that the task of the innovating organization is fundamentally different from that of the operating organization. The innovating task is more uncertain and risky, takes place over longer time periods, assumes that failure in the early stages may be desirable, and so on. Therefore, the organization that performs the innovative task should also be different. Obviously, a firm that wishes to innovate needs both an operating organization and an innovating organization. Let's look at the latter.

STRUCTURE OF THE INNOVATING ORGANIZATION

The structure of the innovating organization encompasses these elements: (1) people to fill three vital roles – idea generators, sponsors, and orchestrators; (2) differentiation, a process that differentiates or separates the innovating organization; and (3) 'reservations,' the means by which the separation occurs – and this may be accomplished physically, financially, or organizationally.

The part that each of these elements plays in the commercialization of a new idea can be illustrated by referring to the case history.

Roles

Like any organized phenomenon, innovation is brought about through

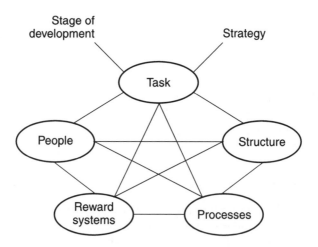

Figure 9.1 **Organization design components**

the efforts of people who interact in a combination of roles. Innovation is not an individual phenomenon. People who must interact to produce a commercial product – that is, to innovate in the sense we are discussing – play their roles as follows:

Every innovation starts with an idea generator or idea champion. In the above example, the field engineer was the person who generated the new idea – that is, the inventor, the entrepreneur, or risk taker on whom much of our attention has been focused. The case history showed that an idea champion is needed at each stage of an idea's or an invention's development into an innovation. That is, at each stage there must be a dedicated, full-time individual whose success or failure depends on developing the idea. The idea generator is usually a low-level person who experiences a problem and develops a new response to it. The lesson here is that many ideas originate down where 'the rubber meets the road.' The low status and authority level of the idea generator creates a need for someone to play the next role.

	Operating Organizations	Innovating Organizations

Structure	Division of labor
	Departmentalization
	Span of control
	Distribution of power
		Roles:
		  Orchestrator
		  Sponsor
		  Idea generator (champion)
		Differentiation
		Reservations

Processes	Providing information and communication Planning and budgeting Measuring performance Linking departments	Planning/funding Getting ideas Blending ideas Transitioning Managing programs
Reward systems	Compensation Promotion Leader style Job design	Opportunity/autonomy Promotion/recognition Special compensation
People	Selection/recruitment Promotion/transfer Training/development	Selection/self-selection Training/development

Figure 9.2 Comparison of components of operating and innovating organizations

Every idea needs at least one sponsor to promote it. To carry an idea through to implementation, someone has to discover it and fund the increasingly disruptive and expensive development and testing efforts that shape it. Thus idea generators need to find sponsors for their ideas so they can perfect them. In our example, the New England sales manager, the European sales manager, and finally the marketing manager all sponsored the field engineer's idea. Thus one of the sponsor's functions is to lend his or her authority and resources to an idea to carry the idea closer to commercialization.

The sponsor must also recognize the business significance of an idea. In any organization, there are hundreds of ideas being promoted at any one time. The sponsor must select from among these ideas those that might become marketable. Thus it is best that sponsors be generalists. (However, that is not always the case, as our case history illustrates.)

Sponsors are usually middle managers who may be anywhere in the organization and who usually work for both the operating and the innovating organization. Some sponsors run divisions or departments. They must be able to balance the operating and innovating needs of their business or function. On the other hand, when the firm can afford the creation of venture groups, new product development departments, and the like, sponsors may work full time for the innovating organization. In the case history, the two sales managers spontaneously became sponsors and the marketing manager was formally designated as a sponsor by the president. The point here is that by formally designating the role or recognizing it, funding it with monies earmarked for innovation, creating innovating incentives, and developing and selecting sponsorship skills, the organization can improve its odds of coming up with successful innovations. Not much attention has been given to sponsors, but they need equal attention because innovation will not occur unless there are people in the company who will fill all three roles.

The third role illustrated in the case history is that of the *orchestrator*. The president played this role. An orchestrator is necessary because new ideas are never neutral. Innovative ideas are destructive; they destroy investments in capital equipment and people's careers. The management of ideas is a political process. The problem is that the political struggle is biased toward those in the establishment who have authority and control of resources. The orchestrator must balance the power to give the new idea a chance to be tested in the face of a negative establishment. The orchestrator must protect idea people, promote the opportunity to try out new ideas, and back those whose ideas prove effective. This person must legitimize the whole process. That is what the president did with the field engineer; before he became involved, the hardware establishment had prevailed. Without an orchestrator, there can be no innovation.

To play their roles successfully, orchestrators use the processes and rewards to be described in the following sections. That is, a person orchestrates by funding innovating activities and creating incentives for middle managers to sponsor innovating ideas. Orchestrators are the organization's top managers, and they must design the innovating organization.

The typical operating role structure of a divisionalized firm is shown in Figure 9.3. The hierarchy is one of the operating functions reporting to division general managers who are, in turn, grouped under group executives. The group executives report to the chief executive officer (CEO). Some of these people play roles in both the operating and the innovating organization.

The innovating organization's role structure is shown in Figure 9.4. The chief executive and a group executive function as orchestrators. Division managers are the sponsors who work in both the operating and the innovating organizations. In addition, several reservations are created in which managers of research and development (R&D), corporate development, product development, market development, and new process technology function as full-time sponsors. These reservations allow the separation of innovating activity from the operating activity. This separation is an organizing choice called differentiation. It is described next.

Differentiation

In the case history we saw that the innovative idea perfected at a remote site was relatively advanced before it was discovered by management. The lesson to be learned from this is that if one wants to stimulate new ideas, the odds are better if early efforts to perfect and test new 'crazy' ideas are differentiated – that is, separated – from the functions of the operating organization. Such differentiation occurs when an effort is separated physically, financially, and/or organizationally from the day-to-day activities that are likely to disrupt it. If the field engineer had worked within the engineering department or at company headquarters, his idea probably would have been snuffed out prematurely.

Another kind of differentiation can be accomplished by freeing initial idea tests from staff controls designed for the operating organization. The effect of too much control is illustrated by one company in which a decision on whether to buy an oscilloscope took about 15 to 30 minutes (with a shout across the room) before the company was acquired by a larger organization. After the acquisition, that same type of decision took 12 to 18 months because the purchase required a capital appropriation request. Controls based on operating logic reduce the innovating organization's ability to rapidly, cheaply, and frequently test and modify new ideas. Thus, the more differentiated an initial effort is, the greater the likelihood of innovation.

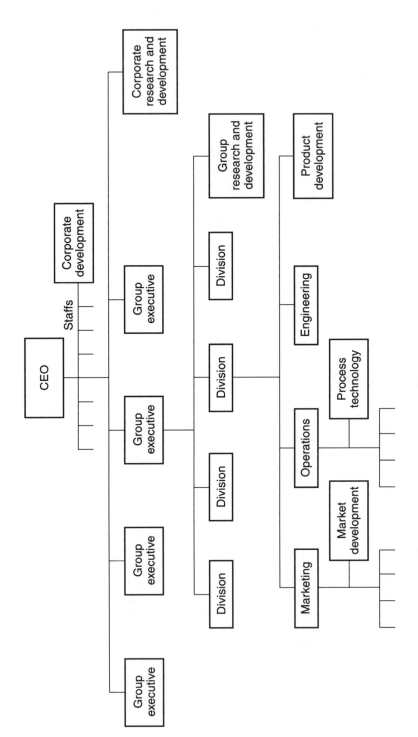

Figure 9.3 **Typical operating structure of divisionalized firm**

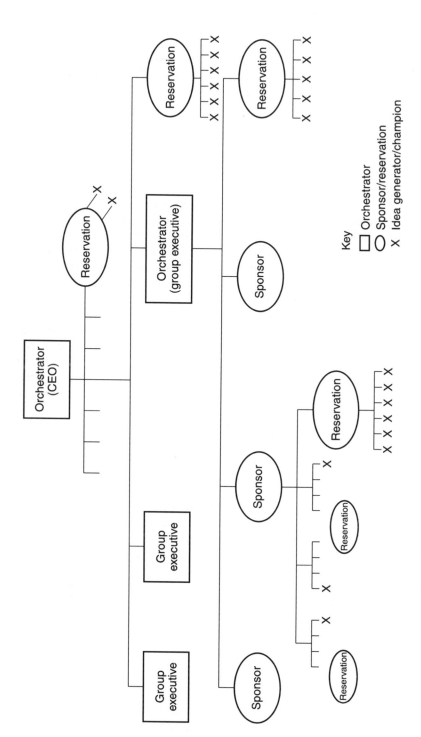

Figure 9.4 An innovation role structure (differentiation)

Key
☐ Orchestrator
◯ Sponsor/reservation
X Idea generator/champion

The problem with differentiation, however, is that it decreases the likelihood that a new proven idea will be transferred back to the operating organization. Herein lies the differentiation/transfer dilemma: the more differentiated the effort, the greater the likelihood of producing a new business idea, but the less likelihood of transferring the new idea into the operation organization for implementation. The dilemma occurs only when the organization needs both invention and transfer. That is, some organizations may not need to transfer new ideas to the operating organization. For example, when Exxon started its information systems business, there was no intention to have the petroleum company run this area of business. Exxon innovators had to grow their own operating organizations; therefore, they could maximize differentiation in the early phases. Alternatively, when Intel started work on the 64K RAM (the next generation of semiconductor memories, this random access memory holds roughly 64,000 bits of information), the effort was consistent with their current business and the transfer into manufacture and sales was critical. Therefore, the development effort was only minimally separated from the operating division that was producing the 16K RAM. The problem becomes particularly difficult when a new product or process differs from current ones but must be implemented through the current manufacturing and sales organizations. The greater the need for invention and the greater the difference between the new idea and the existing business concept, the greater the degree of differentiation required to perfect the idea. The only way to accomplish both invention and transfer is to proceed stagewise. That is, differentiate in the early phases and then start the transition process before development is completed so that only a little differentiation is left when the product is ready for implementation. The transition process is described in the section on key processes (p. 168).

In summary, invention occurs best when initial efforts are separated from the operating organization and its controls – because innovating and operating are fundamentally opposing logics. This kind of separation allows both to be performed simultaneously and prevents the establishment from prematurely snuffing out a new idea. The less the dominant culture of the organization supports innovation, the greater is the need for separation. Often this separation occurs naturally as in the case history, or clandestinely, as in 'bootlegging.' If a firm wants to foster innovation, it can create reservations where innovating activity can occur as a matter of course. Let us now turn to this last structural parameter.

Reservations

Reservations are organizational units, such as R&D groups, that are totally devoted to creating new ideas for future business. The intention is to reproduce a garage-like atmosphere where people can rapidly and frequently test their ideas. Reservations are havens for 'safe learning.' When innovating, one wants to maximize early failure to promote learning. On reservations that are separated from operations, this cheap, rapid screening can take place.

Reservations permit differentiation to occur by housing people who work solely for the innovating organization and by having a reservation manager who works full time as a sponsor. They may be located within division and/or at corporate headquarters to permit various degrees of differentiation.

Reservations can be internal or external. Internal reservations may include some staff and research groups, product and process development labs, and groups that are devoted to market development, new ventures, and/or corporate development. They are organizational homes where idea generators can contribute without becoming managers. Originally, this was the purpose of staff groups, but staff groups now frequently assume control responsibilities or are narrow specialists who contribute to the current business idea. Because such internal groups can be expensive, outside reservations like universities, consulting firms, and advertising agencies are often used to tap non-managerial idea generators.

Reservations can be permanent or temporary. The internal reservations described above, such as R&D units, are reasonably permanent entities. But members of the operating organization may be relieved of operating duties to develop a new program, a new process, or a new product on a temporary basis. When these are developed, they take the idea into the operating organization and resume their operating responsibilities. But for a period of time they are differentiated from operating functions to varying degrees in order to innovate, fail, learn, and ultimately perfect a new idea.

Collectively the roles of orchestrators, sponsors, and idea generators working with and on reservations constitute the structure of the innovating organization. Some of the people, such as sponsors and orchestrators, play roles in both organizations; reservation managers and idea generators work only for the innovating organization. Virtually everyone in the organization can be an idea generator, and all middle managers are potential sponsors. However, not all choose to play these roles. People vary considerably in their innovating skills. By recognizing the need for these roles, developing people to fill them, giving them opportunity to use their skills in key processes, and rewarding innovating accomplishments, the organization can do considerably better than just allowing a spontaneous process to work. Several key processes are part and parcel of this innovating organizational structure. These are described in the next section.

KEY PROCESSES

In our case history, the idea generator and the first two sponsors found each other through happenstance. The odds of such propitious match-ups can be significantly improved through the explicit design of processes that help sponsors and idea generators find each other. The chances of successful match-ups can be improved by such funding, getting ideas, and blending ideas. In addition, the processes of transitioning and program management move ideas from reservations into operations. Each of these is described below.

Funding

A key process that increases our ability to innovate is a funding process that is explicitly earmarked for the innovating organization. A leader in this field is Texas Instruments (TI), a company that budgets and allocates funds for both operating and innovating. In essence the orchestrators make the short-run/long-run tradeoff at this point. They then orchestrate by choosing where to place the innovating funds – with division sponsors or corporate reservations. The funding process is a key tool for orchestration.

Another lesson to be learned from the case history is that it frequently takes more than one sponsor to launch a new idea. The field engineer's idea would never have been brought to management's attention without the New England sales manager. It would never have been tested in the market without the European sales manager. Multiple sponsors keep fragile ideas alive. If engineering had been the only available sponsor for technical ideas, there would have been no innovation.

Some organizations purposely create a multiple sponsoring system and make it legitimate for an idea generator to go to any sponsor who has funding for new ideas. Multiple sponsors duplicate the market system of multiple bankers for entrepreneurs. At Minnesota Mining and Manufacturing (3M), for example, an idea generator can go to his or her division sponsor for funding. If refused, the idea generator can then go to any other division sponsor or even to corporate R&D. If the idea is outside current business lines, the idea generator can go to the new ventures group for support. If the idea is rejected by all possible sponsors, it probably isn't a very good idea. However, the idea is kept alive and given several opportunities to be tested. Multiple sponsors keep fragile young ideas alive.

Getting ideas

The process of getting ideas occurs by happenstance as it did in the case history. The premise of this section is that the odds of match-ups between idea generators and sponsors can be improved by organization design. First, the natural process can be improved by network-building actions such as multidivision or multireservation careers or company-wide seminars and conferences. All of these practices plus a common physical location facilitate matching at 3M.

The matching process is formalized at TI, where there is an elaborate planning process called the objectives, strategies, and tactics or OST system, which is an annual harvest of new ideas. Innovating funds are distributed to managers of objectives (sponsors) who fund projects based on ideas formulated by idea generators, and these then become tactical action programs. Ideas that are not funded go into a creative backlog to be tapped throughout the year. Whether formal, as at TI, or informal, as at 3M, it is noteworthy that these are known systems for matching ideas with sponsors.

Ideas can also be acquired by aggressive sponsors. Sponsors sit at the crossroads of many ideas and often arrive at a better idea by putting two or more together. They can then pursue an idea generator to champion it. Good sponsors know where the proven idea people are located and how to attract such people to come to perfect an idea on their reservation. Sponsors can go inside or outside the organization to pursue these idea people.

And finally, formal events for matching purposes can be scheduled. At 3M, for example, there's an annual fair at which idea generators can set up booths to be viewed by shopping sponsors. Exxon Enterprises held a 'shake the tree event' at which idea people could throw out ideas to be pursued by attending sponsors. The variations of such events are endless. The point is that by devoting time to ideas and making innovation legitimate, the odds that sponsors will find new ideas are increased.

Blending ideas

An important lesson to be derived from our scenario is that it is no accident that a field engineer produced the new product idea. Why? Because the field engineer spent all day working on customer problems and also knew the technology. Therefore, one person knew the need and the means by which to satisfy the need. (An added plus: the field engineer had a personal need to design the appropriate technology.) The premise here is that innovation is more likely to occur when knowledge of technologies and user requirements are combined in the minds of as few people as possible – preferably in that of one person.

The question of whether innovations are need-stimulated or means-stimulated is debatable. Do you start with the disease and look for a cure, or start with a cure and find a disease for it? Research indicates that two-thirds of innovations are need-stimulated. But this argument misses the point. As shown in Figure 9.5(a), the debate is over whether use or means drives the downstream efforts. This thinking is linear and sequential. Instead, the model suggested here is shown in Figure 9.5(b). That is, for innovation to occur, knowledge of all key components is simultaneously coupled. And the best way to maximize communication among the components is to have the communication occur intrapersonally – that is, within one person's mind. If this is impossible, then as few people as possible should have to communicate or interact. The point is that innovative ideas occur when knowledge of the essential specialties is coupled in as few heads as possible. To encourage such coupling, the organization can grow or select individuals with the essential skills or it can encourage interaction between those with meshing skills. These practices will be discussed on p. 176ff.

A variety of processes are employed by organizations to match knowledge of need and of means. At IBM marketing people are placed directly in the R&D labs where they can readily interpret the market requirement documents for researchers. People are rotated through this unit, and a network is created. Wang holds an annual users' conference at which customers and product designers interact and discuss the use of Wang products. Lanier insists that all top managers, including R&D management, spend one day a month selling in the field. It is reported that British scientists made remarkable progress on developing radar after actually flying missions with the Royal Air Force. In all these cases there is an explicit matching of the use and the user with knowledge of a technology to meet the use. Again these processes are explicitly designed to get a user orientation among the idea generators and sponsors. They increase the likelihood that inventions will be innovations. The more complete a new idea or invention is at its inception, the greater the likelihood of its being transferred into the operating organization.

Transitioning

Perhaps the most crucial process in getting an innovative product to market is the transitioning of an idea from a reservation to an operating organization for implementation. This process occurs in stages, as illustrated in the case history. First, the idea was formulated in the field before management knew about it. Then it was tested with a customer, the French bank. And finally, at the third stage, development and full-scale implementation took place. In other cases, several additional stages of testing and scale-up may be necessary. In any case, transitioning should be planned in such stages. At each stage the orchestrator has several choices that balance the need for further invention with the need for transfer. The choices and typical stages of idea development are shown in Table 9.1.

(a) *Linear Sequential Coupling*

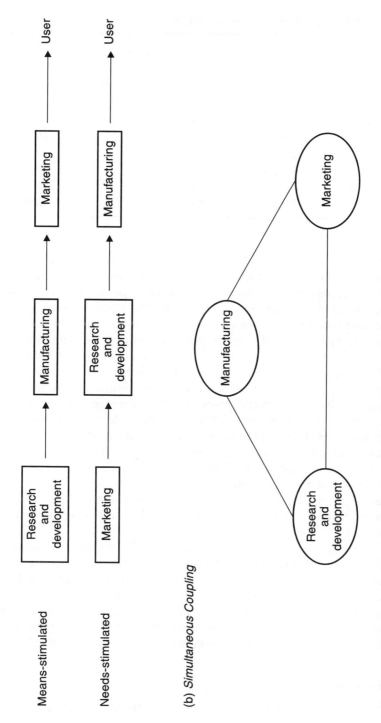

(b) *Simultaneous Coupling*

Figure 9.5 Linear sequential coupling compared with simultaneous coupling of knowledge

Table 9.1 **Transitioning ideas by stages**

| Choices | Stages | | | |
	I	*II*	*Nth*	*Implementation*
Sponsor	Corporate	Corporate	. . .	Division
Champion	Corporate	Corporate	. . .	Division
Staffing	Corporate	Corporate-division	. . .	Division
Location	Corporate	Corporate	. . .	Division
Funding	Corporate	Corporate	. . .	Division
Autonomy	Corporate	Corporate	. . .	Division

At each stage these choices face the orchestrator: Who will be the sponsor? Who will be the champion? Where can staff be secured for the effort? At what physical location will work be performed? Who will fund the effort? How much autonomy should the effort have, or how differentiated should it be? For example, at the initial new idea formulation stage the sponsor could be the corporate ventures group with the champion working on the corporate reservation. The effort could be staffed with other corporate reservation types and funded at the corporate level. The activity would be fully separate and autonomous. If the results were positive, the process could proceed to the next stage. If the idea needed further development, some division people could be brought in to round out the needed specialties. If the data were still positive after the second stage, then the effort could be transferred physically to the division, but the champion, sponsor, and funding might remain at the corporate level. In this manner, by orchestrating through choices of sponsor, champion, staff, location, funding, and autonomy, the orchestrator balances the need for innovation and protection with the need for testing against reality and transfer.

The above is an all-too-brief outline of the transition process; entire books have been written on the subject of technology transfer. The goal here is to highlight the stagewise nature of the process and the decisions to be made by the orchestrator at each stage. The process is crucial because it is the link between the two organizations. Thus to consistently innovate, the firm needs an innovating organization, an operating organization, and a process for transitioning ideas from the former to the latter.

Managing programs

Program management is necessary to implement new products and processes within divisions. At the stage of the process, the idea generator usually hands the idea over to a product/project/program manager. The product or process is then implemented across the functional organization within the division. The systems and organizational processes for managing projects have been discussed elsewhere and will not be discussed here. The point is that a program management process and skill is needed.

In summary, several key processes – that is, funding, getting ideas, blending ideas, transitioning and managing programs – are basic components of the innovating structure. Even though many of these occur naturally in all organizations, our implicit hypothesis is that the odds for successful innovation can be increased by explicitly designing these processes and by earmarking corporate resources for them. Hundreds of people in organizations choose to innovate voluntarily, as did the field engineer in the case history. However, if there were a reward system for people like these, more would choose to innovate, and more would choose to stay in the organization to do their innovating.

REWARD SYSTEM

The innovating organization, like the operating organization, needs an incentive system to motivate innovating behavior. Because the task of innovating is different from that of operating, the innovating organization needs a different reward system. The innovating task is riskier, more difficult, and takes place over longer time frames. These factors call for some adjustment of the operating organization's reward system, the amount of adjustment depending on how innovative the operating organization is and how attractive outside alternatives are.

The functions of the reward system are threefold: First, the rewards must attract idea people to the company and the reservations and retain them. Because various firms have different attraction and retention problems, their reward systems must vary. Second, the rewards provide motivation for the extra effort needed to innovate. After 19 failures, for example, something has to motivate the idea generator to make the 20th attempt. And, finally, successful performance deserves a reward. These rewards are primarily for idea generators. However, a reward-measurement system for sponsors is equally important. Various reward systems will be discussed in the next sections.

Rewards for idea generators

Reward systems mix several types of internal motivators, such as the opportunity to pursue one's ideas, promotions, recognition, systems and special compensation. First, people can be attracted and motivated intrinsically by simply giving them the opportunity and autonomy to pursue their own ideas. A reservation can provide such opportunity and autonomy. Idea people – who are internally driven – such as the field engineer in our story can come in a reservation, pursue their own ideas, and be guided and evaluated by a reservation manager. This is a reward in itself, albeit a minimal reward. If that minimal level attracts and motivates idea people, the innovating organization need go no further in creating a separate reward system.

However, if necessary, motivational leverage can be obtained by promotion and recognition for innovating performance. The dual ladder – that is, a system whereby an individual contributor can be promoted and given increased salary without taking managerial responsibilities – is the best example of such a system. At 3M a contributor can rise in both status and salary to the equivalent of a group executive without becoming a manager. The dual ladder has always existed in R&D, but it is now being extended to some other functions as well.

Some firms grant special recognition for high career performance. IBM has its IBM fellows program in which the person selected as a fellow can work on projects of his or her own choosing for five years. At 3M, there is the Carlton Award, which is described as an internal Nobel Prize. Such promotion and recognition systems reward innovation and help create an innovating culture.

When greater motivation is needed, and / or the organization wants to signal the importance of innovation, special compensation is added to the aforementioned systems. Different special compensation systems will be discussed in the order of increasing motivational impact and of increasing dysfunctional ripple effects. The implication is that the firm should use special compensation only to the degree that the need for attraction and for motivation dictate.

Some companies reward successful idea generators with one-time cash awards. For example, International Harvester's share of the combine market jumped from 12 percent to 17 percent because of the introduction of the axial flow combine. The scientist whose six patents contributed to the product development was given $10,000. If the product continues to succeed, he may be given another award. IBM uses the 'Chairman's Outstanding Contribution Award'. The current program manager on the 4300 series was given a $5,000 award for her breakthrough in coding. These awards are made after the idea is successful and primarily serve to reward achievement rather than to attract innovators and provide incentive for future efforts.

Programs that give a 'percentage of the take' to the idea generator and early team members provide even stronger motivation. Toy and game companies give a royalty to inventors – both internal and external – of toys and games they produce. Apple Computer claims to give royalties to employees who write software programs that will run on Apple equipment. A chemical company created a pool by putting aside 4 percent of the first five years' earnings from a new business venture, which was to be distributed to the initial venture team. Other companies create pools from percentages that range from 2 to 20 percent of cost savings created by process innovations. in any case, a predetermined contract is created to motivate the idea generator and those who join a risky effort at an early stage.

The most controversial efforts to date are attempts to duplicate free-market rewards within the firm. For example, a couple of years ago, ITT bought a small company named Qume that made high-speed printers. The founder became a millionaire from the sale; he had to quit his previous employer to found the venture capital effort to start Qume. If ITT can make an outsider a millionaire, why not give the same change to entrepreneurial insiders? Many people advocate such a system but have not found an appropriate formula to implement the idea. For example, one firm created five-year milestones for a venture, the accomplishment of which would result in a cash award of $6 million to the idea generator. However, the business climate changed after two years, and the idea generator, not surprisingly, tried to make the plan work rather than adapt to the new, unforeseen reality.

Another scheme is to give the idea generator and the initial team some phantom stock, which gets evaluated at sale time in the same way that any acquisition would be evaluated. This process duplicates the free-market process and gives internal people the same venture capital opportunities and risk as they would have on the outside.

The special compensation programs produce motivation and dysfunctions. People who contribute at later stages frequently feel like second-class citizens. Also, any program that discriminates will create perceptions of unfair treatment and possible fallout in the operating organization. If the benefits are judged to be worth the effort, however, care should be taken to manage the fallout.

Rewards for sponsors

The case history also demonstrates that sponsors need incentives, too. In the example, because they were being beaten in the market, the sales people had an incentive to adopt a new product. The point is that sponsors will sponsor ideas, but these may not be innovating ideas unless there's something in it for them. The orchestrator's task is to create and communicate those incentives.

Sponsor incentives take many forms. At 3M, division managers have a bonus goal that is reached if 25 percent of their revenue comes from products introduced within the previous five years. When the percentage falls below the goal, and the bonus is threatened, these sponsors become amazingly receptive to new product ideas. The transfer process becomes much easier as a result. Sales growth, revenue increase, numbers of new products, and so on, may be the bases for incentives that motivate sponsors.

Another company can arise if the idea generators receive phantom stock. Should the sponsors who supervise these idea people receive phantom stock, too? Some banks have created separate subsidiaries so that sponsors can receive stock in the new venture. To the degree that sponsors contribute to idea development, they will need to be given such stock options, too.

Thus, the innovating organization needs reward systems for both idea generators and sponsors. It should start with a simple reward system and move to more motivating, more complex and possibly more upsetting types of rewards only if and when attraction and motivation problems call for them.

PEOPLE

The final policy area to be considered involves people practices. The assumption is that some people who are better at innovating are not necessarily good at operating. Therefore, the ability of the innovating organization to generate new business ideas can be increased by systematically developing and selecting those people who are better at innovating than others. But first the desirable attributes must be identified. These characteristics that identify likely idea generators and sponsors are spelled out in the following sections.

Attributes of idea generators

The field engineer in our case history is the stereotype of the inventor. He is not mainstream. He's hard to get along with, and he wasn't afraid to break company policy to perfect his idea. Such people have strong egos that allow them to persist and swim up-stream. They generally are not the type of people who get along well in an organization. However, if an organization has reservations, innovating funds, and dual ladders, these people can be attracted and retained.

The psychological attributes of successful entrepreneurs include great need to achieve and to take risks. But, to translate that need into innovation, several other attributes are needed. First, prospective innovators have an irreverence for the status quo. They often come from outcast groups or are newcomers to the company; they are less satisfied with the way things are and have less to lose if there's a change. Successful innovators also need 'previous programming in the industry' – that is, an in-depth knowledge of the industry gained through either experience or formal education. Hence, the innovator needs industry knowledge, but not the religion.

Previous startup experience is also associated with successful business ventures. As are people who come from incubator firms (for example high-technology companies) and areas (such as Boston and the Silicon Valley) that are noted for creativity.

The amount of organizational effort needed to select these people varies with the ability to attract them to the organization in the first place. If idea people are attracted through reputation, then by funding reservations and employing idea-getting processes, idea people will, in effect, select themselves – they will want to work with the organization – and over time their presence will reinforce the organization's reputation for idea generation. If the firm has no reputation for innovation, then idea people must be sought out or external reservations established to encourage initial idea generation. One firm made extensive use of outside recruiting to accomplish such a goal. A sponsor would develop an idea and then attend annual conferences of key specialists to determine who was most skilled in the area of interest; he or she would then interview appropriate candidates and offer the opportunity to develop the venture to those with entrepreneurial interests.

Another key attribute of successful business innovators is varied experience, which creates the coupling of a knowledge of means and of use in a single individual's mind. It is the generalist, not the specialist, who creates an idea that differs from the firm's current business line. Specialists are inventors; generalists are innovators. One ceramics engineering firm selects the best and the brightest graduates from the ceramics engineering schools and places them in central engineering to learn the firm's overall system. They are then assigned to field engineering where they spend three to five years with customers and their problems and then they return to central engineering product design. Only then do they design products for those customers. This type of internal coupling can be created by role rotation. Some aerospace firms rotate engineers through manufacturing liaison.

People who have the characteristics that make them successful innovators can be retained, however, only if there are reservations for them and sponsors to guide them.

Attributes of sponsors and reservation managers

The innovating organization must also attract, develop, train and retain people to manage the idea development process. Because certain types of people and management skills are better suited to managing ideas than others, likely prospects for such positions should have a management style that enables them to handle idea people, as well as early experience in innovating, the capability to generate ideas of their own, the skills to put deals together, and generalist business skills.

One of the key skills necessary for operating an innovating organization is the skill to manage and supervise the kind of person who is likely to be an idea generator and champion – that is, people who, among other characteristics, do not take very well to being supervised. Idea generators and champions have a great deal of ownership in their ideas. They gain their satisfaction by having 'done it their way.' The intrinsic satisfaction comes from the ownership and autonomy. However, idea people also need help, advice, and sounding boards. The successful sponsor learns how to manage these people in the same way that a producer or publisher learns to handle the egos of their stars and writers. This style was best described by a successful sponsor:

> It's a lot like teaching your kids to ride a bike. You're there. You walk along behind. If the kid takes off, he or she never knows that they could have been helped. If they stagger a little, you lend a helping hand, undetected preferably. If they fall, you catch them. If they do something stupid, you take the bike away until they're ready.

This style is quite different from the hands-on, directive style of managers in an operating organization. Of course, the best way to learn this style is to have been managed by it and seen it practiced in an innovating organization. Therefore, experience in an innovating organization is essential.

More than the idea generators, the sponsors need to understand the logic of innovation and to have experienced the management of innovation. Its managers need to have an intuitive feel for the task and its nuances. Managers whose only experience is in operations will not have developed the managerial style, understanding, and intuitive feel that is necessary to manage innovations because the logic of operations is counterintuitive in comparison with the logic of innovations. This means that some idea generators and champions who have experienced innovation should become managers as well as individual contributors. For example, the president in our case history was the inventor of the first-generation product and therefore understood the long, agonizing process of developing a business idea. It is also rare to find an R&D manager who hasn't come through the R&D ranks.

The best idea sponsors and idea reservation managers, therefore, are people who have experienced innovation early in their careers and are comfortable with it. They will have been exposed to risk, uncertainty, parallel experiments, repeated failures that lead to learning, coupling rather than assembly-line thinking, long time frames, and personal control systems based on people and ideas, not numbers and budget variances. Sponsors and reservation managers can be developed or recruited from the outside.

Sponsors and reservation managers need to be idea generators themselves. Ideas tend to come from two sources. The first is at low levels of the organization where the problem gap is experienced. The idea generator who offers a solution is the one who experienced the problem and goes to a sponsor for testing and development. One problem with these ideas is that they may offer only partial solutions because they come from specialists whose views can be parochial and local. But sponsors are at the crossroads of many ideas. They may get a broader vision of the emerging situation as a result. These idea sponsors can themselves generate an idea that is suitable for the organization's business, or they can blend several partial ideas into a business-adaptable idea. Sponsors and reservation managers who are at the crossroads of idea flow are an important secondary source of new ideas. Therefore, they should be selected and trained for their ability to generate new ideas.

Another skill that sponsors and reservation managers need is the ability to make deals and broker ideas. Once an idea has emerged, a reservation manager may have to argue for the release of key people, space, resources, charters, for production time, or a customer contact. These deals all require someone who is adept at persuasion. In that sense, handling them is no different than project or product management roles. People do vary in their ability to make deals and to bargain and those who are particularly adept should be selected for these roles. However, those who have other idea management skills may well be able to be trained in negotiating and bargaining.

And, finally, sponsors and reservation managers should be generalists with general business skills. Again, the ability to recognize a business idea and to shape partial ideas into business ideals are needed. Sponsors and reservation managers must coach idea generators in specialisms in which the idea generator is not schooled. Most successful research managers are those with business skills who can see the business significance in the good ideas that come from scientists.

In summary, the sponsors and reservation managers who manage the idea-development process must be recruited, selected, and developed. The skills that these people need relate to their style, experience, idea-generating ability, deal-making ability, and generalist business acumen. People with these skills can either be selected or developed.

Thus some of the attributes of successful idea generators and idea sponsors can be identified. In creating the innovating organization, people with these attributes can be recruited, selected, and/or developed. In so doing, the organization improves its odds at generating and developing new business ideas.

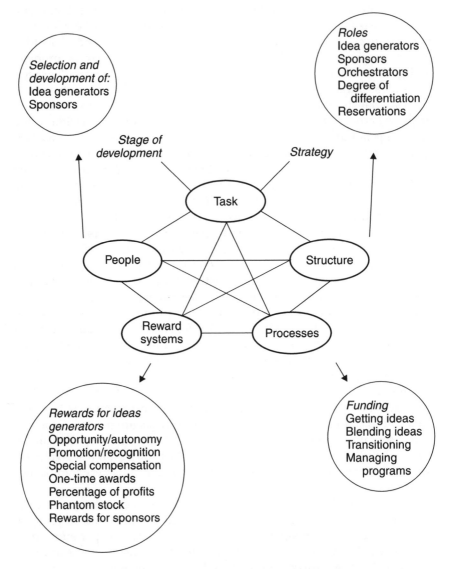

Figure 9.6 **An innovating organization's design components**

SUMMARY

The innovating organization described is one that recognizes and formalizes the roles, processes, rewards, and people practices that naturally lead to innovations. The point we have emphasized throughout this chapter is that the organization that purposely designs these roles and processes is more likely to generate innovations than is an organization that doesn't plan for this function. Such a purposely designed organization is needed to overcome the obstacles to innovation. Because innovation is destructive to many established groups, it will be resisted. Innovation is contrary in operations and will be ignored. These and other obstacles are more likely to be overcome if the organization is designed specifically to innovate.

Managers have tried to overcome these obstacles by creating venture groups, by hiring some entrepreneurs, by creating 'breakthrough funds,' or by offering special incentives. These are good policies but by themselves will not accomplish the goal. Figure 9.1 conveyed the message that a consistent set of policies concerning structure, process, rewards, and people is needed. The innovating organization is illustrated in Figure 9.6. It is the combination of idea people, reservations in which they can operate, sponsors to supervise them, funding for their ideas, and rewards for their success that increase the odds in favor of innovation. Simply implementing one or two of these practices will result in failure and will only give people the impression that such practices do not work. A consistent combination of such practices will create an innovating organization that will work.

SELECTED BIBLIOGRAPHY

The basic ideas of organization design and of blending structure, processes, rewards and people practices are described in my earlier book, *Organization Design* (Addison-Wesley, 1978). The idea of differentiation comes from Paul Lawrence and Jay Lorsch's *Organization and Environment* (Harvard Business School, 1967). One can also find there the basic ideas of contingency theory.

The structure of the innovative organization and the three roles involved are similar to those identified in the investment idea and capital budgeting process. These have been identified by Joseph Bower in *The Resource Allocation Process* (Division of Research at Harvard University, 1968).

Innovation itself has been treated in various ways by many people. Some good ideas about technological innovation can be found in Lowell Steele's *Innovation in Big Business* (Elsevier, 1975).

Chapter 10

Designing collateral organizations

Ralph H. Kilmann

INTRODUCTION

Contemporary organizations are facing increasingly dynamic and changing environments which pose more complex and ill-defined problems than organizations have previously had to address. These problems include: which new international markets to explore, which new technologies should and can be developed, whether organizational goals should be altered, how employees should be motivated more effectively, what social responsibility policies the organization should formulate and implement. But these problems can never be completely resolved since they are always present. Thus, these problems must be managed continually. Furthermore, the information needed to analyze these problems is not generally available nor will the information ever be complete – because the nature of the problem keeps changing. In fact, one might argue that the basic problem is defining what the problem is; then one can begin seeking information, analyzing the problem, and deriving and implementing solutions to manage the problem (Kilmann, 1977a).

Organizations, however, are designed more to perform day-to-day activities and to produce well-defined products and services – not to solve complex and changing problems. In particular, organizations are designed into operational sub-units (e.g. production, marketing, finance, etc.) to pursue well-defined goals and tasks. But how can the organization engage in effective problem solving if it is designed primarily for day-to-day concerns and if complex problems simply do not fit well into the design categories or boxes on the organization's chart? What is needed is a different approach to organizational problem solving – one that may involve the entire organization or at least those persons who are directly affected by complex problems, and one that specifically designs for problem solving. Further, the resultant design should structure objectives, tasks, and people in a manner that does not confine the organization to address complex problems within the day-to-day, operational design (Kilmann, 1977a).

Zand (1974) has suggested such an approach to organization-wide problem solving, referred to as the 'collateral organization'. Zand considers the day-to-day, operational design as dealing with authority-production type problem while a parallel design concentrates on the ill-defined, long-term, system-wide type problems. The members in the collateral design would spend approximately 2–10 hours per week working on such complex problems; the remainder of their time would be spent back in the operational design. Figure 10.1 shows the separateness as well as the linkages between the traditional (operational) and the collateral design.

A major reason for utilizing a parallel structure with overlapping membership is to increase the likelihood that creative and innovative ideas about problems can and will be implemented in the operational design. The trouble with assigning complex issues to staff groups, as is the customary practice, is that these groups are:

1 remote from the source of the problems, and
2 not in any position of line authority to implement their own recommendations.

A collateral organization, in contrast, encourages members and line managers from the operational design to develop creative yet feasible solutions in a more relaxed, fluid, collateral design – and then enables them to return to the operational design and implement their solution from a formal position of authority in the organization. This ongoing cycle of sensing the problem (from the operational design), defining the problem and deriving solutions (in the collateral design) and implementing the solution (back in the operational design), is the foundation of the collateral organization. In addition, the collateral design forms groups of people that cut across the formal departments in the operational design so that a wide array of expertise and information is available in each collateral group. It is less likely, consequently, that important aspects of a problem will be overlooked or treated in a narrow way (as would be done if ill-structured problems were approached by one functional department in the operational design).

DISTINGUISHING DUAL DESIGNS

It is important to distinguish the collateral organization from other design efforts that also create a dual or overlapping structural arrangement. For example, task forces, committees, project teams, and project management are not considered to fall under the heading of collateral organization since these second-order designs are oriented to a well-defined problem in an 'authority-production' type atmosphere. For example, a special task force may be created to study the purchase and renovation of a new

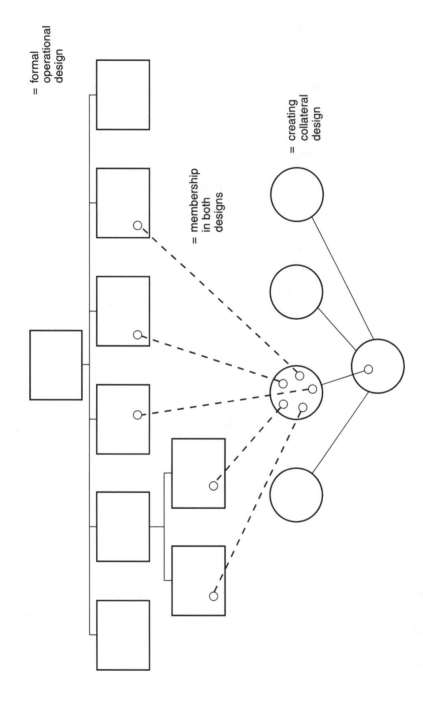

= formal
operational
design

= membership
in both
designs

= creating
collateral
design

Figure 10.1 The collateral organization

building; a project team is created to design and build a prototype labor-saving device; a project management design is developed to devote attention to the marketing of a new line of products for the firm. In general, these dual-design arrangements do not involve a distinction in well-defined vs. ill-defined problems as much as a way of giving special attention to new products, production methods, or facilities development. Stated differently, these dual designs tend to focus on a problem that suggests quite clearly the necessary expertise needed to solve the problem – often a very narrow range of technical expertise. For an ill-defined problem, in contrast, it is not always clear what expertise is needed. (A further discussion of these dual designs can be found in Cleland and King, 1968.)

Another design approach which at first seems to resemble the collateral organization is matrix organization. Matrix has been defined in numerous ways in the literature. Gibson *et al.* (1973) report that terms such as grid structure, multidimensional structure, global matrix, program management, and project management have been used interchangeably with matrix organization. Davis and Lawrence (1977), providing the most comprehensive discussion on matrix to date, define the term by the existence of the two-boss-model – where some people are reporting simultaneously to two superiors, one in the functional design and one in the matrix (business) team. Consequently, if any design were established whereby members would report exclusively to their project manager during the course of the project, this arrangement would not be viewed as matrix. Likewise, any task-force mission that has members working full-time on the task force, reporting to one boss, would not fit the Davis and Lawrence definition of matrix.

A collateral organization has some similarity to the matrix as far as the dual reporting relationship is concerned, with two important exceptions. First, it is possible that several members in the collateral design could have the same boss as in the operational design. Basically, the collateral organization does not establish the equivalent of the business team manager – one who manages the matrix team but does not have a formal position in the functional design. In essence, the persons who manage the groups in the collateral design are also managers in the operation (functional) design. Only those members who come from different divisions or departments than their collateral-design manager would have two bosses.

The second exception to the similarities between a matrix and collateral organization involves a critical difference in focus. In most cases, the matrix teams are oriented to solving 'authority-production' type problems, just as in the functional organization. Matrix organization combines a diversity of expertise within the matrix teams whereas the functional design has its specialized expertise divided into different functional departments. The collateral design, as mentioned earlier, is focused on defining and solving long-term, complex, and ill-defined problems, not authority-production problems.

Another approach to problem solving in groups that bears resemblance to collateral organizations is QWL (Quality of Work Life) programs. Problem-solving groups are established collateral to existing union/ management relationships to solve design, planning, and performance problems at the workplace (Davis, 1977). The various groups are composed of representatives from different parts of the operational design that have some stake in the problem at hand. While these problem-solving groups typically concentrate on rather well-defined work problems, there are examples of using the union/management, cross-membership effort for more ill-defined problems. For example, Davis and Sullivan (1975) report on a joint effort by union and management to design a new chemical plant for Shell Canada, Ltd. The problem-solving groups designed not only the overall structure of the new organization, but also the jobs, the reward system, and the various control mechanisms. In most cases, however, the creation of 'production-oriented' groups – as QWL approaches as the earlier Scanlon Plan (Lesiur and Puckett, 1969), or as the 'new' concept of quality control circles from Japan (Ouchi, 1981) – is centred on well-defined production problems, not ill-defined problems as is intended for the collateral organization.

EXAMPLES OF COLLATERAL DESIGNS

While the concept of collateral organizations is still rather new, it is possible to suggest some missions that would be suited especially well to this problem-solving approach. It has been observed, for example, that strategic planning does not take place well when restricted to the formal (often bureaucratic design) categories on the organization chart (Mitroff *et al.*, 1977). Also, since strategic planning has a bearing on the whole organization, not to mention its long-time frame, a separate collateral design that is special to strategic planning is suggested (rather than attempting to redesign the formal, operational design to make it more responsive overall to such long-term, complex considerations). The same has been discovered for any type of long-term problem focus such as monitoring a complex, multinational environment (Kilmann and Ghgymn, 1976), where a collateral 'intelligence' gathering system can be designed or such as designing an organization-wide, management-information system (MIS) to facilitate and support middle and upper management decision making (Mitroff *et al.*, 1979). The problem of R&D units not providing usable new ideas and products can be approached, for example, by designing a collateral, knowledge utilization design (Kilmann, 1981). In this way, many organizational members would have the dual role of knowledge developers (in the collateral design) and knowledge users (in the formal, operational designs) rather than having a separate group of R&D persons which does not interface well with the rest of the organization (Zaltman, 1977).

Other missions and special purposes might also be approached more effectively with a collateral organization. The question becomes how to create a collateral design so that its potential for managing complex problems is realized. The focus now turns to suggesting a sequence of key steps to consider in designing collateral organizations. These generic steps are based not only on a logical flow of design decisions, but on some of the scientific principles that have been offered for designing effective organizations in general (Bennis, 1966; Kilmann *et al.*, 1976).

CREATING COLLATERAL DESIGNS

Figure 10.2 outlines the 10 basic steps involved in forming an effective collateral organization, based on the research in the field of organization design.

Each step is discussed below, noting the relevant literature where appropriate.

---

1 Recognizing that a special-purpose, collateral design is needed to supplement the operational design for important long-term complex missions.
2 Formulating the special purpose or mission for which a collateral organization will be designed.
3 Specifying objectives that the collateral design will attempt to achieve (5–15 objectives).
4 Specifying tasks that need to be performed in order to achieve each specified objective (30–100 tasks).
5 Identifying people who have the necessary abilities, skills, interests, knowledge and experience to perform the indicated tasks from any division in the organization (10–50 people).
6 Determining the interdependencies of all pairs of tasks; anticipating how people would be working on these tasks in order to achieve the objectives.
7 Forming boundaries around 'clusters' of tasks (denoting each collateral subunit's task environment).
8 Designing the internal-structural characteristics of each collateral subunit, according to the principle of differentiation (i.e. form, policies, and guidelines to fit with each subunit's task environment).
9 Designing the mechanisms to coordinate all collateral subunits into a functioning whole, according to the principle of integration, as well as to coordinate flows between the operational and collateral designs.
10 Implementing, monitoring and evaluating the new collateral design as the mission is being pursued.

Figure 10.2 **The 10 steps for designing collateral organizations**

Step 1: Recognizing complexity

Step 1 emphasizes that organizational members or managers must realize that a particular problem or project will be most difficult to address in the formal, operational design (Zand, 1974). Such a problem or mission would involve several if not many subunits in the formal organization, requiring their frequent or constant interaction. Unless the organization is very flexible, loose, and has been very supportive and rewarding of such interdepartmental interactions, it is unlikely that any creative, effective interchange will develop across these formal units.

Perhaps it should be re-emphasized that departments are oriented primarily to day-to-day concerns and are designed so that they do not have to interact much with other departments. In fact, reward systems of most complex organizations tend to reinforce departmental goals and objectives, even to the detriment of overall organizational goals and objectives (Seiler, 1963; Thomas, 1976).

Step 2: Formulating the mission

With the recognition that some special-purpose, collateral design is needed, Step 2 requires that organizational members specify the primary mission or purpose of the collateral design. Possible missions might include: strategic planning, identifying and solving complex problems that have not been managed well previously, developing an organization-wide information system to aid in the decision-making process of middle managers, planning organizational changes and then guiding the implementation of these changes, evaluating organizational policies, enhancing the organization's responsiveness to its environment, anticipating and monitoring environmental changes, and so on. One might envision a collateral design which first would set priorities on the several possible missions that should be addressed. Thus, determining the long-run strategy of the firm might precede efforts to evaluate organizational policies or to begin designing an organization-wide information system (that assumes a particular strategy for the organization).

It is recommended, therefore, that an organization does not 'jump' into creating one or more collateral designs until the relative importance and priorities of these missions have been established. The organization has to be aware, then, of the Type III error: the probability of solving the wrong problem versus the right problem, or solving the less important versus the most important problems given the limited resources of the organization (Kilmann, 1977a; Mitroff and Fetheringham, 1974). The opposite of not having any collateral design, and assuming that all complex problems or missions can be dealt with in the current operational design, is to create a new collateral design for many or most 'unresolved issues' and thus overwhelm members with many task-force or committee assignments. Rather, the idea is to use collateral designs for what they are intended – the most important, complex undertakings of the organization, which usually have a critical impact on the future of the organization.

The procedure for establishing the importance and priority of several possible missions can be done through an initial collateral design, as noted above, or through an active debate among top management personnel. The judicial-decision process discussed by Wirt (1973) or any version of the Hegelian dialectic (Churchman, 1971) would be useful in this regard. Perhaps a debate on the underlying assumptions which argue for each proposed mission would help management crystallize their priorities (Mason and Mitroff, 1981).

Step 3: Specifying objectives

Once the overall mission for the collateral design has been chosen, Step 3 asks managers to specify, in as much detail as possible, the particular objectives that the collateral design would be designed to achieve. Some possibilities might be: a specific plan or report of the collateral design, a statement or outline of the major problems facing the organization over the next ten years (including priorities), a detailed design of the management-information system, an assessment of R&D's role in the corporate planning, detailing implications regarding human-resource changes in the organization, and so on. In most cases, a complex mission can be subdivided into five to fifteen sub-missions or objectives, indicating the several outcomes expected from the collateral design.

This step involving objectives is somewhat analogous to what generally was intended with 'Management-By-Objectives' or MBO (Reddin, 1972). That is, before an organization engages in any activity, it should be clear about the final outcomes or objectives, and then work backwards to consider the tasks, resources, designs, etc., in order to accomplish these objectives. Specifying objectives at an earlier stage (no matter how tentative for the moment) does not leave members in the collateral design wondering why they were assembled and what it is they really are to do. Surprisingly, committees and task forces often are created to solve a problem that has not been prioritized yet and, in addition, members are not at all clear about what final outcome is expected from them.

Step 4: Specifying tasks

After listing has been made of the several objectives pertaining to the identified mission of the collateral design, Step 4 requires the top managers to indicate the specific tasks that need to be done in order to accomplish the stated objectives. That is, what work has to be done, what information has to be collected, what resources need to be acquired, what decisions have to be made, what actions have to be taken – in order to maximize the probability that the specific objectives, and hence the overall mission, will be achieved. It might be said that one reason for first translating the mission into objectives is to facilitate the listing of specific tasks, which is expected to be easier than going from the mission directly to these tasks.

Any complex mission involving five to fifteen separate objectives is likely to result in anywhere from 30 to 100 tasks. More than 100 tasks generally gets the design process bogged down in too much detail. Some tasks might be as follows: conducting a market survey of consumer interest in this product, asking potential users their opinions on the design of the management-information system, performing the relevant statistical analyses on the survey data, monitoring the pricing changes of major competitors, deciding on the key parameters in the forecasting model, communicating the results of the final report to the relevant external agencies, defining the role of corporate planners regarding the formulation of research projects, taking account of the organization's culture and climate in preparing a plan for implementing a new reward/ incentive system, and so on.

It is important to emphasize that both the list of objectives and the list of tasks should be viewed as comprehensive and complete by a number of top managers responsible for creating the collateral design. This requires that both lists be reviewed a number of times to assure completeness and to guarantee that redundancies, inconsistencies, and jargon have been removed.

Step 5: Identifying people

Step 5 concerns the human-resource aspect of the collateral design. Specifically, given the objectives and tasks, who are the best people to staff the new design, how many are needed, what are their characteristics and areas of expertise, and where in the operational design are they now located? It is only by having these objectives and tasks fairly well specified that one can begin to answer these questions. Naturally, one can always add people to the collateral design as needed, but for efficiency's sake and for the sake of developing cohesive, effective teams in the new design, it is helpful to have planned for the human-resource question well in advance of implementing the collateral organization.

Since, by definition, the missions involve issues that cut across a number of existing organizational departments or subunits, members for the new design would involve people from different parts of the organization. It may even be appropriate, at times, to hire persons from outside of the organization on a temporary basis in order to supply important areas of expertise to the collateral design; expertise that may not be represented in the organization. Outside 'consultants' can be utilized in this manner. Regardless, it seems evident that whatever the tasks and objectives are, the necessary and relevant areas of expertise, information, knowledge, and experience should be included in the pool of human resources for the mission in question.

Thus far, the missions, objectives, tasks, and people for the collateral design have been identified. What is needed now is to consider forming these 'elements' into a particular collateral design: arrangements into subunits. Only if the necessary people for the mission numbered less than 10 would it be feasible to have just one group for the collateral design, similar to a single committee or task force. In most complex, large corporations, the mission may break down into 10 objectives, 60 tasks, and 40 people. This is not an uncommon scope for a mission that is absolutely critical to the long-term survival of the organizations, impacts of most or all major divisions in the operational design, and requires, therefore, a broad base of expertise and representation from all these segments in the organization. But this is precisely why a collateral design is needed and why prior efforts of managing the mission (in the operational design alone) simply have not worked. The next steps of the process draw on organization-design knowledge that provides principles and criteria for subdividing the total set of objectives, tasks, and people into manageable subunits; also providing 'integrators' and mechanisms to coordinate the subunits into a functioning whole.

Step 6: Determining task interdependencies and Step 7: Forming subunit boundaries

Step 6 is perhaps the most difficult and complex part of the design process: to determine (anticipate) all the task interrelationships (interdependencies) that will exist as people begin working on tasks in pursuit of the objectives. Only by knowing the nature and strength of the interdependency for each likely pair of tasks will it be possible to conduct the following step properly: that of determining the way in which the total set of objectives, tasks, and people most optimally divides into separate, manageable subunits.

Thompson's (1976) concept of task interdependencies is very helpful here. Specifically, Thompson defines three types of interdependencies that can take place either within or between organizational subunits: pooled, sequential, and reciprocal. Pooled interdependence is when two or more tasks can be performed relatively independent of one another, and in order to obtain certain outcomes or objectives the separate outputs of each activity can be combined or pooled together at some later time. With pooled interdependence, therefore, there is not much need to coordinate, plan, schedule, or communicate with respect to the separate tasks before the 'pooling' act is performed, and even then, combining is rather straightforward and can be done according to standardized procedures. Sequential interdependencies, however, require that in order for the final outcome or end-product to be achieved, the separate tasks and activities must be combined in a certain sequence. Thus, task A is performed first, then B, then C, which then results in the completion of an overall outcome which, consequently, requires a certain amount of planning and scheduling across several tasks in order to foster efficiency and effectiveness. Finally, reciprocal interdependencies occur when a constant or frequent cycling of interaction and input–output relationships takes place between various tasks so that a 'final' outcome can be achieved. For example, persons performing task A must constantly interact with those performing tasks B and C for the outcome to be completed appropriately. Fostering and managing such ongoing and potentially complex interaction patterns among reciprocal-interdependent tasks, not surprisingly, requires additional coordinating mechanisms beyond procedures, plans, and schedules.

The three types of interdependencies, as implied above, have different costs associated with coordinating tasks in order to achieve a desirable outcome. Specifically, pooled interdependencies are least costly to coordinate because only procedures may have to be instituted at one point in time. Sequential interdependencies are more costly to coordinate due to the planning and scheduling which must take place before and during the performance of the tasks. Reciprocal interdependencies are the most costly since coordination requires constant monitoring, communication, and mutual adjustment (Thompson, 1976).

In order to minimize the general costs of coordinating and managing various tasks, *the most costly forms of interdependencies should be placed within as opposed to between subunit boundaries* (ibid.). Specifically, as far as possible the boundaries of subunits first should contain most or all identified reciprocal interdependencies, then the sequential interdependencies, and finally, the pooled interdependencies can be left between subunit boundaries. In most 'real' settings, however, some sequential and even a few reciprocal interdependencies would be left between subunits since it may be quite impossible to come up with one set of subunit boundaries which contains all interdependencies perfectly.

Step 6 and Step 7 entail identifying all the two-way interdependencies among all the listed tasks so that an 'optimal' design of subunit boundaries can be created for the collateral organization. In addition, these boundaries can be shown not just as the subset of people who are assigned to work on these tasks; they can also show the subset of objectives that the people in each subunit are attempting to accomplish. Thus, a subset of people working on a subset of assigned tasks according to a subset of objectives (as a subset of the total identified mission), constitutes the definition of each subunit in the collateral design. The concept of task interdependencies provides the basic criterion for subdividing tasks, people, and objectives into 'optimal' subunits.

A number of techniques are available for determining task inter-dependencies and then forming the subunits for a collateral design. For example, the 'Q-sort technique' can be utilized by having managers first list each task on a separate 3 × 5 card and then sort the cards into piles representing similar, overlapping, interdependent tasks (Stephenson, 1953). This requires considerable judgement but can be accomplished effectively for small collateral designs (e.g. less than 50 tasks). A variant of this method is suggested by MacKenzie (1978, 1981) in his design technology referred to as 'Organizational Audit and Analysis.' The 'Socio-Technical Systems' approach (Clark, 1972) also requires intuition and judgement in forming groups by examining task flows and tasks interdependencies. Kilmann (1977b) offers a statistical approach by sug-gesting the use of correlational and factor analyses from questionnaire data on respondents' perceptions of task requirements. Using this 'MAPS Design Technology,' a statistical analysis enables a larger set of tasks to be sorted into subunits via computer programs (e.g. 50–150 tasks). Unfortunately, no comparative, empirical study has been done that ex-amines the effects of using these different design technologies for collateral (let alone operational) designing on a number of process and outcome variables. (See MacKenzie, 1981 for a theoretical critique of these different design methods.)

Step 8: Subunit differentiation

Step 8 involves designing the internal-structural characteristics of each subunit in the collateral design, once the subunit boundaries have been determined during the preceding step. The concept of 'differentiation' developed by Lawrence and Lorsch (1967) is relevant to this step of the process.

Differentiation as a design criterion suggests that given a particular set of design categories or subunits of an organization (i.e. given the specifi-cation of subunit boundaries), each subunit should be internally designed to best fit with the characteristics of its task environment. For example, if the task environment or sub-environment facing a subunit is primarily stable, then a highly structured, traditional, bureaucratic design would best foster subunit efficiency and effectiveness (as in most production departments). At the same time, if the members in the subunit are motivated and prefer to work in such a bureaucratic design (because of various motivational and personality characteristics), then the efficiency and effectiveness of the subunit is further enhanced because of this 'fit'

(Lorsch and Morse, 1974). On the other hand, if the task environment facing the subunit is dynamic and changing, then a more loosely structured, non-traditional, organic-adaptive design would be best (Bennis, 1966) (as in some R&D departments). In the latter case, individuals who are motivated and prefer to work in such a fluid design would best contribute to the efficiency and effectiveness of the subunit, given the necessary expertise, etc. It is important to emphasize, however, that the extent to which the various subunits face different environments is the extent that the internal designs of the subunits would be different, ranging from the 'pure' bureaucratic to an extreme organic-adaptive design (as well as suggesting the different types of individuals who are best to staff the various subunits).

Since a collateral organization faces a dynamic, complex, and ill-defined task environment, the internal structure of subunits should be organic-adaptive. The internal characteristics of the operational design should be bureaucratic (consistent with the authority-production forms). Only if the operational design contained subunits that faced a dynamic environment (as in R&D departments) would any subunits in the operational design have an organic-adaptive structure. In fact one might expect that most of the operational design would be bureaucratic (specific rules and procedures, a clear line of authority, well-defined job positions and responsibilities, etc.) and therefore *the design of the collateral organization would be very different from what members are accustomed to in the operation design.*

This creates a special problem for designing collateral organizations. The members must recognize that the structure of the operational design and the collateral design need to be quite different, and the members must be able to operate in these two different 'cultures' as they go back and forth between the two designs. The worst case would be if the collateral design were created with the same type of bureaucratic structure that is found in most operational designs, as a result of familiarity and custom. In this case, by not applying the principles of differentiation, as discussed above, the collateral design would be attempting to define and solve very complex problems within a rigidly defined set of rules, procedures, hierarchy, and job specifications. Besides, it would be a wasted effort to attempt to anticipate all the rules and regulations that are necessary for effective behavior when the task environment of a collateral subunit is so complex and changing, requiring frequent changes in behavior (and thus requiring frequent changes in rules and procedures). Only if one or more subunits in the collateral design were involved with routine tasks (such as information collection and statistical analysis, for example), would a more bureaucratic type of structure be appropriate (for those particular subunits).

With an organic-adaptive design in mind, Step 8 would entail the development of norms, general policies, and guidelines on how each group will proceed. The leadership activities would tend to be more shared than hierarchical in nature, and the influence processes would be based more on expertise, information, persuasiveness, and relevance rather than legitimate power and authority (i.e. personal power vs. positional power). Perhaps the best way of describing the structure and functioning of a collateral subunit (as an organic-adaptive system) is according to professional norms and colleagueship (Bennis, 1966).

Step 9: Subunit integration

Step 9 – how to design the mechanisms to coordinate the residual inter-dependencies of subunits – is handled by the concept of integration (Lawrence and Lorsch, 1967; Lorsch and Lawrence, 1970). It is recognized that even if most of the interdependencies are contained within subunit boundaries, the subunits themselves are still not entirely independent of one another. At a minimum, certain pooled interdependencies would remain, and more often than not, some sequential and even reciprocal independencies would still be present in any complex organization. Integration is concerned with coordinating the subunits into a functional whole. Often the use of a 'loose' management hierarchy would constitute the primary form of integration across collateral groups (i.e. managers being responsible for coordinating the interdependencies of two or more groups). Other integration mechanisms include the 'informal' organiz-ation, overlapping group memberships, as in Likert's (1961) linking pin and specially designed information links. Further, the individuals performing the integrating roles should be ones who appreciate if not possess the variety of skills, styles, goals, etc., that exist within the several groups being coordinated.

An important issue of integration, however, is not so much coordin-ating the activities across the various collateral groups, but the coordination of activities between the collateral design and the operational design. Since the internal structure of these dual designs would be quite different, there is a special problem involved in moving (managing) people across these two different systems. Members involved in both designs must learn to function in two different ways and not be confused by the switch from one culture to another. Furthermore, some integration mechanism should be established to assure that only the ill-defined problems get presented to the collateral design rather than bringing them 'everything' from the operational design. In addition, integration in this context re-quires mechanisms to bring solutions from the collateral design back to the operational design in a well-conceived plan of implementation. Managing this back and forth flow of problems, people, information, solutions, and results necessitates a unique blend of 'integrators' (as persons) and creative linkages in terms of mechanisms, functions, and incentives.

Step 10: Implementation of evaluation

The final step in the design process, Step 10, involves:

1 implementing the collateral organization as designed in the previous nine steps;
2 monitoring and adapting its design as experience in the collateral organization takes place;
3 evaluating how well the collateral design and the design process have fostered the attainment of the stated mission.

In essence, Step 10 puts the collateral organization into action. But an important aspect of this activity is to adjust and modify the design as management and members learn about such organized efforts. There are always unexpected problems that emerge, some of which have to do with members having two positions in the organization, one in the operational design and one in the collateral design. There may also be pressures for members to spend more time in both designs, which is rarely feasible. These sorts of problems have to be worked out in order for both designs to perform as intended.

Step 10 also involves evaluating the results of the design effort, which is especially important if the organization wants to use collateral designs in the future, and therefore wants to learn from its experiences. Further, top management should be interested to learn if the mission was accomplished successfully and what role the collateral design had in the final outcome.

CONCLUSION

It is up to the imagination of organizations and designers to develop numerous uses of collateral, special-purpose designs. This chapter has mentioned only a few but certainly this list extends way beyond these and definitely beyond the single concept of a committee system.

On the other hand, I am not advocating that an organization forms an additional collateral design every time some new problem or purpose emerges. Eventually, members would be confused by such multidesigned organizations (e.g. having membership in four of five collateral designs) and this would approach the feeling of constantly moving from one committee to another as a way of avoiding the real and important issues. It might be argued, therefore, that an organization that finds itself in a very dynamic and changing environment, where new problems and purposes emerge frequently, could have a collateral design concentrating on the initial but critical purpose of problem sorting, problem formulation, problem finding, and the like. Such a 'problem management' design (Kilmann, 1977a) would be a perpetual collateral design (obviously with a very broad range of expertise and wide representation throughout the organization) that would resolve some problems and then go on to others (Bennis, 1966).

The ultimate test of the ideas and suggestions in this chapter remains an empirical question. While I doubt the feasibility of conducting tight, laboratory experiments as a way of examining these complex design issues, it might be possible to conduct some field studies. For example, if several organizations were interested in the general topic of complex problem solving, maybe they would be willing to establish several different efforts; perhaps several different types of collateral design vs. approaching complex problems through staff groups or via traditional operational departments. Although alternative explanations for any finding would be numerous, carefully following and monitoring the processes and outcomes of these various efforts over time could be quite illuminating. Some qualitative or even quantitative assessments could be made which might help develop further knowledge and insights. Certainly, developing this sort of knowledge base is extremely relevant to offering organizations some guidelines and prescriptions for managing increasingly complex problems.

REFERENCES

Bennis, W.G. (1966) *Changing Organizations*. McGraw-Hill, New York.

Churchman, C.W. (1971) *The Design of Inquiring Systems*. Basic Books, New York.

Clark, P.A. (1972) *Organizational Design: Theory and Practice*. Tavistock, London.

Cleland, D.I. and King, W.R. (1968) *Systems Analysis and Project Management*. McGraw-Hill, New York.

Davis, L. (1977) 'Enhancing the quality of working life: developments in the United States', *International Labour Review*, 116, pp. 53–65.

Davis, L. and Sullivan, C. (1975) 'A labor–management contract and quality of working life', *Occupational Behaviour*, 1.

Davis, S.M. and Lawrence, P.R. (1977) *Matrix*. Addison-Wesley, Reading, MA.

Gibson, J.L., Ivancevich, J.M. and Donnelly, Jr, H.H. (1973) 'Organizations: structure, processes, behaviour', *Business Publications*, Dallas.

Kilmann, R.H. (1977a) 'Problem management: a behavioral science approach', in G. Zaltman (ed.) *The Handbook for Managers in Non-profit Organizations*. American Management Association, New York.

Kilmann, R.H. (1977b) *Social Systems Design: Normative Theory and the MAPS Design Technology*. Elsevier North-Holland, New York.

Kilmann, R.H. (1981) 'Organization design for knowledge utilization', *Knowledge: Creation, Diffusion, Utilization*, 3, pp. 211–231.

Kilmann, R.H. and Ghgymn, K. (1976) 'The MAPS design technology: designing strategic intelligence systems for multinational corporations', *Columbia Journal of World Business*, 11, pp. 35–47.

Kilmann, R.H., Pondy, L.R. and Slevin, D.P. (1976) *The Management of Organization Design*, vols I and II. Elsevier North-Holland, New York.

Lawrence, P.R. and Lorsch, J.W. (1967) *Organization and Environment*. Harvard University Press, Boston, MA.

Lesiur, F.G. and Puckett, E.S. (1969) 'The Scanlon plan has proved itself', *Harvard Business Review*, 47, pp. 109–118.

Likert, R. (1961) *New Patterns of Management*. McGraw-Hill, New York.

Lorsch, J.W. and Lawrence, P.R. (1970) *Studies in Organization Design*. Irwin-Dorsey, Homewood, IL.

Lorsch, J.W. and Morse, J.J. (1974) *Organizations and their Members*. Harper & Row, New York.

MacKenzie, K.D. (1978) 'A process based measure for the degree of hierarchy in a group, III: applications to organizational design', *Journal of Enterprise Management*, 1, pp. 175–184.

MacKenzie, K.D. (1981) 'Concepts and measures in organizational development', in J.D. Hogan (ed.) *Dimensions of Productivity Research*, vol. 1. American Productivity Center, Houston, pp. 233–304.

Mason, R.O. and Mitroff, I.I. (1981) *Challenging Strategic Planning Assumptions*. Wiley-Interscience, New York.

Mitroff, I.I. and Fetheringham, T. (1974) 'On systematic problem solving and error of the third kind', *Behavioral Science*, 19, pp. 383–393.

Mitroff, I.I., Barabba, V.P. and Kilmann, R.H. (1977) 'The application of behavioral and philosophical technologies to strategic planning: a case study of a large federal agency', *Management Science*, 24, pp. 44–58.

Mitroff, I.I., Kilmann, R.H. and Barabba, V.P. (1979) 'Avoiding the design of management misinformation systems: a strategic approach', in G. Zaltman (ed.) *The Handbook for Managers in Non-profit Organizations*. American Management Association, New York.

Ouchi, W.G. (1981) *Theory Z*. Addison-Wesley, Reading, MA.

Reddin, W.J. (1972) *Effective Management by Objectives*. McGraw-Hill, New York.

Seiler, J.A. (1963) 'Diagnosing interdepartmental conflict', *Harvard Business Review*, 41, pp. 121–132.

Stephenson, W. (1953) *The Study of Behavior: Q-technique and Its Methodology*, University of Chicago Press, Chicago.

Thomas, K.W. (1976) 'Conflict and conflict management', in M.D. Dunnette (ed.) *The Handbook of Industrial and Organizational Psychology*. Rand McNally, Chicago.

Thompson, J.D. (1976) *Organizations in Action*. McGraw-Hill, New York.

Wirt, J.G. (1973) *A Proposed Methodology for Evaluating R&D Programs in the Department of Health, Education*. The Rand Corporation, Santa Monica, CA.

Zaltman, G. (1977) 'A discussion of the research utilization process', in G. Zaltman and R. Duncan (eds) *Strategies for Planned Change*. Wiley-Interscience, New York.

Zand, D.E. (1974) 'Collateral organization: a new change strategy', *Journal of Applied Behavioral Science*, 10, pp. 63–89.

Chapter 11

Intelligent technology, intelligent workers
A new pedagogy for the high-tech workplace

Gloria Schuck

The Office of Technology Assessment (OTA), which received a charter from the US Congress to investigate the effects of computer-based technologies in industry, released its report in 1984, entitled, *Computerized Manufacturing Automation*. The report paid special attention to the ways in which skill requirements are changed by the use of advanced computer technologies and the ways in which these new skills might be developed in present and future employees. The report said in part:

> Individuals and employers are demanding more from education, training and retraining programs. . . . There is a basic *uncertainty* about how current instructional programs should be revised or expanded to reflect the increased use of advanced technologies and changing skill requirements, given the ongoing nature of technological change.

What is the cause of this widespread uncertainty about instructional programs? In the 'automated factory' the computer does the 'work,' and the worker's role is to monitor the manufacturing process by watching the terminal and reacting to problems by making adjustments to process variables. Essentially, the worker's job involves pushing buttons, and he or she needs to be taught the steps required to react to a problem and regain control of the process. When managers and workers can rely on the 'intelligence' of the computer, little or no uncertainty exists about training programs.

However, automation is only one aspect of technology. My hypothesis is that the uncertainty about training programs originates in another aspect of technology: computer-based information technology not only automates, it also 'informates.' Shoshana Zuboff explains that because it creates more and different information, an informating technology can create an environment for thinking and problem solving. The worker's primary role in an informated environment is not only to push buttons to control process, but also to use the information generated by the technology to 'push the business' – to redefine process variables, to improve quality, and to reduce costs. The intelligence of the worker is as important as, if not more important than, the intelligence of the software. Zuboff writes that the utilization of information technology 'depends uniquely on the worker's quality of mind.' People need 'intellective' skill – abstract thinking, inductive reasoning, and theoretical apprehension – if they are to use information to make a contribution to the business.

Little uncertainty about training arises in an automated environment, because the focus is on operating the terminal and memorizing rules to control the manufacturing process. However, when an organization emphasizes the informating aspects of advanced information technology – when it expects its employees to use information for business insight and innovation – it has made an implicit commitment to developing the intellective skill of its work force.

Over a number of years I have interviewed workers and managers in four industrial organizations in which computer-based technology was being used to automate the manufacturing process. My research focused on the workers – the people who were closest to the point of production and whose jobs had changed the most as a result of computer-based technologies. Their experiences and perceptions offer insights into the process of learning intellective skill and suggest ways in which that learning can be enhanced. This chapter highlights key elements of the learning process and begins to define a philosophy of teaching – a pedagogy that can contribute to the development of intellective skill in an informated work place.

While the term *pedagogy* may be unfamiliar to many people, I use it to convey my view that the approach to learning required in the informated work place is different from what we have come to expect from terms like 'teaching' and 'training.' These words usually connote situations in which there are two clearly defined roles – a teacher who knows and a student who learns. I want instead to invite the reader to consider learning as a collective activity in which the focus is on asking questions and engaging in dialogue – one in which teacher–student roles are not predetermined, but are fluid and are dependent on individuals' expertise and insight in a particular situation. Thus we must think about the values and assumptions we bring to the learning process, rather than the specific tactics of training or teaching.

HIGHER-ORDER COGNITIVE SKILLS AND THE LEARNING PROCESS

Lev S. Vygotsky, an educational psychologist, explains that people learn higher-order cognitive skills by moving from objects and actions to the 'field of meaning.' An object is something that is capable of being seen, touched, or otherwise sensed, and an action is an actual behavior or conduct. 'Field of meaning' refers to abstract thinking, which involves applying relevant concepts in order to make sense of experience. For example, a person who is learning written language first focuses on objects and actions such as tracing letters and memorizing grammatical rules; when the person moves on to constructing and interpreting prose, he or she is then operating in a field of meaning.

Such movement from objects and actions to a field of meaning can also be observed when people learn to use new technology. When automation is introduced into the workplace, learning is typically concerned with 'computer literacy' – a working knowledge of how the computer system operates, general ways in which it can be used, and basic keyboard skills. The worker visualizes *objects* (such as pieces of equipment or the steps in the process) and translates this concrete reality into numbers on the terminal screen, and memorizes *actions*, the standard operating proced-ures necessary to perform the job through the terminal. Performance is evaluated on the basis of how well the worker has learned objects and actions, but he or she may not understand or be able to articulate the underlying rationale or meaning of the task. One worker said:

> I know what buttons to push if things get out of whack, but I really don't know why it happened. If I understood more about the process and the software, maybe I could figure out so I wouldn't keep having the problem.

Of course, workers must learn objects and actions in both automated and informated environments. However, a second step in the learning process is required if information is to be dealt with in any significant way. The worker needs to learn how to translate the information on the terminal screen or printout into insight – to move from objects and actions to a field of meaning. Instead of acting in a preprogrammed way ('If X happens, I do Y'), the worker analyzes the phenomenon and searches the data to establish cause-and-effect relationships. In this way, objects and actions lose their determining force, and workers begin to make sense of the information on the terminal screen. Numbers cease to be mere signs and are transformed into a language of meaning. One worker described this transformation:

> When I used to look at the numbers, I could see the process. But now the numbers talk to me. These numbers are saying 'Hey you might not need that much fuel in the boiler.' That's the kinds of things the numbers are telling me now.

'The numbers talk' when workers make them mean something. Only through the application of intellective skill can people perceive the *meaning* of the data and make conscious and intelligent choices to solve problems or to identify more efficient or effective approaches to the business. The probability that sense making will occur is higher if certain learning conditions are met. Vygotsky found that two of the most important conditions for learning are play and social mediation. These conditions also aid learning in the informated workplace.

'Play' is any behavior that liberates a person from the constraints of objects and actions – behavior that allows a person to create, examine, and redefine meanings. Play leads to learning; it is the pivot from objects and actions to a field of meaning. Initially, play is a recollection and reenactment of real situations but, through the dynamics of imagination and creative thinking, people can remove what John L. Adams calls conceptual blocks – by breaking down the mental walls that prevent them from correctly perceiving a problem or conceiving of its solution. Playful activity lets people approach a situation from different vantage points and increases the likelihood of creative problem solving and innovation. Many workers use play to move from objects and actions to meaning, and they know the value of play in learning. As one worker explained: 'We play around with variables every day . . . [Play] is the most often used learning tool.'

But play has its risks – you can lose the game. Play can shut equipment down and cost the company hundreds, thousands and maybe millions of dollars. Deviation from the rules can have serious consequences for the equipment and process, as well as for the worker. That many workers know that play is serious and has risks is illustrated in the following comment: 'Your level of expertise lets you play. You don't play or fool around if you don't know what you're doing. You have to be competent to fool around.'

The balance between control and play is delicate. But many times 'work' does not allow for any play or even experimentation within the rules. While a manager's demand that workers not play around with the system may be reasonable in a situation of high risk, failure to understand the significance of play can have serious consequences on learning. If opportunities for play are denied, workers probably will not be able to create meaning. When discipline drives out play, workers are likely to develop an 'I'll just do my job' mentality. They may perform the actions necessary to accomplish the work, but may not develop or apply intellective skill to analyze the data and search for new insights. One worker talked about the attitude of indifference that can develop when discipline drives out play:

> I might know it could be better, but I go by the rules. . . . If you don't run by the rules and it screws up, I pay the consequences. Hey, those are the rules, and I just obey the rules. If it costs the company more, well, it's their rules.

But some people are willing to take the risk. In one plant, an expense-tracking system was installed on two machines to give workers information about production costs. Although the system had been billed as a tool for workers, managers were still held accountable for costs and believed that workers did not have the skills to use the technology. The managers imposed strict operating rules for the expense-tracking system, but workers 'played' with it on the graveyard shift – from 10.00 p.m. to 6.00 a.m. – when no managers were around to pressure them. They later presented their discoveries about production costs to managers on the day shift and were equipped with the documentation to back up their suggestions for improvements. To reiterate: play is necessary for the movement from objects and actions to the field of meaning. The challenge for workers and managers is to design learning experiences that minimize risks, encourage imagination, and allow for play.

A second condition for learning is social mediation. Learning is a social experience; it is accomplished through interactions with and assistance from other people. In order to move from objects and actions to meaning, the learner engages in conversation with others to expand his or her boundaries of understanding. In dialogue, ideas and experiences are shared, and the learner poses problems, generates hypotheses, conducts experiments, and reflects on the outcomes. Conversation provides an opportunity for workers to ask 'why' and 'what if' questions. Zuboff described this phenomenon in a discussion of 'the sociality of life at the interface':

> The proper interpretation of information as it appears on a video screen is rarely self-evident. Whenever the viewer perceives something unusual or potentially problematic, there are soon four or five people crowded around the screen, each offering hypotheses and suggesting methods for testing them. In addition, it frequently requires individuals from several disciplines – systems engineers, process operators, instrumentation specialists – to generate the best solutions.

Socially mediated learning often takes place whenever a problem or a crisis arises. Workers gather around the terminal screen to share their experiences and expertise ('What I would do is . . .'), to discuss the interrelationships of process variables ('But if we do that, it will . . .'), to generate hypothetical scenarios ('What would happen if we . . .'), and to point out secondary consequences of proposed actions ('I wouldn't do that because . . .').

Workers also acknowledge times when their collective knowledge is inadequate and someone with a larger repertoire of meanings is required. In the search for meaning, they will sometimes seek out an 'expert' – a person who is capable, knowledgeable, and respected.

> You can work here for years and years and sometimes you can't solve a problem. You exhaust your knowledge and that of your co-workers. That's when you pull your hair out. That's when you need an expert.

In an informed work place, then, the learning process consists of movement and actions and objects ('If X happens, do Y') to the field of meaning ('Why . . . what if?'). If two of the conditions of learning are play and social mediation, do traditional training programs create the conditions necessary for learning intellective skill?

TRADITIONAL TECHNOLOGY TRAINING

The Office of Technology Assessment conducted an in-depth examination of 20 'relatively successful' instructional programs in automated factories. OTA concluded:

> All of the in-plant training programs observed provide job-specific classroom-laboratory training focused on the precise application needs of the plant. . . . In-plant programs are both efficient and effective because they are specifically focused on well-defined application needs.

Typically, training for new technology focuses on precise and well-defined applications. As Arndt Sorge *et al.* explained, training is 'practically oriented and emphasizes the use of equipment'. Instructional programs are designed to provide the 'skills and knowledge required to keep the equipment operating at peak efficiency,' according to Part B of the OTA report.

Training is task-specific, is highly structured, and typically occurs in a classroom setting. Part C of the report described the development of a technology training course in this way:

> The technical specifications written by the engineers were passed along to technical writers. The technical writers developed the technical documentation into a user's manual, written to an eight-grade reading level and broken down into modules, each one covering a specific task. The user manual then became the basis for highly structured lesson plans . . . divided into task modules. . . . Following a 2½-hour terminal operations session, the supervisors trained the workers in precisely those tasks they would be performing.

Thus in typical training courses workers are given information on a 'need to know' basis. They learn just enough about the equipment, the process, and the terminal operations to be able to monitor and control their area of responsibility. Training consists of teaching discrete tasks; its focus is on enhancing an individual's capacity to learn objects and actions. Workers usually learn enough to be able to push buttons, but not enough to be able to push the business. This traditional pedagogy offers little or no opportunity for learning the intellective skill needed to make new meaning out of the data generated by the technology.

An excerpt from the OTA report spoke to the shortcomings of traditional technology training:

They involve us in training – what the new equipment is, what to do to run it. But there's a lot of the theory, the 'whys', the formulae – they don't tell us that. So if a problem happens again, we have to call them to fix it. We don't know why something happened; they didn't educate us. There's no in-depth training. . . . They don't give you the knowledge to think for yourself.

Typically, training is reactive. When the process or the equipment changes, new objects and actions are taught. One worker described training as a reaction to 'trouble':

If the plant is running fine, it's fine. We don't need training resources then. That's management's attitude. When things aren't hunky-dory, they say, 'We need help. We'd better train these folks.' But they don't understand we should have been having training all along. There's always something you can learn, so the resources should be ongoing.

The reaction to 'trouble' usually rehashes the previously taught curriculum – more objects and actions. Seldom is an ongoing, proactive attempt made to provide opportunities for the creation of meaning.

Managers in some plants have recognized the need for ongoing training to increase the knowledge of workers and have designed 'job rotation' or 'cross-skilling' programs in which the worker learns to operate another piece of equipment or to function in a different area in the process. These programs expand the worker's repertoire of objects and actions, but they are of limited value in the informated work place if they do not provide opportunities to learn and use intellective skill.

Traditional training methods are appropriate for teaching people *what* to think. The danger of teaching only objects and actions in an environment of technological change is that workers can become walking encyclopedias of potentially outdated information. If they are to get the most out of informating technologies, people also need to learn *how* to think. Learning how to think means developing the intellective skill required for original, independent problem solving. What pedagogy is necessary to move from the level of objects and actions to the level of meaning?

A PEDAGOGY FOR MEANING

Training for informated workplaces requires a pedagogy – a philosophy of teaching – that creates an environment conducive to the development of intellective skill. A pedagogy for meaning is not a single course or series of training events, but rather involves a reconceptualization of the workplace as a learning environment and a redefinition of the role of manager in the learning process.

An environment of inquiry

In an automated workplace, learning usually begins with ingesting preorganized, predetermined materials and ends with memorizing and regurgitating answers. In contrast, in an informed workplace, there is no end point for learning; more questions can always be asked. Information is a by-product of automation, and it can be continuously reprocessed through dialogue and repackaged as ideas for business improvement.

Inquiry – asking questions – is the first step on the road to creating new meanings and thus new business insights. In an environment of inquiry, people talk to one another and play with ideas. They pose problems, generate hypotheses, test, experiment, and reflect on the outcomes. Questioning information and consciously reflecting on the problem-solving process result in expanded reasoning capabilities.

There are many methods and techniques for problem solving and creative thinking that may be taught in a classroom setting. However, these are of little value if they are taught in a vacuum. Methodologies and techniques cease to constitute inquiry when the teacher is the sole source of problem identification, or when the end product of inquiry (answering) takes precedence over the inquiry process itself (questioning). Situations and information that are real and relevant to the learner are the flesh on the bones of these methodologies. True inquiry is dependent on the motivation and curiosity of the learner, and the best time to learn is at the exact moment when you are faced with a real problem or question.

A pedagogy for meaning focuses on the learner's question and is most concerned with ongoing learning in the natural environment – in this case, the workplace. If 'on-line, interactive *computer* systems' are the buzzwords in the automated workplace, then 'on-line, interactive *learning* systems' should be the buzzwords in the informed workplace. 'On-line' learning means on the job, not just in a formal classroom setting, and 'interactive' learning means dialogue and questions, not lecture and answers.

A pedagogy for meaning does not rigidly adhere to a syllabus or teaching plan. The focus is on the thinking process rather than the curriculum content. What is worth knowing becomes apparent in a very natural way – when a worker is confronted with a problem or has a question. In an environment of inquiry, the question is king and is essential if learning is to occur; therefore, no question is ever irrelevant. As one worker said, 'The only dumb question is the one you didn't ask.'

How can the work environment support inquiry? Some companies, acknowledging that learning is socially mediated, are assigning 'partners' to work together at terminals. In the pursuit of inquiry, people also need access to other resources, either inside or outside the organization; accordingly, a budget for travel to other companies, vendors, or customer organizations may be necessary. The organization also needs to be equipped with a library that makes information and expert knowledge available to workers through a wide variety of media.

Computer technology itself can be a tool for inquiry. For example, computer conferencing is a vehicle for ongoing dialogue either with capable peers or with 'experts' in a particular field of investigation. A computer conference might include an on-line directory of people with special expertise and experience. Computer simulations offer opportunities to play without risk to the business. Well-designed software lets people make conjectures and explore consequences.

Whether people respond to a workplace designed to support inquiry depends largely on the quality of social interactions and attitudes of workers and managers. People must feel free and be eager to ask questions and must demonstrate a willingness to share their knowledge. As one worker put it:

> You should learn with people. 'Let's put our heads together to see what we can do.' That's what we should say. That way, if a person isn't here, the others can handle the problem because they've been taught, they know it from experience. We get other people's experience when we work problems together. You should teach everybody what you know – keep passing the knowledge around.

In an environment where 'you should teach everybody what you know,' what is the appropriate role of a manager?

The manager of inquiry

The beliefs, attitudes, and behaviors of the manager are at the heart of the environment of inquiry. Within a pedagogy for meaning, a manager creates opportunities for learning and becomes an active participant in it. The manager of inquiry encourages people to ask questions and creates an environment in which intellectual play and socially mediated learning are necessary and legitimate components of work.

How does the manager of inquiry function? Workers have described a 'special' manager to me as 'somebody who listens . . . asks me what I think . . . helps me solve problems . . . explains things to me . . . makes me understand . . . makes me think.' Workers respect and seek out such managers because they help them sharpen their intellective skill. Workers can readily approach managers of inquiry to ask questions and test their hypotheses. Typically, such encounters begin with a worker using one of the following conversational openings:

- Can we do . . .?
- How does this work?

- I was thinking about something last night; let me tell you and see what you think.
- I don't understand . . .
- The only explanation I can think of is . . .
- Somebody told me . . . Is that right?

A manager of inquiry deals patiently and thoroughly with all such questions and pushes workers' thinking by listening to their ideas and probing their logic. The manager rarely *tells* workers outright what they want to know, but uses questions to open them to new possibilities. There is a conscious focus on the process of problem solving, not answer giving, because 'answers' can often foreclose further learning. The manager facilitates, nurtures, and leverages the knowledge that people at the point of production already have, and encourages them to become independent thinkers capable of judging the integrity and quality of their own ideas without the presence of an 'authority.'

One of the most important characteristics of a manager of inquiry is humility. Arrogance, whether it stems from the manager's personality or position in the hierarchy, destroys the environment of inquiry. In *Pedagogy of the Oppressed*, Paulo Friere wrote:

> Dialogue cannot exist without humility. . . . Dialogue, as the encounter of men addressed to the common task of learning and acting, is broken if the parties (or one of them) lack humility. How can I dialogue if I always project ignorance onto others and never perceive my own? . . . How can I dialogue if I consider myself a member of the in-group of 'pure' men, the owners of truth and knowledge, for whom all non-members are 'these people' or 'the great unwashed'? How can I dialogue if I am closed to – and even offended by – the contribution of others? . . . Men who lack humility (or have lost it) . . . cannot be partners in naming the world.

A manager of inquiry does not hold a paternalistic view of teacher/student relationships; instead, he or she is an equal partner in the learning process. Managers of inquiry learn with, rather than teach to, workers.

A manager can be evaluated in part by his or her ability to create an environment of inquiry – to facilitate workers' thinking and their contributions to the business. One manager described this role and a reward system based on the ability to 'develop' people:

> My real job is providing leadership . . . to create an environment that supports people and maximizes their contributions. My job is developing people. Managers who can leverage their effectiveness should get rewarded. It would be worth X if you can turn out [business] results, but it would be worth a lot more, X times some number, if you get others to increase their contribution to the business.

How does a manager know if he or she is creating an environment of inquiry in which people can learn and grow? It is not easy to see such a process in action, so how can it be evaluated? Success can best be measured by the behavioral changes observed in workers. Workers in such an environment ask more questions and more cogent questions. They feel free to challenge assertions made by other workers or managers and can clearly articulate the reasoning behind their challenges. They reject answers that in any way resemble 'because we've always done it that way.' They are more willing to listen to others and suspend judgments when they have insufficient data – and they easily modify or otherwise change their position when the data warrant it. 'Changing one's mind' not only is regarded as legitimate, but is interpreted as a sign of growing competence.

The focus on meaning makes it necessary to reconceptualize the workplace as an environment of inquiry and to redefine roles so that managers and workers become partners in an ongoing learning process. With this approach, the probability that the usefulness of information technology will be maximized is substantially higher.

'Environment of inquiry' and 'manager of inquiry' are the cornerstones of a pedagogy for meaning. For organizations that choose to emphasize the informating capacities of computer technology, the challenge will be to continue to develop this philosophy and to identify organizational dynamics that impede or prevent them.

OBSTACLES

There are some brick walls in 'traditional' organizations that can stop a pedagogy for meaning dead in its tracks. An examination of traditional roles and reward systems and their impact on learning can provide insight into the problem and create an awareness of potential obstacles.

Roles

The traditional control model of work-force management described by Richard Walton can heavily influence the opportunity to learn. In this model managers exercise top-down control, seeking subordinates' conformity to their views. Typically, their interactions with workers are concerned with objects and actions – 'Do this . . . do that.' Many of the workers I interviewed expressed frustration with these management declaratives:

> Managers will never ask you if you think that's what should be done or if you have any ideas.

> Managers are not there to ask you what you want to do; they're there to pull you along with a rope.

Managers don't give their expertise to the worker, they give orders.

Declarations or commands can produce action without meaning. A command may be a missed opportunity to allow the worker to articulate his or her own rationale for action. Sometimes managers ask workers to explain the rationale behind their actions, but managerial tone and intent may transform what could have been an inquiry in the pursuit of learning into an inquisition. One worker said: 'It's their [managers'] tone and approach. They don't work problems out with us, they argue. They don't listen, they just get their point across and then cuss us out.' Inquiries become inquisitions when managers ask 'questions' that end with exclamation points instead of question marks. Exclamation points and hostile or challenging tones can turn a potential learning situation into a performance appraisal and thus destroy the opportunity to create an environment of inquiry.

Traditional top-down organizations depend on a historical association between power and hierarchical status that presumes deference to a person in a 'higher' position. A worker described the unwritten rule of deference and obedience: 'Never argue with a manager, no matter how stupid he sounds. Just go on and do it. Agree with him like hell!' Workers who learn to suppress their views and ideas simply don't question the manager – because 'that's the boss.' In a context in which inquiry is considered to be a sign of worker incompetence or defiance, most workers, rather than take a risk, remain silent.

On the other hand, inquiry, which is critical to the creation of meaning, depends on people who are not eager to automatically agree with, submit to, or passively accept the ideas of others. Traditional roles can be counterproductive in an informated workplace, because unilateral authority can impede learning. An environment of inquiry challenges the habits of authority and deference, of imperatives and silence.

Rewards

In addition to traditional roles, formal and informal reward systems may also be obstacles to a pedagogy for meaning. This brick wall is built of the things for which people are punished and rewarded.

For example, pressure can be a powerful deterrent to learning. One worker offered an example of how his peers discouraged him in his pursuit of learning: 'You can't talk to managers because that's "brown-nosing." So now I go about it differently – I go to books, not to managers. You can't "brown-nose" a book.'

Another worker was preparing for a test, the results of which would determine whether he would move to a higher labor and pay grade. He described his attempts to share his new learning with his peers:

I got a copy of the questions on the test to study. I answered all the questions [for the test] and wrote a book with the answers in it. I wanted to share it with the others so they could learn, and I thought I could learn it better by teaching them. They said, 'I don't want to hear that!' They didn't even ask to see the book.

Peer punishment for doing 'better' is at least as old as work itself. Taylorism, with its time-study methods and piece rates, created 'rate busters.' Those who, sometimes unwittingly, cross certain boundaries are typically pulled aside by co-workers and told the rules of the game – 'Don't run too fast; don't produce too much.' The fear is that if one person outperforms the rest, management will begin to expect more from everyone. With new technology this peer culture often persists, but now it is the quality of effort, rather than the quantity of output, that is being contested. One manager expressed belief that the rate-buster phenomenon is at work in the automated factory:

It's like the old union days and workers who operated machines manually. They took enthusiastic people aside and said, 'You don't do that here.' Only it's a more modern approach now; it's more subtle, but that pressure is still there.

In an informed environment, the issue is no longer how much you *do*, but how much you *think*. As one worker said, 'I'm not going to bust my brain, I'm just going to do my job.' The phrases that intellective rate busters hear are, 'Don't learn too much; don't get too smart.'

Workers who want to maintain the status quo are not alone. Managers who do not understand learning and their role in it can also squelch it. Punishment, whether in the form of peer pressure or manager reprimand, will inhibit intellective skill development.

Why would some managers discourage workers from learning? Typically, managers are rewarded for their individual expertise, for having the answers. They are more often rewarded for possessing knowledge than for distributing it. These comments from workers support this idea:

Managers are the technical experts; it's been that way for 30 years. It seems management is afraid we'll learn too much.

Managers want job security, too. They could say, 'I'll teach you all I know,' but then they're afraid they won't have anything to do.

And one manager agreed:

Some managers perceive workers who have information as a threat. I'd love workers to have information to run the day-to-day business so I could work on long-range planning. But managers are afraid of not being the 'experts' – they're used to having everyone come to them and ask questions. All of their time is consumed in fire fighting.

Many formal and informal reward systems are based on traditional roles and do not support inquiry. Rewards are commonly associated with recognition, promotions, and pay increases. That said, the fact remains that opportunities for creating meaning can also be rewarding to managers and workers. Learning can be its own reward, and working in an environment of inquiry can be rewarding in and of itself. A manager spoke about intrinsic rewards: 'You know what really makes me feel good about my job? I have the most fun when workers ask me questions I don't have the answers to. That's exciting, because we all get to learn new things.' However, it would be naive to assume that the intrinsic rewards of learning are enough. Designing formal reward systems that stimulate, encourage, and recognize inquiry and learning is also essential in the informated work place.

SUMMARY

When the focus of technology is on automation, it may be reasonable to have training programs that merely teach workers the objects and actions necessary for them to respond to smart machines. However, as the OTA report clearly points out, 'There is uncertainty about how current instructional programs should be revised or expanded.' This uncertainty comes from the informating function of the technology. As one manager said: 'Our competition can buy the same black boxes that we can. Our future depends on how well our people use the information generated by that technology.'

When the informating quality of the technology is recognized, the importance of smart people becomes apparent. Traditional training, with its focus on objects and actions, is not enough. In the informated environment, on-line, interactive learning is necessary if people are to create new meanings out of the information generated by computer technology.

A pedagogy for meaning is a collective enterprise that can unleash individual and organizational energy in an informated workplace. It has implications for (1) rethinking traditional worker-training and management-education programs, (2) transforming the workplace into a learning environment, (3) reconceptualizing the roles of workers and managers so that they can become partners in creating meaning, and (4) designing rewards for people who create and participate in an environment of inquiry.

A pedagogy for meaning is concerned with people's learning how to learn. A work force that has learned how to learn is one of the most important competitive levers an organization can have in an environment of ongoing technological change.

SELECTED BIBLIOGRAPHY

Three documents generated by the Office of Technology Assessment provided background information for this chapter. The first, published in April 1984 and titled *Computerized Manufacturing Automation: Employment, Education, and the Workplace*, is referred to as the OTA report. The second document, *OTA Working Papers, Part B: Final Report: Education and Training Case Study Series* (June 1984), is referred to as Part B. The third document, *OTA Working Papers Part C: Individual Education and Training Case Studies, C 11* (June 1984), is called Part C in this chapter. All three documents were published by the US Congress, Office of Technology Assessment.

Lev S. Vygotsky's theories on learning can be found in *Mind and Society* (Harvard University Press, 1978). John L. Adams's explanation of how mental blocks are broken down may be found in *Conceptual Blockbusting* (Stanford Alumni Association, 1974).

The description of workers' strategies for getting around managers to use a computerized expense-tracking system comes from Gloria Schuck Bronsema and Shoshana Zuboff's case study, 'The Expense Tracking System at Tiger Creek' (Harvard Business School, 1984). Shoshana Zuboff's article, 'Technologies that Informate: Implications for Human Resource Management in the Computerized Industrial Workplace' (in *Human Resource Management: Trends and Challenges*, edited by R. Walton and P. Lawrence, Harvard Business School Press, 1985), explains why the informating aspect of technology will create vast changes in the way in which people think, work, and are managed.

Arndt Sorge *et al.*'s book, *Microelectronics and Manpower in Manufacturing* (Gower, 1983), discusses how people are trained on new equipment. Richard Walton's control model of management is described in 'From Control to Commitment in the Workplace' (*Harvard Business Review*, March–April 1985).

The need for nontraditional methods of teaching is not unique to the manufacturing milieu. For discussions on teaching and learning about technology in the banking industry, see Gloria Schuck Bronsema's 'Education and Technical Change in the Corporate Context' (Graduate School of Education, Harvard University, 1983), and Bronsema and Peter G. W. Keen's 'Education Intervention and Implementation in MIS' (*Sloan Management Review*, Summer 1983). For more on nontraditional philosophies of teaching, see Paulo Friere's *Pedagogy of the Oppressed* (Herder & Herder, 1972) and Neil Postman and Charles Weingartner's *Teaching as a Subversive Activity* (Dell Publishing, 1969). These two books give an alternative vision, in a more global framework, of what the nature and purpose of teaching should be; Friere's book is considered to be a classic in this area.

Chapter 12

Product development in Ford of Europe
Undoing the past/learning the future

Ken Starkey and Alan McKinlay

Ford is one of the world's largest and most successful corporations. It is associated historically with the development of a distinctive approach to management which bears its name, Fordism, and which some theorists (for example, Piore and Sabel, 1984) argue is *the* typical Western management approach. Fordism is synonymous with 'machine bureaucracy' (Mintzberg, 1983; Morgan, 1986), complex hierarchies organized functionally with top-down decision-making and cost reduction pursued as the main source of competitive advantage so that innovation is sacrificed in favour of efficiency. This model of strategy and organization has proved increasingly dysfunctional.

Western managers have turned to Japan for lessons in world-class manufacturing and for an alternative management system. It is in the auto industry that the effect of Japanese competition has had the most far-reaching ramifications and Ford has led the way in responding to this threat. It has been praised as the Western company most advanced in its efforts to introduce 'lean production', Japan's 'secret weapon' in what has been termed a 'global auto war' (Womack *et al.*, 1990).

Much of the organizational learning at Ford in the 1980s focused on understanding the Japanese challenge. This involved the company's managers in a searching analysis of accepted managerial practice in the company which led to a gradual 'unlearning' of its past competences and to the learning of new modes of managerial behaviour. Ford, therefore, provides a leading example of learning from Japan. Holding a 25 per cent equity stake in the Japanese automobile company Mazda has given it a rare window onto the sources of Japanese competitive advantage.

In this chapter we focus upon product development in Ford of Europe during the 1980s and into the 1990s. Product development includes product planning, car engineering and design. It covers all the activities between the identification of new product concepts through market research, the planning of products to the completed design for production. In Ford of Europe, Product Development – the functional group – 'took the lead in organizational experimenting' during the 1980s. Our analysis is based upon a case study of Ford which itself is based upon extensive interviewing of Ford managers (see Starkey and McKinlay, 1993, for complete details of the study).[1]

The process of engineering an object as complex as today's motor-car demands enormous effort from large numbers of people with a broad range of skills. Mass-production companies have typically tried to solve the complexity problem by finely dividing labour among many engineers with highly specialized expertises (Womack *et al.*, 1990: 63ff). Fordism led to progressive specialization not only of production functions but of knowledge work in product design and development – product engineers specialized in engines, bodies, suspension, electrical systems, even door-handle technology. This replaced the skilled machine-shop owners and the old-fashioned factory foremen of the earlier craft era.

> Those worker-managers had done it all – contracted with the assembler, designed the part, developed a machine to make it, and, in many cases, supervised the operation of the machine in the workshop. The fundamental mission of these new specialists, by contrast, was to design tasks, parts, and tools that could be handled by the unskilled workers who made up the bulk of the new motor-vehicle industry work force.
>
> (Womack *et al.*, 1990: 32–33)

Traditional product development in Ford is described by Don Frey (1991), Vice-President of Product Development at Ford in the 1960s. Frey is highly critical of what was in his time at Ford the 'normal' approach to product development, a process controlled by 'a centralized industrial research organization, typically far-removed from both operations and market' with the 'bean-counters' (Ford's finance staff) the ultimate arbiter of investment decisions (Frey, 1991: 47). As a result quality frequently suffered in the trade-off with cost. Frey illustrates this point in a description of a new car development.

> The quality problems were overwhelming. Someone had to 'dry the car up' – which meant stop it from leaking oil all over the place. I was that someone.
>
>   We attacked the power steering pump, which one of the old hands said was 'a piece of junk.' When I asked how it got that way, he said the 'bean counters' had taken a dime of cost out of assembly each year. I said 'fix it' – and we did. I wondered (in my naivete) how financial planners could have anything to say about the matter in the first place. A bean counter's idea of cost control, I surmised, was to take an inch off the tail pipe every year.
>
> (Frey, 1991: 48)

Finance was not the only function to blame. Research and Development (R&D) people refused to leave the 'lab' and were 'snobbish' about the sales force. So divorced were the design engineers that 'they wouldn't know a customer if they tripped over one'. Senior executives were pre-occupied with political power games. Frey is particularly critical of linear thinking about product innovation which assumes that product development should take place in a staged process in which a breakthrough is made in R&D which is then passed on to be 'reduced' to practice through engineering, manufacture then sales, in that order. A linear process of this kind, he argues, is inherently inefficient because it takes too much time and is prone to failure. It also invites resistance because it tries to work across strong functional barriers, thus threatening to disrupt the power politics of the organization.

Overseeing product development were the architects of the 'total discipline' of the process, the cost analysis experts, whose task was to judge the quality of a component, the most efficient way of producing it and what it would cost. These were the 'high priests' of the old approach. New ideas were treated with 'a scepticism elevated into a system, a Cartesian philosophy anglo-saxon style' (Seidler, 1976: 23) and seldom survived the piercing analysis of the financial equivalent of the test crash at 30 m.p.h. The 'normal' outcome was that innovation crumpled on impact!

Looking back on this approach one older Ford manager commented upon the 'incredible rigidity of this highly compartmentalised design process: even minor changes to single components could take several years: it took just as long to change a door lock as it does to change half a car'. Engineers became extremely specialized. Another manager described the situation in the following terms:

> We had a very strong functional engineering tradition. You had guys at the bottom of the pile engineering individual components like door latches, or rear light fittings, or bumpers. So the whole thing was atomized rather like Henry Ford atomized the production process. So we atomized the engineering process. You'd get these component engineers who'd spent their whole life just engineering these bits, never involved in engineering a car, always just bits of a car.

The crucial emphasis in the system was a concern with control: the system developed 'a design and release manual which included every engineer in the building so that he knew who to blame. You knew who designed the door-lock and on which side of the car. That was the heyday of the hire-and-fire organization.' The system developed the search for the quality into a science.

> The boxes on the organization chart had a double purpose: for the individual they provided the certainty of task and responsibility; for the manager it meant he knew who to kick hardest.

What was lost in this preoccupation with internal control was the product and the customer. As one Ford manager put it:

> while we're doing business with each other the Japanese are getting new products to market.

INSIGHT – STRUCTURE AND PROCESS

1984 was a dismal financial year for Ford of Europe. The core automotive business barely broke even, despite the highest market share ever. Fixed costs were high and marketing expenses 'extraordinary' as the company fought to maintain market share. This was the trigger for a sweeping examination of the company's strategic vision. Product Development led the way in experimenting with a new approach with the 'Insight' project. This comprised interviews with over 200 people within Ford to find out what they considered Ford did well, what they could do better and where change was needed. The Insight project team also talked to people from product development in other companies, most importantly in Mazda.

The message from Insight was a strong indictment of existing best practice. It was summarized in the report as follows:

> increased efficiency can only be achieved by better utilization of available talent through improved teamwork. In our strongly functional organization these improvements require the elimination of artificial barriers to communication and in their place must come a stronger focus on, and identification with, the product and the 'customer'. To facilitate these changes some organization restructuring is needed in order to build cross-functional, multi-discipline teams dedicated to product programs. The organizational change is a means to an end, not an end in itself. Improved efficiencies will result from more delegation, development of broader skills and the substitution of a 'not invented here' attitude by supportive team-goal oriented behaviour.

The comparison with Mazda was crucial to Insight's findings. In Ford of Europe, the project team concluded, there was much evidence of poor communications and inefficiency, due mainly to the 'system' according to which things 'must be done'. The system's formal control was actually dysfunctional in creating blockages in information flow and blockages between different groups who should have been working together: 'Procedure sometimes takes precedence over problem solving.' Mazda, by comparison, had organizational arrangements that functioned smoothly to foster swift flexible responses, employees were involved in making decisions through consensus, and top management was committed to delegating decision-making to the relevant working groups.

Mazda was characterized as having an 'environment of harmony', based on participative management and employee involvement, Ford by an 'environment of competition'. The outcome was a three-fold productivity advantage over Western firms. For Ford managers accustomed to the ubiquity of immutable hierarchies – to 'thinking structurally' – one of the most disconcerting aspects of Mazda organization was that Japanese managers expected to work in flexible and transient project-based teams rather than fixed positions, and 'there was no embarrassment about being a minister without portfolio'.

Product Development's proposed solution to Ford's emerging problems involved a move to a form of matrix management encompassing vehicle design, planning and finance product functions in which the key unit of organization was product development program teams. Program management is defined as

> the process which frames all of the events of the product development process which are dedicated to a specific product program. This process deals with setting and achieving the overall product and timing objectives.

Program management using matrix structures is seen as the necessary antidote to and replacement for the traditional sequential functional approach and as a major step forward in product development 'because it allows us breadth, to carry a portfolio of projects simultaneously, not just one at a time, sequentially'. Two managerial roles were seen as crucial to making program management work – those of functional managers and program managers. Program managers are concerned with meeting 'mission objectives' for a vehicle based on technical, cost and timing targets. Functional managers are concerned with the skills aspect of the program. Their role is to provide people with the appropriate skills to achieve the program's mission. Open communication and information-sharing is seen as essential to achieve mission goals. It is seen as particularly important that variance from plans is surfaced early in the decision-making process. Problem-solving is based on consensus seeking within the parameters for decision-making set by the mission. Process management is geared to positive conflict resolution and the eradication of the negative effects of politics, personalities and win–lose games. Fundamental to success with this approach is a high level of mutual trust, confidence and respect. 'Achieving these ends is perhaps the most significant challenge facing a traditional, bureaucratic organization' (Hopeman, 1989 – external consultant report on the implementation of matrix management).

The goal is for program directors to determine what needs to be done, and when it should be done and the functional managers determine how the tasks should be done, and who should do the tasks. The role of functional management is to provide people with experience, knowledge and skills to support the program director in achieving the mission of the program. Program managers will have an 'integrative', 'mission driven' role. Budgeting previously done by functional unit needs to be transferred to the program team which can contract in functional services. Senior management has to learn how to really devolve responsibility: 'once decisions are made by senior management at a particular point, then the authority and responsibility is delegated to others until the next review point'. The rotation of people between project teams and functional teams serves to avoid the handover problems of 'not invented here' and the movement of managers between project and functional offices for development and career succession purposes.

Restructuring is a typical Ford response to uncertainty.

> In Ford traditionally there's a structural change to meet any and every crisis. We use an organization change as a device to bring about a change in the way we work. It was, in effect, a case of structural change as a substitute for process change.

However, Product Development linked change in organizational structure to the need to develop a new style of management. Process intervention followed, with a workshop for senior management spearheaded by a group of external management consultants geared to enabling teams to function in the new matrix structure (Mumford and Honey, 1986). The goal was the creation of a 'we agree' rather than an 'I tell' decision-making process and culture. In particular the organization learnt that

> the matrix is not an organization, it's not an amended version of the Ford system: it's an enabling mechanism to help the social processes of management. We wanted to change the way we worked together, not the way we directed each other. We're trying to get away from the formal system, the man in the box mentality.

Survival was now seen as depending upon a better quality product and 'more product engineering for less engineering cost'. Overall program mission goals relate to the design, development, manufacturing, sales and service of vehicles. The mission is to design vehicles which can be successfully engineered and manufactured efficiently, 'not just aesthetic masterpieces', to develop new technologies that are marketable not just technically interesting, to engineer vehicles to meet or exceed customer expectations which include quality and reasonable cost, and to manufacture vehicles that are 'good' not merely 'good enough', thus leading not just to satisfied customers but to customers who become repeat purchasers of Ford products and recommend them to others. Underpinning program management is the notion of 'unity':

> Where [program management] is successful there will be a unity in the

vehicle which is evident to everyone: designer, engineer, manufact-urer, sales person, and service personnel. Most importantly, unity in the vehicle will be evident to the customer. Their satisfaction is the fundamental key to the current and future success of Ford Motor Company.

CULTURE CHANGE

The next step was for the rest of Ford of Europe to become convinced that program management was the path to follow. However, this was resisted by Manufacturing. As one manager in Manufacturing described it, using the Ford metaphor of the chimney to describe the irreconcilable divide between different functional groups:

> Because it wasn't invented here, it didn't get any support at all, in fact, quite the reverse. It became a dirty word. It was part of the chimney getting stronger. This was an early attempt to break down the wall of a chimney and it had the opposite effect. It became reinforced. Purely for reasons that it wasn't invented here. And so it worked in PD but it didn't blossom to its full flower.

In a functionally focused organization, operating in a culture where total company objectives are sometimes obscured by the objectives of indi-vidual functions, Ford was grappling with two linked approaches:

- To create cross-functional teams where joint objectives are to address product design and manufacturing issues.
- To define precisely the various development steps and responsibilities.

The problem was that the means of achieving these objectives had yet to become clear. Further learning was necessary.

Major problems post-Insight concerned the lack of clarity of team responsibilities and conflicts between team and existing organizational objectives. The resource demands to support what was seen as incre-mental work seemed exorbitant in some quarters. And there was the added difficulty of actually defining the myriad interfaces between the various functional organizations, particularly Product Development and Manufacturing. There were inevitably conflicting objectives between organizations whose mission definition was functionally based. This, an outcome of the old organizational chimneys, was accepted by Product Development as the real difficulty in its dealings with Manufacturing.

> This, by virtue of management performance and reward/punishment systems that focus sharply on individual, measurable goals, causes the behaviour of leaders of the existing functional organization to be mutu-ally antagonistic. Over time, this behaviour can become a sub-culture

of the two organizations. Attempts to address this problem, including team-building, management behaviour modification and more shared objectives, can go some way towards reducing the organizational conflicts, but the fundamental cultural shifts required to overcome it are long lead and uncertain.

As an aid to understanding the change process it was negotiating, Product Development, with the help of an external consultant, developed a map of the journey it needed to make. The evolution to full program management was seen as a series of seven evolutionary phases. In phase 1, the traditional approach to organization is perceived as problematic. The key issues emerge as the dysfunctional effects of hierarchy, bureaucracy, autocracy, functional myopia and a preoccupation with territorial boundaries. In phase 2 the organization attempts to develop informal ways of coping with these problems, primarily informal team ways of working to promote flexibility and adaptiveness. As a result major issues of authority and responsibility begin to surface. Phase 3 sees the development of more formal arrangements to address these issues. New forms of organization and management are developed, such as program management. A major problem at this stage remains the issue of responsibility/authority. In particular the new program managers 'become concerned about having a lot of responsibility without commensurate authority'. In phase 4, the desired authority shifts finally begin to occur:

> The organization becomes more accustomed to teams, and engages more consistently in participative decision making. The authority to acquire needed resources shifts to the program managers. There are several consequences of this shift which must be resolved regarding authority, responsibility, reward systems, and mechanisms for conflict resolution.

In phase 5 functional units, the previous repositories of power, become 'resource pools' as projects become the key organizational entity. Functional units now become 'the repository of knowledge, skill, experience, and judgment which may be drawn upon to meet program requirements'. In phase 6 program managers become responsible for the management of resources over the life cycles of multiple programs. The key issue now is the balancing of these multiple programs and the efficient allocation of limited resources to their mutual advantage. In phase 7 'the programs flow through the organization, their life cycles balanced. The organization emerges as flexible, adaptive, and mission driven. The organization climate exhibits high degrees of cooperation and integration.' According to a Ford product development manager:

> If your manager starts thinking about totality then we can change the culture.

The legacy of Insight was a measure of culture change but there remained considerable confusion over roles and responsibilities during the attempts to implement program management, leading to problems of 'allegiance'. Program directors complained that the members of their team, drawn from functional organizations, 'cannot deliver their organization' and that they 'only serve as representatives of the functional area'. Another problem to emerge was the lack of a pool of experienced program managers and a turnover of staff that affects program continuity. There was also the problem of a reward structure which was ambivalent in whether it favours functional allegiance or program commitment. This creates tensions in performance appraisal – should it reflect functional or program achievements or some form of combination of the two? Senior management found it a problem stepping back from the day-to-day decision-making arena. The shift of authority from functional manager to program manager remained incomplete. Program managers, crucial players in the new approach, felt that they had considerable responsibility for their programs but insufficient authority to get resources to support their programs. This reflects the problem of shifting authority from functional managers toward the program directors.

SIMULTANEOUS ENGINEERING

The dysfunctions of Ford's product development system again came under the spotlight in a searching report of the late 1980s (the Simultaneous Engineering Study). This study, conducted in 1989, was led by the Vice-President of Manufacturing. His brief was to: 'Recommend changes necessary to facilitate the aims of best product/best process/first time by simultaneous planning and thinking'. For Ford the acceleration of the product development cycle had become a major strategic concern:

> We're talking about survival. It's not about taking two months out of the cycle time, it's much more than that. It's about achieving a quantum leap: we need to take eighteen months out of the cycle time to be competitive. And we can't do that by putting more committees in place. We have to say, 'Stand back, it's fundamental change.' You get small efficiencies by evolutionary change but to get the quantum leap you've got to do something completely different. The Simultaneous Engineering Study team is a concrete manifestation of the company saying, 'Let's stand back and look what's going to get us the quantum leap in organizational process time.'

Simultaneous engineering reflects a growing manufacturing trend, the shift from purely functional forms of organization to more integrated structures (Clark and Fujimoto, 1991: 103). As such it represents a move beyond matrix forms of coordination to actual structural integration of previously separate functional groups, namely Product Development and Manufacturing. The new approach emphasizes communication.

> The distinction between Engineering as we understand it today, (sequential Product and Manufacturing Engineering), and Simultaneous Engineering, is that communication has to be simultaneous, not sequential nor sporadic. Communication is the key to improved relationships and performance at all levels throughout the organizations.
>
> (Clark and Fujimoto, 1991: 103)

The process of product development involves continuous communication from the initial customer requirements fed into the company, through to the complete vehicle delivered to customer requirements. The effectiveness of simultaneity of product and process engineering – working on product and process design in parallel – is dependent upon communication, cooperation and skill (technical and social).

> The parallel approach . . . heightens the importance of coordination and communication between product and process engineering. Product engineering must comprehend implications of their designs for manufacturability, and process engineering must clarify constraints and opportunities in the process and develop a good measure of flexibility to cope with the changes inherent in the product design process. Though it can be a source of improved product quality and lower costs, emphasis on manufacturability without flexibility in the attitudes and skills of process engineers can negatively affect a product's competitiveness. Process engineers dream of product engineers who take manufacturability fully into account in the early stages of development and then freeze the design. But paraphrasing what one process engineer said of this dream: 'If the voice of manufacturing dominates product design, the car may be great in the factory but a dog in the market.'
>
> (Clark and Fujimoto, 1991: 123–124)

Program management had allowed engineering activities to find a better fit of their component efforts into the total vehicle. The extensive use of product-line-focused functional working groups in the matrix structure to communicate and integrate the efforts of various component areas had been effective but it had also increased the number of dedicated coordination resources and non-dedicated time commitment. Program management, the study group concluded, was still some way from realizing its potential due to insufficient isolation of dedicated resources to major programs, especially early in the process, and because of 'a multitude of demanding near-term problems and minor programs'.

Companies successfully using simultaneous engineering possess these features:

- Educational focus on cross-disciplines.
- Geographic co-location for easy communications.
- Reward/incentive systems that rely on team performance vs. individual performance.
- Strong culturally-based sense of interdependence.
- Highly disciplined engineering processes.
- Considerable reliance on *ad hoc* meetings and teams as well as more formal cross-functional teams.

There was no reason why Ford of Europe could not, in theory, achieve all of the above conditions except perhaps those associated with the external Japanese culture. However, in practice, the study argued, Ford at present had very few of the above characteristics. It was also questionable, given the serious competitive deficiency of its total program process versus the Japanese, if it was making the necessary pace of improvement. To implement simultaneous engineering, further cultural change was required involving management leadership, good communication, skilful management of organizational change, and 'training on how to make it happen'.

In the Simultaneous Engineering Study Japan again provided the main point of critical comparison. Mazda, Toyota and Honda were identified as leaders in product development.

> All three companies adopt a structured process for their product programs. The program director works with the functional area to reach a clear understanding on who will contribute what at each point in the program and in this way they construct a structured work plan. This identified the level of achievement which must be reached by the functional area at each stage of the program and becomes the basis for the functional areas to plan their work and control the outcome. In this process the program director acts as a catalyst, one who communicates and coordinates to ensure that the efforts of the functional areas are synchronized.

In Ford, program management (PM) had been implemented in Product Development only. (The study found that Product Development managers were more convinced that PM had become 'embedded in its structure and culture' and that 'participative decision-making at executive level is proven and firmly established'. These views were not shared by Manufacturing.) In Japanese companies program management was company-wide. (Of Ford's European competitors, Opel too had company-wide program management with cross-functional project teams but no formal matrix structure.) Mazda introduced program management into Product Development in 1975 and extended it to embrace Manufacturing in 1979. Mazda also had Product and Manufacturing Engineering on one site with a manufacturing plant. Some Japanese companies had functional organizations but they also had structured cross-functional training and a relatively unitary, integrated company culture.

The Japanese companies have distinctly separate Product Development and Manufacturing Engineering organizational divisions. They rely, very successfully, to judge from results, on their company culture of teamwork, dedication and personal relationships and on Program Management teams to avoid 'chimney' issues with this approach.

Mazda stressed the importance of four factors of successful simultaneous engineering:

Communication	– Co-location, classmates, joint social evenings, to link Product Development/Manufacturing.
Formal cooperation	– Team meetings. Joint Product/Manufacturing management meetings, cross-functional career move planning.
Team culture	– Family loyalty, human values, shared responsibility.
Customer-driven	– Establish process customer relations and agree what is needed.

Simultaneous engineering needs a background of 'suitable conditions'. Mazda enhances communication through a 'classmate system' of recruitment, hiring people from same school or university into interfacing organizations to improve cooperation across functional boundaries. Informal meetings (such as drinking parties) are encouraged to foster team building. In Mazda there is 'No one is a Big Boss', a stark contrast to Mazda's view of the Western firms being over-dependent on the 'Big Boss, with great authority'. In Mazda a leader is not expected to be perfect. All involved in the team share responsibility in an atmosphere of mutual respect. Many joint meetings serve to foster a 'buy-in' philosophy. Every member of the team has full responsibility for the team's success with freedom to criticize and a responsibility to improve.

The power/authority of the program director is an important issue in the Simultaneous Engineering Report. Mazda's view was that the program director is 'powerless'. His main job is to keep channels of communication open. The clear definition of program tasks, including timing and responsibility, which the Japanese achieve at program inception through participation with the functional areas, provides the work plan against which the functional areas themselves can carry out their work and report any off-standard event likely to cause delay and consequently needing management attention. Ford signalled this as a characteristic they should seek to emulate:

The product development process is like Kanban the production process, a self regulating process giving visible control at all times and greatest opportunity for improvement because problems are found and fixed, not concealed and ignored. In such a well regulated environment, power for the program director is irrelevant. There is need to achieve this culture change in Ford. Extend Program Management to Manufacturing and Sales/Marketing.

In Mazda cross-functional training supports this environment. The company's basic training philosophy is summed up as follows:

The Company conducts education and training which it considers necessary for character-building, knowledge acquisition and skill learning of the employees. The upper echelon of employees shall participate actively in the education and training programs and give guidance to the subordinates and junior workers in their respective workplaces.

The study team concluded that fundamental organizational and geographic changes were required to accelerate the process changes that Ford was trying to make. It recommended the extension of program management to include Marketing, Manufacturing and Supply and the need for greater involvement of functional chiefs to resolve areas of conflict with Program Office. There was also a need for stronger leadership of programs to generate early consensus on product and technology strategies. This required Manufacturing involvement from concept stage.

Separate vehicle programs were seen as the means to provide strong, company-wide, product-focused leadership to the Vehicle and Powertrain Divisions through matrix management. The Vehicle Program activity should be separate because:

- Vehicle Division would become too large and dominant if it incorporated Vehicle Programs, and this in turn might lead to a dilution of management focus between manufacturing efficiency and future programs.
- There is a risk that Vehicle Division could over-value internal constraints (e.g. existing facilities versus customers' needs) and less risk that a separate Vehicle Program area would do this.

A vehicle program focus gives a balance so that no single activity can be dominant, with Vehicle Engineering, Design and Finance equally charged with providing services to the program directors for their functions. The matrix structure provides the mechanism to integrate Vehicle Division and Powertrain Division by Vehicle Program with the integration of product and manufacturing engineering activities to the greatest practicable degree in order to eliminate or reduce conflicts caused by differing objectives, to encourage efficient early and informal communications and reduce the complexity of technical interfaces. The extended program management matrix gives responsibility for resolving conflict to the program director who can go to the level of Vice-President as a last resort.

The study group recommendation constituted major surgery. In the words of former Ford of Europe Chairman, Lindsey Halstead,

> We recut the organization which had traditionally been Manufact-uring and PD [Product Development], we sliced it and we took the two heads and said 'You take the vehicle engineering side of the business and you take the production side' and we took the other guy and said 'You take the powertrain and transmission and engines and the manu-facturing'; we also gave him program management responsibility. [The Simultaneous Engineering] study said 'Make three legs, Program Management in the centre, Vehicle and Powertrain'. . . . The key thing is we resliced the organization with two guys who had a reasonable capacity to work together to make it work and some matrix function in this program office in between. That was reorganizing workgroups on a massive scale.

> . . . organization by itself doesn't get you very far. The organization ought to reflect the system, ought to reflect the process first and then decide on the organizational structure.

CONCLUSION

A new sensitivity to learning has emerged in Ford's rethinking of its approach to product development, moving, in the process, the 'balance' of strategic thinking.

> In PD [product development] the balance between innovation and efficiency has changed dramatically. It's not just about cutting cost as an end in itself. It's about cutting cost in relation to the defined output. Now it's 'Let's keep the product exactly the same in terms of quality and specification but cut the cost of development.' So it's no longer a zero-sum trade-off between efficiency and innovation. It used to, but no longer. If we take 25 per cent out of costs through PD or better engineering planning during pre-production then we now plough back 23 per cent to enhance the product. The terms we use, 'efficiency' and 'quality', may sound the same as they did 15 years ago but their meaning has changed.

The strategic need now is to make this newly emerging perspective a permanent and pervasive part of the collective Ford consciousness.

A pyramid-type organization with vertical authority / accountability chimneys is the antithesis of Japanese operating practice. Pressures to achieve consensus and harmony dictate that complete consideration of other functions' views and needs must be incorporated in a plan or idea *before* it goes very far as a proposal.

The Japanese launch 'many trial balloons' that 'are punctured at very low levels before going higher in the organization to a management committee'. By the time the senior executive needs to sanction projects, this approach means that consensus on a best solution is close to emergence. Senior management's function is to 'confirm that the consensus process works and that the proposal is in line with overall policy direction established by the top management and the Executive Committee'.

The traditional Ford approach was to manage *through* levels and tasks, now the intention is to manage *across* levels and projects.

An environment of open communication and sharing of information is seen as essential to achieve mission goals. This requires high levels of trust, respect and confidence. Ford accepts that achieving these ends is perhaps one of the most significant challenges it has to face and that it requires a fundamental shift in organizational values to generate the willingness to pursue cooperation and integration rather than internal competition and separation.

A new way of thinking about product development demands a new way of thinking about products – the car as a 'totality' rather than a 'collection of individual components'. What one sees emerging in product development in Ford of Europe in the 1980s is a new willingness to learn, an acceptance of the need for critical self-analysis and a desire, fragile at first but growing stronger, to innovate. This new will is evident in the constitution of the product development study teams of the period. As a senior Ford manager pointed out: 'For the first time [these used] our stars, our best individuals. For thirty years study teams were used as dumping grounds for under-performers and people about to retire.' 'Study' and 'learning' are no longer marginal activities. They are (at) the heart of strategic thinking.

NOTE

1 Quotations in this chapter, unless otherwise attributed, are taken from interviews conducted by the authors with Ford managers in Europe and the US.

REFERENCES

Clark, K. and Fujimoto, T. (1991) *Product Development Performance. Strategy, Organization and Management in the World Auto Industry*, Cambridge, Mass., Harvard Business School Press.

Frey, D. (1991) 'Learning the ropes: my life as a product champion', *Harvard Business Review*, September–October, 46–56.

Hopeman, R. (1989) 'The evolution of program management', Ford Dagenham, 31 August.

Mintzberg, H. (1983) *Structure in Fives: Designing Effective Organizations*, Englewood Cliffs, NJ, Prentice-Hall.

Morgan, G. (1986) *Images of Organization*, Beverly Hills, Sage.

Mumford, A. and Honey, P. (1986) 'Developing skills for matrix management', *Industrial and Commercial Training*, 18, 5, 2–7.

Piore, M. and Sabel, C. (1984) *The Second Industrial Divide*, New York, Basic Books.

Seidler, P. (1976) *Let's Call It Fiesta. The Autobiography of Ford's Project Bobcat*, Lausanne, Edita.

Starkey, K. and McKinlay, A. (1993) *Strategy and the Human Resource. Ford and the Search for Competitive Advantage*, Oxford, Blackwell.

Womack, J.P., Jones, D.T. and Roos, D. (1990) *The Machine that Changed the World*, London and New York, Rawson Associates/Macmillan.

Chapter 13

Developing the forgotten army
Learning and the top manager

Bill Braddick and David Casey

Serious efforts at management development began about 20 years ago in the UK. It might reasonably be claimed that one important consequence has been that a number of progressive companies now have a more professional management.

Managers in these companies understand the nature of managerial work. They can see it in its wider context. They understand their own role and function. They have acquired a knowledge of the management techniques which are likely to be useful to them. They have developed some of the skills which it is generally agreed that good managers need. To place these managers more accurately – they are usually those at the middle levels or below. Above them there is a forgotten army of senior managers and directors whose development needs have largely been ignored both by their companies and by the educational institutions. They partly have themselves to blame. They didn't get where they are today, they might claim, by going on courses. Certainly they won't get where they want to be tomorrow. They feel that development forces are too theoretical and too lengthy for busy, active people. Management development specialists do not help. Many of them regard it as *lèse-majesté* to suggest that board members need development. The educational institutions themselves have little to offer which makes a contribution to the needs of directors and in any case the effort of bringing a group of directors together is far more expensive than running more conventional courses. Yet the need for training at senior levels has never been more pressing.

Our economic problems are so serious that they can be solved only at strategic level. We approach the millennium facing business problems which will tax the ingenuity of the sharpest intelligence. The problems we have to handle are not only greater in range and depth than hitherto, but they are also different in nature.

Businessmen who matured through the 1960s and early 1970s learned how to live in a world of continuously expanding horizons. They managed with 4 per cent inflation and were horrified at the thought of a rise of 6 per cent. Now they are likely to live with double figure inflation for the rest of their working lives. They have to come to terms with the fact that managing cash flow becomes almost more important than managing profit. They will live for the foreseeable future in a period of stagnation and decline. Competition will grow fiercer each day as they fight for their share in the slack market not only with their usual competitors but with those more recent entrants to the business world from countries whose labour costs give them a sharp competitive edge.

It is easy, even facile, to recite at this point a litany of changes facing us in the next decade, but such a list becomes numbing. We would prefer to summarize just two aspects of change before going on to explore the implications of all this change for management education.

First, radical technological change. Many mature industries find themselves at the mercy of 'invaders' who threaten traditional markets by the application of new and efficient technologies, giving them advantages in price, quality, service, speed – or a combination of them all. Under these circumstances the pressure to diversify into new markets and products is considerable. Risks are high because these activities raise unfamiliar problems – understanding new markets, managing joint ventures, handling mergers, dealing with foreign governments – the list of possible challenges is daunting.

Second, new issues arise from social change. The events of the late 1960s demonstrated that the postwar educational revolution had created expectations concerning participation and involvement which industry was not providing. This problem is nowhere near solution. One would anticipate, as the millennium approaches, that more issues, traditionally regarded as within the managerial prerogative to decide upon, will be jointly shared. One would also anticipate that the typical representative forms of participation which are currently in vogue will have evolved into more complex and subtle shapes. Demands for social accountability will grow in other directions. Educated customers with a knowledge of their rights and the skill to combine to protect and increase them are here to stay. So is the dedicated environmentalist. We must expect increasing pressure to behave with a sense of social responsibility, in relation to investment employment and environment – whatever conflicting demands this places on the organization.

These are formidable challenges and many top managers are ill-equipped to deal with them. Their education and experience has taught them to deal with other issues, but not these.

Members of a board usually get there because they have excelled in their own functional area. But what was once a virtue can become a limitation. Unless the board member is very careful he or she will continue to express a functional point of view – to defend a functional position when what he or she should do is to think strategically. But even functional expertise might be of little use if the company is moving into new fields. In fact fear of the unknown and the threats which might arise are often a potent source of resistance to change and innovation from those who feel their expertise threatened.

Managers sometimes reach board level because they are very competitive and striving. Often they have considerable drive and energy and get to the top by doing everyone else's job as well as their own. These virtues become vices at board level. The competitor does not find it easy to work as a member of a team, but this is vitally necessary at board level. Nor does he or she find it easy to manage through the structure. But this is critical, otherwise the director remains a manager.

Thus, encouraging top managers to learn involves first helping them to 'unlearn' old habits – both in terms of skills and knowledge. They must develop the confidence to abandon old expertise in favour of new. Development is also concerned with helping them to develop the skills of co-operation necessary to effective team membership and the skills of influencing and persuading which are essential to manage effectively through the structure. Any learning design will have to take into account that all we know about top managers suggests that they learn through their work rather than through theoretical discussion; that they learn more from their peers than they do from books and lectures.

These considerations were sharply reinforced by a series of discussions with a number of top industrialists on the theme of Leadership in British Industry in the 1980s (Boyle and Braddick, 1980). These discussions led onto the idea of running some experimental programmes of development for directors which were based on other forms of learning than those traditionally employed. Some form of action learning seemed to be called for.

LOGISTICS

To initiate a programme we wrote to 200 former participants of courses for directors at Ashridge Management College and invited them to one of two evening meetings. About thirty people attended on each occasion. Two difficulties emerged at these meetings.

Although we both have wide experience in management development and one of us is among the most practised action learning set advisers in the country, we had the greatest difficulty in explaining exactly what goes on in an action learning set and what outcomes might be expected. Examples were given and the benefits which others had found were explained, but in the end we had to confess that the only way to experience the advantages of this type of learning is to have a go. Reg Revans, leading exponent of action learning, has always said this (Revans, 1980).

The other problem was possibly allied to the first. Many of the people we talked to associated learning with a syllabus, a lecturer, notes, black-boards, and all the traditional paraphernalia of the classroom. They felt highly suspicious of any other sort of learning. This surprised us since we were both fairly convinced by now that top managers did not learn their business skills in the classroom. It seemed that the mores of school and university education still exerted a very strong influence on this group of people, and no sooner were they seated 'at their desks' in the 'classroom' of an educational institution than all their preconceptions about teaching and learning came flooding back, obliterating what they must have known from experience – that most of their own knowledge of business had been gained in business itself. This group soon dropped out.

But about fifteen people from the original sixty were sufficiently in-trigued to want to go further and we arranged a day when we could all come together and operate in sets to give them a feel for it. This worked well. A couple of hours' work together did far more to convince parti-cipants of the potential value of being able to share strategic problems of their business with their peers from other companies than all our work. Even the earlier fear about difficulties of commercial secrecy soon disappeared.

Finally, one set of five people began and this course ran through the autumn 1980 into New Year 1981, meeting about every six weeks. Three participants were managing directors of subsidiaries of large national and international companies. One ran his own business with a turnover of about £20 million and the fifth was personnel director of a large international organization.

The process of self-selection probably meant that a group of people came together who were willing to experiment and were prepared, for a time at least, to take matters on trust. They were curious people very open to new approaches and ideas. Others had wanted to join us but for a variety of reasons found it impossible. The members of the set held a meeting with these people in the late autumn to explain what was hap-pening. The confusion at the first meeting melted away as each member of the set was able to explain what he or she felt was happening to him/her and what pay-offs he or she was getting. The difficulties and problems of the set were openly explained as well as the advantages, and those who came at least understood clearly what happens in an action learning set.

REFLECTIONS BY THE SET ADVISER (DAVID CASEY)

This set felt quite different from any other in my experience over the last ten years working from time to time in the role of set adviser, and it would be useful as well as interesting to know why. Were the participants more senior or were they older (i.e. at a different life phase), was it the atmosphere of Ashridge or was it because the time between set meetings was longer than usual?

Not much action

The whole basis for the programme was action learning. We had sold the programme as a way of learning and growing which depended cardinally on taking action. We expected that participants would punctuate that action with set meetings at which they would review and evaluate last month's action, before planning next month's. This is what other action learning sets do. But, from the beginning, this set seemed different. We spoke more of life than of business. We were rather 'laid back' when it came to business but highly involved when it came to marriage, the home, our lifestyles, the opportunities missed when the children were growing up, the meaning of success (now that success was here), the imbalance in effort expended on getting to the top compared with the meagre effort expended in building a complete and meaningful existence for ourselves. Bernard Lievegoed's book *Phases – Crisis and Development in the Individual* (Lievegoed, 1979) was the only text I introduced – all of them read it from cover to cover, and it meant a lot. You can't take the same kind of action between set meetings on the phases of your life as you can when your project is dealing with IR on the shop floor. So the action was scant. We didn't put much pressure on each other to take action next week, but the pressure to look life in the face was real enough.

Like everyone else, the set members found themselves prisoners of their own beliefs, and painfully over the life of the set they learned to reframe many problems about their aims and ambitions. Reframing is a difficult process.

I found some help in a book called *Change* written by a team from the Palo Alto Mental Research Institute (Watzlawick *et al.*, 1974). This is a useful theoretical treatment of resistance to change. The authors call up theories from the disciplines of mathematics and formal logic to show that the idea of persistence is just as important as the idea of change itself. The theories suggest that some apparent changes are no more than persistence in disguise. Systems have a tendency to persist and this tendency can be shown to obey certain rules or run on well-worn tracks. Human systems are no exception: four well-worn tracks are identified along which human systems tend to run as a way of thwarting change in the system. The arresting thought which made this book compelling reading for me is that when we attempt to change a human system (for example a marriage, a family or a work group) our very attempts to cause a change often themselves run on those same well-worn four tracks by which the system protects itself from change. So the attempted solution becomes the new problem. A quick example of each of the four deceiving tracks:

1 A person who cannot sleep tries harder to sleep and drives sleep farther away. (The failure of attempting 'more of the same'.)
2 It would be easier to manage well in local government if only local authorities were not pervaded by politics. (The failure of reaching for a utopia that will never exist.)
3 All this company needs to do is communicate better. (The failure of a sweeping simplification associated with a denial that real complex problems exist.)
4 I want my children to want to study. (The failure of setting paradoxes for people.)[1]

In each of these examples an attempted solution has failed and in each case this has made things worse – the innocent attempt to solve the problem (produce change) has built a problem (prevented change).

Here the theories from mathematics and logic come to our aid – because there is another way. Change can be introduced in these cases by stepping right outside the frame of reference which up to this point has been implicitly or explicitly accepted. In mathematics you must take off to the next higher level of logical types. The only activity which will guarantee a change to the original system is an activity which is itself 'meta' to the original system. This is called reframing. The hardest thing of all is that to achieve this one must abandon what has up till now felt like the right approach. First (and most unnaturally) one must stop the current attempts to introduce change, smash the current mould and step out of the current frame. Then one must reframe. So simple to say – so difficult to do. How does the person trying to get to sleep bring himself or herself to accept that the first thing to do is stop trying to get to sleep? How does the local government officer who has spent years hiding behind his utopia syndrome confront the awful truth that utopia will never be?

Our group helped each other to reframe their problems as the weeks went by: first by challenging each other, and then with greater difficulty they began to challenge their own beliefs and to see ways in which they could move forward. As set adviser I sometimes felt lost and confused in a group which came to adopt a highly reflective mode. Where was the line between self-indulgent chatter and a basic re-orientation of thinking about career? How were we to know as a set when success had been achieved if we didn't first define our goals? Let me contrast this with a 'normal' action learning set.

Normal action learning sets

Shaun Harries at the Local Government Training Board has a model of what happens in an action learning set (Harries, 1981), which proposes a Maslow-type hierarchy of activities, as shown in Figure 13.1.

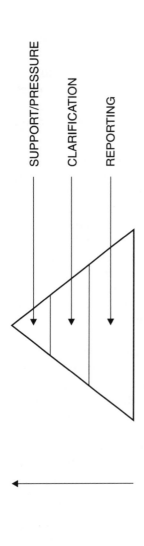

Figure 13.1 **Activities in an action learning set**

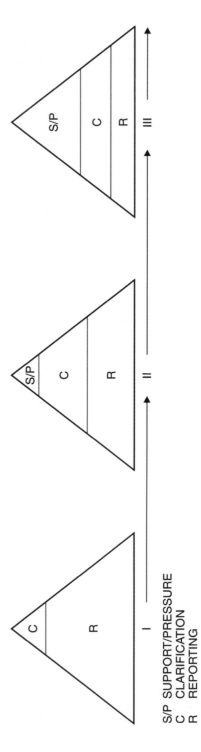

S/P SUPPORT/PRESSURE
C   CLARIFICATION
R   REPORTING

Figure 13.2 **Development of activities in an action learning set**

Shaun's experiences have led him to the empirical finding that the ratio between the three sections changes as time goes by (Figure 13.2).

At the first set meeting there is only reporting, then clarification takes up more time and later support/pressure is brought to bear within the set. This model accords with my own experience of most sets at work, with a gradual shift up the hierarchy from the largely cognitive activity of reporting, to the largely emotional activity of offering support/exerting pressure. Another way to put it is that you can't put pressure on a set member until you have understood (by his/her reporting and your clarification) what he or she is doing.

In the 'normal' set – meeting frequently, getting on with finite projects, taking action between set meetings – members are motivated to achieve success measured as project achievement. The cycle between set meetings is short – typically one week – and activity is at a high pitch.

In terms of the theory of change-and-persistence described earlier, reframing on a week-by-week basis is achieved by the quality of questions asked by the fellow set members. They cannot see the problem in the same frame as the person doing the project, so by challenging that person's every action and proposed solution they can often shake him or her out of the well-worn grooves of his/her attempts to solve the problem: attempts which may be making the problem deeper instead of solving it.

This idea – that the best person to help you with your problem is someone who cannot see your problem in the same frame as you, because he or she is ignorant of your world – is at the heart of Revans' action learning concept. What I now see more clearly is that there are two discreet steps: you must break your old frame by abandoning your current attempts to solve your problem, before reframing as a second step. Someone ignorant of your world is ideally equipped to help you break your old frame.

The set adviser's role here is clear and relatively easy – to encourage iconoclastic smashing of frames by encouraging meta-questions about how the project is being done. These meta-questions have the power to jump the problem from one mathematical group (or one logical level) to the next higher level, by asking about the system and not colluding with the project doer in staying inside the prison of his or her own system. We often call these questions process questions – task process questions – because they are concerned with how the project task is being done.

Less easy – but on precisely the same theoretical basis – the set adviser has a more lonely role to perform in asking meta-questions about feelings. (These are sometimes called maintenance process questions since a group maintains itself as an effective group only if it has a process for dealing with the feelings of individuals.) The purpose of the meta-questions about the task is to enable a reframing to take place. It is a lonelier task for the set adviser because societal norms make such questions taboo in most social transactions – a group of excited managers working on short-term stimulating projects would hardly ever ask each other these questions about their feelings of their own accord. That's why they need a set adviser. So we can sum up this picture of a 'normal' action learning set as something like this:

> The set matures through Harries' stages, moving from cognitive to emotional activity via a very short repeat cycle of action, with frequent and regular set meetings. Individuals are driven to achieve project success and other set members who are 'comrades in adversity', as Revans says, cause them to reframe frequently – by asking high quality meta-questions about how they are going about their projects and how they are feeling.

Our set was different

By contrast with that 'normal' kind of action-packed short-cycling set the experience we had was much more ruminative: there was little action and it was relatively long drawn out, reflective and laid back. The members were driven not by a desire to complete their projects but by a deep-rooted concern for the quality of their total lives. Yet we still followed Harries' empirical pattern of evolution – we still moved from reporting (about ourselves) through clarification, to support/pressure. The emotional pressures were, if anything, heavier than in normal 'action' sets and people went home deeply exhausted. Reframing was heavier too, when it happened, because the picture was a bigger picture and reframing could be a rather massive job. How massive depended on the individual. One managing director presented the problem: 'I have difficulty in communication with some of my staff.' This needed reframing since his solution (*more of the same*) was not working. He reframed to 'What on earth am I going to do with the next major phase of my life?' This man is giving up his job as managing director of a major nationally known company and remustering at age 46 in a quite new career.

Another member of the set reframed from 'How do I pacify this irate group of customers?' to 'Who's managing this company – me or my customers!' He adopted a new stance of confrontation which is paying off in a context wider than dealing with this awkward group of customers.

One of the five was not a managing director but was very senior – the personnel director of a household name public company. He reframed from 'How do I persuade the board to use my professional services more?' (Which had got predictably stuck as a problem – in the groove of *posing a paradox* – 'I want you to want me!') He reframed to 'How much imaginative, heat of the battle work do I need to have and how much direct influence do I need to exert on events?'

We have to admit that one of the five men in the set was apparently untouched by the programme. He was the youngest, running a successful family business which he had turned round in five years, since succeeding his father, from a traditional builder's to a dynamic property development organization. He found it difficult to define a problem at the beginning and didn't reframe at all. The rest of us found this disappointing, but on reflection we asked ourselves – why should he? He really didn't have a problem to reframe! We will refer to this person again later.

DISCUSSION

What did we learn from the programme in retrospect? First that we had described it inaccurately. We all know that there are different forms and modes of learning – learning by doing; learning from active experimentation; learning by reflecting on what we have done; learning by building models and analysing experience through them. We had described what we intended to happen as action learning. We wanted set members to discuss their problems, decide on a course of action, go back to their companies, take action and come back to discuss it. This did happen – but there was far more reflection than action.

The drive of the members of this set was for a deeper understanding of the meaning of their lives and a greater knowledge of themselves. Instead of reframing on a micro scale several times, most of the members of this set reframed once, but on a macro scale. Between set meetings there was little action and the reporting and clarification activities were carried out with reference to large slices of their lives. The content of set discussions tended, therefore, to be more of the 'there and then'; and less of the 'here and now', which is a big contrast with a normal 'action' set. The set adviser's role was less clear and more difficult. The members were senior and seemed to want to deal with concerns of a personal development nature, rather than direct business projects – any issues which started off as business issues tended to finish up as personal issues.

There are at least five areas we want to explore further when our second programme starts. For example, we think there are at least two kinds of set, as shown in Figure 13.3

In attempting to understand the polarity in this figure one must ask the question – why did people come on such a programme as ours, directed as it was to top managers? Perhaps managing directors come to learning events for reasons which are very different from the reasons other managers come? Nobody 'sends' the managing director. Should we be surprised if the managing director wants to focus on his or her own personal development? After all, his or her needs are frequently ignored – simply because the MD is at the top and people either assume he or she has no needs, or lack the appropriate relationship with him to suggest

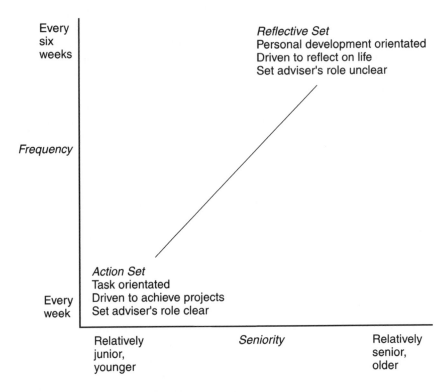

Every
six
weeks

Reflective Set
Personal development orientated
Driven to reflect on life
Set adviser's role unclear

Frequency

Action Set
Task orientated
Every   Driven to achieve projects
week   Set adviser's role clear

Relatively   *Seniority*   Relatively
junior,   senior,
younger   older

Figure 13.3 **Two kinds of action learning set**

that he or she might have. There may be in many top managers a deep isolation and an intense personal need to reframe their lives. Lots of people help them with their business; nobody helps them with their lives and this painful deprivation may have been the subconscious force which brought them to our programme in the first place.

It seems that both kinds of set can be very successful and useful in different ways. Although the differences are very great there is a common core which may represent the essence of this kind of management development. Interestingly enough action does not appear to be part of this essential core,[2] although our programme set out to be an action learning programme.

Perhaps the gem of Revans' ideas is not, after all, action learning – but his other basic idea of comrades in adversity. Certainly what these two very different kinds of set have in common is a group of comrades in adversity (the adversities of a project or the adversities of life itself). This group of comrades is the forum in which meta-questions can be asked which cause the essential smashing of old frames and the building of new. Perhaps it is the power of comrades in adversity causing each other and allowing each other to reframe their ideas, which guarantees the passage from Harries' cognitive first stage to the inevitable engaging of the emotions as set meetings progress, whether in a short-cycle action set or a long-cycle reflective set.

A possible explanation for the young entrepreneur who remained untouched by this experience is that he was in the wrong kind of set. Perhaps a short-cycle action set would have been better for him. Such a set might well have forced him to define a project and get into action on it. Perhaps an action set might have found that he was in a groove (maybe applying 'more of the same' in a fast-changing property market, for instance), and they might have helped him to reframe how he runs his business. The set he found himself in was a reflective set of older people who wanted to reflect on the phases of life and reframe life itself. But for a variety of reasons, perhaps including his relative youth, these were not matters which really engaged him. There may be an important lesson for future set composition here. Certainly it has raised many questions in our minds. How important is the life phase of participants? We now believe the loosely structured experimental mode of this particular set was a direct result of our loosely structured recruitment process. Our open-ended approach to setting up the programme may have given some of the managing directors the opportunity they had been subconsciously searching for to take stock of themselves and their careers at a critical life phase. Our set entrained one younger managing director for whom this was not a need – could we have avoided that?

We sold the programme to top managers as a learning opportunity which depended cardinally on taking action. We also set them and ourselves a paradox, by insisting that they manage their own learning. In the event they decided to change our rules and play down the action bit – but changing our rules was within our rules too, since we had asked them to be a self-managed group! One result for us was a total reframing of our own ideas about learning in small groups. We have unlearned old habits, questioned our old assumptions and reframed our own ideas. And that can't be bad.

NOTES

1 The children are caught in this paradox – if they decide to study is it because they really want to or because they know that I want them to?
2 One could, however, argue that action must eventually be taken as part of a longer cycle, since reframing in itself is not enough and change of behaviour must eventually follow. In this argument both sets follow the same cycle of action, reflection, action – one being a weekly cycle and the other say an annual or even five-year cycle. However, the power of reframing as massive

as that experienced by some members of the Ashridge set may be such that action becomes inescapable simply because it becomes literally impossible to go back to the old frame, which is broken and lost. Since action becomes inevitable there is no need for the set to continue to exist. In this sense it is a reflective set and not an action set.

REFERENCES

Boyle, D and Braddick, W.G (1980) *Challenge of Change*, Aldershot: Gower Press.

Harries, J.M. (1981) 'The role of action learning set advisers', *Training*, vol. 7, no. 2, pp. 7–8.

Lievegoed, B.C.J. (1979) *Phases – Crisis and Development in the Individual*, London: Pharos Paperback, Ruldolf Steiner Press.

Revans, R.W. (1980) *Action Learning*, London: Blond & Briggs.

Watzlawick, P., Weakland, J. and Fisch, R. (1974) *Change – Principles of Problem Formation and Problem Resolution*, New York and London: W.W. Norton.

Chapter 14

GE's Crotonville
A staging ground for corporate revolution

Noel M. Tichy

Radically altering the genetic code of a large, successful corporation requires revolutionary action. Since 1981 John F. Welch, CEO of General Electric, has been struggling to break the company's old genetic code. This code was built around a core set of principles based on growth in sales greater than GNP, with many SBUs (strategic business units), relying on financial savvy, meticulous staff work, and a domestically focused company. The new genetic code is to build shareholder value in a slow-growth environment through operating competitive advantage with transformational level leadership at all levels of the organization.

After five years of this effort – which included downsizing GE by over 100,000 employees, divesting $6 billion and acquiring $13 billion in businesses (RCA being the largest), doubling investment in plant equipment and R&D, and at the same time increasing earnings and shareholder value (GE moved up to no. 3 in the United States in market value from no. 10) – Welch was asked, 'What was your biggest mistake?' He answered, 'I was too timid and cautious. I did not move fast enough . . . bureaucracies need quantum change, not incremental change.' Three years later, in 1989, Welch was still accelerating change at GE.

To accomplish the quantum change in GE, a new breed of leader is required. These are leaders who can:

1 **Transform the organization**; that is, creatively destroy and remake an organization around new visions, supported by revamping the social architecture of the organization. This is needed at all levels of GE and is a continuous process.
2 **Develop global product and service strategies**. As GE more aggressively looks to world markets, it is faced with developing world-class products and services at world-class cost. This means changes in product and service design, production, distribution, and marketing. Leaders must be able to:

   create new forms of design teams;
   make strategic use of sourcing;

drive world-class standards for design, service, and performance.

3 **Develop strategic alliances**. To deliver on global strategies, more and varied alliances are emerging. These alliances are partnerships that are needed to gain market entry, achieve price competitiveness, gain technology, learn more about management, and so on. The success of these alliances will be determined by a set of leadership factors: skill and pre-screening of potential partners, proper negotiation, the right condition for partnering, and good coordination and integration mechanisms.

4 **Devlop global coordination and integration**. As the boundaries of GE span wider geopolitical and cultural diversities, it becomes increasingly difficult to integrate the organization. Better communication and cultural integration will be required since all human resource systems will be impacted by this development.

5 **Develop global staffing and development**. Growing world-class leaders will be the key to competitiveness. Staffing and development systems at GE are outmoded and are undergoing total revamping to develop a new brand of leader.

This chapter chronicles the evolution of a revolutionary agenda at GE. Crotonville, GE's Management Development Institute, is increasingly being used by Welch as a key lever in the radical transformation of the company's culture. The overall Crotonville strategy and particular developmental stagecraft will be discussed. Finally, lessons for other CEOs are articulated. This chapter is based on my two years as leader of the last phase of Crotonville's transformation. I was the manager of GE's Management Development Operation from 1985 through 1987.

THE CROTONVILLE HERITAGE AS A LEVER OF CHANGE

In 1956, when Crotonville launched its first 13-week advanced management program, Ralph Cordiner, who became CEO in 1950, was using development as a direct lever for change. Cordiner believed that decentralization by product line would best position GE to capitalize on the post-World War II market opportunities. He hired Harold Smiddy, a former Booz-Allen consultant, to engineer a massive restructuring. Cordiner and Smiddy quickly saw that GE did not have managerial talent – that is, multi-functional general managers – to run a decentralized company. A major effort was launched to design an advanced management curriculum and build Crotonville, a campus-like-setting in Ossining, New York. The design of the curriculum drew on the expertise of academicians from around the country and resulted in the creation of a multi-volume set of books on how to be a multi-functional general manager in GE. These books were referred to as the 'GE blue books,' which became Crotonville's 'catechism.' The critical point here is that

Crotonville's birth was as a CEO-driven lever for change. This continued under the next CEO, Fred Borch, as Crotonville was used to introduce strategic planning to GE. Borch's successor, Reginald Jones, used Crotonville to round out the strategic planning effort and improve cash management and inflationary accounting practices. In the Welch era, Crotonville again became a centerpiece for the CEO's efforts to make change happen at GE, but on a scale unheard of since Cordiner's days.

THE EARLY WELCH EFFORT

The first act of a transformation is creating a sense of urgency for change and dealing with the inevitable resistance to a new order.[1] From 1981 to 1985 Welch worked closely with Crotonville and its leader, James Baughman, to delayer, downsize, and change GE's portfolio. Baughman revitalized the curriculum, faculty, staff, and the facility to get the message across to thousands of managers, to try to impact their hearts and minds. Baughman joined GE after a year on the Harvard Business School faculty. He had taught at Crotonville since 1968 and was aware of its short-comings as well as its potential. As eager as Baughman was to revitalize Crotonville, he was not prepared for the passion of Welch's challenge to him when they met for the first time in January 1981: 'I want a revolution to start at Crotonville. I want it to be part of the glue that holds GE together.'

Under Baughman's leadership, the first moves were to do a program-by-program upgrade of the faculty, curriculum, and staff, and set the stage for a total revamping of the Crotonville strategy. This resulted in the top-level executive programs being tied directly to the GE succession planning process; thus, there was much more selectivity, with business heads accountable to the CEO for seeing to it that Crotonville development experiences were carefully planned and carried through for their managers. New programs were targeted for populations previously unserved by Crotonville. The first of these was a New Manager Program, targeted to those managers who hire, train, and supervise the vast majority of GE employees. If Welch was to 'drive a stake in the ground' for the new GE culture, this was a critical population to win over.

Another very significant, substantive, and symbolic event was the change in the physical facilities at Crotonville. As GE was going through a very dramatic set of changes, including downsizing, delayering, and divesting, Welch was investing in the future in terms not only of business but also of leadership. The facilities would provide living and development space in the 21st century. This development was Welch's second stake in the ground.

The New Manager Program began the process of shifting Crotonville's focus back toward the new college hire. In addition, during this period horizontal integration began with Crotonville's acquisition of the functional development responsibilities in marketing, finance, computer information systems, and human resources.

By 1985, the Crotonville transformation was well on its way. Two significant changes occurred that year. First, the reporting relationship of Crotonville was shifted from the employee relations organization to the executive management staff. This enabled Crotonville to be better integrated with the succession planning process and the CEO's office. Second, Baughman was promoted to broader responsibilities on GE's Executive Management Staff, and it was his suggestion that his successor be brought in from the outside to keep up the momentum for change and new perspectives. Furthermore, it was proposed that this individual would take on the assignment as a two-year leave of absence from the academic world. Baughman would retain GE oversight of Crotonville, but the person hired would be in full charge of all educational and development programs. Thus, when my two-year assignment began, the revolution had progressed and a vision was emerging for Crotonville. This was a vision that embodied much more than a development agenda; it was a centerpiece in the transformation agendas for GE and its culture. The challenge of leading Crotonville during this historic period was what led me to take a two-year leave of absence from the University of Michigan and join GE.

WELCH'S SECOND ACT: CRYSTALLIZING THE VISION

By 1985, Crotonville was well on its way to becoming once again a lever for change at GE. Ironically, a series of evolutionary experiments and changes led to a revolutionary agenda. Although the following premises were never made explicit by Welch or senior executives in GE, they were clearly implicit, based on the behavior and actions taken regarding the role of Crotonville.

Premise 1: Revolutionaries do not rely solely on the chain of command to bring about quantum change; they carefully develop multichannel, two-way interactive networks throughout the organization. So did Jack Welch.

(a) The chain of command, with its vested interests, is where much of the resistance to change resides. Therefore, there is a need to stir up the populace of the organization and begin developing new leaders for the new regime.
(b) There is a need for a new set of values and templates in the organization.
(c) There is a need for mechanisms to implement all of these changes. Therefore, new socialization and new development processes are required.

Premise 2: Revolutionary change occurs by blending the hard and the soft issues.

(a) Welch understood this blending of hard and soft issues quite well, since it was the hallmark of his experience in building the plastics business in GE. On the one hand, he was a tough person, while on the other he invested a great deal of time and energy in coaching and developing team players and team building. He insisted that those who had to depart were treated compassionately; that is, 'a soft landing.' Thus, the cornerstone of Welch's strategy for building an organization and a winning team is this blending of the hard issues (budget, manufacturing, marketing, distribution, head-count, finance, etc.) and the soft issues (values, culture, vision, leadership, style, innovative behavior, etc.).

(b) Welch felt that US leadership in general and GE leadership in particular were weak on both the hard and the soft issues from World War II through the late 1970s, until increased competition from Japan and elsewhere led to a rude awakening.

(c) Since the early 1980s, GE has been very aggressive about getting strong leadership on the hard issues, such as downsizing, reducing levels of management, and driving productivity. However . . .

(d) Driving solely on the hard issues will only work so long as the primary focus is on bottom-line improvement – and you can only squeeze so far. The long-term need is for top-line growth via new markets, products, innovations, and so on. Driving on the hard issues also takes the excitement out of the organization and can suck the psychological reserve out of people. Thus, the challenge for GE by the mid-1980s was to be strong on the soft issues as well as the hard.

(e) Welch uses Crotonville as a lever for blending the hard and soft, for getting at the hearts and minds of thousands of high-leverage middle managers to test, revise, and inculcate new GE values. It enables him to cut through the chain of command and get at the grass roots, from new college hires up to officers.

Premise 3: Revolutionaries rewrite the textbooks and revamp the education systems. Welch did the same.

The GE 'blue books' – the 25-year-old Crotonville bible – were symbolically burned. Welch has said repeatedly that there are no more textbook answers; leaders must write their own textbooks.

THE NEW CROTONVILLE – GE'S GIANT WORKSHOP FOR STAGING REVOLUTION

Starting in the early 1980s under the leadership of Jim Baughman, the focus at Crotonville moved from the ivory tower end of the training spectrum toward the practical; thus, it became a workshop for wrestling with real organizational and people issues. During this period, more and more live cases from GE were brought into the curriculum; Outward Bound-type activities were introduced for team building; and there was increased personal involvement on the part of the CEO and officers in teaching the programs.

In 1985 this trend was explicitly recognized. A new mission statement and a new management and OD [organization development] strategy were articulated for Crotonville, followed by the aforementioned rapid shift toward the workshop end of the development spectrum.

The mission for Crotonville was spelled out thus:

> To leverage GE's global competitiveness, as an instrument of cultural change, by improving the business acumen, leadership abilities and organizational effectiveness of General Electric professionals.

The management and OD strategy built on a new set of concepts concerning the depth and impact of management and organization development. Out of this effort came a framework, later known as the 'Tichy Development Model,' which provided the concept and rationale for shifting much of the curriculum and emphasis at Crotonville.

Figure 14.1 lays out the strategic framework used to transform Crotonville. This framework conceptualizes development along two dimensions. Along the top of the matrix the focus is on depth of development experience. This ranges from one end of the spectrum, which entails developing awareness, to the opposite end, which entails developing fundamental change. The other dimension refers to the target of the development experience. Here it ranges from change targeted at individuals to change targeted at the organizational level. Historically, at Crotonville, as is true of most university schools of business, the primary focus was on the cognitive understanding of the individual. Managers from all over GE attended Crotonville programs as individuals and participated in classrooms where they learned finance, marketing, accounting, and organizational behavior largely through case studies, reading, discussions, simulations, and so on. The major impact was cognitive understanding with some skill development. The problem with this approach, as with executive education in business schools, is that when the individuals return to their organization, they have difficulty translating their classroom experiences into the work situation because they haven't fundamentally changed and, just as importantly, their organizations often resist individuals with new ideas. These people do not have a support system – a group of co-workers – that has gone through the experience with them. This was the challenge facing Crotonville: how to move development toward the upper left-hand part of the matrix to help deal with the revolutionary agenda of transforming GE. The challenge was to take a large number of participants a year – approximately 8,000 –

in a 53-acre, 145-bed residential educational center and move the development experience as far as possible toward the workshop end, while at the same time dealing with the economies-of-scale issue – which meant that customized workshops were not the answer.

The shift in the Crotonville mindset from a training to a workshop mentality has led to a totally new program design. An increasing number of teams attend sessions whenever possible. Participants bring with them real business problems and leave with action plans, and representatives from various GE businesses bring unresolved live cases to Crotonville for participants to help solve. Leadership behaviors are rated by participants' direct reports, peers, and boss before the program so the change can be linked back to the work setting. Executives consult to real GE businesses on unresolved strategic issues; teams also spend up to a week in the field consulting with these businesses on these issues. As mentioned above, members such as the CEO and officers come to Crotonville to conduct workshops on key GE strategic challenges.

Along the way, participants find the development experiences increasingly unsettling and emotionally charged. They feel uncomfortable with feedback from their back-home organization; they wrestle with very difficult, unresolved, real-life problems, not case studies; and they make presentations to senior executives, argue among themselves, and work through intensive team-building experiences. The measure of program success shifts from participants' evaluation of how good they felt about the learning experience to how the experience impacted on their organization and their leadership behavior over time.

WHO GETS DEVELOPED?

The other key strategic issue was deciding what populations are to participate in the Crotonville experiences. At GE, the assumption is that over 80 per cent of development is through experience, i.e. on-the-job learning. The remaining 20 per cent of formal development occurs out in the various businesses. Therefore, Crotonville represents only a small percentage of the formal development resources. The critical question thus is, 'Who gets to come to Crotonville and at what point in their career?'

This challenge resulted in a reevaluation of leadership development in the 1990s and beyond, from new campus recruits up through to the CEO. The CEO and others worked on the career model of leadership development to identify key transition points in people's careers – that is, 'moments of opportunity' (joining GE as a new recruit, becoming a manager for the first time, and so on) – where they could and should be impacted by a set of shared values and leadership characteristics. The result: by 1986, a core development sequence was implemented. This sequence extends from new college hires up through the officer population.

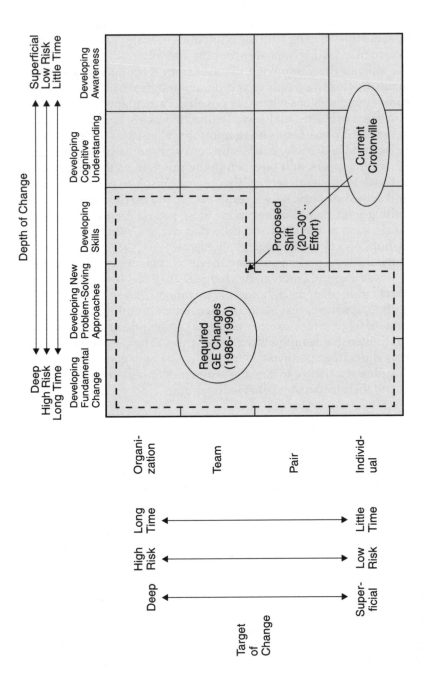

Figure 14.1 **The Tichy development model**

A result of rethinking the strategy was the new, core Crotonville curriculum, shown in Figure 14.2.

Stage I: corporate entry leadership conferences I and II

Close to 2,000 new off-campus hires come to Crotonville within three months of joining GE to learn about global competition, what it takes to win on that global playing field, GE's strategy for winning, and the changing GE values, as well as to undergo a personal examination of their core values *vis-à-vis* GE values. They come in groups of 100. Officers, senior human resource executives, and young managers teach and lead these programs, At the end of each year, 200 facilitators, 30 officers, and 30 human resource executives have taught in this program. All of them are the target of change. As many senior officers comment, 'There is nothing like teaching Sunday School to force you to confront your own values.'

Three years later this group of new hires returns for a program on total business competitiveness. They have real projects to work on, are taught by GE executives, and have to return to their organization with change agendas. These young professionals are again inculcated with a total GE strategy and value mindset. In 1989, the CELC–II program moved out to the businesses as a joint venture with Crotonville.

Stage II: new manager development program

Over 1,000 new managers a year come to Crotonville to learn how to manage and lead in GE. Through a leadership survey they get feedback from their direct reports to help them plan ways of improving their leadership skills. The focus at this stage is making sure that these managers have the right 'soft' people skills for hiring, appraising, developing, motivating, and building the high-performing teams that are needed by this critical group.

Stage III: senior functional programs

Senior functional managers come for several weeks of leadership development in their specific areas – marketing, finance, information systems, human resources, engineering and manufacturing, among others. All the programs involve change projects and some actually require the participants to invite senior line managers (their bosses or major clients) to spend several days at Crotonville to tackle these change projects. Obviously, making real change happen and leadership are the agendas.

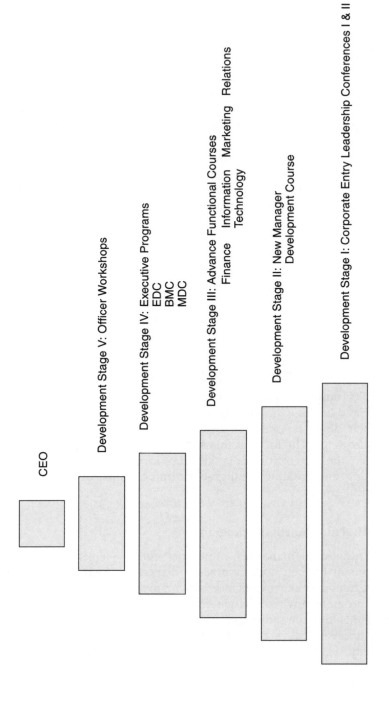

CEO

Development Stage V: Officer Workshops

Development Stage IV: Executive Programs
EDC
BMC
MDC

Development Stage III: Advance Functional Courses
Finance   Information   Marketing   Relations
Technology

Development Stage II: New Manager
Development Course

Development Stage I: Corporate Entry Leadership Conferences I & II

Figure 14.2 **Core development sequence**

Stage IV: executive programs

There are three four-week executive programs for GE managers, which are taken over a five-to-eight-year period. These programs integrate outdoor leadership challenge experiences, consulting team projects, and CEO projects.

One program, the BMC (Business Manager Course), is organized around consulting projects. The head of a GE business presents a difficult, unresolved strategic business problem that is carefully packaged prior to the start of the program; market and industry analysis, financial, and other data are pulled together along with a clear project statement and set of deliverables specified by the head of the business. Teams of BMC managers spend the third week of the program in the field interviewing customers, managers, and competitors, and collecting background information to make recommendations. During the fourth week of the program the heads of the businesses involved with projects come to Crotonville for the presentations. The sessions are electric; the teams, the heads of the businesses, make hard-hitting business recommendations as well as advise on how to implement the recommendations, and they specially emphasize the soft, human side of change.

The participants are also given feedback on both the hard and the soft issues. They debrief their own team members, providing each member with concrete behavioral feedback based on the intense four weeks of teamwork, on how to be a more effective GE leader. The participants and business clients reconvene six months later to follow up on the progress of the implementation, recommendations, and each participant's leadership agenda.

Stage V: officer workshops

Officer workshops, which are held periodically, consist of groups of 20 to 30 officers who wrestle for several days on unresolved, company-wide issues. The CEO actively participates in these sessions.

Elective programs

In addition to the core sequence described above, Crotonville provides a portfolio of elective programs ranging from courses on leading change – similar to the experienced manager program – to functionally specific courses on information systems, marketing, and human resources. This portfolio is constantly changing as the needs of the corporation change.

THE CONTINUED TRANSFORMATION OF CROTONVILLE.

Since 1987 Crotonville has played a key role in both transforming GE and developing a new pipeline for human resources for the future. When I left in 1987, Crotonville's portfolio was enlarged again. All the technical education at GE was brought under Jim Baughman's direction, along with the campus recruiting and early corporate training programs for targeted new college hires. Crotonville thus became GE's integrating device for coordinating developing from off-campus up through the office level.

Figure 14.3 summarizes the agenda for Crotonville as it enters the 1990s. The agenda has three primary development objectives: (1) help develop 'global' maturity and sophistication, (2) help develop technical and business know-how, and (3) help develop leadership abilities. These objectives are worked on differently at each stage of development, from entry-level college hire up through the head of a business.

In 1989 Crotonville is being used by Welch to spearhead an effort to liberate middle management at GE. The 'old way,' hierarchical bureaucracy, needs to be radically altered to create the 'new way,' non-hierarchical, fast-paced, flexible organizations of the future. The transformation must be led from the middle. A series of workshops will provide the catalyst for mobilizing 30,000 to 40,000 middle managers, removing unnecessary carryovers from the past bureaucracy – processes, reports, approvals, measures, and meetings. These workshops will be run in every business and involve the business heads and all their middle-level managers. The process is called 'work out.'

	Developing 'Global' Maturity and Sophistication	Developing Technical and Business Know-How	Developing Leadership Abilities
For Business Leaders			
For Functional Leaders			
For Experienced Managers			
For New Managers			
For Functional Contributors			
At Entry-Level			

Figure 14.3 **The development challenge – who and what?**

LESSONS FOR OTHER CEOs

Crotonville is not unique. It does not require a large campus and bricks and mortar investment to use development as a tool for both bringing about quantum change in an organization and developing future generations of leaders. For this to happen, the leadership challenge for a CEO must entail the following.

Vision

For the CEO to leverage change via development, he or she must have a reasonably clearly articulated future vision for the company. This vision must include the organization culture and shared values that will likely be needed in the future. Such a vision must go well beyond the faddish articulation of values triggered by the 'excellence' fad of the early 1980s, when everyone had a list of company values that read like the Boy Scout handbook. The values must be closely integrated with the imperatives of winning in the marketplace.

Leadership characteristics

The CEO must be able to articulate the appropriate characteristics of leaders; that is, the characteristics that will fit with the culture and shared values of the future organization. All too often, companies undertake competency studies focusing on who are the successful managers and leaders of today. This will only ensure that development is focused backward on yesterday's successes, not on the harder task of thinking through what is the new template for leadership in the future. This is not a task to be delegated to human resource staff people, who often have little idea of where the industry, the business, and the company are headed. Only the CEO can lead this effort, albeit with strong staff support.

Career transition points

To maximize the impact of any formal development experience, timing is critical. The challenge here is to have clearly articulated 'theory of the case.' This enables the organization to deal with the 80/20 dilemma; that is, the 80 per cent of development that really takes place as a result of life experiences and on-the-job development; and the 20 per cent that takes place via formal development programs. Again, this is a responsibility of the CEO, with strong human resource support. The company must have a framework that provides guidelines in blending on-the-job development and other developmental tools, such as secondary assignment activities and coaching and counseling emphases, with formal development experiences. At each career phase, what tools are to be used for what purposes must be identified.

CEO involvement

For development to leverage the kind of change and impact discussed in this chapter, the CEO must visibly lead the development process by participating in the overall design and architecture, delivery, and integration of the development process as it gets tied to succession planning and rewards. This is not a voluntary, open university-type approach to development. It is a very personal tool of the top leadership of the organization as well as a very central part of organization effectiveness.

CEO role model

No CEO should undertake the challenge of using development as a lever for change and as a creator of the new shared values in leadership without also understanding that such a process will put more pressure on the senior leadership to demonstrate personal adherence to those values. An open-dialogue, interactive development process also means that top management must be able to take criticism. Hypocrisy will be uncovered and a great deal of subtle pressure placed on leaders to overcome the schizophrenia often found in changing cultures; that is, where people in the middle rightfully point out that top management gives a great deal of lip service to change but in reality their practice is 'Do as I say, and not as I do.' The CEO must lead a critical group of senior executives to undergo the same kind of rigorous self-examination as do participants in the development process. For example, if middle managers are being asked to have subordinates fill out surveys of their management practices, the CEO and the top team must do the same.

Organizational resistance

Perhaps the final and real test of the CEO is how he or she deals with resistance to change, as well as how he or she handles the transition from the more comfortable awareness and cognitive learning portion of the matrix in Figure 14.1 to the area of fundamental change, in which a great deal of emotion and turmoil are stirred up. This means that the development and human resource staff will have to deal with the fact that the daily 'smile sheet' – that is, evaluation of how happy participants are with each day of the program – tends to go up and down during a real transformation experience. Not everyone is always happy; officers have to wrestle with business problems with participants and are made to feel uncomfortable (and sometimes accused of hypocrisy), and there is a tendency for some people to think that things are getting out of hand. It is here that the CEO must stay the course. At times such as this it might serve well to remember that no one ever gave a high rating to his drill sergeant during the middle of boot camp.

CONCLUSION

In this chapter I have laid out a challenge to those CEOs who are wrestling with the transformation of their organizations for global competitiveness. It is my contention that one of the most underutilized levers for change is the rather elaborate investment in development that most large corporations make. One reason why it is so underutilized is that there is little or no personal commitment or involvement by the CEO. Obviously, the challenges laid out here are not for everyone. Once the CEO decides to use development as a lever of change, he or she must make the commitment and follow through on the size principles outlined above. Doing so will be a real test of leadership for all involved.

NOTE

1 *The Transformational Leader*, Noel Tichy and Mary Anne Devanna, Wiley, 1986.

Part III

Leadership and the learning process

Introduction

Part III focuses upon the link between strategy, leadership and learning. There is a plethora of prescriptive models of how do strategy, framed in terms of different forms of environmental (industry and market) analysis and in different approaches to analysing firm strengths and weaknesses, linking these, again in a prescriptive sense, to the kind of generic strategies firms should pursue. But facts concerning the practical effects of these models are hard to come by. For example, it is still impossible to prove that planning does pay. Mintzberg (1991) argues that studies of successful strategic management in practice – rare though they are – do provide one lesson and that is that learning is more effective than planning ('Learning 1, Planning 0').

A key case here is Pascale's (1984) study of Honda's successful entry into the US motorcycle market. What is especially fascinating about this account is that it stands in sharp contrast to the brilliantly rational strategy imputed to Honda by the Boston Consulting Group who based their analysis upon 'objective' data and their own portfolio planning prescriptions but, unlike Pascale, did not actually ask Honda managers how and why they thought and acted as they did! The Boston Consulting Group's 'explanation' portrayed Honda as a firm dedicated to being the low cost producer, utilizing its dominant position in Japan to force entry into the US market using a clever marketing strategy and exploiting its comparative advantage by aggressive pricing and advertising.

Pascale's alternative explanation highlights learning rather than a streamlined strategy. Honda's success was based not upon a pristine plan for market entry, building to market dominance. The strategy evolved/ emerged as a result of a series of unpredictable events and chance discoveries. The final strategy was 'backed into reluctantly' by managers who felt themselves 'entirely in the dark'. What made the strategy possible was a culture and managerial leadership that fostered the unfolding of the learning process.

Mintzberg argues strongly that we want to be rational but that it is difficult to deal with our complicated world in a rational fashion. What we need is a management process that is sensitive both to the need for emergent learning and to the practical possibilities, and limitations, of deliberate planning. 'If we have discovered anything at all, these many years, it is, first, that the conception of a novel strategy is a creative process (of synthesis), for which there are no formal techniques (analysis), and second, that to program these strategies throughout complex organizations, and out to assenting environments, we often require a good deal of formal analysis. So the two processes can intertwine' (Mintzberg, 1991: 465). Strategic learning cannot be formalized. As the Honda case demonstrates, strategy has to be conceived informally before it can be programmed formally. We have to guard against being seduced by the siren call of 'science' or the false simplicity of 'facts'.

In the first chapter in Part III, 'Management and the learning process', David Kolb, one of the most influential writers on managerial learning, argues that learning is at the heart of a successful management process. The ability to learn at the individual and organizational levels is the basis of the capability to adapt to and master changing circumstances and, as such, lies at the root of effective strategy. Kolb's major contribution has been his elucidation of the learning process in terms of a model of experiential learning, experiential because his theory emphasizes experience as a stimulus to learning rather than cognition. At the core of this model is the concept of the learning cycle composed of four stages in which experience leads to reflection and theory building. Theory provides the basis for action by a process in which action is mediated and guided by hypotheses based upon the implications of theory. During learning, action and reflection form part of an iterative process that leads to new possibilities of action. Creative thought and action involve a process of unlearning. One needs to learn to experience 'anew', i.e. one has to liberate one's capacity for experience from the constraints of existing theory, otherwise new ways of thinking and acting are impossible.

Kolb also analyses learning styles using a Learning Style Inventory which measures the relative emphasis the individual learner attaches to concrete experience, reflective observation, abstract conceptualization and active experimentation. In general, managers tend to emphasize active experimentation over reflective observation. (Theorists of management tend to stress reflective observation and abstract conceptualization!) Learning style determines how individuals deal with new experiences when new facts do not fit existing theory or plans. Innovation is associated with divergent rather than convergent styles of thinking. The innovator is prepared to consider facts that challenge and necessitate the rethinking of existing theories. For the converger the converse applies – the facts have to be made to fit the extant theory. Innovation requires flexibility rather than rigidity, and open- rather than closed-mindedness.

Kolb's work has important implications for management education.

Academic education generally rewards reflection and analysis rather than concrete goal-directed action. Good management education requires the blending of the reflective examination of experience with the application of knowledge to action and the integration of the scholarly and the practical. In experiential learning both 'teacher' and 'student' reflect upon experience. The teacher's role is to develop the capacity for self-direction in learning that combines the abstract and the practical to create the practicable. Organizations are constituted of different groups with different orientations to experience and learning. Effective organizational learning, like individual learning, depends upon action and reflection, concrete involvement and analytical detachment. Organizations need to critically reflect upon their ability to learn and to synthesize the outcomes of different forms of learning to create a whole that is greater than the sum of its parts.

Peter Senge, in the next chapter, 'The leader's new work: building learning organizations', makes the critical link between learning and leadership, arguing that truly learning organizations will remain only a distant vision until the leadership skills they require are more readily available. The key constraint, therefore, on the development of learning organizations is management skill and a new sort of management development is necessary that focuses upon the skills necessary for leadership in learning organizations. First of all, we have to overcome our obsession with control and the notion that people are to be rewarded only for conforming to the rules of others rather than for developing better rules themselves. An external locus of control is a recipe for stasis and, in the long run, mediocrity. (And, of course, the long run is getting shorter and shorter!)

Competitive advantage increasingly depends upon 'experimentation', the continuous exploration of opportunity. This experimentation requires generative rather than adaptive learning. Adaptive learning accepts the world as it is. It is reactive to external events. Generative learning involves recreating the world. It gets below the surface of events to look for underlying patterns and below those the underlying structures (systems) that condition events. The ability to build learning organizations requires a new vision of leadership. The traditional view sees the leader as someone special, usually male (macho management), who chooses the goals and motivates followers through charisma. The new leadership needs to reorientate our thinking. It needs to address our fear of freedom (Fromm, 1941).

The new leaders will be designers, teachers and stewards with a range of new skills that recreate 'followers' as active participants in their own destiny. Such leaders will be designers of the 'social architecture' of organization, responsible for fostering the governing ideas of purpose, vision and values and then translating these governing ideas into business decisions via policies, strategies and structures. Policy and structure represent the 'institutional embodiment of purpose'. Leadership is also about ensuring that processes exist so that policies, structures and strategies are continually improved. This means surfacing, challenging and changing, where necessary, managers' mental models of their business. In this process the leader acts as teacher, coach, guide or facilitator, focusing attention upon the generative systemic structures upon which organizations depend. Organizations need to develop a range of skills/disciplines. These are: self-mastery, shared vision, mental models, team learning and systems thinking.

Ray Stata takes as the starting point of the next chapter, 'Organizational learning: the key to management innovation', the argument that one of the most serious problems in declining industries can be traced to a lack of management innovation, embodied in new knowledge and new learning methods (knowledge technologies). It is management innovation that allows Japan to take advantage of technology innovation. Chairman of a company in a knowledge-intensive industry, Stata is a practitioner member of Peter Senge's MIT New Management Style Project. He argues that this project, a partnership of practitioners and academics, can serve as a prototype for industry/university partnerships.

Stata builds upon Senge's view that organizational learning can only take place through shared insights, knowledge and mental models. His vision of the learning organization is one that integrates systems thinking, planning, quality improvement, organizational behaviour and information systems. Change will not occur unless the major decision-makers participate in a shared learning process. Stata emphasizes the top management role of design for operations – the design of the organization structure and policies so as to realize the organization's mission.

The chapter provides us with a case study of how the author's own company, Analog Devices, using the Shell notion of 'planning as learning' (see de Geus, Chapter 6 of Part I), transformed itself into a learning organization. Crucial to this change was the learning that took place which convinced the company, contrary to conventional business strategy wisdom, that it could be both a product innovator and low-cost producer. In doing this, the company replaced another piece of conventional strategy wisdom, the Boston Consulting Group's 'experience curve' argument that learning occurs as a function of cumulative production volume, with the discovery that learning is crucially related to time and the rate of learning, a qualitative rather than quantitative denominator.

Analog Devices also set about learning how to balance the autonomy of their divisional structure with cooperation between divisions. New values of teamwork, openness and objectivity were promulgated. A new management process based upon information and reason replaced an emphasis upon control. New information systems were important here. The crucial challenge of new information technology is to decide what information and knowledge is needed and – remembering Marshall McLuhan's injunction that 'the medium is the message' – in what form. The creative use of the possibilities offered by new information technologies is crucial because, like any innovation process, management innovation requires new technology and new ideas and the rapid diffusion of the new knowledge through the organization to inform and create new practice.

In the next chapter, 'Second thoughts on teambuilding', Bill Critchley and David Casey address the vexed question of teambuilding in the top management context. They start with a searching analysis of when teamwork is necessary. This might seem somewhat counter-intuitive as a starting point since teamwork is extolled as a panacea for so many contemporary management ills. But Critchley and Casey are persuasive in their argument that teamwork is not something to strive for in all circumstances. However, having said that, they do demonstrate that teamwork is crucial under certain conditions.

First of all we have to be clear what characterizes teamwork. In a properly functioning team there is a sense of belonging to a collective enterprise and members have a shared sense of a common fate and care for each other. There is a high level of trust which leads to openness and truthfulness in communications. Decisions are made by consensus and conflict is confronted. Members share ideas, tasks and feelings. However, many managerial decisions and actions organizations do not require deep attention to interpersonal process. In conditions where technical expertise is sufficient, for example when one is synchronizing sales and production schedules, teamwork involving the whole management team is not necessary providing that members of the top management team trust the expertise of the managers in production, sales and finance.

Teamwork is at a premium, though, in strategic decisions when the future fate of the whole organization is at issue. Consensus based on teamwork is important here otherwise different functional groups will not 'buy into' whatever decisions are made. Strategic work is characterized by high levels of choice and conditions of great uncertainty. There is a temptation to approach these issues in an operational manner, by forcing them to fit into existing strategy frameworks for example, but this is usually dysfunctional because it tends to oversimplify the problems the organization has to face. It is crucial in the strategic dialogue between top managers that they expose/share their uncertainties and their own subjective views of the world. Out of such frank dialogues teams can build common perceptions and a new sense of possibility.

In conditions of shared uncertainty new management processes are needed, new skills and a new mode of leadership. In working with uncertainty people's feelings – anxiety, excitement and trust – are as important as the 'objective' facts and the leader has to work with the group to contain high levels of feeling that can threaten the integrity of the task at hand, the decisions about the future. The leader has to cultivate the interpersonal skills that are necessary to fulfil the process – for example empathy, cooperation, communication, listening, hearing, sharing. The leader has to serve as a catalyst in a cyclical process. Shared uncertainty leads to shared cooperation, leads to unshared certainty and the operationalization of the decision. In the healthy organization the process repeats itself in a virtuous circle.

One criticism levelled against theories of the learning organization is that they ignore organizational politics, 'the processes whereby differentiated but interdependent individuals or interest groups exercise whatever power they can amass to influence the goals, criteria, or processes used in organizational decision making to advance their own interests' (Miles, 1980: 154). This issue is critically examined in the next chapter, John Coopey's 'Crucial gaps in "the learning organization": power, politics and ideology', which argues that power is omnipresent, that the learning organization ignores the reality of asymmetries of power and that political activity is likely to impede learning.

Power is exercised to secure sectional goals. Theories of the learning organization assume a unitarist perspective in which goals are shared, levels of trust are high and differences are treated and resolved rationally. According to a political model of organization, top management constructs disciplinary practices to control employee performance and one can construe the new emphasis upon learning as, beneath the veneer of responsible autonomy, a more subtle way of exercising control. A case of *plus ça change, plus c'est la même chose*. The rewards of improved performance remain uneven and even inequitable. Much employee learning, Coopey suggests, is itself about learning new modes of defence against the exercise of the managerial imperative. The learning organization might disguise the underlying structure of relationships but it does not fundamentally change them.

This argument poses a real challenge to proponents of the learning organization. Information does not circulate freely. Rather, it is used strategically, even cynically, for sectarian purposes. Groups jealously guard their knowledge and use it to defend their positions rather than to promote the good of the whole (Crozier, 1964). Access to information is controlled and restricted by senior managers. The learning organization perspective assumes that knowledge will be shared and that the process of incorporating the discoveries of any group into common policy will not be problematic. This view underestimates the strain of coping in an organization which is in constant turbulence. The ideology of learning, like that of 'organizational culture' which it is fast replacing, provides an antidote to these tensions, legitimizing the organizational dynamism necessary to respond internally. But, again, the ideology serves as a device to preserve managerial hegemony, further 'enforcing' individual dependence upon the organization. The emphasis upon learning and on *one* ideology might also, paradoxically, serve to suppress fruitful dissidence.

In the next chapter, 'Executive tourism: the dynamics of strategic leadership in the MNC', Ken Starkey explores the complications affecting the diffusion of learning in the context of the multinational corporation in a perspective that emphasizes the important role of the top management team dynamic in enabling or in inhibiting learning. Starkey's focus is two-fold. He first examines the factors that contributed to Ford's spectacular turnaround in the US, emphasizing the importance of a new sense of mission, new values and new guiding principles of organization and management. He then examines why the learning process that Ford went through in the US failed in Europe. Ford of Europe plunged from record profits in 1988 to record losses in 1991.

A variety of reasons explain this strange loss of competitiveness. The changes in product development, analysed by Starkey and McKinlay in Part II, had not been successful quickly enough in replenishing Ford of Europe's range of cars. There was cultural resistance to American change initiatives. Indeed, Europeans in general seem to have a form of cultural antipathy to the very idea of an explicit mission and problems with more participative forms of management. But the primary reason, according to Starkey's analysis, has to do with the demise of strategic leadership in Europe committed to the new management agenda.

Ford, like other US firms, tends to use foreign subsidiaries as staging posts in the career development of high-fliers who spend relatively short terms of duty on overseas assignments before returning to bigger and better things in the US. It is difficult for these 'executive tourists' to have an impact upon a situation that they experience only briefly and at a distance, both mentally and geographically. Such managers lack local knowledge and it is frequently more sensible from the standpoint of the individual career not to attempt change. As a result, without high-level integrated championship of new agendas, the status quo tends to prevail. The major issue here is how to find the means of diffusing innovation across national divides. These barriers of geography and culture form a more potent obstacle to change than functional divides. In a major recent reorganization Ford has tried to do away such divisions by integrating its operations both functionally and globally.

In 'Top management teams and organizational renewal', David Hurst, James Rush and Rod White bring the book to a fitting end with a critical examination of the effects of the composition of top management teams, in particular their range of cognitive skills, upon strategic renewal. In the process, they also propose a new model of management (creative management) as an alternative/antidote to conventional thinking about strategic management. They critique the conventional approach to strategy for concentrating upon incremental improvements of existing practices to the neglect of the new ideas and innovations necessary to renew established businesses.

The conventional approach is predicated upon a rational view of strategic decision-making grounded in clearly definable predispositions and acts of planning, choice and action. Intuition and feelings are alien to this view. The problem with the conventional view is that it ignores the differences of orientation of individual managers. It is based upon a simplistic view of the process of decision-making. It is deficient in its implicit assumptions about human cognitive abilities. For example, it assumes that reality exists as a 'given' 'out there' to be apprehended by our senses. An approach based upon logic and rationality cannot deal with the intangibles of the creative process demanded by innovation. The creative management model, by contrast, starts with the assumption that reality is actually a social construction. The environment is 'enacted' by the interaction of actions, events and cognitions. Innovation involves 'creating' a new reality, or, at least, convincing people that they need to reconfigure their expectations about existing and future products and services. Radical innovation involves a clear break with past thinking and creative learning about future possibilities.

Intuition allows people to see/feel what has not been seen/felt before. It taps into our tacit, hidden knowledge. Creative management espouses and validates new ways of seeing things (new visioning), in particular in early stages of organizational and strategic renewal when managers have to respond creatively to ambiguity and uncertainty. It gives rise to new metaphors that liberate our thinking and new organizational myths that inspire people to come up with new ideas by promoting collaborative efforts in conditions of uncertainty. Having stimulated a range of new ideas/possibilities the intuitive stage of strategy cedes centre stage to a feeling stage during which the work of management is to work with people's emotions to align motivation with the choice of a new strategic direction that is acceptable to a range of actors who might start this stage with differing views of which option to choose.

In top management teams one needs to create a climate in which one can tap into the positive force of intuition and feelings. This demands a broadening of the power base for decision-making. It also requires that imagination and motivation are given as much salience as planning, action and evaluation. In terms of their demographics, top management teams need to be constituted to contain a variety of cognitive types so that no single cognitive mode dominates. The ideal top management team needs a mix of people, who individually and collectively are adept in both sensing and thinking and in intuition and feeling. Top management teams need thinkers and sensors, intuitives and feelers, if they are to generate new ideas and to infuse these ideas with value. Crucially, they need to synthesize differences into a creative unity.

REFERENCES

Crozier, M. (1964) *The Bureaucratic Phenomenon*, Chicago, University of Chicago Press.

Fromm, E. (1941) *Escape from Freedom*, New York, Rinehart.

Miles, R.H. (1980) *Macro Organizational Behavior*, Glenview, Ill., Scott, Foresman.

Mintzberg, H. (1991) 'Learning 1, Planning 0: reply to Igor Ansoff', *Strategic Management Journal*, 12, 463–466.

Pascale, R.T. (1984) 'Perspectives on strategy: the real story behind Honda's success', *California Management Review*, 26, 47–72.

Chapter 15

Management and the learning process

David A. Kolb

Today's highly successful manager or administrator is distinguished not so much by any single set of knowledge or skills but by the ability to adapt to and master the changing demands of his or her job and career – by the ability to learn. The same is true for successful organizations. Continuing success in a changing world requires an ability to explore new opportunities and learn from past successes and failures. These ideas are neither new nor particularly controversial. Yet it is surprising that this ability to learn, which is so widely regarded as important, receives so little explicit attention from managers and their organizations. There is a kind of fatalism about learning. One either learns or one doesn't. The ability to consciously control and manage the learning process is usually limited to such schoolboy maxims as 'Study hard' and 'Do your homework.'

Part of the reason for this fatalism lies, I believe, in a lack of understanding about the learning process itself. If managers and administrators had a model about how individuals and organizations learn, they would better be able to enhance their own and the organization's ability to learn. This chapter describes such a model and attempts to show some of the ways in which the learning process and individual learning styles affect management education, managerial decision making and problem solving, and organizational learning.

THE EXPERIENTIAL LEARNING MODEL

Let us begin with a model of how people learn, which I call the experiential learning model. The model is labelled 'experiential' for two reasons. The first is historical, tying it to its intellectual origins in the social psychology of Kurt Lewin in the 1940s and the sensitivity training and laboratory education work of the 1950s and 1960s. The second reason is to emphasize the important role that experience plays in the learning process, an emphasis that differentiates this approach from other cognitive theories of the learning process. The core of the model is a simple description of the learning cycle – how experience is translated into concepts, which in turn are used as guides in the choice of new experiences (Figure 15.1).

Learning is conceived of as a four-stage cycle. Immediate concrete experience is the basis for observation and reflection. These observations are assimilated into a theory from which new implications for action can be deduced. These implications or hypotheses then serve as guides in acting to create new experiences. Learners, if they are to be effective, need four different kinds of abilities – *concrete experience* (CE), *reflective observation* (RO), *abstract conceptualization* (AC), and *active experimentation* (AE). That is, they must be able to involve themselves fully, openly, and without bias in new experiences (CE); reflect on and observe these experiences from many perspectives (RO); create concepts that integrate their observations into logically sound theories (AC); and use these theories to make decisions and solve problems (AE).

Yet how difficult this ideal is to achieve! Can anyone become highly skilled in all of these abilities, or are they necessarily in conflict? How can one act and reflect at the same time? How can one be concrete and immediate and still be theoretical? Indeed, a closer examination of the four-stage learning model reveals that learning requires abilities that are polar opposites and that the learner, as a result, must continually choose which set of learning abilities to bring to bear in any particular learning situation.

More specifically, there are two primary dimensions to the learning process. The first dimension represents the concrete experiencing of events at one end and abstract conceptualization at the other. The other

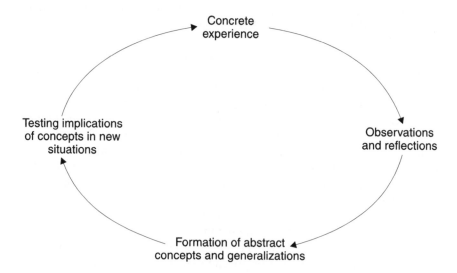

Figure 15.1 **The experiential learning model**

dimension has active experimentation at one extreme and reflective experimentation at the other. Thus, in the process of learning one moves in varying degrees from actor to observer, from specific involvement to general analytic detachment.

Most cognitive psychologists see the concrete/abstract dimension as a primary dimension on which cognitive growth and learning occurs (Flavell, 1963; Bruner, 1960, 1966; Harvey et al., 1961). Goldstein and Scheerer (1941: 4) suggest that greater abstractness results in the development of the following abilities: to detach our ego from the outer world or from inner experience; to assume a mental set; to account for acts to oneself, to verbalize the account; to shift reflectively from one aspect of the situation to another; to hold in mind simultaneously various aspects; to grasp the essential of a given whole – to break up a given into parts to isolate and synthesize them; to abstract common properties reflectively, to form hierarchic concepts; to plan ahead ideationally, to assume an attitude toward the more possible, and to think or perform symbolically. Concreteness, on the other hand, represents the absence of these abilities, the immersion in and domination by one's immediate experiences.

Yet as the circular model of the learning process would imply, abstractness is not exclusively good and concreteness exclusively bad. To be creative requires that one be able to experience anew, freed somewhat from the constraints of previous abstract concepts. In psychoanalytic theory this need for a concrete, childlike perspective in the creative process is referred to as regression in service of the ego (Kris, 1952). In his essay on the conditions for creativity, Bruner (1966) further emphasizes the dialectic tension between abstract detachment and concrete involvement. For him the creative act is a product of detachment and commitment, of passion and decorum, and of a freedom to be dominated by the object of one's inquiry.

The active/reflective dimension is the other major dimension of cognitive growth and learning. As growth occurs, thought becomes more reflective and internalized, based more on the manipulation of symbols and images than covert actions. The modes of active experimentation and reflection, like abstractness/concreteness, stand in opposition to one another. Reflection tends to inhibit action and vice versa. For example, Singer (1968) has found that children who have active internal fantasy lives are more capable of inhibiting action for long periods of time than are children with little internal fantasy life. Kagan has found, on the other hand, that very active orientations toward learning situations inhibit reflection and thereby preclude the development of analytic concepts (Kagan et al., 1964). Herein lies the second major dialectic in the learning process – the tension between actively testing the implications of one's hypotheses and reflectively interpreting data already collected.

INDIVIDUAL LEARNING STYLES

As a result of our hereditary equipment, our particular past life experience, and the demands of our present environment most people develop learning styles that emphasize some learning abilities over others. We come to resolve the conflicts between being active and reflective and between being immediate and analytical in characteristic ways. Some people develop minds that excel at assimilating disparate facts into coherent theories, yet these same people are incapable of or uninterested in deducing hypotheses from their theories. Others are logical geniuses but find it impossible to involve and surrender themselves to an experience, and so on. A mathematician may come to place great emphasis on abstract concepts, while a poet may value concrete experience more highly. A manager may be primarily concerned with the active application of ideas, while a naturalist may develop his or her observational skills highly. Each of us in a unique way develops a learning style that has some weak and some strong points.

For some time now I have been involved in a program of research studies aimed at identifying different kinds of learning styles and their consequences. The purpose of this research is to better understand the different ways that people learn and solve problems so that we can both make individuals aware of the consequences of their own learning style and of the alternative learning modes available to them, and improve the design of learning experiences to take into account these learning-style differences. In this work we have developed a simple self-description inventory, the Learning Style Inventory (LSI), which is designed to measure an individual's strengths and weaknesses as a learner. The LSI measures an individual's relative emphasis on the four learning abilities described earlier, concrete experience (CE), reflective observation (RO), abstract conceptualization (AC) and active experimentation (AE) by asking him or her, several different times, to rank in order four words that describe these different abilities. For example, one set of four words is 'feeling' (CE), 'watching' (RO), 'thinking' (AC), and 'doing' (AE). The inventory yields six scores, CE, RO, AC, and AE plus two combination scores that indicate the extent to which the individual emphasizes abstractness over concreteness (AC–CE) and active experimentation over reflection (AE–RO).

The LSI was administered to 800 practicing managers and graduate students in management to obtain a norm for the management population. In general these managers tended to emphasize active experimentation over reflective observation. In addition, managers with graduate degrees tended to rate their abstract learning skills higher (Kolb, 1971; Kolb et al., 1971). While the managers we tested showed many different patterns of scores on the LSI, we have identified four dominant types of learning styles that occur most frequently. We have called these four styles the converger, the diverger, the assimilator, and the accommodator. (The reason that there are four dominant styles is that AC and CE are highly negatively correlated as are RO and AE. Thus individuals who score high on both AC and CE or on both AE and RO occur with less frequency than do the other four combinations of LSI scores.)

The converger's dominant learning abilities are AC and AE. His or her greatest strength lies in the practical application of ideas. We have called this learning style the converger because a person with this style seems to do best in situations such as conventional intelligence tests, where there is a single correct answer or solution to a question or problem (Torrealba, 1972). The converger's knowledge is organized in such a way that, through hypothetical-deductive reasoning, he or she can focus it on specific problems. Hudson's research on this style of learning shows that convergers are relatively unemotional, preferring to deal with things rather than people (Hudson, 1966). They tend to have narrow technical interests and choose to specialize in the physical sciences. Our research shows that this learning style is characteristic of many engineers.

The diverger has the opposite learning strengths of the converger. Divergers are best at CE and RO. Their greatest strength lies in their imaginative ability. They excel in the ability to view concrete situations from many perspectives. We have labelled this style diverger because a person with this style performs better in situations that call for generation of ideas such as a 'brainstorming' session. Hudson's (1966) work on this learning style shows that divergers are interested in people and tend to be imaginative and emotional. They have broad cultural interests and tend to specialize in the arts. Our research shows that this style is characteristic of managers from humanities and liberal arts backgrounds. Personnel managers tend to be characterized by this learning style.

The assimilator's dominant learning abilities are AC and RO. Assimilators' greatest strength lies in the ability to create theoretical models. They excel in inductive reasoning – in assimilating disparate observations into an integrated explanation. Like convergers, assimilators are less interested in people and more concerned with abstract concepts, but they are less concerned with the practical use of theories. For them it is more important that the theory be logically sound and precise. As a result, this learning style is more characteristic of the basic sciences rather than the applied sciences. In organizations this learning style is found most often in the research and planning departments.

The accommodator has the opposite learning strengths of the assimilator. Accommodators are best at CE and AE. Their greatest strength lies in doing things, in carrying out plans and experiments and getting involved in new experiences. The accommodator tends to be more of a risk taker than people with the other three learning styles. We have labelled this style accommodator because these people tend to excel in situations where they must adapt to specific immediate circumstances. In situations where the theory or plans do not fit the facts, they will most likely discard the plan or theory. (The opposite style type, the assimilator, would be more likely to disregard or reexamine the facts.) Accommodators are at ease with people but are sometimes seen as impatient and 'pushy.' Their education background is often in technical or practical fields such as business. In organizations people with this learning style are found in action-oriented jobs, often in marketing or sales.

These different learning styles can be illustrated graphically (Figure 15.2) by plotting the average LSI scores for managers in our sample who reported their undergraduate college major (only those majors with more than ten people responding are included). Before interpreting these data, some cautions are in order. First, it should be remembered that all of the individuals in the sample are managers or managers-to-be. In addition, most have completed or are in graduate school. These two facts should produce learning styles that are somewhat more active and abstract than the population at large (as indicated by total sample mean scores on AC–CE and AE–RO, +4.5 and +2.9 respectively).

The interaction between career, high level of education, and under-graduate major may produce distinctive learning styles. For example, physicists who are not in industry may be somewhat more reflective than those in this sample. Second, undergraduate majors are described only in the most general terms. There are many forms of engineering or psychology. A business major at one school can be quite different from that at another. However, even if we take these cautions into consideration, the distri-bution of undergraduate majors on the learning style grid is strikingly consistent with theory (Kolb, 1971). Undergraduate business majors tend to have accommodative learning styles, while engineers on the average fall in the convergent quadrant. History, English, political science, and psychology majors all have divergent learning styles, along with eco-nomics and sociology. Physics majors are very abstract, falling between the convergent and assimilative quadrants. What these data show is that one's undergraduate education is a major factor in the development of learning style. Whether this is because individuals' learning styles are shaped by the fields they enter or because of selection processes that put people into and out of disciplines is an open question at this point. Most probably both factors are operating – people choose fields that are con-sistent with their learning styles and are further shaped to fit the learning norms of their field once they are in it. When there is a mismatch between the field's learning norms and the individual's learning style, people will either change or leave the field. Plovnick's research indicates that the latter alternative is more likely (Plovnick, 1971). He studied a major university physics department and concluded that the major emphasis in

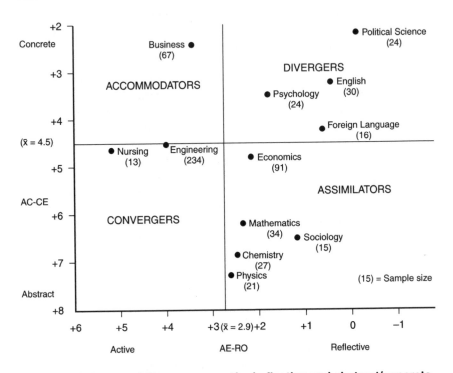

Figure 15.2 Average LSI scores on active/reflective and abstract/concrete by undergraduate college major

physics education was on convergent learning. He predicted that physics students who had convergent learning styles would be content with their majors, whereas physics majors who were divergent in their learning style would be uncertain of physics as a career and would take more courses outside of the physics department than their convergent colleagues. His predictions were confirmed. Those students who are not 'fitted' for the convergent learning style required in physics tend to turn away from physics as a profession.

These results pose something of an educational dilemma for the physics department. To contribute in physics today one must know many facts, so learning content is important; and this takes time, time that might be spent developing the convergent skills of divergers. So isn't it simpler to select (implicitly or explicitly) people who already possess these convergent experimental and theoretical skills? Perhaps, but in the process the creative tension between convergence and divergence is lost. The result of this process may be a program that produces fine technicians but few innovators.

Kuhn (1952) put the issue this way: 'Because the old must be revalued and reordered when assimilating the new, discovery and invention in the sciences are usually intrinsically revolutionary. Therefore they do demand just that flexibility and open-mindedness that characterize and indeed define the divergent.' It just may be that one of the reasons why creative contributions in the sciences are primarily by younger people is that the learning styles of older people have been shaped by their professional training and experience so that they adapt well to the inquiry norms of their profession, but the creative tension is lost (Lehman, 1953).

LEARNING STYLES IN MANAGEMENT EDUCATION

Differences in learning style create similar problems for management education. Managers who come to the university for mid-career education experience something of a culture shock. Fresh from a world of time deadlines and concrete, specific problems that they must solve, they are suddenly immersed in a strange, slow-paced world of generalities where the elegant solution to problems is sought even when workable solutions have been found. One gets rewarded here for reflection and analysis rather than concrete goal-directed action. Managers who 'act before they think – if they ever think' meet scientists who 'think before they act – if they ever act'.

Our research on learning styles has shown that managers on the whole are distinguished by very strong active experimentation skills and are very weak on reflective observation skills. Business school faculty members usually have the reverse profile. To bridge this gap in learning styles the management educator must somehow respond to pragmatic demands for relevance and the application of knowledge while encouraging the reflective examination of experience that is necessary to refine old theories and to build new ones. In encouraging reflective observation the teacher often is seen as an interrupter of action – as a passive, 'ivory tower' thinker. Indeed, this is a critical role to be played in the learning process. Yet if the reflective observer role is not internalized by the students themselves, the learning process can degenerate into a value conflict between teacher and student, each maintaining that theirs is the right perspective on learning.

Neither the faculty nor student perspective alone is valid, in my view. Managerial education will not be improved by eliminating theoretical analysis or relevant case problems. Improvement will come through *integration of the scholarly and practical learning styles*. My approach to achieving this integration has been to apply directly the experiential learning model in the classroom (Kolb *et al.*, 1971). To do this we created a workbook providing games, role plays, and exercises (concrete experiences) that focus on fifteen central concepts in organizational psychology.

These simulations provide a common experiential starting point for managers and faculty to explore the relevance of psychological concepts for their work. In traditional management education methods the conflict between scholar and practitioner learning styles is exaggerated because the material to be taught is filtered through the learning style of the faculty member' lectures or presentation and analysis of cases. Students are 'one down' in their own analysis because their data are second-hand and already biased.

In the experiential learning approach this filtering process does not take place because both teacher and student are observers of immediate experiences, which they both interpret according to their own learning styles. In this approach the teacher's role is that of a facilitator of a learning process that is basically self-directed. The teacher helps students to experience in a personal and immediate way the phenomena in his or her field of specialization, providing observational schemes and perspectives from which to observe these experiences. The teacher stands ready with alternative theories and concepts as students attempt to assimilate their observations into their own conception of reality. The teacher also assists in deducing the implications of the student's concepts and in designing new experiments to test these implications through practical, 'real world' experience.

There are two goals in the experiential learning process. One is to learn the specifics of a particular subject. The other goal is to learn about one's own strengths and weaknesses as a learner – learning how to learn from experience. When the process works well, managers finish their educational experience not only with new intellectual insights, but also with an understanding of their own learning style. This understanding of learning strengths and weaknesses helps in the application of what has been learned and provides a framework for continuing learning on the job. Day-to-day experience becomes a focus for testing and exploring new ideas. Learning is no longer a special activity reserved for the classroom; it becomes an integral and explicit part of work itself.

LEARNING STYLES AND MANAGERIAL PROBLEM SOLVING

We have been able to identify relationships between managers' learning style and their educational experiences, but how about their current behavior on the job? Do managers with different learning styles approach problem solving and decision making differently? Theoretically, the answer to this question should be yes, since learning and problem solving are not different processes but the same basic process of adaptation viewed from different perspectives. To illustrate this point I have overlaid in Figure 15.3 a typical model of the problem-solving process on the experiential learning model (Pounds, 1965). In this figure we can see that the stages in a problem-solving sequence generally correspond to the learning-style strengths of the four major learning styles described previously. The accommodator's problem-solving strengths lie in executing solutions and initiating problem finding based on some goal or model about how things should be. The diverger's problem-solving strengths lie in identifying the multitude of possible problems and opportunities that exist in reality ('compare model with reality and identify differences'). The assimilator excels in the abstract model building that is necessary to choose a priority problem and alternative solutions. The converger's strengths lie in the evaluation of solution consequences and solution selection.

To date, two studies have been conducted to discover whether there is anything to this theoretical model. The first was conducted by Stabell in the trust department of a large Midwestern bank (Stabell, 1973). One aim of his study was to discover how the learning styles of investment portfolio managers affected their problem solving and decision making in the management of the assets in their portfolios. While his study involved

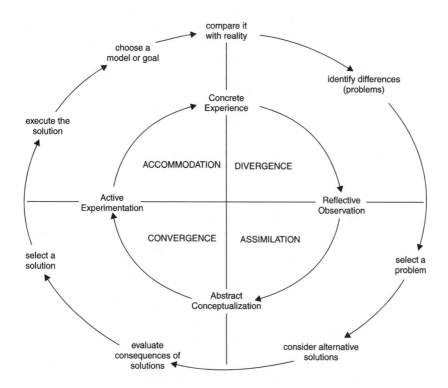

Figure 15.3 **Comparison of the experiential learning model with a typical model of the problem-solving process**

only thirty-one managers, he found a strong correspondence between the type of decisions these managers faced and their learning styles. More specifically, he found that nearly all of the managers in the investment advisory section of the department, a high-risk, high-pressure job (as indicated by a large percentage of holdings in common stock, a large percentage of discretionary accounts, and a high performance and risk orientation on the part of clients), had accommodative learning styles (scoring very high on the AE and CE LSI scales). On the other hand, the men in the personal trust section, where risk and performance orientations were low and there were few discretionary accounts and fewer holdings in common stock, scored highest on reflective observation. This finding supports our earlier analysis that high-pressure management jobs develop and select for active experimentation learning skills and inhibit reflective observation learning skills.

Stabell was interested in whether he could identify differences, on the basis of their LSI scores, in the way managers went about making investment decisions. He focused his research on differences between managers with CE learning skills and AC learning skills. He asked these managers to evaluate the importance of the information sources they used in making decisions and found several interesting differences. First, CE managers cited more people as important sources (colleagues, brokers, and traders), while the AC managers listed more analytically oriented printed material as sources (economic analyses, industry and company reviews). In addition, it seemed that CE managers sought services that would give them a specific recommendation that they could accept or reject (a potential list), while the AC managers sought information they could analyze themselves in order to choose an investment. This analytic orientation of the AC managers is further illustrated by the fact that they tended to use more information sources in their decisions than the CE managers. These data fit well with the learning/problem-solving model in Figure 15.3. The concrete managers prefer go/no go implementation decisions based on personal recommendations, while the abstract managers prefer to consider and evaluate alternative solutions themselves.

The second study of the relationship between learning styles and managerial problem solving was a laboratory computer simulation of a production 'trouble-shooting' problem where the problem solver had to determine which specific type of 'widget' was failure-prone. This experiment, which is a modification of an earlier problem-solving experiment by Bruner and associates (1956), was conducted by Grochow as part of his doctoral dissertation (Grochow, 1973). His subjects for the experiment were twenty-two middle-level managers at MIT's Sloan Fellows program. Grochow was particularly interested in the different types of problem-solving strategies that assimilators and accommodators would use to solve this problem. He predicted that the accommodators would use a strategy that called for little complexity in use and interpretation, little inference from the data, and little cognitive strain in assimilating information, while assimilators would prefer a strategy that had the opposite characteristics – more complex use and interpretation and more assimilation strain and required inference. The former strategy, called successive scanning, was simply a process whereby the problem solvers scan the data base of widgets for a direct test of their current hypothesis. It requires little conceptual analysis, since the current hypothesis is either validated or not in each trial. The latter strategy, called simultaneous scanning, is in a sense an optimal strategy in that each data point is used to eliminate the maximum number of data points still possible. This strategy requires considerable conceptual analysis, since the problem solver must keep several hypotheses in his or her head at the same time and deduce the optimal widget to examine in order to test these hypotheses.

The results of Grochow's experiment confirmed his hypothesis that accommodators would use successive scanning, while assimilators would use the more analytical simultaneous scanning strategy. He further found that managers with accommodative learning styles tended to show more inconsistency in their use of strategies, while the assimilative managers were quite consistent in their use of the simultaneous scanning strategy. The accommodative managers seemed to be taking a more intuitive approach, switching strategies as they gathered more data during the experiment. Interestingly, Grochow found no differences between accommodative and assimilative managers in the amount of time it took them to solve the problem. Though the two groups used very different styles, in this problem they performed equally well.

The results of both of these studies are consistent with the learning/problem-solving model. Managers' learning styles are measurably related to the way in which they solve problems and make decisions on the job and in the laboratory.

THE ORGANIZATION AS A LEARNING SYSTEM

Like individuals, organizations learn and develop distinctive learning styles. They do so through their transactions with the environment and through their choice of how to relate to that environment. This has come to be known as the 'open systems' view of organizations. Since many organizations are large and complex, the environment they relate to becomes highly differentiated and diverse. The way the organization adapts to this external environment is to differentiate itself into units, each of which deals with just one part of the firm's external conditions. Marketing and sales face problems associated with the market, customers, and competitors. Research deals with the academic and technological worlds. Production deals with production equipment and raw materials sources. Personnel and labor relations deal with the labor market, and so on.

Because of this need to relate to different aspects of the environment, the different units of the firm develop characteristic ways of thinking and working together, different styles of decision making and problem solving. These units select and shape managers to solve problems and make decisions in the way their environment demands. In fact, Lawrence and Lorsch define organizational differentiation as 'the difference in cognitive and emotional orientation among managers in different functional departments' (1967: 11).

If the organization is thought of as a learning system, then each of the differentiated units that is charged with adapting to the challenges of one segment of the environment can be thought of as having a characteristic learning style that is best suited to meet those environmental demands. The LSI should be a useful tool for measuring this organizational differentiation among the functional units of a firm. To test this we studied approximately twenty managers from each of five functional groups in a Midwestern division of a large American industrial corporation (Weisner, 1971; I have reanalyzed Weisner's data for presentation here). The five functional groups are described below, followed by my hypothesis about the learning style that should characterize each group given the environments to which they relate.

1 Marketing (n = 20). This group is primarily former salesmen. They have a nonquantitative, intuitive approach to their work. Because of their practical sales orientation in meeting customer demands, they should have accommodative learning styles – concrete and active.

2 Research (n = 22). The work of this group is split about evenly between projects. The emphasis is on basic research. Researchers should be the most assimilative group – abstract and reflective, a style fitted to the world of knowledge and ideas.

3 Personnel/Labor Relations (n = 20). In this company men from this department serve two primary functions: interpreting personnel policy and promoting interaction among groups to reduce conflict and disagreement. Because of their people orientation these men should be predominantly divergers, concrete and reflective.

4 Engineering (n = 18). This group is made up primarily of design engineers who are quite production oriented. They should be the most convergent subgroup – abstract and active – although they should be less abstract than the research group. They represent a bridge between thought and action.

5 Finance (n = 20). This group has a strong computer/information-systems bias. Finance men, given their orientation toward the

mathematical task of information-system design, should be highly abstract. Their crucial role in organizational survival should produce an active orientation. Thus, finance group members should have convergent learning styles.

Figure 15.4 shows the average scores on the active/reflective (AE–RO) and abstract/concrete (AC–CE) learning dimensions for the five functional groups. These results are consistent with the above predictions with the exception of the finance group, whose scores are less active than predicted; thus, they fall between the assimilative and the convergent quadrant (Weisner, 1971). The LSI clearly differentiates the learning styles that characterize the functional units of at least this one company. Managers in each of these units apparently use very different styles in doing their jobs.

But differentiation is only part of the story of organizational adaptation and effectiveness. The result of the differentiation necessary to adapt to the external environment is the creation of a corresponding internal need to integrate and coordinate the different units. This necessitates resolving

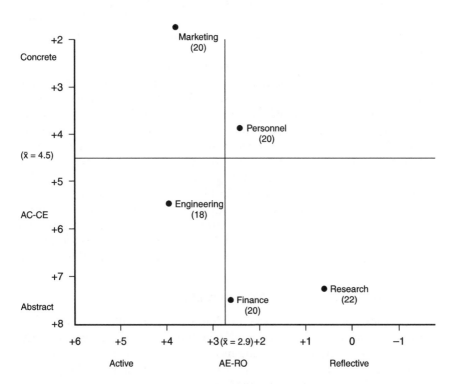

Figure 15.4 **Average LSI scores on active/reflective and abstract/concrete by organizational function**

in some way the conflicts inherent in these different learning styles. In actual practice this conflict gets resolved in many ways. Sometimes it is resolved through dominance by one unit over the other units, resulting in an unbalanced organizational learning style. We all know of organizations that are controlled by the marketing department or are heavily engineering-oriented, and so forth. This imbalance can be effective if it matches environmental demands in a stable environment; but it can be costly if the organization is called upon to learn to respond to changing environmental demands and opportunities.

One important question concerns the extent to which the integrative conflict between units is a function of managers' learning styles rather than merely a matter of conflicting job and role demands. To get at this question we asked the managers in each of the five functional units in the preceding study to rate how difficult they found it to communicate with each of the other four units. If integrative communication is a function of learning style, there should be a correspondence between how similar two units are in their learning style and how easy they find it to communicate. When the average communication difficulty ratings among the five units are compared with differences in unit learning styles, we find that in most cases this hypothesis is confirmed – those units that are most different in learning style have more difficulty communicating with one another.[1]

To test this notion more rigorously we did a more intensive study of communication between the two units that were most different in learning styles: marketing and research. To ascertain whether it was the manager's learning style that accounted for communication difficulty we divided managers in the marketing unit into two groups. One group had learning styles that were similar to those managers in research (assimilators), while the other group had accommodative learning styles typical of the marketing function. The research group was divided similarly. The results of this analysis are shown in Figure 15.5. When managers have learning styles similar to another group they have little trouble communicating with that group. When style differences are great, communication difficulty rises. These results suggest that managers' learning styles are an important factor to consider in achieving integration of functional units.

MANAGING THE LEARNING PROCESS

To conclude, let us return to the problem we began with – how managers and organizations can explicitly manage their learning process. We have seen that the experiential learning model is useful not only for examining the educational process but also for understanding managerial problem solving and organizational adaptation.

But how can an awareness of the experiential learning model and our

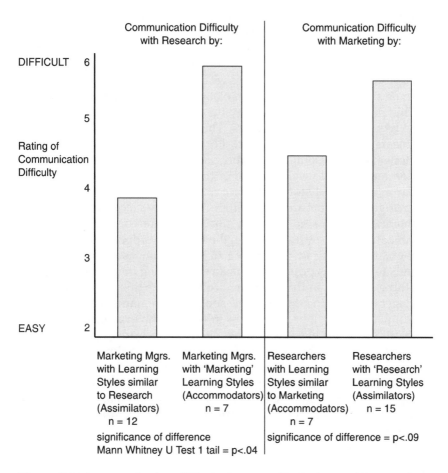

Figure 15.5 **Communication difficulty between Marketing and Research as a function of learning style**

own individual learning style help improve individual and organizational learning? Two recommendations seem important.

First, learning should be an explicit objective that is pursued as consciously and deliberately as profit or productivity. Managers and organizations should budget time specifically to learn from their experiences. When important meetings are held or important decisions made, time should be set aside to critique and learn from these events. In my experience all too few organizations have a climate that allows for free exploration of such questions as, What have we learned from this venture? Usually active experimentation norms dictate – We don't have time; let's move on.

Which leads to the second recommendation. The nature of the learning process is such that opposing perspectives, action and reflection, concrete involvement and analytical detachment, are all essential for optimal learning. When one perspective comes to dominate others, learning effectiveness is reduced in the long run. From this we can conclude that the most effective learning systems are those that can tolerate differences in perspective.

This point can be illustrated by the case of an electronics firm that I have worked with over the years. The firm was started by a group of engineers with a unique product. For several years they had no competitors and when some competition entered the market they continued to dominate and do well because of their superior engineering quality. Today is a different story. They are now faced with stiff competitors in their original product area. In addition, their very success has caused new problems. They are no longer a small, intimate company but a large organization with several plants in the US and Europe. The company has had great difficulty in responding to these changes because it still responds to problems primarily from an engineering point of view. Most of the top executives in the company are former engineers with no formal management training. Many of the specialists in marketing, finance, and personnel who have been brought in to help the organization solve its new problems feel like second-class citizens. Their ideas just don't seem to carry much weight. What was once the organization's strength – its engineering expertise – has become to some extent its weakness. Because engineering has flourished at the expense of the development of other organizational functions, such as marketing and the management of human resources, the firm is today struggling with rather than mastering its environment.

NOTE

1 't' tests for significance of difference between groups on the abstract/concrete dimension yield the following one-tail probabilities that are less than 0.10. Marketing is more concrete than personnel ($p<0.10$), engineering ($p<0.05$), research ($p<0.005$), and finance ($p<0.005$). Finance and research are more abstract than personnel (on both comparisons $p<0.005$). On the active/reflective dimension, research is more reflective than marketing ($p<0.05$), engineering ($p<0.05$), and to a less extent finance ($p<0.10$).

REFERENCES

Bruner, J.S. (1960) *The Process of Education* (New York: Vintage Books).
Bruner, J.S. (1966) *Essays for the Left Hand* (New York: Atheneum).
Bruner, J.S., Goodnow, J.J. and Austin, G.A. (1956) *A Study of Thinking* (New York: Wiley & Sons).
Flavell, John (1963) *The Developmental Psychology of Jean Piaget* (New York: Van Nostrand Reinhold).

Goldstein, K. and Scheerer, M. (1941) 'Abstract and Concrete Behavior: An Experimental Study with Special Tests,' *Psychological Monographs*, p. 4.

Grochow, Jerrold (1973) 'Cognitive Style as a Factor in the Design of Interactive Decision-Support Systems,' PhD thesis, MIT Sloan School.

Harvey, O.J., Hunt, David and Schroder, Harold (1961) *Conceptual Systems and Personality Organization* (New York: John Wiley).

Hudson, L. (1966) *Contrary Imaginations* (Harmondsworth: Penguin Books).

Kagan, Jerome, Rosman, Bernice L., Day, Deborah, Alpert, Joseph and Phillips, William (1964) 'Information Processing in the Child: Significance of Analytic and Reflective Attitudes,' *Psychological Monographs*.

Kolb, David A. (1971) *Individual Learning Styles and the Learning Process*, MIT Sloan School Working Paper No. 535–71.

Kolb, David, Rubin, Irwin and McIntyre, James (1971) *Organizational Psychology: An Experiential Approach* (Englewood Cliffs, NJ: Prentice-Hall).

Kris, Ernst (1952) *Psychoanalytic Explorations in Art* (New York: International Universities Press).

Kuhn, Thomas (1952) *The Structure of Scientific Revolutions* (Chicago: University of Chicago Press).

Lawrence, Paul and Lorsch, Jay (1967) *Organization and Environment* (Boston: Division of Research, Graduate School of Business Administration).

Lehman, H.C. (1953) *Age and Achievement* (Princeton, NJ: Princeton University Press).

Plovnick, M.S. (1971) 'A Cognitive Ability Theory of Occupational Roles,' MIT School of Management, Working Paper No. 524–71, Spring.

Pounds, William (1965) 'On Problem Finding,' Sloan School Working Paper No. 145–65.

Singer, J. (1968) 'The Importance of Daydreaming,' *Psychology Today*, pp. 18–26.

Stabell, Charles (1973) 'The Impact of a Conversational Computer System on Human Problem Solving Behavior,' unpublished working paper, MIT Sloan School.

Torrealba, David (1972) 'Convergent and Divergent Learning Styles,' MS thesis, MIT Sloan School.

Weisner, F. (1971) 'Learning Profiles and Managerial Styles of Managers,' S.M. thesis, Sloan School of Management, MIT.

Chapter 16

The leader's new work
Building learning organizations

Peter M. Senge

Human beings are designed for learning. No one has to teach an infant to walk, or talk, or master the spatial relationships needed to stack eight building blocks that don't topple. Children come fully equipped with an insatiable drive to explore and experiment. Unfortunately, the primary institutions of our society are oriented predominantly toward controlling rather than learning, rewarding individuals for performing for others rather than for cultivating their natural curiosity and impulse to learn. The young child entering school discovers quickly that the name of the game is getting the right answer and avoiding mistakes – a mandate no less compelling to the aspiring manager.

'Our prevailing system of management has destroyed our people,' writes W. Edwards Deming, leader in the quality movement.[1] 'People are born with intrinsic motivation, self-esteem, dignity, curiosity to learn, joy in learning. The forces of destruction begin with toddlers – a prize for the best Hallowe'en costume, grades in school, gold stars, and on up through the university. On the job, people, teams, divisions are ranked – reward for the one at the top, punishment at the bottom. MBO, quotas, incentive pay, business plans, put together separately, division by division, cause further loss, unknown and unknowable.'

Ironically, by focusing on performing for someone else's approval, corporations create the very conditions that predestine them to mediocre performance. Over the long run, superior performance depends on superior learning. A Shell study showed that, according to former planning director Arie de Geus, 'a full one-third of the Fortune "500" industrials listed in 1970 had vanished by 1983.'[2] Today, the average lifetime of the largest industrial enterprises is probably less than *half* the average lifetime of a person in an industrial society. On the other hand, de Geus and his colleagues at Shell also found a small number of companies that survived for seventy-five years or longer. Interestingly, the key to their survival was the ability to run 'experiments in the margin,' to continually explore new business and organizational opportunities that create potential new sources of growth.

If anything, the need for understanding how organizations learn and accelerating that learning is greater today than ever before. The old days when Henry Ford, Alfred Sloan, or Tom Watson *learned for the organization* are gone. In an increasingly dynamic, interdependent, and unpredictable world, it is simply no longer possible for anyone to 'figure it all out at the top.' The old model, 'the top thinks and the local acts,' must now give way to integrating thinking and acting at all levels. While the challenge is great, so is the potential payoff. 'The person who figures out how to harness the collective genius of the people in his or her organization,' according to former Citibank CEO Walter Wriston, 'is going to blow the competition away.'

ADAPTIVE LEARNING AND GENERATIVE LEARNING

The prevailing view of learning organizations emphasizes increased adaptability. Given the accelerating pace of change, or so the standard view goes, 'the most successful corporate of the 1990s,' according to *Fortune* magazine, 'will be something called a learning organization, a consummately adaptive enterprise.'[3] As the Shell study shows, examples of traditional authoritarian bureaucracies that responded too slowly to survive in changing business environments are legion.

But increasing adaptiveness is only the first stage in moving toward learning organizations. The impulse to learn in children goes deeper than desires to respond and adapt more effectively to environmental change. The impulse to learn, at its heart, is an impulse to be generative, to expand our capability. This is why leading corporations are focusing on *generative* learning, which is about creating, as well as *adaptive* learning, which is about coping.[4]

The total quality movement in Japan illustrates the evolution from adaptive to generative learning. With its emphasis on continuous experimentation and feedback, the total quality movement has been the first wave in building learning organizations. But Japanese firms' view of serving the customer has evolved. In the early years of total quality, the focus was on 'fitness to standard,' making a product reliably so that it would do what its designers intended it to do and what the firm told its customers it would do. Then came a focus on 'fitness to need,' understanding better what the customer wanted and then providing products that reliably met those needs. Today, leading edge firms seek to understand and meet the 'latent need' of the customer – what customers might truly value but have never experienced or would never think to ask for. As one Detroit executive commented recently, 'You could never produce the Mazda Miata solely from market research. It required a leap of imagination to see what the customer *might* want.'[5]

Generative learning, unlike adaptive learning, requires new ways of looking at the world, whether in understanding customers or in understanding how to better manage a business. For years, US manufacturers sought competitive advantage in aggressive controls on inventories, incentives against overproduction, and rigid adherence to production forecasts. Despite these incentives, their performance was eventually eclipsed by Japanese firms who saw the challenges of manufacturing differently. They realized that eliminating delays in the production process was the key to reducing instability and improving cost, productivity, and service. They worked to build networks of relationships with trusted suppliers and to redesign physical production processes so as to reduce delays in materials procurement, production set up, and in-process inventory – a much higher-leverage approach to improving both cost and customer loyalty.

As Boston Consulting Group's George Stalk has observed, the Japanese saw the significance of delays because they saw the process of order entry, production scheduling, materials procurement, production, and distribution *as an integrated system*. 'What distorts the system so badly is time,' observed Stalk – the multiple delays between events and responses. 'These distortions reverberate throughout the system, producing disruptions, waste, and inefficiency.'[6] Generative learning requires seeing the systems that control events. When we fail to grasp the systemic source of problems, we are left of 'push on' symptoms rather than eliminate underlying causes. The best we can ever do is adaptive learning.

THE LEADER'S NEW WORK

'I talk with people all over the country about learning organizations, and the response is always very positive,' says William O'Brien, CEO of the Hanover Insurance companies. 'If this type of organization is so widely preferred why don't people create such organizations? I think the answer is leadership. People have no real comprehension of the type of commitment it requires to build such an organization.'[7]

Our traditional view of leaders – as special people who set the direction, make the key decisions, and energize the troops – is deeply rooted in an individualistic and nonsystemic worldview. Especially in the West, leaders are *heroes* – great men (and occasionally women) who rise to the fore in times of crisis. So long as such myths prevail, they reinforce a focus on short-term events and charismatic heroes rather than on systemic forces and collective learning.

Leadership in learning organizations centers on subtler and ultimately more important work. In a learning organization, leaders' roles differ dramatically from that of the charismatic decision maker. Leaders are designers, teachers, and stewards. These roles require new skills: the ability to build shared vision, to bring to the surface and challenge prevailing mental models, and to foster more systemic patterns of thinking. In short, leaders in learning organizations are responsible for *building organizations* where people are continually expanding their capabilities to shape their future – that is, leaders are responsible for learning.

CREATIVE TENSION: THE INTEGRATING PRINCIPLE

Leadership in a learning organization starts with the principle of creative tension.[8] Creative tension comes from seeing clearly where we want to be, our 'vision,' and telling the truth about where we are, our 'current reality.' The gap between the two generates a natural tension (see Figure 16.1).

Creative tension can be resolved in two basic ways: by raising current reality toward the vision, or by lowering the vision toward current reality. Individuals, groups, and organizations who learn how to work with creative tension learn how to use the energy it generates to move reality more reliably toward their visions.

The principle of creative tension has long been recognized by leaders. Martin Luther King, Jr., once said, 'Just as Socrates felt that it was necessary to create a tension in the mind, so that individuals could rise from the bondage of myths and half truth . . . so must we . . . create the kind of tension in society that will help men rise from the dark depths of prejudice and racism.'[9]

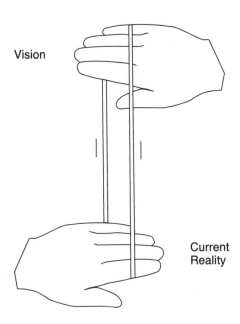

Figure 16.1 **The principle of creative tension**

Without vision there is no creative tension. Creative tension cannot be generated from current reality alone. All the analysis in the world will never generate a vision. Many who are otherwise qualified to lead, fail to do so because they try to substitute analysis for vision. They believe that, if only people understood current reality, they would surely feel the motivation to change. They are then disappointed to discover that people 'resist' the personal and organizational changes that must be made to alter reality. What they never grasp is that the natural energy for changing reality comes from holding a picture of what might be that is more important to people than what is.

But creative tension cannot be generated from vision alone; it demands an accurate picture of current reality as well. Just as King had a dream, so too did he continually strive to 'dramatize the shameful conditions' of racism and prejudice so that they could no longer be ignored. Vision without an understanding of current reality will more likely foster cynicism than creativity. The principle of creative tension teaches that *an accurate picture of current reality is just as important as a compelling picture of a desired future.*

Leading through creative tension is different than solving problems. In problem solving, the energy for change comes from attempting to get away from an aspect of current reality that is undesirable. With creative tension, the energy for change comes from the vision, from what we want to create, juxtaposed with current reality. While the distinction may seem small, the consequences are not. Many people and organizations find themselves motivated to change only when their problems are bad enough to cause them to change. This works for a while, but the change process runs out of steam as soon as the problems driving the change become less pressing. With problem solving, the motivation for change is extrinsic. With creative tension, the motivation is intrinsic. This distinction mirrors the distinction between adaptive and generative learning.

NEW ROLES

The traditional authoritarian image of the leader as 'the boss calling the shots' has been recognized as oversimplified and inadequate for some time. According to Edgar Schein, 'Leadership is intertwined with culture formation.' Building an organization's culture and shaping its evolution is the 'unique and essential function' of leadership.[10] In a learning organization, the critical roles of leadership – designer, teacher, and steward – have antecedents in the ways leaders have contributed to building organizations in the past. But each role takes on new meaning in the learning organization and, as will be seen in the following sections, demands new skills and tools.

LEADER AS DESIGNER

Imagine that your organization is an ocean liner and that you are 'the leader.' What is your role?

I have asked this question of groups of managers many times. The most common answer, not surprisingly, is 'the captain.' Others say, 'the navigator, setting the direction.' Still others say, 'the helmsman, actually controlling the direction,' or, 'the engineer down there stoking the fire, providing energy,' or, 'the social director, making sure everybody's enrolled, involved, and communicating.' While these are legitimate leadership roles, there is another which, in many ways, eclipses them all in importance. Yet rarely does anyone mention it.

The neglected leadership role is the *designer* of the ship. No one has a more sweeping influence than the designer. What good does it do for the captain to say, 'Turn starboard 30 degrees,' when the designer has built a rudder that will only turn to port, or which takes six hours to turn to starboard? It's fruitless to be the leader in an organization that is poorly designed.

The functions of design, or what some have called 'social architecture,' are rarely visible; they take place behind the scenes. The consequences that appear today are the result of work done long in the past, and work today will show its benefits far in the future. Those who aspire to lead out of a desire to control, or gain fame, or simply to be at the center of the action, will find little to attract them to the quiet design work of leadership.

But what, specifically, is involved in organizational design? 'Organization design is widely misconstrued as moving around boxes and lines,' says Hanover's O'Brien. 'The first task of organization design concerns designing the governing ideas of purpose, vision, and core values by which people will live.' Few acts of leadership have a more enduring impact on an organization than building a foundation of purpose and core values.

In 1982 in the USA, Johnson & Johnson found itself facing a corporate nightmare when bottles of its best-selling Tylenol were tampered with, resulting in several deaths. The corporation's immediate response was to pull all Tylenol off the shelves of retail outlets. Thirty-one million capsules were destroyed, even though they were tested and found safe. Although the immediate cost was significant, no other action was possible given that the firm's credo states that permanent success is possible only when modern industry realizes that:

- service to its customers comes first;
- service to its employees and management comes second;
- service to the community comes third; and
- service to its stockholders, last.

Such statements might seem like motherhood and apple pie to those who have not seen the way a clear sense of purpose and values can affect key business decisions. Johnson & Johnson's crisis management in this case was based on that credo. It was simple, it was right, and it worked.

If governing ideas constitute the first design task of leadership, the second design task involves the policies, strategies, and structures that translate guiding ideas into business decisions. Leadership theorist Philip Selznick calls policy and structure the 'institutional embodiment of purpose.'[11] 'Policy making (the rules that guide decisions) ought to be separated from decision making,' says Jay Forrester.[12] 'Otherwise, short-term pressures will usurp time from policy creation.'

Traditionally, writers like Selznick and Forrester have tended to see policy making and implementation as the work of a small number of senior managers. But that view is changing. Both the dynamic business environment and the mandate of the learning organization to engage people at all levels now make it clear that this second design task is more subtle. Henry Mintzberg has argued that strategy is less a rational plan arrived at in the abstract and implemented throughout the organization than an 'emergent phenomenon.' Successful organizations 'craft strategy' according to Mintzberg, as they continually learn about shifting business conditions and balance what is desired and what is possible.[13] The key is not getting the right strategy but fostering strategic thinking. 'The choice of individual action is only part of . . . the policymaker's need,' according to Mason and Mitroff.[14] 'More important is the need to achieve insight into the nature of the complexity and to formulate concepts and world views for coping with it.'

Behind appropriate policies, strategies, and structures are effective learning processes; their creation is the third key design responsibility in learning organizations. This does not absolve senior managers of their strategic responsibilities. Actually, it deepens and extends those respon-sibilities. Now, they are not only responsible for ensuring that an organiz-ation has well-developed strategies and policies, but also for ensuring that processes exist whereby these are continually improved.

In the early 1970s, Shell was the weakest of the big seven oil companies. Today, Shell and Exxon are arguably the strongest, both in size and financial health. Shell's ascendance began with frustration. Around 1971 members of Shell's 'Group Planning' in London began to foresee dra-matic change and unpredictability in world oil markets. However, it proved impossible to persuade managers that the stable world of steady growth in oil demand and supply they had known for twenty years was about to change. Despite brilliant analysis and artful presentation, Shell's planners realized, in the words of Pierre Wack, that they 'had failed to change behavior in much of the Shell organization.'[15] Progress would probably have ended there, had the frustration not given way to a radically new view of corporate planning.

As they pondered this failure, the planners' view of their basic task shifted: 'We no longer saw our task as producing a documented view of the future business environment five or ten years ahead. Our real target was the microcosm (the "mental model") of our decision makers.' Only when the planners reconceptualized their basic task as fostering learning rather than devising plans did their insights begin to have an impact. The initial tool used was 'scenario analysis,' through which planners encouraged operating managers to think through how they would manage in the future under different possible scenarios. It mattered not that the managers believed the planners' scenarios absolutely, only that they became engaged in ferreting out the implications. In this way, Shell's planners conditioned managers to be mentally prepared for a shift from low prices to high prices and from stability to instability. The results were significant. When OPEC became a reality, Shell quickly responded to increasing local operating company control (to enhance manoeuvrability in the new political environment), building buffer stocks, and accelerating development of non-OPEC sources – actions that its competitors took much more slowly or not at all.

Somewhat inadvertently, Shell planners had discovered the leverage of designing institutional learning processes, whereby, in the words of former planning director de Geus, 'Management teams change their shared mental models of their company, their markets, and their competitors.'[16] Since then, 'planning as learning' has become a byword at Shell, and Group Planning has continually sought out new learning tools that can be integrated into the planning process. Some of these are described below.

LEADER AS TEACHER

'The first responsibility of a leader,' writes retired Herman Miller CEO Max de Pree, 'is to define reality.'[17] Much of the leverage leaders can actually exert lies in helping people achieve more accurate, more insightful, and more *empowering* views of reality.

Leader as teacher does *not* mean leader as authoritarian expert whose job is to teach people the 'correct' view of reality. Rather, it is about helping everyone in the organization, oneself included, to gain more insightful views of current reality. This is in line with a popular emerging view of leaders as coaches, guides, or facilitators.[18] In learning organizations, this teaching role is developed further by virtue of explicit attention to people's mental models and by the influence of the systems perspective.

The role of leader as teacher starts with bringing to the surface people's mental model of important issues. No one carries an organization, a market, or a state of technology in his or her head. What we carry in our heads are assumptions. These mental pictures of how the world works have a significant influence on how we perceive problems and opportunities, identify courses of action, and make choices.

One reason that mental models are so deeply entrenched is that they are largely tacit. Ian Mitroff, in his study of General Motors, argues that an assumption that prevailed for years was that, in the United States, 'Cars are status symbols. Styling is therefore more important than quality.'[19] The Detroit automakers didn't say, 'We have a *mental model* that all people care about is styling.' Few actual managers would even say publicly that all people care about is styling. So long as the view remained unexpressed, there was little possibility of challenging its validity or forming more accurate assumptions.

But working with mental models goes beyond revealing hidden assumptions. 'Reality,' as perceived by most people in most organizations, means pressures that must be borne, crises that must be reacted to, and limitations that must be accepted. Leaders as teachers help people *restructure their views of reality* to see beyond the superficial conditions and events into the underlying causes of problems – and therefore to see new possibilities for shaping the future.

Specifically, leaders can influence people to view reality at three distinct levels: events, patterns of behavior, and systemic structure.

Systemic Structure
(Generative)
↓
Patterns of Behavior
(Responsive)
↓
Events
(Reactive)

The key question becomes: *where do leaders predominantly focus their own and their organization's attention?*

Contemporary society focuses predominantly on events. The media reinforces this perspective, with almost exclusive attention to short-term, dramatic events. This focus leads naturally to explaining what happens in terms of those events: 'The Dow Jones average went up sixteen points because high fourth-quarter profits were announced yesterday.'

Pattern-of-behavior explanations are rarer, in contemporary culture, than event explanations, but they do occur. 'Trend analysis' is an example of seeing patterns of behavior. A good editorial that interprets a set of current events in the context of long-term historical changes is another example. Systemic, structural explanations go even further by addressing the question, 'What causes the patterns of behavior?'

In some sense, all three levels of explanation are equally true. But their usefulness is quite different. Event explanations – who did what to whom – doom their holders to a reactive stance toward change. Pattern-of-behavior explanations focus on identifying long-term trends and assessing their implications. They at least suggest how, over time, we can respond to shifting conditions. Structural explanations are the most powerful. Only they address the underlying causes of behavior at a level such that patterns of behavior can be changed.

By and large, leaders of our current institutions focus their attention on events and patterns of behavior, and, under their influence, their organizations do likewise. That is why contemporary organizations are predominantly reactive, or at best responsive – rarely generative. On the other hand, leaders in learning organizations pay attention to all three levels, but focus especially on systemic structure; largely by example, they teach people throughout the organization to do likewise.

LEADER AS STEWARD

This is the subtlest role of leadership. Unlike the roles of designer and teacher, it is almost solely a matter of attitude. It is an attitude critical to learning organizations.

While stewardship has long been recognized as an aspect of leadership, its source is still not widely understood. I believe Robert Greenleaf came closest to explaining real stewardship, in his seminal book *Servant Leadership*.[20] There, Greenleaf argues that 'The servant leader *is* servant first . . . It begins with the nature feeling that one wants to serve, to serve *first*. This conscious choice brings one to aspire to lead. That person is sharply different from one who is leader first, perhaps because of the need to assuage an unusual power drive or to acquire material possessions.'

Leaders' sense of stewardship operates on two levels: stewardship for the people they lead and stewardship for the larger purpose or mission that underlies the enterprise. The first type arises from a keen appreciation of the impact one's leadership can have on others. People can suffer economically, emotionally, and spiritually under inept leadership. If anything, people in a learning organization are more vulnerable because of their commitment and sense of shared ownership. Appreciating this naturally instills a sense of responsibility in leaders. The second type of stewardship arises from a leader's sense of personal purpose and commitment to the organization's larger mission. People's natural impulse to learn is unleashed when they are engaged in an endeavor they consider worthy of their fullest commitment. Or, as Lawrence Miller puts it, 'Achieving return on equity does not, as a goal, mobilize the most noble forces of our soul.'[21]

Leaders engaged in building learning organizations naturally feel part of a larger purpose that goes beyond their organization. They are part of changing the way businesses operate, not from a vague philanthropic urge, but from a conviction that their efforts will produce more productive organizations, capable of achieving higher levels of organizational success and personal satisfaction than more traditional organizations. Their sense of stewardship was succinctly captured by George Bernard Shaw when he said,

> This is the true joy in life, the being used for a purpose you consider a mighty one, the being a force of nature rather than a feverish, selfish clod of ailments and grievances complaining that the world will not devote itself to making you happy.

NEW SKILLS

New leadership roles require new leadership skills. These skills can only be developed, in my judgment, through a lifelong commitment. It is not enough for one or two individuals to develop these skills. They must be distributed widely throughout the organization. This is one reason that understanding the *disciplines* of a learning organization is so important. These disciplines embody the principles and practices that can widely foster leadership development.

Three critical areas of skills (disciplines) are building shared visions, surfacing and challenging mental models, and engaging in systems thinking.[22]

Building shared visions

How do individual visions come together to create shared visions? A useful metaphor is the hologram, the three-dimensional image created by interacting light sources.

If you cut a photograph in half, each half shows only part of the whole image. But if you divide a hologram, each part, no matter how small, shows the whole image intact. Likewise, when a group of people come to share a vision for an organization, each person sees an individual picture of the organization at its best. Each shares responsibility for the whole, not just for one piece. But the component pieces of the hologram are not identical. Each represents the whole image from a different point of view. It's something like poking holes in a window shade; each hole offers a unique angle for viewing the whole image. So, too, is each individual's vision unique.

When you add up the pieces of a hologram, something interesting happens. The image becomes more intense, more lifelike. When more people come to share a vision, the vision becomes more real in the sense of a mental reality that people can truly imagine achieving. They now have partners, co-creators; the vision no longer rests on their shoulders alone. Early on, when they are nurturing an individual vision, people may say it is 'my vision.' But, as the shared vision develops, it becomes both 'my vision' and 'our vision.'

The skills involved in building shared vision include the following:

- **Encouraging personal vision**. Shared visions emerge from personal visions. It is not that people only care about their own self-interest – in fact, people's values usually include dimensions that concern family, organization, community, and even the world. Rather, it is that people's capacity for caring is *personal*.
- **Communicating and asking for support**. Leaders must be willing to continually share their own vision, rather than being the official representative of the corporate vision. They also must be prepared to ask, 'Is this vision worthy of your commitment?' This can be difficult for a person used to setting goals and presuming compliance.
- **Visioning as an ongoing process**. Building shared vision is a never-ending process. At any one point there will be a particular image of the future that is predominant, but that image will evolve. Today, too many managers want to dispense with the 'vision business' by going off and writing the Official Vision Statement. Such statements almost always lack the vitality, freshness, and excitement of a genuine vision that comes from people asking, 'What do we really want to achieve?'
- **Blending extrinsic and intrinsic visions**. Many energizing visions are extrinsic – that is, they focus on achieving something relative to an outsider, such as a competitor. But a goal that is limited to defeating an opponent can, once the vision is achieved, easily become a defensive posture. In contrast, intrinsic goals like creating a new type of product, taking an established product to a new level, or setting a new standard for customer satisfaction, can call forth a new level of creativity and innovation. Intrinsic and extrinsic visions need to coexist; a vision solely predicated on defeating an adversary will eventually weaken an organization.
- **Distinguishing positive and negative visions**. Many organizations only truly pull together when their survival is threatened. Similarly, most social movements aim at eliminating what people don't want: for example anti-drugs, anti-smoking, or anti-nuclear arms movements. Negative visions carry a subtle message of powerlessness: people will only pull together when there is sufficient threat. Negative visions also tend to be short term. Two fundamental sources of energy can motivate organizations: fear and aspiration. Fear, the energy source behind negative visions, can produce extraordinary changes in short periods, but aspiration endures as a continuing source of learning and growth.

Surfacing and testing mental models

Many of the best ideas in organizations never get put into practice. One reason is that new insights and initiatives often conflict with established mental models. The leadership task of challenging assumptions without invoking skills is possessed by few leaders in traditional controlling organizations.[23]

- **Seeing leaps of abstraction**. Our minds literally move at lightning speed. Ironically, this often slows our learning, because we leap to generalizations so quickly that we never think to test them. We then confuse our generalizations with the observable data upon which they are based, treating the generalizations *as if they were data*. The frustrated sales rep reports to the home office that 'customers don't really care about quality, price is what matters,' when what actually happened was that three consecutive large customers refused to place an order unless a larger discount was offered. The sales rep treats her generalization, 'customers care only about price' as if it were absolute fact rather than an assumption (very likely an assumption reflecting her own views of customers and the market). This thwarts future learning because she starts to focus on how to offer attractive discounts rather than probing behind the customers' statements. For example, the customers may have been so disgruntled with the firm's delivery or customer service that they are unwilling to purchase again without larger discounts.
- **Balancing inquiry and advocacy**. Most managers are skilled at articulating their views and presenting them persuasively. While important, advocacy skills can become counterproductive as managers rise in responsibility and confront increasingly complex issues that require collaborative learning among different, equally knowledgeable people. Leaders in learning organizations need to have both inquiry *and* advocacy skills.[24]

  Specifically, when advocating a view, they need to be able to:

  - explain the reasoning and data that led to their view;
  - encourage others to test their view (e.g. Do you see gaps in my reasoning? Do you disagree with the data upon which my view is based?); and
  - encourage others to provide different views (e.g. Do you have either different data, different conclusions, or both?).

  When inquiring into another's views, they need to:

  - actively seek to understand the other's view, rather than simply restating their own view and how it differs from the other's view; and

- make their attributions about the other and the other's view explicit (e.g. Based on your statement that . . .; I am assuming that you believe . . .; Am I representing your views fairly?).

If they reach an impasse (others no longer appear open to inquiry), they need to:

- ask what data or logic might unfreeze the impasse, or if an experiment (or some other inquiry) might be designed to provide new information.

- **Distinguishing espoused theory from theory in use**. We all like to think that we hold certain views, but often our actions reveal deeper views. For example, I may proclaim that people are trustworthy, but never lend friends money and jealously guard my possessions. Obviously, my deeper mental model (my theory in use) differs from my espoused theory. Recognizing gaps between espoused views and theories in use (which often requires the help of others) can be pivotal to deeper learning.
- **Recognizing and defusing defensive routines**. As one CEO in our research program puts it, 'Nobody ever talks about an issue at the 8.00 business meeting exactly the same way they talk about it at home that evening or over drinks at the end of the day.' The reason is what Chris Argyris calls 'defensive routines,' entrenched habits used to protect ourselves from the embarrassment and threat that come with exposing our thinking. For most of us, such defenses began to build early in life in response to pressures to have the right answers in school or at home. Organizations add new levels of performance anxiety and thereby amplify and exacerbate this defensiveness. Ironically, this makes it even more difficult to expose hidden mental models, and thereby lessens learning.

  The first challenge is to recognize defensive routines, and then to inquire into their operation. Those who are best at revealing and defusing defensive routines operate with a high degree of self-disclosure regarding their own defensiveness (e.g. I notice that I am feeling uneasy about how this conversation is going. Perhaps I don't understand it or it is threatening to me in ways I don't yet see. Can you help me see this better?).

Systems thinking

We all know that leaders should help people see the big picture. But the actual skills whereby leaders are supposed to achieve this are not well understood. In my experience, successful leaders often *are* 'systems thinkers' to a considerable extent. They focus less on day-to-day events and more on underlying trends and forces of change. But they do this almost completely intuitively. The consequence is that they are often unable to explain their intuitions to others and feel frustrated that others cannot see the world the way they do.

One of the most significant developments in management science today is the gradual coalescence of managerial systems thinking as a field of study and practice. This field suggests some key skills for future leaders:

- **Seeing interrelationships, not things, and processes, not snapshots**. Most of us have been conditioned throughout our lives to focus on things and to see the world in static images. This leads us to linear explanations of systemic phenomenon. For instance, in an arms race each party is convinced that the other is *the cause* of problems. They react to each new move as an isolated event, not as part of a process. So long as they fail to see the interrelationships of these actions, they are trapped.
- **Moving beyond blame**. We tend to blame each other or outside circumstances for our problems. But it is poorly designed systems, not incompetent or unmotivated individuals, that cause most organizational problems. Systems thinking shows us that there is no outside – that you and the cause of your problems are part of a single system.
- **Distinguishing detail complexity from dynamic complexity.** Some types of complexity are more important strategically than others. Detail complexity arises when there are many variables. Dynamic complexity arises when cause and effect are distant in time and space, and when the consequences over time of interventions are subtle and not obvious to many participants in the system. The leverage in most management situations lies in understanding dynamic complexity, not detail complexity.
- **Focusing on areas of high leverage**. Some have called systems thinking the 'new dismal science' because it teaches that most obvious solutions don't work – at best, they improve matters in the short run, only to make things worse in the long run. But there is another side to the story. Systems thinking also shows that small, well-focused actions can produce significant, enduring improvements, if they are in the right place. Systems thinkers refer to this idea as the principle of 'leverage.' Tackling a difficult problem is often a matter of seeing where the high leverage lies, where a change – with a minimum of effort – would lead to lasting, significant improvement.
- **Avoiding symptomatic solutions**. The pressures to intervene in management systems that are going awry can be overwhelming. Unfortunately, given the linear thinking that predominates in most organizations, interventions usually focus on symptomatic fixes, not

underlying causes. This results in only temporary relief, and it tends to create still more pressures later on for further, low-leverage intervention. If leaders acquiesce to these pressures, they can be sucked into an endless spiral of increasing intervention. Sometimes the most difficult leadership acts are to refrain from intervening through popular quick fixes and to keep the pressures on everyone to identify more enduring solutions.

While leaders who can articulate systemic explanations are rare, those who *can* will leave their stamp on an organization. One person who had this gift was Bill Gore, the founder and long-time CEO of W. L. Gore and Associates (makers of Gore-Tex and other synthetic fiber products). Bill Gore was adept at telling stories that showed how the organization's core values of freedom and individual responsibility required particular operating policies. He was proud of his egalitarian organization, in which there were (and still are) no 'employees,' only 'associates,' all of whom own shares in the company and participate in its management. At one talk, he explained the company's policy of controlled growth: 'Our limitation is not financial resources. Our limitation is the rate at which we can bring in new associates. Our experience has been that if we try to bring in more than a 25 percent per year increase, we begin to bog down. Twenty-five percent per year growth is a real limitation; you can do much better than that with an authoritarian organization.' As Gore tells the story, one of the associates, Esther Baum, went home after this talk and reported the limitation to her husband. As it happened, he was an astronomer and mathematician at Lowell Observatory. He said, 'That's a very interesting figure.' He took out a pencil and paper and calculated and said, 'Do you realize that in only fifty-seven and a half years, everyone in the world will be working for Gore?'

Through this story, Gore explains the systemic rationale behind a key policy, limited growth rate – a policy that undoubtedly caused a lot of stress in the organization. He suggests that, at larger rates of growth, the adverse effects of attempting to integrate too many new people too rapidly would begin to dominate. (This is the 'limits to growth' systems archetype explained below.) The story also reaffirms the organization's commitment to creating a unique environment for its associates and illustrates the types of sacrifices that the firm is prepared to make in order to remain true to its vision. The last part of the story shows that, despite the self-imposed limit, the company is still very much a growth company.

The consequences of leaders who lack systems thinking skills can be devastating. Many charismatic leaders manage almost exclusively at the level of events. They deal in visions and in crises, and little in between. Under their leadership, an organization hurtles from crisis to crisis. Eventually, the worldview of people in the organization becomes dominated by events and reactiveness. Many, especially those who are deeply committed, become burned out. Eventually, cynicism comes to pervade the organization. People have no control over their time, let alone their destiny.

Similar problems arise with the 'visionary strategist,' the leader with vision who sees both patterns of change and events. This leader is better prepared to manage change. He or she can explain strategies in terms of emerging trends, and thereby foster a climate that is less reactive. But such leaders still impart a responsive orientation rather than a generative one.

Many talented leaders have rich, highly systemic intuitions but cannot explain those intuitions to others. Ironically, they often end up being authoritarian leaders, even if they don't want to, because only they see the decisions that need to be made. They are unable to conceptualize their strategic insights so that these can become public knowledge, open to challenge and further improvement.

NEW TOOLS

Developing the skills described above requires new tools – tools that will enhance leaders' conceptual abilities and foster communication and collaborative inquiry. What follows is a sampling of tools starting to find use in learning organizations.

Systems archetypes

One of the insights of the budding, managerial systems-thinking field is that certain types of systemic structures recur again and again. Countless systems grow for a period, then encounter problems and cease to grow (or even collapse) well before they have reached intrinsic limits to growth. Many other systems get locked in runaway vicious spirals where every actor has to run faster and faster to stay in the same place. Still others lure individual actors into doing what seems right locally, yet which eventually causes suffering for all.[25]

Some of the system archetypes that have the broadest relevance include:

- **Balancing process with delay**. In this archetype, decision makers fail to appreciate the time delays involved as they move toward a goal. As a result, they overshoot the goal and may even produce recurring cycles. Classic example: real estate developers who keep starting new projects until the market has gone soft, by which time an eventual glut is guaranteed by the properties still under construction.
- **Limits to growth**. A reinforcing cycle of growth grinds to a halt, and may even reverse itself, as limits are approached. The limits can be

resource constraints, or external or internal responses to growth. Classic examples: product life cycles that peak prematurely due to poor quality of service, the growth and decline of communication in a management team, and the spread of a new movement.

- **Shifting the burden.** A short-term 'solution' is used to correct a problem, with seemingly happy immediate results. As this correction is used more and more, fundamental long-term corrective measures are used less. Over time, the mechanisms of the fundamental solution may atrophy or become disabled, leading to even greater reliance on the symptomatic solution. Classic example: using corporate human resource staff to solve local personnel problems, thereby keeping managers from developing their own interpersonal skills.

- **Eroding goals.** When all else fails, lower your standards. This is like 'shifting the burden,' except that the short-term solution involves letting a fundamental goal, such as quality standards or employee morale standards, atrophy. Classic example: a company that responds to delivery problems by continually upping its quoted delivery times.

- **Escalation.** Two people or two organizations, who each see their welfare as depending on a relative advantage over the other, continually react to the other's advances. Whenever one side gets ahead, the other is threatened, leading it to act more aggressively to reestablish its advantage, which threatens the first, and so on. Classic examples: arms race, gang warfare, price wars.

- **Tragedy of the commons.**[26] Individuals keep intensifying their use of a commonly available but limited resource until all individuals start to experience severely diminishing returns. Classic examples: shepherds who keep increasing their flocks until they overgraze the common pasture; divisions in a firm that share a common salesforce and compete for the use of sales reps by upping their sales targets, until the salesforce burns out from overextension.

- **Growth and underinvestment.** Rapid growth approaches a limit that could be eliminated or pushed into the future, but only by aggressive investment in physical and human capacity. Eroding goals or standards cause investment that is too weak, or too slow, and customers get increasingly unhappy, slowing demand growth and thereby making the needed investment (apparently) unnecessary or impossible. Classic example: countless once successful growth firms that allowed product or service quality to erode, and were unable to generate enough revenues to invest in remedies.

The archetype template is a specific tool that is helping managers identify archetypes operating in their own strategic areas (see Figure 16.2).[27] The template shows the basic structural form of the archetype but lets managers fill in the variables of their own situation. For example, the shifting the burden template involves two balancing processes ('B') that compete for control of a problem symptom. The upper, symptomatic solution provides a short-term fix that will make the problem symptom go away for a while. The lower, fundamental solution provides a more enduring solution. The side effect feedback ('R') around the outside of the figure identifies unintended exacerbating effects of the symptomatic solution, which, over time, make it more and more difficult to invoke the fundamental solution.

Several years ago, a team of managers from a leading consumer goods producer used the shifting the burden archetype in a revealing way. The problem they focused on was financial stress, which could be dealt with in two different ways: by running market promotions (the symptomatic solution) or by product innovation (the fundamental solution). Marketing promotions were fast. The company was expert in their design and imple-

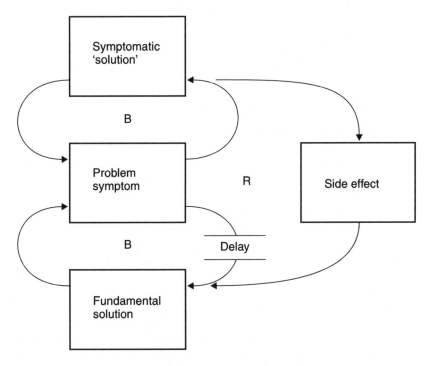

In the 'shifting the burden' template, two balancing processes (B) compete for control of a problem symptom. Both solutions affect the symptom, but only the fundamental solution treats the cause. The symptomatic 'solution' creates the additional side effect (R) of deferring the fundamental solution, making it harder and harder to achieve.

Figure 16.2 **'Shifting the burden' archetype template**

mentation. The results were highly predictable. Product innovation was slow and much less predictable, and the company had a history over the past ten years of product-innovation mismanagement. Yet only through innovation could they retain a leadership position in their industry, which had slid over the past ten to twenty years. What the managers saw clearly was that the more skillful they became at promotions, the more they shifted the burden away from product innovation. But what really struck home was when one member identified the unintended side effect: the last three CEOs had all come from the advertising function, which had become the politically dominant function in the corporation, thereby institutionalizing the symptomatic solution. Unless the political values shifted back toward product and process innovation, the managers realized, the firm's decline would accelerate – which is just the shift that has happened over the past several years.

Charting strategic dilemmas

Management teams typically come unglued when confronted with core dilemmas. A classic example was the way US manufacturers faced the low cost/high quality choice. For years, most assumed that it was necessary to choose between the two. Not surprisingly, given the short-term pressures perceived by most managements, the prevailing choice was low cost. Firms that chose high quality usually perceived themselves as aiming exclusively for a high quality, high price market niche. The consequences of this perceived either–or choice have been disastrous, even fatal, as US manufacturers have encountered increasing international competition from firms that have chosen to consistently improve quality *and* cost.

In a recent book, Charles Hampden-Turner presented a variety of tools for helping strategic management teams confront strategic dilemmas creatively.[28] He summarizes the process in seven steps:

- **Eliciting the dilemmas**. Identifying the opposed values that form the 'horns' of the dilemma, for example, cost as opposed to quality, or local initiative as opposed to central coordination and control. Hampden-Turner suggests that humor can be a distinct asset in this process since 'the admission that dilemmas even exist tends to be difficult for some companies.'
- **Mapping**. Locating the opposing values as two axes and helping managers identify where they see themselves, or their organization, along the axes.
- **Processing**. Getting rid of nouns to describe the axes of the dilemma. Present participles formed by adding 'ing' convert rigid nouns into processes that imply movement. For example, central control versus local control becomes 'strengthening national office' and 'growing

local initiatives.' This loosens the bond of implied opposition between the two values. For example, it becomes possible to think of 'strengthening national services from which local branches can benefit.'

- **Framing/contextualizing**. Further softening the adversarial structure among different values by letting 'each side in turn be the frame or context for the other.' This shifting of the 'figure–ground' relationship undermines any implicit attempts to hold one value as intrinsically superior to the other and thereby to become mentally closed to creative strategies for continuous improvement of both.
- **Sequencing**. Breaking the hold of static thinking. Very often, values like low cost and high quality appear to be in opposition because we think in terms of a point in time, not in terms of an on-going process. For example, a strategy of investing in new process technology and developing a new production-floor culture of worker responsibility may take time and money in the near term, yet reap significant long-term financial rewards.
- **Waving/cycling**. Sometimes the strategic path toward improving both values involves cycles where both values will get 'worse' for a time. Yet, at a deeper level, learning is occurring that will cause the next cycle to be at a higher plateau for both values.
- **Synergizing**. Achieving synergy where significant improvement is occurring along all axes of all relevant dilemmas. (This is the ultimate goal, of course.) Synergy, as Hampden-Turner points out, is a uniquely systemic notion, coming from the Greek *syn-ergo* or 'work together.'

'The left-hand column': surfacing mental models

The idea that mental models can dominate business decisions and that these models are often tacit and even contradictory to what people espouse can be very threatening to managers who pride themselves on rationality and judicious decision making. It is important to have tools to help managers discover for themselves how their mental models operate to undermine their own intentions.

One tool that has worked consistently to help managers see their own mental models in action is the 'left-hand column' exercise developed by Chris Argyris and his colleagues.[29] This tool is especially helpful in showing how we leap from data to generalization without testing the validity of our generalizations.

When working with managers, I start this exercise by selecting a specific situation in which I am interacting with other people in a way that is not working, that is not producing the learning that is needed. I write out a sample of the exchange, with the script on the right-hand side of the page. On the left-hand side, I write what I am thinking but not saying at each stage in the exchange (see Figure 16.3).

Imagine my exchange with a colleague, Bill, after he made a big presentation to our boss on a project we are doing together. I had to miss the presentation, but I've heard that it was poorly received.

Me: How did the presentation go?

Bill: Well, I don't know. It's really too early to say. Besides, we're breaking new ground here.

Me: Well, what do you think we should do? I believe that the issues you were raising are important.

Bill: I'm not so sure. Let's just wait and see what happens.

Me: You may be right, but I think we may need to do more than just wait.

Now, here is what the exchange looks like with my 'left-hand column':

What I'm thinking	What is said
Everyone says the presentation was a bomb.	*Me*: How did the presentation go?
Does he really not know how bad it was? Or is he not willing to face up to it?	*Bill*: Well, I don't know. It's too early to say. Besides, we're breaking new ground here.
	Me: Well, what do you think we should do? I believe that the issues you were raising are important.
He really is afraid to see the truth. If he only had more confidence, he could probably learn from a situation like this.	*Bill*: I'm not so sure. Let's just wait and see what happens.
I can't believe he doesn't realize how disastrous that presentation was to our moving ahead.	*Me*: You may be right, but I think we may need to do more than just wait.
I've got to find some way to light a fire under this guy	

Figure 16.3 **The left-hand column: an exercise**

The left-hand column exercise not only brings hidden assumptions to the surface, it shows how they influence behavior. In the example, I make two key assumptions about Bill: he lacks confidence and he lacks initiative. Neither may be literally true, but both are evident in my internal dialogue, and both influence the way I handle the situation. Believing that he lacks confidence, I skirt the fact that I've heard the presentation was a bomb. I'm afraid that if I say it directly, he will lose what little confidence he has, or he will see me as unsupportive. So I bring up the subject of the presentation obliquely. When I ask Bill what we should do next, he gives no specific course of action. Believing he lacks initiative, I take this as evidence of his laziness; he is content to do nothing when action is definitely required. I conclude that I will have to manufacture some form of pressure to motivate him, or else I will simply have to take matters into my own hands.

The exercise reveals the elaborate webs of assumptions we weave, within which we become our own victims. Rather than dealing directly with my assumptions about Bill and the situation, we talk around the subject. The reasons for my avoidance are self-evident: I assume that if I raised my doubts, I would provoke a defensive reaction that would only make matters worse. But the price of avoiding the issue is high. Instead of determining how to move forward to resolve our problems, we end our exchange with no clear course of action. My assumptions about Bill's limitations have been reinforced. I resort to a manipulative strategy to move things forward.

The exercise not only shows the need for skills in surfacing assumptions, but that we are the ones most in need of help. There is no one right way to handle difficult situations like my exchange with Bill, but any productive strategy revolves around a high level of self-disclosure and willingness to have my views challenged. I need to recognize my own leaps of abstraction regarding Bill, share the events and reasoning that are leading to my concern over the project, and be open to Bill's views on both. The skills to carry on such conversations without invoking defensiveness take time to develop. But if both parties in a learning impasse start by doing their own left-hand column exercise and sharing them with each other, it is remarkable how quickly everyone recognizes their contribution to the impasse and progress starts to be made.

Learning laboratories: practice fields for management teams

One of the most promising new tools is the learning laboratory or 'micro-world': constructed microcosms of real-life settings in which management teams can learn how to learn together.

The rationale behind learning laboratories can best be explained by analogy. Although most management teams have great difficulty learning (enhancing their collective intelligence and capacity to create), in other domains team learning is the norm rather than the exception – team sports and the performing arts, for example. Great basketball teams do not start off great. They learn. But the process by which these teams learn is, by and large, absent from modern organizations. The process is a continual movement between practice and performance.

The vision guiding current research in management learning laboratories is to design and construct effective practice fields for management teams. Much remains to be done, but the broad outlines are emerging.

First, since team learning in organizations is an individual-to-individual and individual-to-system phenomenon, learning laboratories must combine meaningful business issues with meaningful interpersonal dynamics. Either alone is incomplete.

Second, the factors that thwart learning about complex business issues must be eliminated in the learning lab. Chief among these is the inability to experience the long-term, systemic consequences of key strategic decisions. We all learn best from experience, but we are unable to experience the consequences of many important organizational decisions. Learning laboratories remove this constraint through system dynamics simulation games that compress time and space.

Third, new learning skills must be developed. One constraint on learning is the inability of managers to reflect insightfully on their assumptions, and to inquire effectively into each other's assumptions. Both skills can be enhanced in a learning laboratory, where people can practice surfacing assumptions in a low-risk setting. A note of caution: it is far easier to design an entertaining learning laboratory than it is to have an impact on real management practices and firm traditions outside the learning lab. Research on management simulations has shown that they often have greater entertainment value than educational value. One of the reasons appears to be that many simulations do not offer deep insights into systemic structures causing business problems. Another reason is that they do not foster new learning skills. Also, there is no connection between experiments in the learning lab and real-life experiments. These are significant problems that research on learning laboratory design is now addressing.

DEVELOPING LEADERS AND LEARNING ORGANIZATIONS

In a recently published retrospective on organization development in the 1980s, Marshall Sashkin and W. Warner Burke observe the return of an emphasis on developing leaders who can develop organizations.[30] They also note Schein's critique that most top executives are not qualified for the task of developing culture.[31] Learning organizations represent a potentially significant evolution of organizational culture. So it should come as no surprise that such organizations will remain a distant vision until the leadership capabilities they demand are developed. 'The 1990s may be the period,' suggest Sashkin and Burke, 'during which organization development and (a new sort of) management development are reconnected.'

I believe that this new sort of management development will focus on the roles, skills, and tools for leadership in learning organizations.

Undoubtedly, the ideas offered above are only a rough approximation of this new territory. The sooner we begin seriously exploring the territory, the sooner the initial map can be improved – and the sooner we will realize an age-old vision of leadership:

The wicked leader is he who the people despise
The good leader is he who the people revere
The great leader is he of whom the people say, 'We did it ourselves.'

– Lao-Tzu

Learning at Hanover Insurance

Hanover Insurance has gone from the bottom of the property and liability industry to a position among the top 25 percent of US insurance companies over the past twenty years, largely through the efforts of CEO William O'Brien and his predecessor, Jack Adam. The following comments are excerpted from a series of interviews Senge conducted with O'Brien as background for his book.

Senge: Why do you think there is so much change occurring in management and organizations today? Is it primarily because of increased competitive pressures?
O'Brien: That's a factor, but not the most significant factor. The ferment in management will continue until we find models that are more congruent with human nature.

One of the great insights of modern psychology is the hierarchy of human needs. As Maslow expressed this idea, the most basic needs are food and shelter. Then comes belonging. Once these three basic needs are satisfied, people begin to aspire toward self-respect and esteem, and toward self-actualization – the fourth- and fifth-order needs.

Our traditional hierarchical organizations are designed to provide for the first three levels, but not the fourth and fifth. These first three levels are now widely available to members of industrial society, but our organizations do not offer people sufficient opportunities for growth.

Senge: How would you assess Hanover's progress to date?
O'Brien: We have been on a long journey away from a traditional hierarchical culture. The journey began with everyone under-standing some guiding ideas about purpose, vision, and values as a basis for participative management. This is a better way to begin building a participative culture than by simply 'letting people in on decision making.' Before there can be meaningful participation, people must share certain values and pictures about where we are trying to go. We discovered that people have a real need to feel that

they're part of an ennobling mission. But developing shared visions and values is not the end, only the beginning.

Next we had to get beyond mechanical, linear thinking. The essence of our jobs as managers is to deal with 'divergent' problems – problems that have no simple answer. 'Convergent' problems – problems that have a 'right' answer – should be solved locally. Yet we are deeply conditioned to see the world in terms of convergent problems. Most managers try to force-fit simplistic solutions and undermine the potential for learning when divergent problems arise. Since everyone handles the linear issues fairly well, companies that learn how to handle divergent issues will have a great advantage.

The next basic stage in our progression was coming to understand inquiry and advocacy. We learned that real openness is rooted in people's ability to continually inquire into their own thinking. This requires exposing yourself to being wrong – not something that most managers are rewarded for. But learning is very difficult if you cannot look for errors or incompleteness in your own ideas.

What all this builds to is the capability throughout an organization to manage mental models. In a locally controlled organization, you have the fundamental challenge of learning how to help people make good decisions without coercing them into making *particular* decisions. By managing mental models, we create 'self-concluding' decisions – decisions that people come to themselves – which will result in deeper conviction, better implementation, and the ability to make better adjustments when the situation changes.

Senge: What concrete steps can top managers take to begin moving toward learning organizations?

O'Brien: Look at the signals you send through the organization. For example, one critical signal is how you spend your time. It's hard to build a learning organization if people are unable to take the time to think through important matters. I rarely set up an appointment for less than one hour. If the subject is not worth an hour, it shouldn't be on my calendar.

Senge: Why is this so hard for so many managers?

O'Brien: It comes back to what you believe about the nature of your work. The authoritarian manager has a 'chain gang' mental model: 'The speed of the boss is the speed of the gang. I've got to keep things moving fast, because I've got to keep people working.' In a learning organization, the manager shoulders an almost sacred responsibility: to create conditions that enable people to have happy and productive lives. If you understand the effects the ideas we are discussing can have on the lives of people in your organization, you will take the time.

NOTES

1 P. Senge, *The Fifth Discipline: The Art and Practice of the Learning Organization* (New York: Doubleday/Currency, 1990).
2 A.P. de Geus, 'Planning as Learning,' *Harvard Business Review*, March–April, 1988, pp. 70–74.
3 B. Domain in *Fortune*, 3 July 1989, pp. 48–62.
4 The distinction between adaptive and generative learning has its roots in the distinction between what Argyris and Schon have called their 'single-loop' learning, in which individuals or groups adjust their behavior relative to fixed goals, norms, and assumptions, and 'double-loop' learning, in which goals, norms, and assumptions, as well as behavior, are open to change (e.g. see C. Argyris and D. Schon, *Organizational Learning: A Theory-in-Action Perspective* (Reading, Massachusetts: Addison-Wesley, 1978).
5 All unattributed quotes are from personal communications with the author.
6 G. Stalk, Jr, 'Time: The Next Source of Competitive Advantage,' *Harvard Business Review*, July–August 1988, pp. 41–51.
7 Senge (1990).
8 The principle of creative tension comes from Robert Fritz' work on creativity. See R. Fritz, *The Path of Least Resistance* (New York: Ballantine, 1989) and *Creating* (New York: Ballantine, 1990).
9 M.L. King, Jr, 'Letter from Birmingham Jail,' *American Visions*, January–February 1986, pp. 52–59.
10 E. Schein, *Organizational Culture and Leadership* (San Francisco: Jossey-Bass, 1985). Similar views have been expressed by many leadership theorists. For example, see: P. Selznick, *Leadership in Administration* (New York: Harper & Row, 1957); W. Bennis and B. Nanus, *Leaders* (New York: Harper & Row, 1985); and N.M. Tichy and M.A. Devanna, *The Transformational Leader* (New York: John Wiley & Sons, 1986).
11 Selznick (1957).
12 J.W. Forrester, 'A New Corporate Design,' *Sloan Management Review* (formerly *Industrial Management Review*), Fall 1965, pp. 5–17.
13 See, for example, H. Mintzberg, 'Crafting Strategy,' *Harvard Business Review*, September–October 1985, pp. 73–89.
14 R. Mason and I. Mitroff, *Challenging Strategic Planning Assumptions* (New York: John Wiley & Sons, 1981), p. 16.
15 P. Wack, 'Scenarios, Uncharted Waters Ahead,' *Harvard Business Review*, September–October 1985, pp. 73–89.
16 de Geus (1988).
17 M. de Pree, *Leadership is an Art* (New York: Doubleday, 1989), p. 9.
18 For example, see T. Peters and N. Austin, *A Passion for Excellence* (New York: Random House, 1985) and J.M. Kouzes and B.Z. Posner, *The Leadership Challenge* (San Francisco: Jossey-Bass, 1987).
19 I. Mitroff, *Break-Away Thinking* (New York: John Wiley & Sons, 1988), pp. 66–67.
20 R.K. Greenleaf, *Servant Leadership: A Journey into the Nature of Legitimate Power and Greatness* (New York: Paulist Press, 1977).
21 L. Miller, *American Spirit: Visions of a New Corporate Culture* (New York: William Morrow, 1984), p. 15.
22 These points are condensed from the practices of the five disciplines examined in Senge (1990).
23 The ideas below are based to a considerable extent on the work of Chris Argyris, Donald Schon, and their Action Science colleagues: Argyris and

Schon (1978); C. Argyris, R. Putnam and D. Smith, *Action Sciences* (San Francisco: Jossey-Bass, 1985); C. Argyris, *Overcoming Organizational Defenses* (Englewood Cliffs, New Jersey: Prentice-Hall, 1990).

24 I am indebted to Diana Smith for the summary points below.

25 The system archetypes are one of several systems diagramming and communication tools. See D.H. Kim, 'Toward Learning Organizations: Integrating Total Quality Control and Systems Thinking' (Cambridge, Massachusetts: MIT Sloan School of Management, Working Paper No. 3037–89–BPS, June 1989).

26 This archetype is closely associated with the work of ecologist Garrett Hardin, who coined its label: G. Hardin, 'The Tragedy of the Commons,' *Science*, 13 December 1968.

27 These templates were originally developed by Jennifer Kemeny, Charles Kiefer, and Michael Goodman of Innovation Associates, Inc., Framingham, Massachusetts.

28 C. Hampden-Turner, *Charting the Corporate Mind* (New York: The Free Press, 1990).

29 See note 23.

30 M. Sashkin and W.W. Burke, 'Organization Development in the 1980s' and 'An End-of-the-Eighties Retrospective,' in *Advances in Organization Development*, ed. F. Masarik (Norwood, New Jersey: Ablex, 1990).

31 E. Schein (1985).

Chapter 17

Organizational learning
The key to management innovation

Ray Stata

For more than fifteen years, Analog Devices grew consistently at a rate of about 25 percent per year. Then for the first time, between 1982 and 1987, we missed our five-year goals – and by a country mile. True enough, like other semiconductor companies we were affected by the malaise in the US electronics industry and by the strong dollar. But the external environment was only part of the problem: something was also wrong internally, and it had to be fixed.

But what was the problem? We had the largest share of our niche market in high-performance linear integrated circuits. We had the best designers and technologies in our business. We had excellent relations with a highly motivated workforce. We were not guilty of under-investment, nor of managing for short-term profits. The only conclusion was that there was something *about* the way we were managing the company that was not good enough. So I set about to understand what was wrong and how to make it better.

In the 1980s, our plight was not uncommon in corporate America. Companies that for decades enjoyed world leadership in their markets were being brought to their knees. Of course, there are many purported reasons for the loss of US competitiveness. The high cost of capital, an overvalued dollar, a deteriorating education system, overconsumption at the expense of investment, government regulations, misplaced emphasis on military as opposed to economic security, and undisciplined government spending certainly all contributed to this decline. However, many who have studied the situation believe that the root of the problem is our declining rate of innovation. If this is true, then the challenge lies in better understanding innovation and in determining how to do more of it.

Usually we think of innovation in terms of technologies that give rise to a new class of products or to improvements in the design and manufacture of existing products. The bottleneck is management innovation.

Peter Drucker points out that the rise to industrial dominance of Great Britain, Germany and the United States was based on technological innovation in engines, electricity, chemistry, aviation, agriculture, optics and so forth.[1] Japan is the first nation whose rise to industrial power was clearly based on management innovation, not technological innovation in the traditional sense.

Michael Cusumano reinforces this point in analyzing Japan's conquest of the automobile industry.[2] In the early years of the Japanese industry, small Japanese automakers, especially Toyota, beat out their giant US competitors not with product innovation, superior manufacturing technology, or greater capital investment per employee. They did it with management innovations that turned their presumed disadvantage of lower production volume and smaller lot sizes into an advantage: shorter manufacturing cycles, lower inventories and (eventually) higher quality and lower cost.

Certainly management innovation alone is not enough. As Utterback and Abernathy point out, the optimum blend of product, process, and (I would add) management innovation depends on the circumstances of a particular industry.[3] But I would argue that where many US firms lag most today is in the *management innovation* required to take fullest advantage of their *technology leadership*.

Until very recently management innovation received little serious consideration either from corporations or academic researchers, especially in comparison with the resources invested in product and process innovation. The results of this neglect are evident in the competitive crises facing US industries.

Management innovation, like product and process innovation, depends on new technology. New technology for management, as for engineering, comes in the form of new knowledge, tools, and methods. In my quest to improve the performance of Analog Devices, I began to search for new technologies and ideas that would change, if not revolutionize, the way we were managing our company.

Around that time I had the good fortune to meet MIT's Jay Forrester and Peter Senge and learn of their work in applying system dynamics to the analysis and design of complex social systems.[4] For thirty years Professor Forrester has pioneered the use of feedback theory and systems analysis to examine the behavior of systems not only in management, but also in politics, economics, medicine, and the environment. He has created a whole new field of knowledge that is only now finding its way into management practice.

Peter Senge invited me to join eight other organizational leaders in what was called the 'New Management Style Project.'[5] We have met on a semiannual basis over the past four years, and this collaboration has proven to be fruitful for all of us, practitioners and academics alike. As I shall point out later, this project can serve as a prototype for industry/ university partnerships, which are needed to accelerate management innovation.

ORGANIZATIONAL LEARNING

The initial focus of the New Management Style group was on using system dynamics to improve our thinking about complex organizations. But as time progressed, we began to explore systems thinking in a broader context. About this time Arie de Geus, director of group planning for Shell International, joined the group because of his interest in system dynamics as a tool to accelerate organizational learning. As we listened to de Geus's ideas and his experiences at Shell, organizational learning emerged as a fundamental concept; it not only helped us to better appreciate the power of system dynamics, but also to integrate a broader range of management tools and methods to facilitate organizational change and improvement.

In an even broader context, as I come to understand this concept more fully, I see organizational learning as the principal process by which management innovation occurs. *In fact, I would argue that the rate at which individuals and organizations learn may become the only sustainable competitive advantage, especially in knowledge-intensive industries.*

What is organizational learning, and how does it differ from individual learning? We tend to think of learning as a process by which individuals gain new knowledge and insights and thereby modify their behavior and actions. Similarly, organizational learning entails new insights and modified behavior. But it differs from individual learning in several respects. First, organizational learning occurs through shared insights, knowledge, and mental models. Thus organizations can learn only as fast as the slowest link learns. Change is blocked unless all of the major decision makers learn together, come to share beliefs and goals, and are committed to take the actions necessary for change. Second, learning builds on past knowledge and experience – that is, on memory. Organizational memory depends on institutional mechanisms (e.g. policies, strategies, and explicit models) used to retain knowledge. Of course, organizations also depend on the memory of individuals. But relying exclusively on individuals risks losing hard-won lessons and experiences as people migrate from one job to another.

The challenge, then, is to discover new management tools and methods to accelerate organizational learning, build consensus for change, and facilitate the change process. Let me share some of the specifics of how organizational learning is serving as an umbrella to unify my approach to systems thinking, planning, quality improvement, organizational behavior, and information systems.

SYSTEMS THINKING

Systems thinking, and in particular system dynamics, is a powerful tool to facilitate both individual and organizational learning. One of the early lessons learned from system dynamics is that organizations are like giant networks of interconnected nodes. Changes intended to improve performance in one part of the organization can affect other parts of the organization with surprising, often negative consequences. That is, decisions based solely on information at the local level, which is often the only information available, can be counterproductive to the system as a whole. The undesirable buildup of inventory in distribution channels is a well-known example of what happens when local managers do not understand the conditions of the total environment in which they are operating.

Human cognitive capabilities limit our ability to understand what is actually going on in complex organizations. In fact, recent experimental studies by John Sterman at MIT show that decision makers consistently misjudge complex systems with multiple feedback processes and delays.[6] Fortunately, owing to the work of Forrester and others in system dynamics, tools to analyze and design complex electronic and mechanical systems have been adapted to perform the same functions in complex organization systems. Using these tools and desktop computers, we can simulate organizational behavior and show how the structure and policies of companies may generate undesirable performance that is often blamed on the external environment. We can also demonstrate how decisions that improve performance in the short term sometimes only make it worse in the long term.

Forrester and Senge make the point that the role of organizational leaders is undergoing dramatic change. Historically leaders were referred to as 'captains of the ship' to denote their role in operating the vessel entrusted to their care. But future leaders must be both designers and operators. Their principal contribution will be to shape the design of the organization structure and policies so as to best fulfil the corporate mission. Expertise in organization design will be a critical skill – a skill that will require considerable technical knowledge about how to analyze, modify, and simulate the behavior of complex human systems.

Let us take one of the most elementary concepts of feedback theory as applied to organizational design. That is, when you model organizational behavior, one basic characterization of a system is the delay time between cause and effect – for example, between when an order is received and when it is shipped, when you start manufacturing a product and when you finish, when you start to design a new product and when you introduce it to the market, or when you receive a request for information and when you respond. Using system dynamics to simulate organizational behavior, you find that often one of the highest leverage points for improving performance is the minimization of these system delays. In designing the organization, the leader should focus on optimizing the response times to changes in the external environment, with minimum overshoot and undershoot of output from the desired goals (see Figure 17.1, p. 321).

You might argue that this is an obvious conclusion and that you don't need system dynamics to prove it. What is *not* obvious is the magnitude of loss from excessive inventories, excessive lead time, and poor customer service that result from these system delays. Only when the loss is quantified does its critical importance strike home. To put it another way, if these conclusions are so obvious, then why did it take US manufacturers so long to grasp the critical importance of manufacturing cycle time and to focus on reducing time to market? It certainly was not obvious to me five years ago that excessive manufacturing cycle time was the principal cause of our poor delivery performance. And even now that it is obvious, there is considerable debate at Analog Devices about when you reach the point of diminishing returns in driving down cycle time as a means of improving on-time delivery, product quality, and cost.

Another important use of system dynamics is as a training tool. Once we have decided the correct policy on cycle time, for example, how do we help the organization learn how the policy works best and why? By explicitly revealing our mental model of how we believe the organization works or should work (that is, how the 'nodes' in the organization are connected and what factors govern their interaction), we create a precise language with which to share our understanding. By comparing our model with others, we provide a mechanism not only to converge on a shared model, but also to communicate to younger, less experienced managers the organization's stored experience and knowledge. System dynamics has the same teaching potential in management schools as it does in industry. In fact, MIT recently introduced system dynamics as a teaching tool to augment the case study method. Students use a model developed by John Sterman to learn how flawed business policies led to the dramatic rise and fall of People Express Airlines.

PLANNING AS LEARNING

My approach to strategic planning for our most recent five-year plan, 1988 to 1992, was strongly influenced by discussions with Arie de Geus in the New Management Style Project. De Geus suggested that the benefits accruing from planning are not just the objectives and strategies that emerge, but the learning that occurs during the planning process.[7] He contends that one form of organizational learning results from understanding the changes occurring in the external environment and then adapting beliefs and behavior to be compatible with those changes. If learning is a goal, then the way you structure the planning process and who you involve in it can make an important difference.

Analog Devices is a highly decentralized company; in the past, top management set the broad corporate objectives and assumptions, but most of the detailed strategic planning was carried out in the divisions. But this time, in order to encourage organizational learning, we formed fifteen corporate-wide product, market and technology task forces that drew together 150 professionals from throughout the company. We wanted to better understand the opportunities we faced as a corporation and how we needed to change to fully exploit those opportunities. The result of twelve months of deliberations was a delineation of nine imperatives for change, as well as specific recommendations for how to bring about those changes. An even more important result was that a broad cross-section of our top professionals understood why some basic beliefs and assumptions that had served us well in the past needed modification.

For example, one of our strongest beliefs was that the best way to organize our resources was to use relatively small, autonomous divisions. However, as we worked our way through the planning process, it became clear to all of us that our most fanatical commitment to decentralization was impeding progress. We concluded that we needed to coordinate technology development across divisions and to centralize certain aspects of manufacturing, especially wafer fabrication. We also had to better coordinate product planning to capitalize on the combined strength of our diverse product and technology base in penetrating new markets. We had to learn to present ourselves as a single vendor to our key accounts instead of as a collection of autonomous divisions, often competing with each other. We all realized that in accepting these conclusions we had unleashed powerful forces that would change the culture, structure, and behavior of the company in ways not yet foreseen.

Another strong belief that melted under scrutiny was that we had to choose between a proprietary, differentiated product strategy and a low-cost producer strategy. This either/or choice has proven to be a false and misleading alternative not only for Analog Devices, but for many other US companies as well. We had always taken pride in technology leadership and focused on opportunities where customers would pay high margins for performance, usually in applications with modest volume requirements. Now some of these applications were developing high-volume potential. Moreover, applications for our products and technology were emerging in computer peripherals, communications networks, and even consumer products like digital audio, and customers were demanding low prices in return for high volume.

We decided that our long-term strategy should be to serve certain selected high-volume applications where our technology provides unique benefits, lest competitors capture these markets, learn our technology, and eventually use a lower cost structure to penetrate our traditional lower-volume industrial and military markets. This strategy change was drastic. Only through a process of open deliberation, during which the

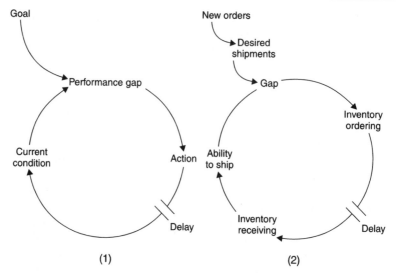

(1)

(2)

1. Basic balancing process with delay

2. Balancing process with delay in production distribution system

Balancing or adjustment processes are a universal feature of complex human and social systems. The human body dilates and expands capillaries, opens and closes skin pores, sweats and shivers to maintain body temperature in the face of changing environmental temperatures. Corporations likewise respond to gaps between desired and actual levels of performance.

The purpose of internal adjustment processes is to maintain desired balances in the face of environmental changes. However, adjustment mechanisms can also become the source of unintended and unwanted instabilities, especially when there are long delays between action and consequence (see '1' above). In the presence of delays, an action that persists until a performance gap is eliminated will result in overshoot and oscillation; thus a bather gets scalded by overadjusting a shower that responds slowly to the faucet setting.

The principle of delays and instabilities has many applications in corporate systems. For years executives and master's students in MIT's introductory System Dynamics courses have done a product-distribution simulation, affectionately known as the 'Beer Game.' In the simulation, retailers and wholesalers, distributors, and factories interact through ordering and shipping cases of beer to meet changing patterns of customer demand. In the process, the players unintentionally generate uncontrolled cycles in production, inventories, and orders because they fail to take into account the delays that intervene between inventory ordering and inventory receiving (see '2' above).

There are two basic design improvements to reduce instabilities created by delays in adjustment processes: modulate the decision makers' actions or shorten the delays. In the beer game, about 10 percent of the teams achieve stable outputs because they don't overreact in ordering inventory. However, the resulting product-distribution system is still sluggish in response to large changes in customer demands. In real industrial systems, where information systems and means of production and distribution can be redesigned, the leverage often lies in shortening delay times so that the system can be both stable and highly responsive.

Figure 17.1 **Systems principles: delays and instabilities**

consequences of the alternatives became very clear, did the organization 'buy into' this new direction.

Once a decision was made, the organization enthusiastically turned its attention to learning what it would take to win in certain selected high-volume applications that we were well aware of but had long ignored. In less than a year we were selling digital-to-analog converters to compact audio disc player manufacturers in Japan and Korea, and we had a research effort under way to develop a monolithic analog-to-digital converter for high-definition television.

We now have confidence that we can develop high-volume manufacturing capability to serve these new markets profitably, and we are busy putting these resources in place. We also believe we can and must be both product innovators and lower-cost producers. This change in beliefs has greatly expanded our vision of opportunity and of the types of customers and markets we will serve in the future.

These examples illustrate just a few of the dramatic changes taking place at Analog Devices. I believe our approach to planning as a learning process has greatly facilitated our ability to forge a consensus for change among those who must make it happen. It has also helped reduce the obstacles and resistance to change, that is, outdated beliefs and assumptions created by past success.

QUALITY IMPROVEMENT: A METHODOLOGY FOR CHANGE

Even when there is a strong consensus for change, achieving it is easier said than done. For example, another imperative reinforced by the planning process at Analog Devices was the need to improve customer service, product quality, and yields. Of course this concern was not new. Since the early 1980s, as our customers have gotten a taste of what Japanese electronic companies could deliver, and as just-in-time (JIT) programs have become more prevalent, pressure has mounted to improve performance. What was new was the realization of just how much we had to improve to meet our customers' expectations, and how little time we had to do it. On-time delivery of products that work has become the major factor in vendor selection and performance evaluation. We can no longer win by the sheer force of being first to market with the latest products and technology.

Quality improvement, or total quality control as it is often called, is a management methodology for achieving improvement and change.[8] In 1983 we began to introduce quality improvement methods at Analog Devices. We decided to focus our attention on product quality, on-time delivery, lead time, yields, and new-product time to market. We went to seminars, read books, gave speeches, and introduced information systems to measure our performance. But three years into the mission we were not getting very far very fast. I had an uneasy feeling that I did not know what I was supposed to be doing to lead this effort and that there were a lot of other dedicated managers in the same boat.

We knew all about error detection and correction and about doing it right the first time. But we did not have any notion of what rate of improvement was satisfactory or what we could do to accelerate the improvement process. Considering that many Japanese companies had been working the quality improvement game for more than twenty years and that they are not standing still even now, we had a justifiable sense of discomfort.

Because of our 'lean and mean' attitude toward staff functions, we had resisted the addition of quality improvement staff. Line managers were expected to learn on their own. But learn from where, learn from whom? Reading books and going to seminars was not enough. So we finally broke down and recruited a quality improvement professional to teach us how to tap the mainstream of experience and knowledge that is rapidly accumulating in this field and to help our managers become more expert practitioners. Only then did the organization begin to see real progress. One of the early lessons I learned from our quality guru was that there is a rational basis on which to set standards for rates of improvement. From his consulting experience, our director of quality improvement had documented case histories where quality improvement methodology had worked. What these cases showed was that while the rate of improvement varies from case to case, the rate in each case is remarkably consistent over an extended time period. Figure 17.2 shows three actual businesses' learning rates. Note that in the first case, performance improved by 50 percent every 10.4 months, in the second case every 7.8 months, and in the third case every 3.6 months. He called this characteristic slope of improvement the *half life*.

An analysis of a larger number of case studies indicated that the half life for improvement fell within a relatively narrow range, usually six to twelve months, across a wide range of applications.[9] The reason for this phenomenon is clear enough when you understand the method by which quality improvement is achieved.

The method is deceptively simple. For example, as I mentioned, one of our goals was to reduce the percentage of orders shipped late. To do this we assembled a team from various organizations involved with customer service to analyze the causes of lateness. For each late shipment we determined the cause, and then we plotted their distribution. We found that a relatively small number of causes was responsible for 50 percent of the problems.

Next we assembled problem-solving teams to attack these major causes of lateness. When the cycle was completed, we repeated the process by prioritizing the causes for 50 percent of the remaining problems and then eliminating the causes. This cycle was repeated again and again; each time the most important remaining problems were identified and resources were focused on solving them.

In this example, as in others using this method, the slope of the learning curve is determined by how long it takes to identify and prioritize the causes of the problem and to eliminate those causes. The skills of the people and the level of resources do have an impact, but surprisingly the time required for each cycle of improvement is largely a function of the complexity and bureaucracy of the organization. Or, to put quality improvement in the larger context of this chapter, the slope of the characteristic half-life curve is determined by the rate of organizational learning.

Notice that this theory of learning differs from the Boston Consulting Group (BCG) 'experience curve' theory that says learning occurs as a function of cumulative production volume, independent of lapsed time. The quality improvement theory says that learning, properly managed, occurs as a function of time, independent of cumulative volume. How else can we explain the success of the Japanese automobile industry which learned faster than the US industry with substantially less cumulative volume? If we combine the two ideas, we can say more accurately that the slope of the BCG experience curve is determined by the rate of organizational learning. A steeper experience curve occurring at lower production volume can soon overcome a more shallow experience curve occurring at higher volume.

We know that communication across organizational boundaries is less effective than within organizational boundaries and that many problems accumulate because of poor communication. Quality improvement is a way to create temporary organizational structures, or teams, that cut horizontally across organizational boundaries and enhance communication and cooperation. It is a way to get people to think about problems and issues objectively and quantitatively instead of subjectively and politically. It is a way to separate the vital few problems from the trivial many – and to focus organizational resources on resolving them. In short, quality improvement is a way to accelerate organizational learning.

Using the half-life concept, at Analog Devices we set very aggressive five-year goals for quality improvement (see Table 17.1). The results of continuous improvement with nine-to-twelve-month half lives over an extended period are awesome. The first reaction of our organization was to recoil from what looked like unrealistic objectives. But we reminded our managers that if a company really gets its quality improvement act together, there is no fundamental reason why these goals cannot be achieved. There are companies in Japan already operating at these levels on some of these measures.

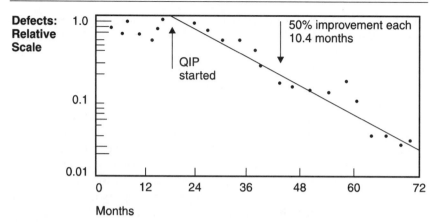

Figure 17.2(a) **Examples of quality improvement versus time product defect rate**

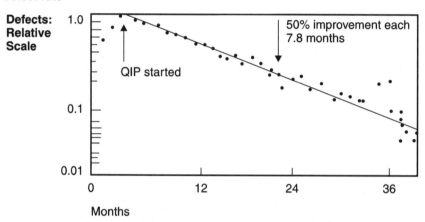

Figure 17.2(b) **Average defects per unit**

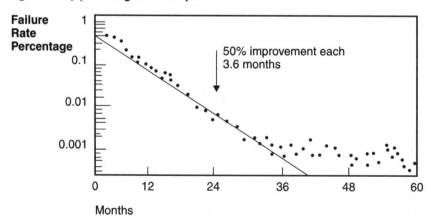

Figure 17.2(c) **Failure rate improvement**

BEHAVIORAL INFLUENCES ON THE LEARNING PROCESS

The values and culture of an organization have a significant impact on the learning process and on how effectively a company can adapt and change. In particular, poor communication between people and between organizations can be a major block to learning and quality improvement.

We decided another imperative for change at Analog Devices was to elevate teamwork as a virtue in our culture. We hoped to better balance our historical bias toward divisional autonomy with the recognition that many high-priority changes require interdivisional cooperation. If teamwork was our goal, then other virtues had to be emphasized. We tried to capture the essence of these virtues in the concepts of *openness* and *objectivity*. By openness, we mean a willingness to put all the cards on the table, eliminate hidden agendas, make our own motives, feelings, and biases known, and invite other opinions and points of view – thereby engendering trust in relations between people. By objectivity, we mean searching for the best answers based on reasoned positions and objective criteria, as opposed to political influence and parochial interests. We also mean making judgments based on facts, not opinions or rumors.

In order to encourage teamwork, openness, and objectivity, we have included these attributes in our performance appraisal process and our criteria for hiring and promotion. Moreover, during performance reviews we solicit feedback from peers and subordinates on these and other competencies. It is only when you tie pay and promotion to these in-

Table 17.1 Analog devices: quality improvement program goals

Measurement	1987	Half life (in months)	1992
External			
On-time delivery	85%	9	> 99.8%
Outgoing defect level	500 ppm	9	< 10 ppm
Lead time	10 weeks	9	< 3 weeks
Internal			
Manufacturing cycle time	15 weeks	9	4–5 weeks
Process defect level	5000 ppm	6	< 10 ppm
Yield	20%	9	> 50%
Time to market	36 months	24	6 months

tangible factors that the organization knows you are serious and begins to modify its behavior.

The concept of teamwork has many dimensions. We have found that the best way to introduce knowledge and modify behavior is by working with small teams that have the power and resources to enact change. For example, quality improvement training starts with the division manager and his or her direct reports [those who report directly to him/her]. The group not only develops a common understanding of new concepts and language, but peer pressure can also help to bring along skeptics who might otherwise block progress. Moreover, the new knowledge can be immediately transformed into action as an integral part of training. This approach, in contrast with sending people individually to centralized training programs, highlights the distinction between individual and organizational learning.

INFORMATION SYSTEMS: A HELP OR HINDRANCE TO LEARNING

Information, of course, is essential to the learning process. It is helpful to think about information *systems* in terms of whether they help or hinder organizational learning. Let me give a few examples to illustrate this point.

Many companies distribute their products through international sales affiliates. Product divisions 'sell' their output to sales affiliates at some transfer price. The affiliates, in turn, resell at the highest price the local market will bear. Each group is measured separately on 'sales' and 'profits,' but the company's *real* sales and profits are the combination of the two, with proper accounting eliminations. Analog Devices got started this way because we initially used a network of trading companies and representatives to distribute our products internationally. Over time we replaced these independent agencies with wholly owned sales affiliates, but the original organization and information system remained intact for years.

The system worked extremely well so long as there were enough profits to satisfy the goals of both organizations. But as competition intensified, more and more time was spent in haggling over the transfer prices between divisions, instead of in figuring out how to retain our market share in a competitive world. The system actually encouraged managers to hide the facts and play games to increase their share of the profit pie. So this year we threw out our old management information system, disbanded transfer prices (except for tax purposes), and went to worldwide product line reporting. Now both affiliates and product divisions operate from the same set of books.

Under the new system, division managers see results on a worldwide basis segmented by territory – with direct visibility, although not complete control, of end-customer sales revenues and distribution costs. By the same token, affiliate managers also see worldwide results with profit and cost visibility segmented by product division.

Under the old system, the only people who saw the worldwide results were the corporate accountants; even then the results were aggregated, rather than segmented by product line. No one in the corporation actually knew the real worldwide sales and profits for any product.

The worldwide product line management system focuses division and affiliate managers on common goals and performance measures that encourage cooperation rather than conflict. Separate information systems that hide interdependence and give a false sense of control are not realistic. As you might expect, though, our managers ask, 'How can we be responsible for what we can't control?' The answer is that we can influence others with information and reason. Control is an illusion – compelling in the short term, but unachievable in the long term. Information systems that hide this dilemma do not get at the problems. Already I can tell you that, since we started using worldwide product line information, a lot of thoughtful discussions have taken place around the company, and some constructive behavior changes have occurred. The new information system is helping managers on both sides to understand their businesses better and to make better decisions.

Another problem with management information systems is that they are strongly biased toward reporting financial information to stockholders and government agencies. Unless quality improvement and other more fundamental performance measures are elevated to the same level of importance as financial measures, when conflicts arise, financial considerations win out. To address this issue, we designed what we call a division scorecard that reports only the barest of financial information and places greater emphasis on quality improvement goals. This scorecard is used not only to evaluate division performance, but also to structure division bonus plans.

How information is displayed makes an incredible difference. Consider, for example, the format we use to display on-time delivery information (see Figure 17.3). This simple summary replaces pages of information that used to be circulated to managers. With all these pages, the most crucial information was missing – namely, the half-life trend. Because the information is plotted on a log-linear scale, the trend is readily discernible. For management purposes, displaying all divisions together on a single page has great motivational value. A high level of internal competition exists to generate the fastest learning curve; it is obvious and embarrassing when you are not performing.

Management information systems transform data into information and then help managers transform information into knowledge and knowledge into action. The challenge is deciding what information and knowledge – in what form – are needed. If we keep organizational learning in mind as a goal of information systems design, then we are more likely to generate the information and knowledge that managers need to take effective action.

We still have only a primitive knowledge of how organizations learn and of how to overcome obstacles to organizational change. Industry and universities need to work together developing tools and concepts that facilitate the process of change.

THE NEED FOR COLLABORATIVE RESEARCH

Among engineers and scientists there is a consensus that collaborative university–industry research promotes innovation and competitiveness. The National Science Foundation's Engineering Research Center (ERC) program, patterned on MIT's interdisciplinary research centers, is an attractive prototype partnership. The criteria in winning ERC grants include cross-disciplinary research, industry participation, new knowledge generation, improvement of the United States' competitive position, and linkage to the education system. If we broaden the concepts of innovation and technology to embrace management, then the need for collaborative research in management is no less than it is in engineering. Perhaps it is even greater.

Japanese industry is concentrated in huge, vertically integrated corporations, whereas the United States has a fragmented industry structure, especially in knowledge-intensive industries. In fact, six of the world's ten largest corporations are Japanese; only three are American. Because of their size, these mega-corporations can be more self-sufficient in technical and managerial research, education, and training. America's superior research universities could potentially offset this advantage, but only if they work closely with industry.

The New Management Style Project closely follows the ERC model and offers an excellent prototype for the development of collaborative partnerships between business schools and industry. We have learned from this experience that an effective partnership should include the following characteristics.

- *Focus on critical management problems.* Academics and industrialists should work together to identify critical issues of practical significance to practicing managers. They must be issues for which academic research can add to the store of knowledge and tools, codify industry

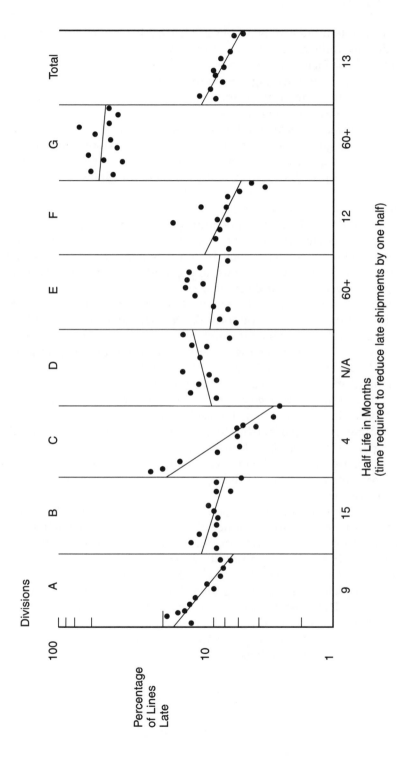

Figure 17.3 **Analog Devices on-time customer service performance**

practice into more widely usable and teachable form, or both. In order to do this, universities may need to rethink their research agenda, as well as how faculty contributions and performance are evaluated. It may also require a willingness on the part of universities to set aside their preference for tidy 'academic research,' and, instead, confront messy, real-life management issues.

- *Develop and disseminate new learning tools and methods.* One important partnership goal is the broad dissemination of new tools and concepts in both management education and practice, either through academic research or through discovery and documentation of the best industry practices.

- *Test tools and methods in practice.* Some of the companies in the New Management Style Project are testing new concepts by serving as experimental laboratories. The real value of *new* management ideas can be determined only when they are put into practice. Research partnerships provide a unique opportunity to perform controlled experiments in real-world settings.

- *Provide cross-organizational learning.* An important benefit for the industrial partners is the opportunity to share experiences and learn from each other – not superficially, but with the benefit of thoughtful discussion. I certainly learned a great deal from my partners in the New Management Style Project, and so did the academics who heard firsthand about common issues and concerns.

- *Use a cross-disciplinary approach.* Important problems are generally complex; they do not align themselves with a single technology or discipline. Thus a partnership focused on real-world problems should bring together specialists from several related disciplines. MIT has done this very successfully in science and engineering through interdisciplinary research centers. This approach is promising for management schools as well.

- *Provide cooperative education opportunities for students.* One objective of the partnership is to introduce the most current knowledge and methods into management education, but these partnerships could also provide a unique opportunity for cooperative education. That is, during the summer months, students could become involved with research projects already being undertaken by the university and the company. These work assignments could lead to a thesis or study project that is part of the academic program. Blending theory and practice in an internship program is perhaps the best approach to professional graduate education.

CONCLUSIONS

Five years ago Analog Devices had no conceptual framework for the kind of thinking outlined in this chapter and no prayer of making the kind of improvements that are essential to our survival. Now I believe we are on the right track, and we are seeing real progress across a broad front. But the question remains, are we learning fast enough? Or will one of our competitors, either here or abroad, learn even faster in the future? That unsettling question concerns me most of all.

Management innovation is already an important aspect of industrial competitiveness, and it will surely become even more of a factor in the future. Like any innovation process, management innovation requires new technology and new ideas and then the rapid diffusion of the new knowledge into practice. These results do not come free; they require a major investment of time and resources. We have to ask ourselves, as a company and as a nation, are we investing enough in management innovation? Do we even know how much or how little we are investing? I suspect we are not investing nearly enough and, as a result, the huge sums we are pouring into product and process development will not produce anywhere near their full potential. Clearly, industry has a vested interest in working more closely with universities to advance the state of management technology and practice.

Our research universities must also play a major role in boosting management innovation and restoring competitiveness. One way, as proposed here, is to work with industry to develop better management tools and concepts and to help companies put these ideas into practice. Better understanding of how to accelerate organizational learning and adapt to a changing world environment would be a good place to start.

NOTES

1 P.F. Drucker, 'Management and the World's Work,' *Harvard Business Review*, September–October 1988, pp. 65–76.
2 M.A. Cusumano, 'Manufacturing Innovation: Lessons from the Japanese Auto Industry,' *Sloan Management Review*, Fall 1988, pp. 29–39.
3 J.M. Utterback and W.J. Abernathy, 'A Dynamic Model of Process and Product Innovation,' *OMEGA*, 3 (1975): 639–656.
4 J.W. Forrester, 'Counterintuitive Behavior of Social Systems,' *Technology Review*, January 1971, pp. 52–68.
5 P.M. Senge, 'The New Management: Moving from Invention to Innovation,' *New Management*, Summer 1986, pp. 7–13.
6 J. Sterman, 'Misperceptions of Feedback in Dynamic Decision Making,' *Organizational Behavior and Human Decision Processes*, 43, April 1989.
7 A.P. de Geus, 'Planning as Learning,' *Harvard Business Review*, March–April 1988, pp. 70–74.

8 K Ishikawa, *What is Total Quality Control? The Japanese Way*, trans. D.J. Lu (Englewood Cliffs, NJ: Prentice-Hall, 1985).
9 A.M. Schneiderman, 'Setting Quality Goals,' *Quality Progress*, April 1988, pp. 51–57.

Chapter 18

Second thoughts on teambuilding

Bill Critchley and David Casey

PART 1: TEAMBUILDING – AT WHAT PRICE AND AT WHAT COST?

It all started during one of those midnight conversations between consultants in a residential workshop. We were running a teambuilding session with a top management group and something very odd began to appear. Our disturbing (but also exciting) discovery was that for most of their time this group of people had absolutely no need to work as a team; indeed the attempt to do so was causing more puzzlement and scepticism than motivation and commitment. In our midnight reflections we were honest enough to confess to each other that this wasn't the first time our teambuilding efforts had cast doubts on the very validity of teamwork itself, within our client groups.

We admitted that we had both been working from some implicit assumptions that good teamwork is a characteristic of healthy, effectively functioning organizations. Now we started to question those assumptions. First, we flushed out what our assumptions actually were. In essence it came down to something like this:

> We had been assuming that the top group in any organization (be it the board of directors or the local authority management committee or whatever the top group is called) should be a team and ought to work as a team. Teamwork at the top is crucial to organizational success, we assumed.

We further assumed that a properly functioning team is one in which:

- people care for each other;
- people are open and truthful;
- there is a high level of trust;
- decisions are made by consensus;
- there is strong team commitment;
- conflict is faced up to and worked through;
- people really listen to ideas and to feelings;

- feelings are expressed freely;
- process issues (task and feelings) are dealt with.

Finally, it had always seemed logical to us that a teambuilding catalyst could always help any team to function better – and so help any organization perform better as an organization. Better functioning would lead the organization to achieve its purposes more effectively.

The harsh reality we came up against was at odds with this cosy view of teams, teamwork and teambuilding. In truth the Director of Education has little need to work in harness with his fellow chief officers in a county council. He or she might need the support of the Chief Executive and the Chair of the elected members' Education Committee, but the other chief officers in that local authority have neither the expertise nor the interest, nor indeed the time, to contribute to what is essentially very specialized work.

Even in industry, whilst it is clear that the marketing and production directors of a company must work closely together to ensure that the production schedule is synchronized with sales forecasts and the finance director needs to be involved – to look at the cash flow implications of varying stock levels – they don't need to involve the *whole* team. And they certainly do not need to develop high levels of trust and openness to work through those kinds of business issues.

On the other hand, most people would agree that *strategic* decisions, concerned with the future direction of the whole enterprise, should involve all those at the top. Strategy should demand an input from every member of the top group, and for strategic discussion and strategic decision-making, teamwork at the top is essential. But how much time do most top management groups actually spend discussing strategy? Our experiences, in a wide variety of organizations, suggest that 10 per cent is a high figure for most organizations – often 5 per cent would be nearer the mark. This means that 90–95 per cent of decisions in organizations are essentially operational; that is decisions made within departments based usually on a fair amount of information and expertise. In those conditions, high levels of trust and openness may be nice, but are not necessary; consensus is strictly not an issue and in any case would take up far too much time. There is therefore no need for high levels of interpersonal skills.

Why, then, is so much time and money invested in teambuilding, we asked ourselves. At this stage in our discussions we began to face a rather disturbing possibility. Perhaps the spread of teambuilding has more to do with teambuilders and *their* needs and values rather than a careful analysis of what is appropriate and necessary for the organization. To test out this alarming hypothesis we each wrote down an honest and frank list of reasons why we ourselves engaged in teambuilding. We recommend this as an enlightening activity for other teambuilders – perhaps, like us, they will arrive at this kind of conclusion: teambuilders work as catalysts to help management groups function better as open teams for a variety of reasons, including the following:

- They like it – enjoy the risks.
- Because they are good at it.
- It's flattering to be asked.
- They receive rewarding personal feedback.
- Professional kudos – not many people do teambuilding with top teams.
- There's money in it.
- It accords with their values: for instance democracy is preferred to autocracy.
- They gain power. Process interventions are powerful in business settings where the client is on home ground and can bamboozle the consultant in business discussions.

All those reasons are concerned with the needs, skills and values of the *teambuilder* rather than the management group being 'helped'. This could explain why many teambuilding exercises leave the so-called 'management team' excited and stimulated by the experience, only to find they are spending an unnecessary amount of time together discussing other people's departmental issues. Later on, because they cannot see the benefit of working together on such issues, they abandon 'teamwork' altogether. Such a management group has been accidentally led to disillusionment with the whole idea of teamwork and the value of teambuilding.

We began to see, as our discussions went through the small hours, that there is a very *large* proportion of most managers' work where teamwork is not needed (and to attempt to inculcate teamwork is dysfunctional). There is, at the same time, a very *small* proportion of their work where teamwork is absolutely vital (and to ignore teamworking skills is to invite disaster). This latter work, which demands a team approach, is typified by strategic work but not limited to strategic work. It is any work characterized by a high level of choice and by the condition of maximum uncertainty.

Most people find choice and uncertainty uncomfortable. Many senior managers attempt to deny the choice element by the employment of complex models and techniques. We don't think most people's management experience teaches them to make choices about the future for instance; it puts the main emphasis on establishing as many facts as possible and reviewing options in the light of past experience. That's why models like, for example, the Boston portfolio model and the General Electric matrix are so popular. They provide comforting analytic frameworks for looking at strategic options, but they are appealing really to our operational mentality. The hope often is that they will magic up a solution to the strategic question. But of course they can't make choices for people and they don't throw any light on the future.

The top team of an organization, if it is to achieve quality and commitment in its decisions about future directions, will need to pool the full extent of each individual's wisdom and experience. That means something quite different from reacting to a problem in terms of their own functional knowledge and experience. It means *exposing fully* their uncertainties, taking unaccustomed risks by airing their own subjective view of the world and struggling to build some common perceptions and possibilities. This is where that much abused word 'sharing' really comes into its own. In this context it is not merely a value-laden exhortation: it is vital to the future of the organization. Ideas and opinions are all we have to inform our view of the future, but if we are to take a risk with a fragile idea or opinion, unsubstantiated by facts, we will only take it if the climate is right. Conversely, if we take the risk and the sheer airiness and vulnerability of the idea attracts a volley of ridicule and abuse, then it will die on the instant, lost forever, snuffed out like Tinkerbell.

Most functional executives, brought up in the hurly-burly of politics and inter-functional warfare, find the transition from functional to strategic mode very difficult to make. They do not always see the difference, and if they do, they are reluctant to leave their mountain top, the summit of knowledge, experience and hence power, for the equality and shared uncertainty of strategic decision making. And yet this is one area where real teamwork is not only necessary but vital.

We had now got ourselves thoroughly confused. We seemed to be forcing teambuilding on groups which had no need to be a team and missing the one area where teamwork is essential – because choice and uncertainty are at a maximum and for this very reason managers were shying away from the work – work which can *only* be done by a team. We resorted to diagrams to help clear our minds and these new diagrams form the basis of Part 2 of this chapter.

PART 2: THEORETICAL CONSIDERATIONS CONCERNING MANAGEMENT GROUPS

We found these kinds of discussions taking us farther and farther away from teambuilding and closer and closer to an understanding of why management groups work, or don't work, in the ways they do. In the end, we developed two basic diagrams, showing the relationships between a number of variables which operate in management groups:

– the degree of uncertainty in the management task;
– the need for sharing in the group;
– modes of working;

- different kinds of internal group process;
- different levels of interpersonal skills;
- the role of the leader.

We would now like to present these two framework diagrams as diagnostic tools, which a dozen or so management groups have found very useful in coming to terms with how they work and why. These simple diagrams are helping groups see what kind of groups they are and when and if they want to be a team, rather than jumping to the conclusion that all groups need teambuilding.

Throughout the discussion, we will be talking about the management group – that is the leader plus those immediately responsible to him or her, perhaps five to ten people in all, at the top of their organization or their part of the organization.

The first diagram (Figure 18.1) shows the relationship between the level of uncertainty inherent in any group task and the need for members of that group to share with each other. Expressed simply – 'The more uncertainty – the more need to share.' Everyday examples of this truism are: children holding hands for comfort in the dark or NASA research scientists brainstorming for fresh ideas on the frontiers of human knowledge – any uncertainty, emotional, physical or intellectual, can best be coped with by sharing.

However, the converse is also true – where there is less uncertainty, there is less need to share. The same children will feel no need to hold hands round the breakfast table where all is secure; the NASA scientists during the final launch will each get on with their own well-rehearsed part of the launch programme in relative isolation from each other. Only if something goes wrong (uncertainty floods back) will they need to share, quickly and fully. It took us a long time to realize the full significance of that in terms of the need to share in a management group.

We are dealing here only with the top group of the organization where task is the dominant imperative. There are other situations in which other objectives demand sharing: for instance if one is dealing with the whole fabric of a complete organization and attempting a global shift in attitudes, then culture-building may become the dominant imperative and sharing at all levels in that organization may become necessary. But that is a different situation – we are focusing here on the top management group where task must be the dominant imperative.

In Figure 18.1 we have used Revans' powerful distinction between problems (no answer is known to exist) and puzzles (the answer exists somewhere – just find it) to describe different levels of uncertainty. To illustrate the difference between a problem and a puzzle – deciding about capital punishment is a problem for society; tracking down a murderer is a puzzle for the police.

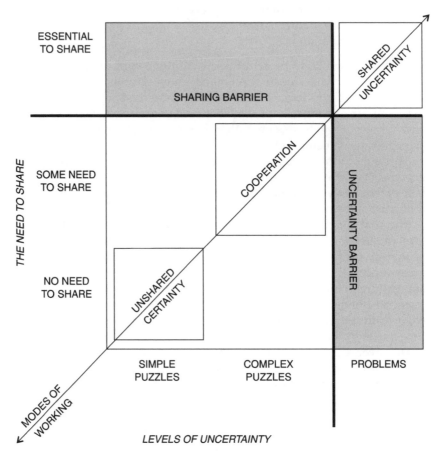

Figure 18.1 **The more uncertainty in its task, the more any group has to share**

Work groups dealing with genuine problems (of which strategy is only one example) would be well advised to share as much as possible with each other. They should share feelings to gain support, as well as ideas to penetrate the unknown. Figure 18.1 shows two shaded areas: *these shaded areas must be avoided.* The shaded area on the right indicates the futility of tackling real problems unless people are prepared to share. The shaded area at the top indicates that there is no point in sharing to solve mere puzzles.

Two 'barriers' appear on our model; they indicate that a positive effort must be made if a breakthrough to a new level of working is to be accomplished. For instance the uncertainty barrier represents a step into the unknown – a deliberate attempt to work in areas of ambiguity, uncertainty and ambivalence. To avoid the shaded areas and arrive in the top righthand corner, the group break through *both* barriers at the *same* time. This is the *only* way to solve genuine problems. Most management groups stay behind both barriers in Figure 18.1 and handle work which is in the nature of a puzzle – and to achieve this they cooperate, rather than share with each other. As long as they continue to limit their work to solving puzzles, they are quite right to stay within the sharing and uncertainty barriers of Figure 18.1.

As teambuilders, we now see that we must spend time identifying which modes of working any management group operates. The three modes of working come out in Figure 18.1 as the diagonal and we would like to describe each mode, by working up the diagonal from left to right:

Mode of unshared certainty. The proper mode for simple puzzles of a technical nature in everyday work where every member of the group is relatively competent within his/her field and speaks from the authority of his/her specialism. Ideal when the work issues are independent of each other – as they often are. A healthy attitude is, 'I will pull my weight and see that my part is done well.' Attitudes can become unhealthy if they move towards 'my interests must come first'.

Mode of cooperation. The appropriate mode for complex puzzles which impinge on the work of several members of the management group. In this mode (very common in local authorities) group members recognize the need for give-and-take, cooperation, negotiation and passing of information on a need-to-know basis. The attitude is, 'I'll cooperate for the good of the whole and because other members of this group have their rights and problems too.' Sharing is restricted to what is necessary and each group member still works from the security (certainty) of his/her own professional base, recognizing the professional bases of colleagues.

Mode of shared uncertainty. A rare mode. Partly because it is appropriate only for genuine problems (such as strategy) where nobody knows what to do, uncertainty is rife and full sharing between members is the only way out; partly because, even when it is the appropriate mode, many management groups never reach these professional heights. The attitude of members has to be 'the good of the whole outweighs any one member's interests – including mine. I carry an equal responsibility with my colleagues for the whole, and for this particular work I am not able to rely on my specialism, because my functional expertise is, for this problem we all face, irrelevant.'

Clearly this top mode of 'shared uncertainty' is extremely demanding and it is not surprising that many management groups try hard to avoid it. We know several boards of directors and even more local authority management 'Teams' who have devised a brilliant trick to avoid handling genuine problems requiring genuine sharing in the top mode. Quite simply – they turn all strategic problems into operational puzzles! How? There are very many variations of this trick available:

- Appoint a working party
- Ask a consultant to recommend
- Recruit a corporate planner
- Set up a think-tank, etc.

To make sure the trick works, the terms of reference are – 'Your recommendation must be short and must ask us to decide between option A or option B.' Choosing between A and B is an operational puzzle they *can* solve and it leaves them with the comfortable illusion that they have actually been engaging in strategic problem resolution work, whereas the truth is they have avoided uncertainty, avoided sharing their fears and ideas, avoided their real work, by converting frightening problems into management puzzles. And who can blame them!

We don't feel we have the right to censure top groups for not working in the top mode of shared uncertainty. We do feel we have the obligation to analyse quite rigorously how top groups actually work, before we plunge in with our teambuilding help.

In Figure 18.1 the size of the box for each mode indicates very roughly how frequently each mode might be needed by most management groups. Sadly, we see many management groups working in modes which are inappropriate to the work being done. It is not just that many top groups fail to push through a lot of the time, when they should be working in the middle mode. On the other hand other groups go through a pantomime of sitting round a table trying to work in the middle mode, but in truth feeling bored and uninterested because the middle mode is inappropriate and each member of the group could carry on separately with his or her own work, without pretending to share it with colleagues, who don't need to know anyway. In other words their appropriate mode is unshared certainty and attempts at sharing are boring or frustrating facades.

Figure 18.1 shows an arrow on both ends of the diagonal to illustrate that all three modes of working are necessary at different times and effective work groups can and should slide up and down the diagonal. We do not see any management group working in one mode all the time – the really effective group is able to move from mode to mode as the *task* requires. Although it may think of itself as a management 'team', a top group will be truly functioning as a team only when it is operating in the top mode.

We use the word team here, in the sense used in the first part of this chapter, which we believe is the sense used by most teambuilders in teambuilding work. Because we now believe that working in the top mode of shared uncertainty is called for infrequently – by the nature of the work – and is actually practised even less frequently, we now doubt the value of teambuilding work with most management groups, when there is so much more urgent work to be done with these groups.

We found in Figure 18.1 that when we plot the level of uncertainty in the work against the need to share we discover three modes of working, on the diagonal of Figure 18.1. These three modes of working are:

Unshared certainty
Cooperation
Shared uncertainty

We now want to go on to answer the questions 'How does a management group work in each of these modes? What *processes* are needed, what *skills* are required, and how does the *leader* function?

The format of Figure 18.2 is the same as Figure 18.1, only the variables are different. The vertical axis of Figure 18.2 is the diagonal lifted from Figure 18.1 (modes) and two new variables are introduced – *processes* is on the horizontal axis and *interpersonal skills* becomes the new diagonal.

Processes

To start with the horizontal axis – processes. We distinguish three levels of process in any group. At the most perfunctory there are *polite social processes*, very important to sustain the social lubrication of a healthy group but not focused on the work itself. The work is accomplished largely via *task processes* – the way work is organized, distributed, ideas generated and shared, decisions made and so forth. The third level of process concerns people's feelings (*feelings processes*) and how these are handled – by the people themselves and by others.

Reference to Figure 18.2 will make it clear that as the mode of working becomes more difficult, ascending the vertical axis, from unshared certainty towards shared uncertainty, so the processes needed to accomplish this more difficult work also become more difficult, as the group moves along the horizontal axis from simple basic social processes, through task processes, towards the much more difficult processes of working with people's deeper feelings.

Many groups never reach the top mode of shared uncertainty, where people's feelings are actually *part of the work* and all is uncertainty, excitement and trust.

The shaded areas are to be avoided (as in Figure 18.1). The righthand shaded area indicates that it is absurd to indulge in work with people's feelings if the group is working only in the two lower modes of unshared certainty and cooperation – to engage in soul-searching to accomplish this kind of work is ridiculous and brings teambuilding into disrepute. The top shaded area indicates similarly that there is no need to share deeply when only the two lower levels of processes (basic social processes and task processes) are operating.

However, a management group faced with the need to tackle uncertainty can either funk the whole thing, by staying safely behind the barriers (which is what most management groups appear to do), or it can have the courage to break through both barriers simultaneously, arriving (breathlessly) in the top righthand corner where the mode of working is shared uncertainty and the necessary processes are task *and* feelings processes together. Those few management groups which accomplish this become *teams*.

Interpersonal skills

The final variable is the diagonal of Figure 18.2 – 'interpersonal skills' – and clearly there is an ascending order of skill from the lowest (but *not* least important) level of polite social skills to the highest possible level of interpersonal skills required in the rarefied atmosphere of highest uncertainty and real teamwork. But, for the middle mode, a solid raft of straightforward interpersonal skills is needed by all managers – empathy, cooperation, communication, listening, negotiating and many more. We have come to believe that here is the greatest area of need.

The leader's role

The group leader and group leadership have not been mentioned so far, in an attempt to keep things simple. The whole question of leadership is fundamental to the operation of all management groups and we would like to make some observations now.

Leader's role in the mode of unshared certainty

The leader is hardly needed at all in the unshared certainty mode and, indeed, the social lubrication processes of a group working in this mode may well be carried out much better by an informal leader – there is nothing so embarrassing as the formal group leader bravely trying to lead the group through its Christmas lunch in the local pub!

Some local authority chief executives (so called) suffer an even worse fate – they cannot find a role at all, because the members of their management team (so called) steadfastly refuse to move out of the bottom mode of working, tacitly deciding *not* to work together and denying the Chief Executive any place in the organization at all! This is not uncommon.

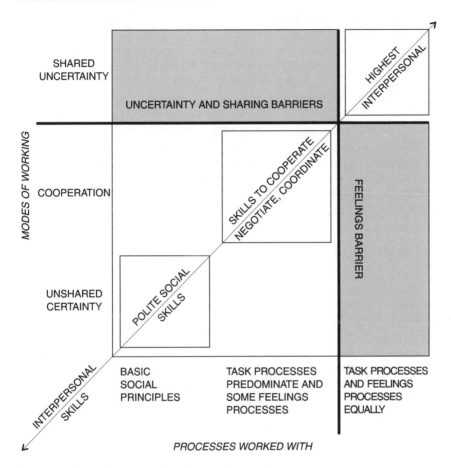

Figure 18.2 Different modes of working require different processes

Leader's role in the mode of cooperation

The leader's role in the central (cooperation) mode is well established in management convention. For example, a clear role at meetings has been universally recognized as that of enabling the leader to manage the *task* processes in particular. This role is of course the chairperson. Coordination of the task is at its core and most group leaders find this role relatively clear.

Leader's role in the mode of shared uncertainty

No such role has yet been universally recognized to deal with the processes in the highest mode, of shared uncertainty. In Britain, we have the added difficulty of our cultural resistance to working with feelings (in action learning language 'No sets please, we're British'). In this sophisticated mode of working, the word 'catalyst' seems more appropriate than the word chairperson and often a teambuilder is invited in to carry out this role. But where does this leave the group leader? All management group leaders have learned to be the chairperson; very few have yet learned to be the catalyst. And in any case, to be the catalyst and the leader at the same time is to attempt the north face of the Eiger of interpersonal skills. It can be done, but not in carpet slippers. If, on the other hand, the role of catalyst is performed by an outsider, the leadership dynamic becomes *immensely* complex and adds a significant overlay of difficulty when working in a mode which we have already shown to be extremely difficult in the first place. No wonder teambuilding often fails.

CONCLUSIONS

Many teambuilders are unaware of the shaded no-go areas and dreamily assume that any progress towards open attitudes, free expression of feelings and genuine sharing in any management group is beneficial. This is not so – to be of benefit there needs to be a very delicate and deliberate balance between what *work* the group has decided to pursue (what level of *uncertainty*) and the degree of sharing and expression of feelings the group is prepared for, to accomplish that work. Only if the balance is right will the management group be able to aim accurately at the top righthand corner of Figures 18.1 and 18.2 and succeed in breaking through all the barriers at the same time, to experience real teamwork. Attempts to push through only *one* barrier (trying to handle uncertainty without sharing; sharing for the sake of sharing; being open for the sake of being open) will fail and in failing will probably make things worse for that management group.

Strategic planners are often guilty of pushing management groups towards handling uncertainty *without* the commitment abilities to share and work with feelings. Teambuilders are often guilty of the converse sin – pushing management groups to be open and share their feelings, when the group has no intention whatever of getting into work where the level of uncertainty is high. Neither will succeed. It is no coincidence that both strategic planning and teambuilding can fall quickly into disrepute; it may be too late to save strategic planning from the management scrapheap – it is not too late to save teambuilding.

SUMMARY: PUTTING TEAMBUILDING IN ITS PLACE

The problems we described in Part 1 of this chapter centre round the dangers of consultants imposing their own values on a client management group when they engage in teambuilding work, instead of first finding out how that management group actually works, its context within the organization, and hence what it really needs.

In Part 2 we developed a diagnostic tool, in the form of two figures, which in the hands of a management group will enable it to understand how it actually works, and will provide it with a means of articulating the kind of group it wants to become, starting unequivocally from an analysis of its role and purpose and the work it has to do, rather than from some prior assumptions or values about how a management group 'should' work.

Some people will argue that management groups cannot even begin to engage with each other in any kind of serious work, such as for example establishing what the key tasks are, until they have first built a degree of openness and trust. We would disagree on two counts.

In the first place, as our figures illustrate, high levels of openness and trust are only rarely needed, and management groups get most of their work done very well without them, preferring for safety and comfort to remain relatively closed, and, covertly at least, distrustful. To ask such groups to make a major cultural shift, to take such big risks with each other as to be fully open and trusting, requires some mighty cogent justification.

Secondly, we have a theoretical objection to starting with feelings. Most management groups are likely to be task-centred, to be working at an intellectual rather than an emotional level. Approaching such a group suddenly at an emotional level will either generate shock, pain, distrust and confusion, or will produce a warm, cosy, euphoric, one-off experience. In either case it will often be followed by rejection of the approach and its sponsor, the teambuilder.

So we are suggesting to all would-be teambuilders, that if their purpose is to be one of real *value to their clients*, they start by encouraging their clients to clarify the role and purpose of the management group in question, to identify the nature of the tasks which they need to address *as a group* – complex puzzles or real problems – and then to consider the appropriate modes of working, and the skills and processes which go with them. When we have reached this stage, most of us have the skills and technologies to provide what is needed. What is often left out is the diagnostic work that gets us to this stage.

Chapter 19

Crucial gaps in 'the Learning Organization'

Power, politics and ideology

John Coopey

> Learning is about getting to like what you get.
>
> (with apologies to George Bernard Shaw)

Learning has a long history as a concept in organization theory. The essential concern is to enhance processes of learning which can be used within organizations to improve individual and collective actions through better knowledge and understanding (Shrivastava, 1983; Fiol and Lyles, 1985). The notion of the Learning Organization has emerged more recently, focusing on organizations designed deliberately to facilitate the learning of their members and, hence, much freer collective adaptation (Revans, 1982; Garratt, 1987; Pedler *et al.*, 1988, 1989, 1991). It can be defined as:

> An organization that facilitates the learning of all its members *and* continuously transforms itself.
>
> (Pedler *et al.*, 1991: 1; original emphasis)

Three longstanding themes are brought together: how to structure organizations to enhance performance; how to facilitate individual learning and development in a corporate setting; and how to ensure that organizations adapt quickly to changes in their external environment.

Theorizing about learning organizations which emphasizes their potential for transformation fits into a diverse array of recent approaches to achieving greater flexibility, to 'find ways of managing an unprecedented degree of economic uncertainty deriving from a need for continuous rapid adjustment to a market environment that seems to have become permanently more turbulent than in the past' (Streeck, 1987: 295).

In this chapter the most thoroughly worked out model of a learning organization is summarized and placed within a framework of assumptions about power and political activity seemingly lacking in the literature. Arguments are developed regarding the likely incidence of political activity within a learning organization and its implications for employee empowerment deemed important for learning. Finally, we examine the potential use of the language and symbolism of the Learning Organization to create new ideological representations.

The most detailed exposition of the Learning Organization, used as the main focus of the chapter, is by Pedler *et al.* (1988, 1989, 1991). Part metaphor, part prescription and called by them a 'learning company', its theoretical framework was sketched in from the organizational learning literature and developed through a Manpower Services Commission project involving managers, consultants and academics. Other sources drawn on are Garratt (1987) and Hawkins (1991). To facilitate the discussion in this chapter the terms Pedler *et al.* use and the relationships between the terms which the authors assert or seem to imply are summarized in a model represented in Figure 19.1. Shown are eleven characteristics of a learning organization, several intervening variables at the level of the individual and the organization, and output variables subsumed under the term 'competitive advantage'. The causal relationships implied in the model are mediated by a control process. Greater detail of the eleven characteristics is provided in Figure 19.2.

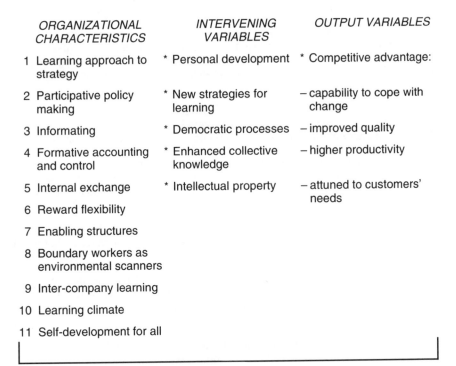

ORGANIZATIONAL CHARACTERISTICS	*INTERVENING VARIABLES*	*OUTPUT VARIABLES*
1 Learning approach to strategy	* Personal development	* Competitive advantage:
2 Participative policy making	* New strategies for learning	– capability to cope with change
3 Informating	* Democratic processes	– improved quality
4 Formative accounting and control	* Enhanced collective knowledge	– higher productivity
5 Internal exchange	* Intellectual property	– attuned to customers' needs
6 Reward flexibility		
7 Enabling structures		
8 Boundary workers as environmental scanners		
9 Inter-company learning		
10 Learning climate		
11 Self-development for all		

CONTROL PROCESS

Figure 19.1 **The Learning Organization**

* **A learning approach** to strategy requires that the various aspects of forming policy and strategy are structured as a learning process allowing ongoing development and revision of business plans.

* **Participative policy making** ensures that all organizational members can contribute to major policy decisions.

* **Informating** assumes new ways will be found of using information technology not only to provide a model of organizational processes required for control (the cybernetic model) but also to make widely available 'the kind of knowledge [which] will enable competent participation in the processes associated with making things' (Zuboff, 1988: 57).

* **Formative accounting and control** ensures that accounting and budgeting systems meet the information needs of all internal clients of those systems so as to strengthen the 'ethos of self-responsibility' fostering semi-autonomous individuals and groups.

* **Internal exchange** implies that all departments and units relate to each other as potential customers and suppliers within a partly regulated internal market exchanging information on expectations, negotiating, contracting and providing feedback. Collaboration rather than competition is the keynote, yielding positive-sum instead of zero-sum outcomes.

* **Reward flexibility**, within a general framework of Human Resource Management, ensures flexibility in the types of rewards used and in the way in which systems of financial rewards are structured and delivered, requiring that assumptions underlying reward systems are made public and reviewed collectively.

* **Structures** take temporary forms (e.g. Hedberg *et al.*, 1976) which, while catering for current needs, can be shaped through experimentation to respond easily to future changes in the internal and external environments.

* All **boundary workers** are **environmental scanners**, not just those who traditionally have been accorded a scanning role, providing a corpus of information on developments in the external environment for use in strategy formulation.

* **Inter-company learning** carries the learning ethos to suppliers, customers and even competitors through, for example, joint training, shared investment and R&D.

* A **learning climate** is necessary to facilitate individual learning, essentially a cultural template designed around a questioning frame of mind, tolerance of experiments and mistakes, the essential need for differences and the idea of continuous improvement.

* **Self-development opportunities** are available for all, sufficient to allow people to take advantage of the enabling climate.

Figure 19.2 **Learning Organization characteristics**

Central to the model is the 'control' learning which takes place at three levels, broadly as defined by Argyris and Schon (1978). At level I, or 'operational' learning, performance errors are corrected against norms built into operating plans (Garratt, 1987; Pedler *et al.*, 1991); level II, or 'strategic learning', occurs when existing goals and transformation processes are modified to match perceived changes in the external environment (Garratt, 1987); at level III, learning is related to questions of purpose (Pedler *et al.*, 1991) such that an organization's leaders share the perspective of others in the wider community, tapping new sources of spiritual energy (Hawkins, 1991: 183).

POWER AND POLITICS WITHIN A LEARNING ORGANIZATION

The assumptions which seem to underlie a learning organization are now reviewed against a framework of power and political behaviour summarized in Figure 19.3. Central is Giddens' (1976, 1979) concept of power, chosen for three reasons: first, its rigour; second, its potential for resolving the duality as between individual agency and the power implicit in the bias built into institutions; and, third, because its use of the notion of 'transformative capacity' relates well to key aspects of the learning organization. Later we draw on Clegg (1989) for a more thoroughly developed analysis of the environmental context through which agency and structure are dynamically related. Within the institutional setting are symmetries in the distribution of resources, in actors' access to existing resources and in their scope to create and use new ones. The outcome is a pattern of relative advantage favouring one or more dominant groups. In Figure 19.3 this notion is summed up in the term *institutional bias*.

At the level of individual strategy actors intervene in the course of events, producing certain outcomes through the deployment of their various capabilities denoted by the term *transformative capacity*. Giddens argues that power is expressed in interactions where that capacity is harnessed to actors' attempts to get others to comply with their wants. *Power*, in this relational sense, 'concerns the capability of actors to secure outcomes where the realization of those outcomes depends on the agency of others'. Its use in interaction 'can be understood in terms of the facilities that participants bring to and mobilise as elements in the production of that interaction' (Giddens, 1979: 93).

The structural and action-based levels, of institutional bias and transformative capacity respectively, are mediated through control over *resources* already existing in the institutional setting and created afresh through the application of transformative capacity.

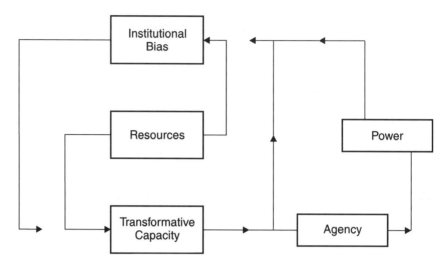

Figure 19.3 **Transformative capacity and agency**

CONTROL AND POLITICAL ACTIVITY

Central to Giddens' framework are issues of control and political activity on which the learning organization literature seems confused. Pedler *et al.* (1991) focus explicitly on one aspect of control, concerned with ensuring that the learning process develops according to their prescription. They seem not to acknowledge the tension between control and learning, that 'to focus on learning without taking into account legitimate need for control is to embark on a romantic and usually fruitless exercise' (Argyris and Schon, 1983: 4).

Consistent with their egalitarian stance, Pedler *et al.* stress the importance of control of the learning process but do not prescribe who should exercise control; implicit, however, is that 'managers' will play key roles. Garratt (1987) is unashamedly elitist; of the three necessary roles – operational planning and action, external monitoring and integrating and direction-giving – the latter is the directors' 'brain function', that 'monitors what is happening in day-to-day operations, checks what is happening in the wider environment, and then takes decisions on how best to deploy the limited resources it controls to achieve its objectives in the given conditions' (Garratt, 1987: 33). He rates as effective those directors who 'set out to design their world in the way they want it. They act on George Bernard Shaw's maxim: "Get what you like or you get to like what you get"' (ibid., p. 54).

To Garratt's 'brain-function' category Hawkins (1991) adds the 'Business

Soul': connecting level II and level III learning it incorporates 'the men and women of wisdom an organization needs on its board, among its trustees and facilitating its learning environment' (p. 183).

Giddens' (1979) approach to control is pluralist. Actors are involved in a 'dialectic of control', attempting to maintain some semblance of control over their own work, taking advantage of imbalances in personal access to existing resources and scope to create new ones. Differences of 'wants' as between individuals and of 'interests' between groups are expressed in attempts to exert control over patterns of work through relationships of mutual dependency.

How does Giddens' view square with relationships envisaged within a learning organization? Pedler *et al.* acknowledge plurality but only as regards learning; essential differences are an important element in the framework of a learning organization's internal market, any conflicts which arise are to be settled via constant dialogue. Collaboration based on trust rather than competition in search of advantage is the essence, enabling conflict to be used constructively. So, whilst control is an essential element it is not an overtly political process in the terms used by Giddens. Despite the rhetoric the Learning Organization seems to be placed within a unitarist framework of relationships, a utopia to be ushered in through the pursuit of shared goals in a climate of collaborative high trust and a rational approach to the resolution of differences.

Such an approach based on principles of fairness, mutual respect and trust might well yield unobtrusive control devices, mitigating the level of political activity. But in circumstances of external turbulence and internal transformation, where greater uncertainty and dissensus might be expected, such devices are not likely 'to be wholly effective in producing a coherent and unified set of goals and definitions of technology'. Instead action will 'result from bargaining and compromise [where] those individuals or groups with access to the greatest power will receive greatest rewards from political interplay' (Pfeffer, 1981: 28). This position is supported by Kanter's (1989) finding that, in new forms of organization designed to deal with external turbulence, political action increases considerably and political skills are at a premium. Such an outcome fits Clegg's (1989) view that political activity is premised on organizations as loci of decisions and action. Decision making and political activity are correlated because of the effect decisions generally have on resource allocation and, consequently, on power relationships.

Pfeffer (1981) suggests ways of moderating the extent of political activity. Slack resources can be created to reduce competition for them; a set of decision makers can be established, homogeneous in respect of attitudes and skill level; and the importance of decisions can be reduced. How far these steps are possible or desirable in a learning organization is questionable. If slack resources existed organizational leaders might perceive a turbulent external environment as less threatening and conceive of more conventional, less risky ways of adapting to it than implied in a learning organization. Second, homogeneity in decision makers would potentially threaten the very interpersonal differences judged so essential to learning and creativity. Finally, it might be possible to reduce the importance of decisions – for example by avoiding them, re-labelling them, breaking them down into less crucial elements – but scope for such tactics would probably be limited in a learning organization where decision making to create new meanings is, presumably, central.

Within the political model managers construct and operate disciplinary practices to ensure that employees perform as expected and to sanction certain forms of creativity (Clegg, 1989). Such creativity-enabling processes are at the heart of a learning organization, as managers seek to construct consent without recourse to cruder forms of control used widely within bureaucracies. But in constructing permissive forms of control they face a tension in the employment relationship, seeking to minimize unit labour costs in the owners' interests as against the employees' interest in maximizing financial rewards. This conflict complicates managerial efforts to ensure employees commit and contribute to the organization while constraining their behaviour in the light of economic realities (Keenoy, 1992).

Employees can draw on two sources of resistance: an ability to regulate the productive use of their capacities and to use their discursive capacity to prevent others' attributing and fixing unacceptable meanings to organizational events (Clegg, 1989). 'Discursive penetration' is a vital element of this process, consisting of knowledge of the structural framework which all actors possess to a degree because 'they draw upon that framework in producing their action at the same time as they reconstitute it through that action' (Giddens, 1979: 144). Within a learning organization employees' discursive penetration would presumably be enhanced through 'informating' – providing an understanding of structures and systems of which the organization is composed – and opportunities to develop 'intellective skills' of abstraction, explicit inference and procedural reasoning (Pedler et al., 1991).

From this reading of a learning organization we can infer that it is a 'form of high discretionary strategic agency . . . for which power will be less prohibitive and more productive', the pattern typically of 'the classical conception of the professional discipline as a vocation' (Clegg, 1989: 199). Mutual investment in the process of learning on the part of management and other employees should enable the former to move the frontier of control as noted by Buchanan (1992) in his study of a computer manufacturer, where 'boundaries of what were once considered acceptable work control are being expanded by new environmental pressures' (p. 138).

Despite this, we should note how important it was for those business-men consulted by Pedler *et al.* (1988), and for those with whom Garratt (1987) regularly works, that any changes proposed within the context of a learning organization should create increased productivity. This implies that, wherever the frontier of control is drawn, time will be a critical term in constructing forms of control. Even given accounting systems which are user oriented, learning organizations will probably not escape the pressures to introduce further time-related techniques in oper-ations, in managing people generally and in strategic evaluation. The likely outcome is more automation or techniques such as 'Just in Time', enabling increased control of operations; the employment of time-related indices to regulate the efficient use of white collar staff; further inroads of 'chronarchy' into managerial autonomy through devices such as 'time management' (Scarborough and Corbett, 1992); and, at the strategic level, techniques such as 'Shareholder Value Analysis' (Coopers and Lybrand / MORI, 1991) or the monthly monitoring of 'key control ratios' which Garratt (1987) recommends to his client directors.

These pressures might moderate how far the frontier of control will be displaced within learning organizations in practice, certainly those in the private sector who, Pedler *et al.* claim, have shown considerable interest in the concept. This is consistent with Keenoy's (1990) view that Human Resource Management (placed by Pedler *et al.* at the centre of their model) is neutral as regards the benefits to employees of any particular strategy followed. What makes HRM strategic 'is not how personnel management policies translate into practice but whether or not those policies represent a good *fit* with the prevailing product and labour market constraints' (Keenoy, 1990: 6; original emphasis). The example Keenoy quotes is the withdrawal of recognition from trade unions, an action which supported the overall business strategy. So, the notional moving outwards of bound-aries of control implied in a learning organization can be seen as a dependent variable, one of a variety of strategies available to organiz-ations in response to environmental turbulence. Hence the Learning Organization, like the notion of Organizational Culture (Meyerson, 1991), might well be destined to be transformed from a root metaphor, helping to explain the nature of organizational activities and performance, to a mechanism through which managerial control is improved under drama-tically changed external circumstances. If this were so, employees could be expected to resist managerial pressures to conform, using their trans-formative capacity in defensive ways inimical to the aims of a learning organization.

POWER AND AGENCY IN A LEARNING ORGANIZATION

In this section the institutional setting derived from the work of Giddens

and Clegg is used to examine how the members of a learning organization, especially its senior managers, might use their power in order to
maintain or enhance their control of the work context. Members will use
their discursive capacities and discursive penetration of the organization's structures and systems in attempts to build up agency, alone and
in collaboration with others. While Pedler *et al.* do not discriminate
between the degree of discursive penetration which different actors or
groups enjoy or require, or the level of skills they bring to social relationships, Hawkins (1991) differentiates between the penetration sufficient to
handle operations at level I of learning, to enhance organizational
effectiveness at level II, and to relate the organization to evolutionary
needs at level III. The position assumed by Hawkins is a specific example
of the general proposition that discursive penetration is limited in terms
of 'the situated character of the action [and] the degree to which tacit
knowledge can be articulated in discourse' (Giddens, 1979: 144).

Wherever they are situated participants will attempt to articulate their
knowledge, developing explanations for the activities in which they are
involved and persuading others to accept their rationalizations. Given
that learning organizations are, by design, less structured than more
traditional forms, and that structures themselves provide socially accepted
rationalizations for specific types of activity, we should probably expect
to find a high volume of informal communications as people seek to
resolve the uncertainty created by ambiguous situations and the relative
dearth of structural cues to behaviour (Pfeffer, 1981). As Kanter (1989)
noted, managers engaged in informal networks to achieve influence within
'modern' organizations with less structure and more flexible systems
than usual. Within such networks those who have a high level of Giddens'
(1979) discursive capacity are more likely to build up a reputation for
persuasiveness, for creating new knowledge successfully through their
skills in presentation, argumentation and debate (Pfeffer, 1981).

Other personal characteristics which are important in influencing
collective meanings include actors' self-efficacy and associated beliefs in
the validity of positions they are proposing; through such self-confidence
considerable commitment is built up so that conscious self-dealing is
rarely necessary. Knowledge of the distribution of interests and power is
also an advantage, and of decision processes, as a basis for successful
political activity – providing cues to deciding where to invest resources
and with whom to collaborate in agency building (Pfeffer, 1981). Such
'cynical knowledge' – though likely to be viewed with suspicion in a
high-trust learning organization – is part of Giddens' discursive penetration.

While the personal characteristics referred to are likely to differentiate
one actor from another in their potential to build up a reputation as
'influential' – even offsetting to some extent the effect of institutional bias
– probably more crucial is the access to penetrative knowledge gained via

the position occupied in the organization's structure. But even though learning organizations are likely to be less hierarchical than conventional forms, with fewer managerial levels and positions, the incumbents of such positions will typically occupy quite crucial roles at internal and external boundaries, giving them access to deeper penetrative knowledge than is open to most non-managerial colleagues. This will be in addition to any formal authority they are granted, enabling them to command other people and to allocate conventional, collective resources.

Clegg (1989) would argue that, potentially, such managers are a 'key agency', with scope to further their interests through control of membership and meaning within alliances and coalitions, because they operate at organizational 'nodal points' where two circuits of power intersect:

- circuits of 'dispositional power' out of which organizational forms are created based on membership and shared meanings, and
- circuits of 'facilitative power' through which socially derived forces flow in the external environment, engendering innovation in techniques of production and discipline.

Within the learning organization Pedler *et al.* (1991) argue that all members who operate at the external boundary should act as 'environmental scanners', bringing their interpretations of events in the outside world back into the organization as potentially useful knowledge. But this formulation obscures the degree of penetration which their different roles allow. Boundary roles give varied scope for the accumulation of discursive penetration and for accruing personal influence. It is one thing, for example, to bring back information about the pattern of a competitor's prices in a local market, but insights into that organization's overall market strategy, or the Government's position on competition policy as it affects that market, would constitute much more significant knowledge. This conclusion is most important when focusing on the power of managers at the apex of an organization. At key nodal points in the interlocking circuits of power they can maintain formal and informal social structures which provide essential continuity in the internal organization of people's capacities whilst shaping the collective transformation which takes place under the perceived pressure of competitive trends in the external environment.

The set of institutions which constitute the pathways of the facilitative circuit of power in the wider society and, hence, the external environment of any one organization, has its own structure of rules, resources and systems regulating relationships between the separate institutions. As at the level of the single institution, there are symmetries which favour certain organizations over others in, for example, their dealings with Government or the financial system. In effect, at societal level, networks of agencies control nodal points within an economy's circuits of power so as to establish relatively stable and privileged sets of relationships which enable them to safeguard their access to power and, hence, to build and maintain formal organizational structures. As Scarborough and Corbett (1992) recognize, 'the considerable power which management exercise over technology, for instance, is linked to their relations with external constituencies of owners, technology suppliers and providers of capital' (p. 26).

Senior managers are almost certainly at the most salient nodes when considering strategic decisions involved in raising finance, securing new markets, reaching agreements with major suppliers, and influencing Government. This seems to be the reality of Hawkins' (1991) levels II and III of a learning organization, concerned with strategy and evolution. Individuals operating at those levels can use increments of corporate knowledge created through the learning process in their dealings with other agencies in the external environment. It is a conclusion which parallels Kanter's (1989) finding that chief executives of modern forms of organization tend to retain their identity, status and control, occupying positions which still yield considerable power, despite the difficulties they face in creating agency through networks of stakeholders rather than simply controlling subordinates.

Here are reflected Giddens' and Clegg's institutional bias in the distribution of resources and access to them. And since knowledge is such an important resource in a learning organization we might expect much political activity to be associated with how it is acquired and stored and how access to the collective data bank is controlled. Despite Pedler's protestations that information will be widely available in a learning organization, limitations are inevitable. Organizations are, after all, social arrangements in which specialist roles are coordinated to achieve the creation and use of knowledge, overcoming in this way constraints of individuals' bounded rationality and limited cognitive capacities (Simon, 1976). Such specialization is modelled on the development of a corporate information system built up from individual contributions but into which 'the rules expressing hierarchical access to information have come to be incorporated in the provision of levels of access and "security", complete with elaborate passwords and gates' (Scarborough and Corbett, 1992: 14). The 'rationality' embedded in the protocols gives potential power to those experts who devise and incorporate the rules into the system and to their client senior managers who make decisions as to access. They will probably be the only ones able to penetrate in a holistic way the knowledge which can be used to provide meaning for the organization's members in a strategic and evolutionary sense.

Directors' access to the increasing stock of collective knowledge intended to be generated in a learning organization and their control of nodal points of relationships within the broader circuits of facilitative power will enable them to consolidate the membership of existing agencies, to recruit new members to them, and to set up new agencies. In Clegg's (1989) terms their nodal positions, and the internally derived knowledge and control of discourse to which these give access, should enable them to 'translate phenomena into resources, and resources into organization networks of control, of alliance, of coalition, of antagonism, of interest and of structure' (Clegg, 1989: 204).

Kanter (1984) provides an example of this process, describing how the 'integrated' flexible organizational forms which she surveyed facilitated innovation in the body of the organization which could then form part of corporate learning. 'Experiments by middle-level innovators make possible the formulation of a new strategy to meet a sudden external challenge of which even the middle-level innovators might have been unaware. Then the new strategy, in effect, elevates the innovator's experiments to the level of policy' (Kanter, 1984: 290). If a learning organization operates as expected this, presumably, is how powerful people would translate internal phenomena into resources to use in exerting stronger agency in the internal and external environment. By rewarding so tangibly the internal innovators, by bringing their 'brain-children' centre stage, the latter would probably be incorporated into the agency of the top strategists, turning latent opposition into support.

The relatively sparse structure of a learning organization will advantage some and disadvantage others. Those who might lose managerial positions in any structural change would probably attempt to create alternative sources of advantage and power, an assumption supported by Kanter's (1989) insights into managerial behaviour in modern forms of organization. Giddens (1979) argues that 'in modern bureaucracies there are more openings for those in formally subordinate positions to acquire or regain control over organizational tasks than Weber recognized. The more tightly-knit and inflexible the formal relations of authority within an organization, in fact, the more the possible openings for circumventing them' (Giddens, 1979: 147). If this is the case it is not surprising that some members of a learning organization might feel vulnerable within its supposedly more open and facilitative framework. As Kanter (1989) observes, while hierarchy might be a thing of the past in the modern organizations she studied, senior managers wielded power in ways which their subordinates perceived as arbitrary.

The lack of protective structure might also go some way to explaining why those individuals and groups who fear losing their sole rights over a certain body of knowledge – and hence their influence over those dependent on that expertise – might attempt to retain it at the tacit level, or to restrict its use in discourse to oral transmission as in the case of maintenance engineers in Crozier's (1964) classic study of a tobacco plant. Such defensive behaviour is more likely in groups of managers and experts who have the generic knowledge required to make effective choices about technology and structure and who are under pressure from movements in the boundary of control, such as those involving users in decisions about technology (Scarborough and Corbett, 1992), a trend which would probably evolve further in a learning organization. For example, a group of managers with technical expertise were shown not to favour decentralized control of technology by operators (Mueller *et al.*, 1986 quoted by Scarborough and Corbett, 1992) and the introduction of 'quality circles' has to be seen against the background of managers who 'tend to appropriate knowledge to themselves and to disclaim the value of knowledge possessed by other groups' (Scarborough and Corbett, 1992: 132). In such situations of dominant technical rationality, technology is implemented which symbolizes that superiority, signifying meanings which reinforce the domination of systems specialists and associated managers.

In summary, the agency that individuals and groups might be able to build up in a learning organization depends on a variety of factors. Personal characteristics such as learning style and self-efficacy will determine to some extent the influence which can be exerted through relationships. Probably more important will be the level of discursive penetration which individuals, making use of their unique qualities, are able to develop through formal position, boundary spanning activities and expert technical knowledge. Those at the apex, despite the difficulties they might face in exerting control in a learning organization, could be expected to have their power enhanced through occupation of nodal points of power and the holistic nature of the discursive penetration which this makes possible. Their cooptation and patronage of lower-level innovators would also probably enable them to disarm those with expertise critical to the extension of their agency. Others sited less advantageously in a learning organization would probably be active in developing their own agency through similar but less potent tactics. People perceiving themselves to be especially disadvantaged might defend any erosion of their status and influence by restricting the scope for their tacit knowledge to be translated into objective collective knowledge which, potentially, others can use within the dialectic of control. Overall the effect would be, again, to diminish the potential for individual and collective learning as prescribed by proponents of learning organizations.

IDEOLOGY AND THE LEARNING ORGANIZATION

Much new knowledge generated by members of an organization attempting to deal with perceived turbulence in the external environment will probably have a strong normative element, concerned with values and beliefs deemed relevant to solving problems posed by that turbulence

(Schein, 1985). In this section we consider how the use made of new knowledge might be constrained by an ideology constructed from the language in which the concepts of a learning organization are couched.

For Geertz (1964), systems of cultural symbols are the stuff of ideology, providing guides for behaviour, thought or feeling – poems and maps for navigating through terrain which is strange, emotionally and topographically. The 'ornate, vivid' style of ideological language, and the psychological pressure of the rituals and settings within which it is employed, helps the construction of situations which encourage commitment and motivate action. In contrast, science seeks intellectual clarity by avoiding semantic devices which construct moral feeling. Like ideology, its focus is a problematic situation, providing information which is lacking. But where science 'is the diagnostic, the critical, dimension of culture, ideology is the justificatory, the apologetic one – it refers to that part of culture which is actively concerned with the establishment and defense of patterns of belief and value' (Geertz, 1964: 71–72).

Geertz construes ideology as a means of reducing social strain and individual tension in times of turbulence when the level of cultural, social and personal dislocation is such that patterns of shared understanding start to break down and newer ideologies can become crucial as sources of revised individual and collective meaning. The concept of a learning organization fits well into this strain theory of ideology. Managements are offered a new formula for dealing with organizational strain produced by turbulence in the external environment, enabling employees to be given some means of reducing the personal tension brought about by that same turbulence. Corporate reassurance is provided by the belief that organizational flexibility and responsiveness will be enhanced by collective learning. Its source in the learning of individual members will enable them to feel more secure about their own identity, especially as it is fixed by their employment, work status and career prospects.

A learning organization can fulfil the four functions of ideology identified by Geertz (1964). There could be a 'cathartic displacement of emotions' onto 'symbolic enemies', in this case those over whom the proposed arrangements should yield competitive advantage. Morale could be sustained by legitimizing the perceived strains in terms of higher values of personal development and spirituality. Solidarity could be engendered in the face of disruptive turbulence, bolstered by the symbols associated with individual and collective learning practices. And, finally, by articulating the relationship between turbulence and learning, those who publicize the learning organization 'state the problems for the larger society, take sides on the issues involved and present themselves in the ideological market place' (Geertz, 1964: 55).

None of the designers of the Learning Organization seem to claim that it is based on scientific principles. In fact, Pedler et al. (1989) note that the

Learning Company can be perceived as scientific hypothesis without empirical evidence. On the other hand, the concept is expressed in language which Geertz might describe as 'ornate, vivid, deliberately suggestive'. Garratt (1987) claims that learning organizations can 'concentrate on their firm's hearts . . . people can get enthused, and the dread Kafkaesque stereotype of organizations dispelled' (p. 134). In Pedler *et al.* (1989) 'the Learning Company is the new frontier and the scouts are busy bringing back reports. In short, we are now standing at the "vision" end of the vision-to-reality sequence in bringing the idea into being' (p. 1). Hawkins' (1991) focus 'is the spiritual learning in worldly organizations, rather than the Ashram' (p. 177) which will require that we 'replace "helicopter thinking" with "satellite thinking"' (p. 179).

Within his strain theory of ideology Geertz (1964) accepts that it is possible to argue that 'interest based' process through which a resolution of the conflicting interests of key actors determines the course of events during a time of rapid change, when political tactics and strategy become paramount. In a turbulent period, competing individuals and groups attempt to enrol others to the values and beliefs which they offer as explanations of collective experience – i.e. to emergent elements of ideology (Giddens, 1979; Clegg, 1989). But the playing field is not level in this competition; instead there are institutional symmetries, created historically through 'economic-based structures and systems of discursive monopoly', which provide the management of organizations with tactical and strategic advantage (Deetz, 1992).

As argued in the previous section, there seems no reason why a learning organization as defined should differ in this respect. Existing symmetries of power are likely to be buttressed by the learning process, giving senior managers access to newly generated corporate knowledge and language, strengthening their hands in internal and external dealings. Through their control of strategic planning activities, senior managers should be able to influence strongly insiders' perceptions of the external environment and outsiders' reciprocal perceptions, moderating any strain and tension by marginalizing representation of interests other than their own, reducing unacceptable alternative courses of action to economic costs (e.g. the time-consuming aspects of worker participation in management), by further socialization of members, and by shifting extra responsibility to the individual (Deetz, 1992).

In this context the language of ideology mediates between individuals and the conditions of their existence. They are positioned as subjects and, as such, assume that they are the authors of the ideology which they speak, as if in control of the meanings which that ideology carries (Deetz, 1992). To this end the management of a learning organization could embark on a process of re-socialization within an overall 'ethos of self-responsibility' fulfilled through collaboration rather than competition.

The organization's members would probably be encouraged to see themselves as critical providers of organizational knowledge through their enhanced learning capability; as responsible for experimentation; as wise interpreters of collective knowledge; as honoured participants in decision making; as responsive to the needs of internal and external customers. In imagining themselves as these types of people, individuals would be accepting a revised personal identity, taking on more responsibility for providing solutions to corporate problems and for self-surveillance, enforcing norms which constrain the expression of doubts or disloyalties reflecting differing belief structures. In the process the increased level of organizational commitment induced in employees might place at risk some of their other commitments, e.g. to family and close friends (Randall, 1987). 'To increase organizational commitment involves creating a greater tension and, by implication, places a strain on the other life-worlds in which there is partial inclusion' (Hopfl, 1992).

This perspective takes account of the language used in proposals for a learning organization; but equally important is what is not said, especially about goals and preferences, their origins and the criteria used in decision making to further their achievement (Pfeffer, 1981). Directorial competence in these areas is not questioned by Garratt (1987), Hawkins (1991) or Pedler et al. (1991). As for managerial prerogatives, Hawkins' (1991) hierarchical view provides implicit support for the notion, while Garratt (1987) does not question directors' prerogatives, seeing learning organizations as a means of improving directors' performance through better control over organizations made much more productive via individual and collective learning. Pedler et al. (1988, 1989, 1991) do not address the issue directly, blurring distinctions between managers and other employees. 'Managerial acts are seen as conscious experiments rather than set solutions', as part of 'the learning approach to strategy' (1991: 18) and all members of the company have a chance to take part, to discuss and contribute to major policy decisions (p. 19). In any but the smallest organizations this would seem to be impracticable and implies only a process of consultation.

Pedler et al. provide an example of the constraints managerial prerogative places on employee discretion even within a learning organization. In reviewing the implications of an extensive learning initiative in the Rover Car Group its Chairman, Graham Day, is quoted as saying, 'We realize that by encouraging continuous learning and development among all our employees, they will start to question more and more the way we manage things. We will have to learn to respond appropriately to that, but we are not a democracy – the buck stops with management' (Pedler et al., 1991: 195).

Ideology is expressed not only in language but in artifacts, especially those which constitute an organization's technology. Those who are privileged in the design and implementation of technology are well placed to translate their interests into ideologies, embedded and invisible in the technological process. All those who use the technology are then influenced strongly by the ideology of its controlling logic, made subject to it. There is a circuit of meaning: ideology helps to shape the meanings and perceptions of technology; these influence the development of technological artifacts and language; and in turn, these reflect and reinforce ideology as a natural, taken-for-granted part of the control process (Scarborough and Corbett, 1992).

Whether the ethos of a learning organization takes root or not will depend crucially on its adoption by those who make key decisions at the design and implementation stages in the introduction or modification of technology. If committed to the learning ethos of Pedler *et al.* (1991) they are likely to involve users in the design stage, providing scope for operator discretion, allowing for experimentation and learning, 'informating' as well as automating. But there is a long history of the hegemony of rational, science-based principles, of people's subordination to the ideology of scientific rationality, to the conservative values and rationality of science and its enframement of the technology process (Scarborough and Corbett, 1992: 89).

In summary, ideology is central to questions of choice and especially whether choices are to be made privately by members of dominant coalitions or as the outcome of some more public challenges within an open democratic process. Potentially, the ethos and language of the Learning Organization provide ideological raw material which people in organizations can use to accommodate to the collective and personal strains of an external environment perceived as turbulent. The language and symbolism, explicitly or by omission, upholds managerial prerogatives in expressing strategic preferences and in pursuing goals. Within the framework of explicit and tacit legitimation which the metaphor of a learning organization provides, those managements who realize its ideological potential will be able to make use of the prescribed language and practices to maintain their hegemony. In the process, employees risk being subjected to further socialization, encouraged to adopt aspects of identity which, as Clegg (1989) anticipates, would ensure their continued obedience, not only in a prohibitive sense, but also creatively.

CONCLUSIONS

This chapter has enabled certain problematic aspects of the Learning Organization to be considered within a theoretical framework related to power, politics and ideology. A confusion in the literature was examined, concerning the extent of political activity within a 'dialectic of control' and where the 'control boundary' between management and other employees might be drawn. Given continuing pressures on organizations operating in turbulent conditions to become ever more productive it was argued that boundaries are unlikely to be moved anything like as far as implied in the more utopian prescriptions, with consequent effects on the scope for individual and collective learning.

This conclusion leads on to a further point about the likely effect of the characteristics of a learning organization on the distribution of power. It seems that the changes in structure and the increments in collective knowledge associated with this and other features will tend to favour those formally appointed as managers, especially at the apex of organizations. In making use of their enhanced discursive penetration at the nodal points where internal and external circuits of power intersect they are likely to build up and safeguard their power. Others who feel that their power is threatened will probably behave defensively, placing restrictions on the possibilities for collectively productive learning.

Finally, it is likely that senior managers within enterprises where the principles of a learning organization are put into practice will be able to bolster and safeguard their prerogatives by articulating aspects of the ideology implicit in the literature of the Learning Organization. This leads us to conclude that those who propagate the principles of a learning organization risk opening the latest phase of a long history of metaphors which have been used manipulatively (Giddens, 1979) by managers with a long pedigree of instrumental interest in social science as a means of solving industrial problems (Pfeffer, 1981). The force of the metaphors employed stems from the rational, conscious level of explanation and at a deeper level where versions of social science – 'the orthodox consensus' – provide commonsense explanations of lived experience which it serves to justify (Giddens, 1979).

Earlier metaphors proposed by social scientists – most recently 'Organizational Culture' – have served to 'transform compliance into cooperation, consent into commitment, discipline into self-discipline, the goals of the organization into the goals of the employee' (Hollway, 1991: 94). The metaphor of 'Learning Organization' could well suffer the same fate, translated into an instrument for control so that the ambiguities of organizational life, potentially fruitful for learning and creativity, are suppressed in favour of a dominant and stable set of beliefs and interests (Meyerson, 1991).

REFERENCES

Argyris, C. and Schon, D.A. (1978) *Organizational Learning: A Theory of Action Perspective*, Reading, MA: Addison-Wesley.

Argyris, C. and Schon, D.A. (1983) Editorial. *Journal of Management Studies*, 20(1), 3–5.

Buchanan, D.A. (1992) 'High Performance: New Boundaries of Acceptability in Worker Control', in G. Salaman, S. Cameron, H. Hamblin, P. Iles, C. Mabey and K. Thompson (eds) *Human Resource Strategies*, London: Sage.

Clegg, S.R. (1989) *Frameworks of Power*, London: Sage.

Committee on the Financial Aspects of Corporate Governance (1992) *Draft Report*, London.

Coopers and Lybrand/MORI (1991) *Shareholder Value Analysis Survey*, Spring, London: Coopers and Lybrand.

Crozier, M. (1964) *The Bureaucratic Phenomenon*, Chicago: University of Chicago Press.

Deetz, S. (1992) 'Disciplinary Power in Modern Corporations', in M. Alvesson and H. Willmott (eds) *Critical Management Studies*, London: Sage.

Fiol, C.M. and Lyles, M.A. (1985) 'Organizational Learning', *Academy of Management Review*, 10(4), 803–813.

Garratt, B. (1987) *The Learning Organization*, London: Fontana.

Geertz, C. (1964) 'Ideology as Cultural System', in D.E. Apter (ed.) *Ideology and Discontent*, New York: The Free Press.

Giddens, A. (1976) *New Rules of Sociological Method*, London: Hutchinson.

Giddens, A. (1979) *Central Problems in Social Theory*, London: Macmillan.

Hawkins, P. (1991) 'The Spiritual Dimension of the Learning Organisation', *Management Education and Development*, 22(3), 172–187.

Hedberg, B., Nystrom, P. and Starbuck, W. (1976) 'Camping on Seesaws: Prescriptions for a Self-Designing Organization', *Administrative Science Quarterly*, 21, 41–65.

Hollway, W. (1991) *Work Psychology and Organizational Behaviour*, London: Sage.

Hopfl, H. (1992) 'The Making of the Corporate Acolyte: Some Thoughts on Charismatic Leadership and the Reality of Organizational Commitment', *Journal of Management Studies*, 29(1), 23–33.

Kanter, R.M. (1984) *The Change Masters: Corporate Entrepreneurs at Work*, London: George Allen & Unwin.

Kanter, R.M. (1989) 'The Managerial Work', *Harvard Business Review*, Nov./Dec., 85–92.

Keenoy, T. (1990) 'HRM: A Case of the Wolf in Sheep's Clothing?' *Personnel Review*, 19(2), 3–9.

Keenoy, T. (1992) 'Constructing Control', in J.F. Hartley and G.M. Stephenson (eds) *Employment Relations*, Oxford: Blackwell.

Meyerson, D.E. (1991) 'Acknowledging and Uncovering Ambiguities in Cultures', in P.J. Frost, L.F. Moore, M.R. Louis, C.C. Lundberg and J. Martin (eds) *Reframing Organizational Culture*, Newbury Park, CA: Sage.

Mueller, W.S., Clegg, C.W., Wall, T.D., Kemp, N.J. and Davies, R.T. (1986) 'Pluralist beliefs about new technology within a manufacturing organisation', *New Technology, Work and Employment*, 1, 127–139.

Pedler, M., Boydell, T. and Burgoyne, J. (1988) *Learning Company Project Report*, Sheffield: Manpower Services Commission.

Pedler, M., Burgoyne, J. and Boydell, T. (1989) 'Towards the Learning Company', *Management Education and Development*, 20(1), 1–8.

Pedler, M., Burgoyne, J. and Boydell, T. (1991) *The Learning Company: A Strategy for Sustainable Development*, Maidenhead: McGraw-Hill.

Pfeffer, J. (1981) *Power in Organizations*, Cambridge, Mass: Ballinger.

Randall, D.M. (1987) 'Commitment and the Organization: The Organization Man Revisited', *Academy of Management Review*, 12(3), 460–471.

Revans, R.W. (1982) *The Origins and Growth of Action Learning*, Chartwell-Bratt.

Scarborough, H. and Corbett, J. Martin (1992) *Technology and Organization*, London: Routledge.

Schein, E.H. (1985) *Organizational Culture and Leadership*, San Francisco: Jossey-Bass.

Shrivastava, P. (1983) 'A Typology of Organizational Learning Systems', *Journal of Management Studies*, 20(1), 7–28.

Simon, H.A. (1976) *Administrative Behaviour*, 3rd edn, New York: Free Press.

Streeck, W. (1987) 'The Uncertainties of Management in the Management of Uncertainty: Employers, Labour Relations and Industrial Adjustment in the 1980s', *Work, Employment and Society*, 1(3), 281–308.

Zuboff, S. (1988) *In the Age of the Smart Machine*, London: Heinemann.

Chapter 20

Executive tourism
The dynamics of strategic leadership in the MNC

Ken Starkey

In the 1980s Ford Motor Company enacted one of the most spectacular turnarounds in corporate history. Ford's US transformation, however, was not replicated in Europe. This chapter analyses Ford's US turnaround and the problems Ford experienced in repeating the experience in Europe, arguing that the roots of these problems lay in leadership and learning.[1]

FORD MOTOR COMPANY – THE US EXPERIENCE

The key strategic question that came to the fore at Ford in the late 1970s was 'How good are we as a world class manufacturer?' The answer, after Japan, was 'Not good enough.' The beginning of the 1980s found the company bereft of attractive product and moving ever more deeply into loss. Don Petersen, who became Ford Chairman and CEO in 1985, describes the company's situation when he became company President and Chief Operating Officer in 1980 in a triumph of understatement: 'Ford was operating in difficult times back then.' Its market share was slipping steadily. Ford was rated lowest among the Big Three US automakers in the quality and styling of its cars. Japanese automakers had gained a substantial edge in the quality of their products and the efficiency of their factories. The growing sense that the company could not continue in the way it had always done, incrementally improving on the way it had done things in the past, led to a fundamental re-examination of the Ford mission and management style. Ford's response was a commitment to radical change.

Pascale (1990: 119–121) concludes his study of a range of American companies – 'Ford stands alone in appearing to have truly transformed itself.' From a loss of $3.3 billion between 1980 and 1982, Ford moved to profits in 1986 that surpassed General Motors for the first time since 1924. In 1987, Ford broke all previous industry records for profitability. In his own analysis of Ford's US turnaround, Don Petersen describes how top management initiated change. 'You have to create a sense of urgency that will dramatize what you're up against and convince everyone that important changes must be made in order to improve' (Petersen, 1991: 18). A top management team set about examining the key concepts they wanted the company to express with a view to putting these on paper in a new mission statement. A Ford task force examined what they considered 'outstanding' American companies and concluded that these companies had ten things in common:

1 Each firm circulated a statement of corporate goals and values, and executives spent a majority of their time outside their offices, trying to communicate those ideas to their employees.
2 All six emphasized the importance of people and respect for the individual.
3 They substituted trust for strict rules and controls.
4 Every firm made a big fuss about being customer-driven.
5 All six used teamwork, particularly multidepartmental teams, to develop cutting edge products and services.
6 They tried to eliminate levels of management and to drive down authority.
7 The companies emphasized free, open, face-to-face communications.
8 Team players were promoted over individualists.
9 All six offered sophisticated training for managers as well as hourly employees.
10 Managers made a habit of asking their people, 'What do you think?'

Ford top management then decided, after much internal dialogue, that Ford's core values could be encapsulated in 'three p's' – people, products and profits. They went on to develop a new statement of Ford's mission, its values and guiding principles of behaviour. The major organizational challenges that top management set itself to support its strategic agenda were employee involvement (EI) and participative management (PM). EI – 'the process by which employees are provided with the opportunities to contribute their minds, as well as their muscles, and hopefully their hearts, to the attaining of individual and Company goals' (Banas and Sauers, 1989) – had as its goal the development of a cooperative employee relations environment. PM had a dual agenda: first, to complement employee involvement by developing the skills that managers need to provide employees and fellow managers with opportunities to participate in the managerial processes (planning, goal setting, problem solving, and decision making); and second, the integration of managerial effort across rigid functional barriers. The latter is the main focus of this chapter.

According to Petersen (1991: 52), PM is 'simply a style of operating in which you give your peers and subordinates an opportunity to say what they think, and you include their ideas in the overall decision-making process'. Former Ford Vice-President of Product Development, Don Frey

(1991: 56), describes the managerial legacy of Fordism: 'Watching the company under Mr Ford during the 1970s, I alternated between sorrow and outrage over what was happening. The company grew only more Byzantine, with a chief executive fighting with his president and principal lieutenants who were, at best, inwardly focused; people who fostered functional isolation among the company's best employees, usually to divide and diffuse power – all antithetical to innovation.' In Ford the propensity of different functional groups to become introverted and self-seeking in their dealings with other units at the expense of the common good is captured in the image of 'organizational chimneys' – an organization structured for vertical relationships *within* functions that work against horizontal linkages *between* functions. Participative management has as one of its main goals the changing of managerial attitudes and the dismantling of what is now perceived as dysfunctional structures. Its aims are to simplify managerial control, devolve authority and break down the barriers between managerial groups which have their basis in hierarchy, functional specialization, organizational culture and managers' cognitions.

Participative management is of crucial strategic significance. The success of Ford's strategic shift towards innovation hinged on the integration of design, manufacture and sales and marketing. Japanese companies, Ford learnt, owe much of their success to the degree to which they are able to manage their inter-management relationships in a way that facilitates responsiveness to increasingly turbulent market conditions. Responsiveness, based on managerial flexibility, is something which a traditionally organized, tightly controlled, bureaucratic, hierarchical company finds extremely difficult (Piore, 1986: 158). President, and later Chairman, Harold 'Red' Poling described the importance of PM as a guiding principle of behaviour: 'there was a time when many found satisfaction in guarding their own turf . . . those days are over. Interpersonal skills and team effort are now a key part of the performance review process. All of us – including me – will be judged on success in this area.' PM and product development came together for Ford in a new strategic vision of the company as design leader. Ford's turnaround in the US was design-led with the new Taurus/Sable range. The company hit rock-bottom in 1980 the year it initiated the Taurus and Sable program in a 'bet the company strategy' (Halberstam, 1987: 647). With participation and involvement came the opportunity to experiment and design innovative products. Creativity was no longer stifled by bureaucracy. Involvement and participation were used to engender a new sense of responsibility for and joint ownership of product development programs and effective collaboration across organizational divides – employee with employee, employee with manager, manager with manager, function with function. This proved much more difficult to do in Europe.

STRATEGIC LEADERSHIP – FORD US

Explanations of Ford's transformation in the United States during the 1980s have emphasized the role of top management and the top team dynamic. Pascale (1990) emphasizes the relationship of Don Petersen, President from 1980 to 1985 and Chairman between 1985 and 1990, and Harold 'Red' Poling, Vice-President, Ford North American Automotive Operations, then President from 1984 until he became Petersen's successor as Chairman in 1989. Petersen provided the 'visionary' leadership (Westley and Mintzberg, 1989), Poling kept the company's 'feet on the floor'. One individual alone was not enough. Petersen was responsible for the motivation and excitement of individuals and changing their goals, needs and aspirations through the redefinition of company mission and values. Poling provided the instrumental leadership responsible for making sure that behaviour throughout the organization was consistent with the new goals necessary to transform the company, concentrating on the quantifiable, on getting the quality and the numbers right, ruthlessly benchmarking against key competitors. Petersen dealt with the unquanti-fiable such as issues of PM and the harnessing of hearts and minds to innovative product development. The complementarity of the top management team is unambiguously regarded as crucial: 'Ford was lucky to have this dynamic of individuals who somehow complemented each other. . . . While Red looked after the North American cost structure, Pete became an EI/PM diplomat.' Petersen's own view (1991: 55–56) is that he and Poling became a team whose ability exceeded the sum of the parts.

Having emphasized the complementarity of their roles one does have to stress the importance of Petersen's role in transforming Ford's management process. Petersen was responsible for disrupting conventional thinking in Ford, for getting Ford managers to think the 'unthinkable' and for shifting the focus from the *functional* to the *strategic*. To facilitate this attack upon Ford's conventional, traditional and now outmoded management approach, Petersen's most significant contribution was to set in place the participative approach to top decision-making, thus broadening, deepening and enriching the company's strategic decision-making. He himself became the living proof of PM. 'He lives and breathes participative management, taking to heart suggestions from vice presidents and assembly line workers. Most remarkably, he subordinates his ego to the needs of the company' (Pascale, 1990: 159).

Petersen also stressed the importance of a balanced management team that was comfortable with its own internal differences. Difference was to be encouraged as a virtue rather than excoriated as a threat. Insight into his own personality and that of his peers helped Petersen refine the management process of Ford's top management group. An important part of the development of a new management style was the introduction of the participative management approach to the workings of the top decision-making forums of the company, such as the crucial Policy and Strategy Committee. When Petersen joined this committee in 1975 as head of Diversified Products the approach was non-participative in the sense that committee members spoke only about their own businesses and did not intrude on the views expressed by members from other areas. For example, the rule was that if the manager in charge of cars was discussing product problems, it was inappropriate for Petersen himself to contribute to the discussion, despite his experience in product development. The way the dynamics of the Policy and Strategy Committee were changed to encourage greater participation paralleled the approach used at the plant and operations levels. Poling and Petersen himself held back from expressing their opinions at the beginning of the discussion. Petersen also made a point of telling the committee members that they should feel encouraged to speak up regardless of the subject, something they found very difficult at first, and often polled the members individually for comments and suggestions, in effect serving as the facilitator (Petersen, 1991: 61). To further facilitate the free exchange of ideas committee meetings were sometimes conducted away from traditional committee meeting venues such as the board of directors' room. Breakfast meetings were particularly successful in this respect and top management meetings were conducted off-site with the participants dressed in sweaters and slacks – relaxing the 'dress code' – to generate franker discussion. The shedding of conventional modes of behaviour was symbolic of a shift in thinking about strategy and management style. Petersen feels that these measures led to 'some of the most candid conversations in Ford's history' (Petersen, 1991: 61–62).

AMERICAN INITIATIVES, EUROPEAN RESPONSES

Ford of Europe appeared very successful for much of the 1980s. In 1988 it recorded record profits but since 1989 it has under-performed in a market struggling with the effects of a deepening recession. In 1991 the company achieved record sales in Europe but went into loss. 1992 saw record losses. The company continues to face the twin strategic imperatives of cost reduction and innovation. Its product development record throughout the 1980s was patchy.

Ford of Europe's problems of the late 1980s were exacerbated by its top management's slow awakening to the magnitude of the change agenda it had to address. In the early 1980s there was little generally felt need for fundamental change. The belief persisted that the company only needed to do better what it had always done well. This was, with the benefit of hindsight, shortsighted. In the words of one senior Ford of Europe manufacturing manager: 'When you're making two billion dollars a year it's tough to say our system is inadequate. And suddenly when you're not making two billion dollars profit it's too late.'

In 1979, Ford of Europe initiated its 'After Japan' [AJ] campaign, an internal study of Ford's productivity levels which was the direct response to the company's new awareness of the Japanese competitive edge. The origins of AJ lay in a visit to Japan by Bill Hayden, Ford of Europe Vice-President of Manufacturing, from which he returned, in his own words, in 'a state of shock'. Japan was the crucible of change for Ford. In 1992 Hayden acknowledged how fundamentally Japan had changed the rules of competition.

> The most important change [of the 1980s] is that the company no longer believes today – as it did ten years ago – that its quality was sufficient to match the competition, that customers were loyal to Ford and that our efficiency was more than a match for the rest of the world. It's as basic and fundamental as that. The Japanese have caused us to completely rethink our policies and behaviour patterns and that's what we're desperately trying to do.

This acceptance of the need for radical change was a long time coming. AJ did not go far enough. In the opinion of Lindsey Halstead, Chairman of Ford of Europe from 1988 to 1992, AJ's great limitation was that it 'looked at the world through Ford's eyes'. It was driven by a primary focus on cost differences and a belief that the old Ford system, if intensified, was still capable of matching the Japanese. In this sense, it contributed little to understanding *why* the productivity and quality gap existed between Ford and Japan. The conclusion Ford of Europe's top management derived from AJ was the need for efficiency improvement and lowering the company's breakeven point. The challenge of AJ was to accelerate 'towards greater efficiency *within* our established system: to take the Ford system to its limits'. 'AJ was about cost reduction – it [was] how Ford has always responded to the unknown. . . . AJ was a typical Ford drive to streamline the organization.' In the words of Lindsey Halstead:

> Because it didn't diagnose that we had a fundamental cultural change problem . . . it didn't focus on cultural change . . . AJ didn't take us far enough . . . it was a hell of a good start. But I don't know that before we did MVGP [the introduction of the new missions, values and guiding principles statement in the US] we knew what a fundamental change [we really needed], how thorough throughout the organization it had to become.

AJ strengthened the managerial emphasis on control. It did nothing to challenge the dysfunctions of Ford's Finance-dominated culture.

The tradition in Ford has been for functional heads to come to planning meetings with their own plans to defend. It was an adversarial system. And in an organization like Ford where Finance had been top-dog for so long, figures weren't used to improve the quality of decision-making but as weapons to gain a sectional advantage irrespective of what the overall cost was.

The adversarial nature of managerial relations was captured in a joke of the early 1980s: 'the difference between the West and Japan is that they both have boats of eight but in Japan you have seven oarsmen and one cox whereas in the West you have one oarsman and seven coxes!' The joke also captures another crucial issue: the unfavourable ratio of direct to indirect workers in Ford compared to Japanese companies.

AJ was succeeded in Europe by the American change initiative based upon the new company Statement of Mission, Values and Guiding Principles and the new managerial emphasis on teamwork, employee involvement and participative management. In the words of an American human resource manager on secondment to Ford of Europe, 'The idea was to achieve a quick transfusion of the American experience into the European company.' Various barriers to participative management had to be con- fronted. There were turf battles between functional groups, structural barriers ('chimneys') between functions and an inevitable resistance to change. There was also an important leadership issue. Top management endorsement and leadership in getting the whole organization aligned and working towards the same goal was felt to be lacking.

Pascale (1990) emphasizes the creative tension that existed in the top management team at Ford in the US. What one sees as a result is the complicated working out of a dialectic between old and new, the outcome of which was a synthesis. If Petersen was the champion of the new guard, Poling represented the best of the old with his emphasis on efficiency and discipline. In Europe it was a very different story because there was no comparable balance of champions. Differences in the constitution and dynamics of the top management groups in Ford of Europe and in the US which had a significant effect upon the unfolding of the new management agenda. As a result there are no top-level champions of the new change agenda in Europe with the experience or enough power to make this the centre of Ford of Europe's management agenda.

What we find is a marked difference in top management tenure of position in Ford of Europe compared with the US. European postings are used as career staging-posts by fast-track American executives. In Ford of Europe Europeans refer to American managers as 'executive tourists' – 'This is seen as a place that people need to come for experience to move them up the ladder in the US'. The same contrast of stability in the US and turnover in Europe existed in the positions of Vice-President, *with one crucial exception.* Bill Hayden was Vice-President of Manufacturing in Ford of Europe from 1974 until 1991 when he became the first Ford Chairman of Jaguar after its acquisition. With this steady turnover in Ford's European top management cadre, Hayden, despite the fact that he was never Chairman, exerted a disproportionate influence, not only by sheer force of personality and the iron control he exercised over Manufacturing but also because he had been a source of stability in an otherwise rapidly changing executive team.

Hayden represented the old discipline, the emphasis on efficiency and control as the basis of strategy. He was quite willing to innovate in search of cost-reduction, as with the 'After Japan' initiative, but was more wary of other kinds of innovation. His role in Europe was comparable to that of Poling in the US – incidentally, he declares himself Poling's 'biggest fan' – but in Europe there was no strong countervailing force for change, no Petersen.

> Europe didn't have a Petersen, it didn't have a big name champion of change throughout the 80s in anything like the same way [as the US] so it missed out on that healthy tension, it remained cost-driven. There were change initiatives, there wasn't the same advocacy of change.

Hayden was associated with the urge to centralized control.

> He [ran] Manufacturing in a way which is almost unbelievable that one man could run an organization that large in such a centralized way . . . you would find it difficult to believe how all the decisions have been funnelled into him. . . . Extremely centralized. And of course a man of tremendous ability, not many like him.

One senior manufacturing executive offered the following anecdote as encapsulating the deep-seated tensions of the period in Europe.

> There is conflict between quality and cost. We were having a discussion about our objective of being the lowest-cost vehicle producer in Europe and was that right or should we really be designing the best quality vehicles and sales would come from that rather than cost? Lou Lataif [then President] made a statement that our objective was to be the lowest-cost producer but also the best-quality producer. Bill Hayden stood up and said, 'Yes, I agree with you Lou, but Manufacturing is totally committed to being the lowest cost vehicle producer in Europe.' And Lou Lataif said, 'Thank you Bill, would anyone in Manufacturing who disagrees with Bill please stand up . . .' It was a nice blend of Bill saying, 'This is Manufacturing, and this is what we do' and Lou saying, 'Well, perhaps there should be some debate about that.' Everyone laughed because everyone knew damn well that nobody would stand up and contradict Bill. To me it was indicative of some of the conflicts

between what we say we're trying to do and what we actually do, especially at the highest level!

One can construe this dialogue in a variety of ways. There are none of the subtleties of 'problem-solving' and 'dilemma management' in the participative management mode. It represents the old politics – the Manufacturing function protecting its power base within the corporation. When Product Development wanted Manufacturing to participate in program management groups, it was Hayden who said 'No'!

This is not to suggest that Hayden was the 'villain of the piece'. It is far more complex than that. In psychodynamic terms Ford needed and, indeed, had created Hayden as a crucial point of stability but top US management, ultimately responsible for Ford of Europe, had not created the necessary countervailing force for new thinking in Europe. As a result commitment to the implications of Ford's new mission and the values and principles of behaviour necessary to support it, such as PM, was only skin-deep. Lindsey Halstead's description of the topography of the boardroom when he arrived in Europe in 1988 is indicative of the quality of the top management process.

> [How was it possible] to be able to answer any questions in that damn boardroom? . . . There was a horseshoe table and a hierarchy of seating. It's a very cold room. We used to assign seats literally, by tradition, because the damn thing is arranged this way. There would be a name card and the Chairman would sit there, and so it went down in pecking order. We stopped this. We created another conference room. It's got a round table. We don't have any assigned seats, deliberately, we sit wherever there's an empty chair. That's what I would call PM in action, it's living it . . . it makes a statement.

The top management group in Europe was insulated from the reality of European operations both by experience and by its *modus operandi*.

> There is a huge gap between the Ford of Europe Executive Committee and most of the rest of the company . . . there's a vacuum. They travel as a cloistered group around Europe and the world and they try to make contact with the rest of management but I don't think it's very successful. They'll never meet plant managers, for example. They're like high-level tourists. Even if we wanted to give them bad news – and we don't – we don't have the opportunity. They receive their information . . . in sound-bites, half-hour briefings. But the budget process, the hard figures are pored over for weeks on end. We're still driven by the numbers at the executive level no matter how hard we try.

The lack of a top management team with a long-term stable membership creates particular problems of institutionalizing change. If the tenure of change agents is transitory then the ownership of the change process becomes difficult if not impossible.

The upshot of the impermanence in the top echelons in Europe was that, in some senses, Hayden was operating in a top management vacuum. He himself says of his experience in the Ford of Europe boardroom:

> Ford of Europe is not a very stable organization. By that I mean if you look at the number of chairmen and presidents of the organization over the last twenty-odd years then there's been a change of personnel every two or three years. And it's not like an ordinary organization where the guy tends to come up [through the ranks]. They've come over and gone back. If you come up through the ranks then you're part of the culture and you're less of a shock to the system . . . [they] arrive and you've never met, never worked for or with them. . . . It slows down the decision-making process. Because when people arrive they have to buy into the current agenda. Unsettling is a strong word but if you're setting long-term objectives and changing three of the top five players in Europe every other year then it makes it very difficult.

He found the effort of keeping up with the changes in top management personnel an increasing chore.

> I had met most of them in Dearborn [Ford's US headquarters], but it wasn't a working relationship. We didn't *know* each other, hadn't worked together. When they arrived I'd usually go and introduce myself. But with time – it would register that a new guy had arrived – but I didn't bother going down the corridor to knock on his door. The business went on as before, new Chairman or not.

The emphasis on cost and efficiency that Hayden represents, the strength of this mind-set and the weakness in political terms of the new change perspective also have to be seen in terms of the relationship between Europe and the parent company. There were pressures from the US that slowed down the European change process.

> I think probably that the pressures even from Dearborn caused it to be that way. . . . Remember Europe was producing profit, it was sort of salvaging North America, the rest of the company was in significantly difficult shape. Part of that you can explain away by the economic conditions and the fact that the Japanese hadn't attacked here. There's a whole bunch of reasons. Therefore I don't think that there was that pressure for change even from Dearborn. The pressure was to keep producing profit and keep doing the job that you're doing. You're doing it well so keep at it, guys. Well what kind of pressure was that? That was a cost-profit pressure, primarily.

Europe was acting as Ford's 'cash cow'.

'We must throw a bridge between Europe and the United States of America' – this was Henry Ford himself as long ago as 1924. In conjunction with its US parent, Ford of Europe still has to negotiate an appropriate governance process at the highest level that will allow it to optimize its development. For the company as a whole 'breaking down the division . . . the barriers between countries' remains a strategic imperative. From a strategic leadership perspective the major factor contributing to the weakness of the impetus to diffuse the successful US initiatives (the new mission, values, guiding principles, participative management, employee involvement) to Europe was the dynamic of Ford of Europe's top management group, in itself a reflection of the group's composition and tenure which themselves reflected the way in which Ford's top US management used Ford of Europe as a convenient 'staging-post' in American top management development. In the US there were the top-level champions, 'competing' perspectives had the time to gel, and operating management was brought into the process as were top union representatives. In short, the process was managed. This just did not happen in Europe in the same coherent manner. It was not made to happen.

CONCLUSION

The Ford experience of the 1980s raises a variety of questions about the dynamics of strategic leadership in the MNC. The 'executive tourist' phenomenon requires further research to chart its prevalence and to assess its effects. More generally, further empirical evidence is needed on how the composition and dynamics of top management teams in MNCs affect strategy and performance. Order is more a matter of beliefs than of structures. Disorder can result when differing top management beliefs and actions prove incompatible or impede necessary change. Of course, one cannot generalize from one case study. A larger sample of cases is needed to uncover patterns of similarity and difference, for example in the balance of locals and 'tourists' at top management level, with a view to developing perhaps a classification of types of career development strategies in the MNC and an explicit statement of testable hypotheses. We need further understanding before the 'experimental' stage is reached and, in this author's opinion, comparative case studies will provide the basis for developing our understanding.

It is perhaps ironic in the Ford case that 'Red' Poling is of the opinion that you have to spend at least four years in a position to get anything out of it and that Don Petersen himself thinks he changed jobs too often – more than fifteen positions in his first twenty years at Ford! But tenure in company alone as a measure needs to be supplemented by the analysis of tenure and movement through positions in the company – for example, functional experience and overseas tours of duty – and with a combined 'measure' of top team experience and outlook. Defining leadership 'periods' and strategic 'eras' solely in terms of the period of office of the CEO is far from ideal (Thomas, 1988: 399). Individual tenure measures on their own are not very helpful in capturing the experience of individuals and its effects or the dynamic nature of the strategy process which is an outcome of team interactions. One also needs to incorporate some measure of individual personality characteristics into the emerging 'equation'. Don Petersen stresses the interaction of personality types in Ford's top team. He used the Myers-Briggs typology [see Hurst *et al.*, next chapter] to teach Ford managers about the differences between themselves and to illustrate how different types of individuals operate differently. Petersen himself brought to Ford's top team an intuitive and feeling approach to decision-making, something which is rarely found at that level.

Creating the right organizational context for transnational learning depends upon developing managers with broadly-based perspectives and relationships and fostering supportive organizational norms and values that are sensitive to but not submerged by local management dynamics. A firm's ability to develop general managers or program managers is crucial to its capacity for adapting to changing competitive pressures. Effective teams require a variety of legitimate difference if they are to avoid groupthink manifested in the tendency for a few individuals to dominate discussions and decision-making, insularity, the restricted generation and assessment of alternatives, and, ultimately, inferior decision-making. The strategic mode of decision-making is best managed by a heterogeneous group in which diversity of opinion, knowledge and background allows a thorough voicing of alternatives. In terms of the dynamics of such a process one is talking about what one might term 'constructive dissent' that challenges the status quo in a positive way, not the rather more prevalent 'defending turf'. Such heterogeneity is necessary in a turbulent environment. The crucial strategic leadership skill in the MNC will be the ability to synthesize difference and interdependence.

POSTSCRIPT

Henry Ford's project of nearly three-quarters of a century ago still remains – the building of a bridge between Ford in the US and Ford in Europe. Ford still has to develop an appropriate management process that will allow it to optimize its development in Europe. In April 1994 the company announced the biggest structural change in its history: its decision to abandon its regional approach to organization with the merging of European and North American operations to create Ford Automotive Operations. The goal is to become a truly global organization based upon five global product lines/vehicle programs, all reporting to a Vice-President of Product Development in the US. The aim is to integrate all automotive processes and eliminate duplication of effort across the company, thus substantially reducing costs by a predicted $2–3 billion a year.

On 1 January 1995, Ford of Europe ceased to exist as a profit centre and as an identity. (Part of the rationale behind the current changes is to 'wipe out the separate profit centre mentality'.) The reorganization is an implicit admission that managing on the basis of senior US staff on temporary secondment to Europe cannot cope with the complexities of this form of regional organization. Indeed, the reorganization is also an admission that the regional approach to organization is itself too complex. Product development across regional divides, as pioneered in the Mondeo/Contour/Mystique development, is too expensive and takes too long. The company is still not competitive in production costs with GM in Europe or with the revitalized Chrysler in the US.

In 1967, with the establishment of Ford of Europe, the European national companies (Ford U.K. and Ford Germany) were asked to 'think Europe not Britain or Germany'. In 1995 the injunction is to 'think global'. The new senior management for the new Ford Automotive Operations (FAO) has been selected on the basis of its technical and leadership capability. Only one of this new management team is European. The joke doing the rounds during the last days of Ford of Europe was that FAO actually means 'For Americans Only'!

NOTE

1 Further details of the study upon which this chapter is based can be found in Starkey and McKinlay (1993). Quotes, unless otherwise attributed, are from interviews conducted in the company by the author.

REFERENCES

Banas, P. and Sauers, R. (1989) 'The relationship between Participative Management and Employee Involvement', Dearborn, Ford Motor Company.
Frey, D. (1991) 'Learning the ropes: my life as a product champion', *Harvard Business Review*, September–October, 46–56.
Halberstam, D. (1987) *The Reckoning*, London, Bloomsbury.
Pascale, R. (1990) *Managing on the Edge*, New York, Viking.
Petersen, D.E. (1991) *A Better Idea. Redefining the Way Americans Work*, Boston, Houghton-Mifflin.
Piore, M. (1986) 'Perspectives on labor market flexibility', *Industrial Relations*, 25, 2, 146–166.
Starkey, K. and McKinlay, A. (1993) *Strategy and the Human Resource. Ford and the Search for Competitive Advantage*, Oxford, Blackwell Business.
Thomas, A.B. (1988) 'Does leadership make a difference to organizational performance?', *Administrative Science Quarterly*, 33, 388–400.
Westley, F. and Mintzberg, H. (1989) 'Visionary leadership and strategic management', *Strategic Management Journal*, 10, Special Issue, 17–32.

Chapter 21

Top management teams and organizational renewal

*David K. Hurst, James C. Rush and
Roderick E. White*

Increasingly the makeup of the top management group is believed to
affect the development, identification and exploitation of strategic opportunities. This chapter explains a creative management model, which goes
beyond conventional strategic management, and identifies the
behaviours of top managers needed for the ongoing renewal of their
business. It is proposed that these behaviours cluster and can be aligned
with different and distinct cognitive styles or types. The implication is
that top management groups should be composed of a mix of types. This
chapter posits a mix of Jungian types: Intuitives, Feelers, Thinkers and
Sensors. This diversity can yield great strength if the differences can be
focused and unified. Propositions and suggestions for further empirical
research are developed.

The strategic management (SM) framework which has evolved over
the past 40 years and has come to dominate North American thinking
about the principal functions of senior managers has, more recently, been
the subject of a good deal of criticism, both from practitioners (Peters and
Waterman, 1983) and theoreticians (Weick, 1979; Pascale, 1984). It seems
that while the conventional SM process allows managers to maintain,
direct and improve existing activities, it is less able to promote and
accommodate the radical ideas and innovative behaviours needed to
renew established businesses. Indeed it may be counterproductive in this
regard.

With its emphasis on problem-solving, the SM framework implicitly
stresses the role of the senior, synoptic, singular executive: one individual, or group with an established understanding of how the business
functions. Within this group there exists a shared 'cause map' (Weick,
1979) or 'dominant logic' (Prahalad and Bettis, 1986): a structure of
knowledge about their business, which for them defines 'rationality'.
Facts which can be plotted onto this map of the business are accepted;
data which cannot be assigned coordinates are not perceived, are ignored
if they are perceived or are treated as an aberration.

For the top management group, behaviours consistent with rational thought are implied. Individuals predisposed to plan, act and evaluate would fit; others, with different behavioural predispositions, would not. Intuition, insight and feelings are suppressed because they do not fit within the accepted SM process. Individuals openly exhibiting these types of behaviours cannot be accommodated within the conventional SM framework and are often excluded from the process, even though their contributions may be valuable. SM fits the people within its rational-analytic procedures, rather than expanding the process to fit the people, and their different abilities, predispositions and preferences.

For these reasons dissatisfaction with the SM framework has increased, resulting in a renewed focus on the top management group, the dominant coalition (Cyert and March, 1963), as it impacts firm strategy and organizational performance. As Hambrick (1987: 88) explains: 'This view contends that performance of an organization is ultimately a reflection of its top managers.' Implicitly this view holds that when it comes to understanding strategy and performance, the people are equally as important, and perhaps more important, than the process. But neither is this view entirely satisfactory, for it ignores the processes needed by any large organization to make decisions and take concerted action. Even more importantly, it lacks a sense of the role and function of the executive group.

The composition or form of the top management group needs to be related to its function. Barnard (1938: 215) contends: 'Executive work is not that of the organization, but the specialized work of maintaining the organization in operations.' When narrowly interpreted, this view can be construed as supporting the limited plan–act–evaluate functions for the executive implicit in the SM model. However, in any changing, competitive environment, long-term maintenance/existence of the business requires the ongoing (re)creation of the business and the logic by which it is managed. This renewal, too, is a critical executive function.

Large organizations require a process for taking concerted actions. The broad-based adoption of SM technology suggests it has fulfilled a need in this regard. We must be careful not to discard, out of hand, even a partially useful process. The SM model is powerful because it prescribes a process, as well as a function (or functions), for the top management group within that process. However, the process and prescribed functions are limited and do not take advantage of the full range of human cognitive abilities. The SM framework is not so much incorrect as incomplete. A broader perspective on the top management process, an enhanced model, taking more complete advantage of the human potential, could help bridge the gap between the appropriate function of the executive and the makeup of the top management group.

BEYOND STRATEGIC MANAGEMENT

Stepping back and viewing the question from a philosophical perspective, the SM framework's principal shortcoming is its base in a naive realism. It tacitly assumes that reality is given which exists 'out there' and is accessible through our senses. These sensations, these supposed objective perceptions or facts, can then be subjected to rational thought. Although the need for action is recognized, it is regarded largely as the servant of thought. Facts evaluated by a rational analytic thinking process are regarded as more important than insight, feelings and even empirical experience! The classic SM framework emphasizes the use of conscious, analytic thought processes to the exclusion of any other, even though non-rational or, to use Barnard's word, 'non-logical' processes and their importance have long been recognized (Barnard, 1938; McKenny and Keen, 1974; Mintzberg, 1976).

Hurst (1986) suggested that the emphasis of the SM framework on logic and rationality precludes it from being helpful in the innovative, creative processes which allow organizations to enact fundamental change, to renew themselves. Logic and rationality depend upon normative structures based in the past, and methodologies such as SM which appeal to norms of rationality – measurability, efficiency, consistency – perpetuate the past. In short, because SM is based on a logic developed from past experiences, it is an appropriate methodology for defending an established business, but is less able to prospect. It cannot deal well with novelty and ambiguity; it cannot bring into being these new activities which lie outside the structure of the managers' current understanding of their existing business but which may well be required as part of tomorrow's business.

A classic example of a flawed logic based upon past experiences is illustrated by the actions of Sewell Avery, CEO of Montgomery Ward following World War II. Avery convinced himself, based upon a study of economic history and his own experiences after World War I, that economic depressions followed wars. Based on this logic, Montgomery Ward, in the years following 1945, did not expand, and even deferred basic maintenance expenditures in order to preserve cash for the anticipated depression. Meanwhile Robert Wood at Sears correctly perceived the 'tremendous foundation of purchasing power that had been held back by the war'. Sears expanded aggressively to become the dominant US department store chain. Avery was forced to depart Wards in 1955 (Worthy, 1984: 219).

The Avery story provides a simple, yet dramatic, example of a flawed logic retrospectively derived from past experiences. The complex of logics and their relationships underlying a sophisticated SM approach in any large organization are many, subtle and difficult to surface. However, business redefinition requires a shift in the logic that is embedded in any well-developed SM process. Conventional SM incorporates no means to unlearn what has been learnt, although there have been developments in this direction (de Geus, 1988). To deal conceptually with this short-coming, Hurst (1986) has extended the SM framework to encompass what he calls the creative management model (CMM).

The creative management model

The creative management (CM) model is built on the philosophical assumption that the real world which surrounds the organization is a dynamic construct enacted by the members of the organization over time. This view is shared by Weick (1979: 228). As he explains: 'the environment is viewed as an output rather than an input. On the basis of enactments and interpretations people construct a belated picture of some environment that could have produced these actions.' Organizational realities, like personal realities, consist of complex interactions of the objective, tangible ('out there') and the subjective, cognitive ('in here') elements.

Implicit in the CM model is the assertion that organizations capable of creating tomorrow's businesses while maintaining today's will require a diverse group of senior managers, able to perceive the world differently, yet able to participate in the process that transcends these different views to enact a complex organizational reality. In the CM framework the emphasis is on top management teams which can envision, or recognize and frame, new opportunities, as well as solve or exploit them (Bower, 1982). By embracing recognition, opportunity-framing and problem-solving, the CM model subsumes strategic management and provides additional insights into the composition, leadership and processes of top management teams.

As illustrated in Figure 21.1, the CM process is conceived of as passing though four levels or modes of cognition. When (subjective) time is considered, the model incorporates seven recursive and not necessarily completely sequential stages whereby an original idea is transformed from an intuitive insight, a vision, into action, eventually to become a remembered 'reality'. Tracking the progress of an idea from its original conception to its final realization helps to explain the model. The classic SM model deals explicitly with only Stages 3 through 5, the 'plan–act–evaluate' stages. Because it does not consider the cognitive levels of intuition and feeling, the SM framework is unable to supply insight into the nature of recognition by organizations. How do organizations come to fundamentally new approaches to the way they go about their business? How do they learn? By ignoring the other stages in the process and overemphasizing the linear, in what is in fact recursive process, the SM paradigm misses key aspects of the creative learning process.

The CM model makes it clear that strategic thinking (Stage 3) does not take place without antecedents. It is based heavily upon earlier expectations and past experiences (Stages 4 through 7), modified by what happens in Stages 1 and 2. In addition, rationality depends on logic structures developed after action. People, and organizations, truly understand (Stage 5) only after they act (Stage 4), not before. Anything else is speculation. The model makes it clear that radical innovation (Stage 1) represents a break with the thought structures, the logic of the past. Initially, an innovation will not be based on rationality and logic because the supporting conceptual structures are not yet in place. Conversely, highly structured thought, as well as tradition, can interfere with, and inhibit, insight and innovation.

Thus, in the CM model a strategy is initially a *post hoc* rationalization of a successful activity. As Weick (1979: 188) explains:

> The only thing that can be selected and preserved is something that is already there. This simple reality keeps getting lost amidst the preoccupation of people in organizations with planning, forecasting, anticipating and predicting. . . . Organizations formulate strategy after they implement it, not before. . . . The more common (and misleading) way to look at this sequence in organizations is to say that first comes strategy and then comes implementation. That commonplace recipe ignores the fact that meaning is always imposed after elapsed actions are available for review.

As the activity becomes standardized, feedback from Stage 5 to Stage 3 occurs. Successful behaviours are interpreted into a causal model which drives the organization's routines and corrects deviations from course.

By making explicit the dimension of time the CM model allows the renewal function to be seen as a learning process. The time dimension in Figure 21.1 is not the objective time of physics but subjective time, views of the future and memories of the past as seen from the perpetual 'now' in which all human cognitive systems function (Jaques, 1982). With subjective time the creative process can be seen to be a learning process whereby successful innovations within an organization, new logics for doing business, are institutionalized and made routine. Not all organizations, and more particularly not all top management groups, are necessarily equally adept at, and receptive to, the development of new logics. These biases may be reflected in the organization's pattern of actions: its strategy.

There is more to the CM model than the capacity for prospective or retrospective thought. The model, as shown in Figure 21.1, contends that different modes of cognition are dominant at different levels in the process. These different modes are believed to have an underlying relationship with subjective time orientation; sensing may be associated more with the present, intuition more with the future (Mann et al., 1971) and one might

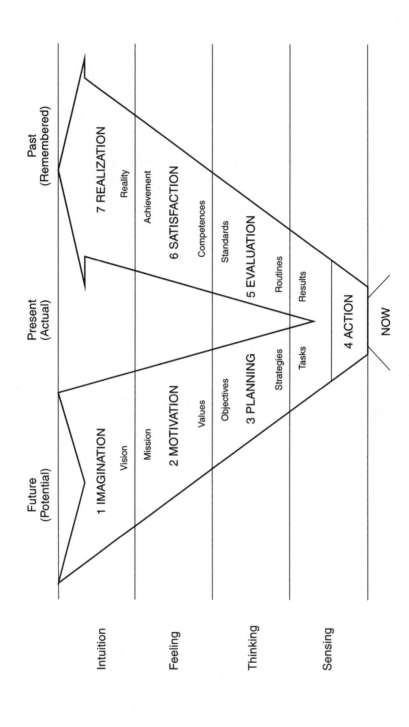

Figure 21.1 The creative management model

also suspect with the remembered past (in contrast to the experience of the present). But, more fundamentally, these different modes are believed to represent distinct cognitive preferences.

Cognitive modes

The different levels in the CM model are related to and emphasize different modes of cognition corresponding to the four fundamental psychological functions outlined by Jung (1960).

These processes are arranged by CM level and function in Table 21.1. Jung contends that while all individuals have the capacity for, and make use of, all four modes, each has a dominant function. The Myers–Briggs Type Indicator (MBTI) (Myers, 1962) has been used extensively as a measure of an individual's preference on each of these four functions.

The two information gathering modes are Sensation (S) and Intuition (N). Sensation mediates the perception of physical stimuli via the five senses. Through Sensation an individual becomes conscious that something exists physically. Intuition, on the other hand, mediates perception via what is thought to be an unconscious patterning process – the individual goes beyond the differentiations yielded by the Sensation process to see the whole of physical phenomena (Extrovert preference), or the world of ideas (Introvert preference). By allowing the detection of gaps between perceived parts this mode gives individuals the ability to see unrealized potential within the stream of events which surround them. Sensation and Intuition then are opposite but complementary mental processes used to gather information about the world.

The two information evaluation modes are Thinking (T) and Feeling (F). Each mode appeals to a different type of evaluative process. Thinking links ideas impersonally using logic and notions of cause and effect. Feeling, on the other hand, bases evaluation on personal and group values. As Jung makes clear, Thinking and Feeling are complementary functions for the evaluation of information, just as Sensing and Intuition are complementary processes used in the gathering of information. Each

Table 21.1 **Level in the CM and cognitive model**

	Function	
CM level	Information gathering	Information evaluation
I	INTUITION	
II		FEELING
III		THINKING
IV	SENSATION	

process within a pair is in tension with the other, but it can be a creative tension. Subjective time is the dimension which mediates the tension. It is these functions or layers which creative management must transcend.

The levels in the CM process are layered to reflect the renewal function of the executive as it relates to Jung's cognitive functions. Sensing deals with physical stimuli, action and reaction, in the here and now. Behaviours based simply on sensation can be thought of as reflexive; a stimulus evokes an instinctive or reflex response. Actions, other than reflex responses, have input from higher levels. For example, the thinking-planning level will, based upon accepted logics, delineate tasks to guide action. The results of actions taken also feed back into the thinking / evaluation activity. Sensing and thinking are adjacent layers in the model because, prescriptively, prospective thinking precedes, and retrospective analysis, or sensemaking, follows action.

At the intuitive level a vision or insight into a new way of doing business does not by itself result in action. Because it is outside the established logic of the business, it cannot be evaluated by the thinking process. Therefore its worth, whether positive or negative, cannot be logically derived and must be based upon personal or group values. A positive feeling must be created for the idea if it is to overcome the established logic, result in action and thus change the understanding of the business. Accordingly, the Feeling mode is positioned between the Intuition and Thinking layers in the model.

The layering in the CM model is based upon Jung's conception of the 'psychological functions' for several reasons. This conception may be related to basic human physiology. As Taggart and Robey (1981: 189) point out, 'Jung's theory of personality identifies two dimensions of human information processing that seem directly related to right and left brain activity.' Typically, Sensing and Thinking are left hemisphere related and Intuition and Feeling right hemisphere related. This duality and Jung's conception may have deep and perhaps related roots in human information processing, psychology and philosophy. Although there are other cognitive typologies (Hampden-Turner, 1981; Gardener, 1985) on which a model of creative management could be built, in our estimation none has as strong a conceptual and philosophical base for this application. However, in the last analysis this model will be judged by its utility; the meaningful implications it has for the practice of management.

Top managers' behaviours and cognitive preference

The conceptual linkages between the creative management process, cognitive mode and behaviours are sketched in Table 21.2. Although the empirical relationships require further validation the table is adapted from existing empirical evidence (Myers, 1962; Keirsey and Bates, 1978;

Macdaid *et al.*, 1986). There are other possible arrangements of type (Mitroff and Kilmann, 1975; Keirsey and Bates, 1978). However, they tend to be finer-grained, employing more mixed preferences than the four utilized in Table 21.2, which seem to depict the most natural flow through the stages of the creative management process.

The cognitive preferences, or types, outlined above cover the spectrum of ways in which information is gathered and evaluated by individuals. In Table 21.2 each type has been associated with a particular cluster of behaviours and positioned within the layers of the CM model. The implication is that to effectively handle a creative process a management group needs these different behaviours, and accordingly should be composed of

Table 21.2 Relationship between cognitive preferences and behaviours

Level in CM process	Cognitive preference	Concerned with	Handle these with	Tends to be	Examples of behaviours
I	Intuition	Possibilities and patterns, ideas	Metaphors and symbols	Ingenious and integrative	Sees what others do not. Espouses new ways of working at things. Proposes new ideas. Disregards practical details. Describes with metaphors and symbols. Creates organizational stories and myths.
II	Feeling	People and values	Force of personality	Enthusiastic and insightful	Inspires peers and subordinates. Responds to a challenge. Sponsors new ideas. Shares information, power and resources. Brings people together. Rewards with recognition and praise. Promulgates organizational stories and myths.
III	Thinking	Cause and effect things	Regulations and language	Reliable and orderly	Matches goals and resources to results (i.e. plans). Organizes people; coordinates. Balances novel with routine. Rewards when outcome exceeds plan.
IV	Sensation	Activities, events	Spontaneity and action	Adaptable and practical	Matches skills to tasks. Attention to practical details. Makes things work. Describes what has occurred in concrete terms. Results are their own reward.

Source: Adapted from Myers (1962) and Keirsey and Bates (1978)

individuals with the different cognitive preferences. Although individuals may be able to exhibit a variety of behaviours it is unlikely they will be equally able at each set of behaviours, or indifferent amongst them. They will have a preference.

Of course, cognitive preference is not the only factor to consider in forming a top management team. The model does not indicate the sources of the raw material for cognition, what information is gathered (and evaluated). However, it is reasonable to expect that, within limits, variety in output (actions) is related to variety of input (information). Much of the information available to a top management group will be directly related to the personal background and experience of team members. Simon (1988: 16) contends that 'expertness is the prerequisite to creativity'. He suggests that experts have 50,000 'chunks' of knowledge in their area of expertise which it takes at least 10 years of experience to acquire. But not every expert (with 50,000 chunks of knowledge in a given area) can necessarily use that knowledge creatively.

Indeed, as Koestler (1976) reports, often the insight occurs after the idea generators have dissociated themselves from the specifics of the puzzle they are attempting to solve. James Watson (1969), whose insight uncovered the double-helix structure of DNA, recounts his need to remove himself from data derived from months of chemical and X-ray experiments, while Francis Crick, his co-researcher, felt a need to remain immersed in the data. (Sensation-Thinking Preference versus Intuition-Thinking Preference?)

> The next few days saw Francis becoming increasingly agitated by my failure to stick close to the molecular models. . . . Almost every afternoon, knowing that I was on the tennis court, he would fretfully twist his head away from his work to see the polynucleotide backbone unattended . . . Francis' grumbles did not disturb me, however, because further refining of our latest backbone without a solution to the bases would not represent a real step forward.
>
> (Watson, 1969: 114)

None of this is to diminish the importance of expertise acquired through diligence and hard work, but rather to suggest that other factors are also at work. We would argue that individual cognitive preference merits consideration. The involvement of different cognitive preferences at different stages in the process and linking the stages together over time has not received the attention it deserves, either in theory or in practice.

Creative management: a need for integration

The argument has been made above that an effective CM process requires different behaviours, and therefore cognitive styles consistent with the roles implicit in the different layers of the CM model. With such differentiation in cognitive orientations comes a need for integration (Lawrence and Lorsch, 1969) – a way of allowing for, or facilitating, the exchanges necessary to bring about coherent action. The most efficient means of achieving the required integration depends on the type of interdependence (Thompson, 1967; Galbraith, 1973). As illustrated in Table 21.3, the CM process presents different types of interdependences between its different levels.

In explaining the interdependences it is helpful to make the simplifying assumption of a different individual at each level. Even though radically new ideas may be stimulated by certain antecedent conditions, they seem to be the independent creation of a single mind (with intuitive preferences and abilities) (Koestler, 1976). Generating new insights is not thought to be a group activity. Once discerned, the exchange between the intuitive, idea generator, and the feeler would appear to be reciprocal. If the feeler is to inspire and energize the organization, the feeler and idea generator must talk face to face. (They can, of course, be one and the same person.) The feeler must appreciate the idea sufficiently well to move it forward. This requires the feeler to listen to, and question, the idea generator. Also it is likely that articulating the idea causes the idea generator to better define his or her 'vision'.

Table 21.3 Integrating cognitive types and levels within the creative management process

Level	Cognitive type	Concern	Integrative mechanism	Type of interdependence
I	Intuitive	Patterns and ←— possibilities, ideas	Individual's perceptive abilities	Independent
		\←———————	Informal, face-to-face	Reciprocal
II	Feeler	People		
		\←———————	Task forces	Reciprocal/ sequential
III	Thinker	Cause and effect, plans		
		\←———————	Policies, procedures, rules, hierarchy	Sequential
IV	Sensor	Activities, events		

Because the idea cannot be evaluated logically the feeler must not only communicate it to the thinker, but also create a sense of energy and excitement about the idea. The thinker can then prepare for implementation. This relationship is also a reciprocal type of interdependence, but may tend towards the sequential as the link between idea generator and feeler may need to be richer impersonally than the link between feeler and thinker. Given the nature of the task, and their concern for people, feelers are likely to use task forces to accomplish the necessary integration.

The link between thinkers and sensors can be more sequential. Once the thinker has 'planned' for implementation, the sensor's role (doing) can be communicated by policy, procedures, rules and specification of tasks (hierarchy). However, to the extent that the new idea requires new tasks which are in conflict with established and accepted routines it will be important for the sensor also to have enthusiasm for the initiative.

Such sequencing of interdependent activities may represent a normative ideal; it is not necessarily descriptive of practice. For example, feelers may bypass thinkers, interacting directly with sensors, 'bootlegging' the initial implementation of the creative idea. At the thinking level plans may be developed only after early implementation, not before. Of course, this is more likely to happen when the thinkers in the top management group are wedded to their established plans based upon existing logics and are unwilling to experiment with novel approaches.

This sequence also recognizes that the dominant coalition may not be a group in the social psychological sense, where all members have frequent face-to-face interactions. Rather, it may be a series of interchanges over (objective) time between individuals, each with a predisposition for certain behaviours. These interchanges are the result of complex stimuli, and detailed consideration of them is beyond the scope of this chapter. However, evidence from Belbin's (1981) work with groups of managers in a business simulation suggest that effective groups had members (Belbin called them Chairman and Teamworker) concerned with transcending individual differences and facilitating the process. In our framework such individuals would be oriented towards integrating the levels of the CM process amongst people and organizational units, and over time.

Power and influence in the creative management process

The CM model has significant implications for the study and practice of processes through which power and influence are exercised within organizations. In the SM model the communication channels and relationships considered important in the exercise of power are those of the formal organization hierarchy. This is consonant with the framework's underlying philosophy – if reality exists objectively and is accessible to rational instruments, then where else can the many partial views be integrated except in the synoptic mind of the CEO/strategist? For only he or she has the panoramic view of reality by virtue of a superior position at the apex of the organization. Information flows up, directives down. In contrast the CM model stresses rich and fluid communication channels and relationships making up the 'neural' network, a cognitive framework within which the organization will scan, describe and develop its version of reality.

How then should an organization in search of renewal proceed? The interaction patterns required for renewal assume a broad distribution of influence within the management team, and that all cognitive types are represented. No single cognitive mode dominates the ongoing negotiation process. In support of this view Friedlander (1983: 200) states that sustained 'power imbalances diminish [the benefits of] heterogeneity and contact and thereby diminish system learning'.

This does not necessarily mean power should, or will, be uniformly and statically distributed. Rather, power must shift according to the 'authority of the situation' (Follett, 1941). At the outset, when the issue is highly ambiguous, the intuitive mode is required and those individuals with significant capacity in this area should assume more influence, regardless of their hierarchical level within the formal organization. As the renewal process moves to the feeling dimension the motivation of the team becomes critical. Individuals capable of evoking and expressing shared values should now have more influence. The intuitives, while still involved, would exhibit less influence. Subsequently as the task shifts to planning and action the process requires that thinkers and sensors become predominant. Thus, in an ideal process, each cognitive type assumes influence as determined by the needs of the evolving renewal process. The relationship between the individual in the (temporarily) dominant role and the rest of the team has been described by Greenleaf (1977) as *primus inter pares*, first amongst equals. Like strands in a tapestry, now in the front, now in the back, individuals of the team together weave a cognitive fabric, the pattern of which will express their version of a renewed organizational reality.

What happens when a cognitive type is not available on the team? Theoretically, a cognitive (and therefore behavioural) void exists. There is no one with the cognitive preference needed to influence the renewal process in the desired way at a particular stage. If, however, there exists within the group an awareness of the need for different types of cognition and behaviour, as well as some capacity to perform the role, then it is possible that one or more members of the team may spontaneously assume the 'vacant' role. In this process of self-organization the renewal process proceeds by evoking the needed but less preferred cognitive processes from members of the management team. Organizational adaption and individual learning are combined.

Implications for top management groups

The CM model generates a number of insights into the composition of, and processes within, top management teams. From a prescriptive point of view, the CM model suggests that an 'ideal' top management group would be made up of individuals capable of functioning in each of the four cognitive modes. Since individuals seem to have stable cognitive preferences (Myers and McCaulley, 1985), an 'ideal' team needs several different 'types' of individuals to assume the variety of roles required. The general implication is that in addition to the Sensing and Thinking modes implied by the SM model, Intuition and Feeling modes are required by the CM model. All four modes need to be represented within the effective top management group and utilized in the management process.

From a descriptive point of view, cognitive composition might be expected to evolve as an organization matures. One would expect founders of organizations to be predominantly intuitive in their gathering of information, and to evaluate information using the feeling mode. As organizations mature, intuition and feeling would be expected to give way to sensation and thinking. Although it need not necessarily be the case, the latter style can easily drive out the former. This occurs most dramatically when founders leave (or are forced out) and replaced by 'professional managers', those trained in the SM methodology. More generally, differences in composition within the top management group can be expected to change as an organization develops, and these differences are expected to yield different patterns of behaviour. However, the actions of an organization are not directly impacted by the cognitive preferences of this group and the integration of these behaviours into a pattern of organizational actions which impacts strategy and performance.

BUSINESS STRATEGY AND THE CREATIVE MANAGEMENT MODEL

The CM model is basically an adaptive process and, as such, relates best to strategy concepts, which share this perspective. For example, Miles and Snow (1978: 21) recognized that 'The strategic-choice approach essentially argues that the effectiveness of organizational adaption hinges on *the dominant coalition's perceptions* of environmental conditions and the decisions it makes concerning how the organization will cope with these conditions' (emphasis added). Based upon their empirical observations,

Miles and Snow (1978: 14) identified four patterns of behaviour which they reduced to four strategic archetypes, 'representing alternative ways of moving through the adaptive cycle'. These are defender, prospector, analyser and reactor. Unfortunately, Miles and Snow do not link these types to their underlying concern with the perceptual abilities of the dominant coalition. And while they recognize prospectors as more innovative and willing to experiment with new ideas than their other strategy types, they do not provide much insight into how perceptions impact this process. Furthermore, there is little sense of how established business logics are changed, how unconventional ideas are incorporated into established business strategies. They do not directly address the question of renewal.

In our view, truly prospecting organizations have dominant coalitions which search for new ways of doing business and continually use visions of possible futures, ideas about new and different ways of doing business, to feed forward into present behaviour and actions. By contrast, in preserving organizations past norms and traditions feed back to dominate present behaviour. As shown in Figure 21.2, when viewed in this way, the CM model can be used to distinguish between organizations with a preference for either prospecting or preserving strategies.

The management groups in both prospecting and preserving organizations are oriented towards the intuition and feeling levels of the CM model. Preserving managements are able, with their intuitive ability, to perceive patterns in past decisions, actions and events: and by way of their feeling level they extract and express meaning from their firm's past. They have a strong sense of history and tradition; 'what we have been'. Their orientation is towards the past. Prospective management use the same cognitive abilities (intuition and feeling) but focus them on the future; 'what we might become'. Although both types of organization must function in the perpetual 'now', they do so with different (subjective) time orientations; the managements of prospecting organizations are oriented towards the potential of what might be, the future; in the preserving organization the orientation is towards the remembrance of what has been, the realized vision, the past.

Prospecting organizations can be expected to be radical innovators, willing to experiment with new ideas that do not fit within the accepted logic for business. In preserving organizations realized vision and tradition guide action, resulting in an adherence to past strategies; even incremental adjustments may be difficult because intentions and results are evaluated against values (at the feeling level), not standards derived from a logic (at the thinking level). Both of these strategies, because vision and values drive behaviours, often lack the coherence in their actions that is provided by the thinking-planning level. Furthermore, these organizations are not highly responsive to direct environmental stimuli.

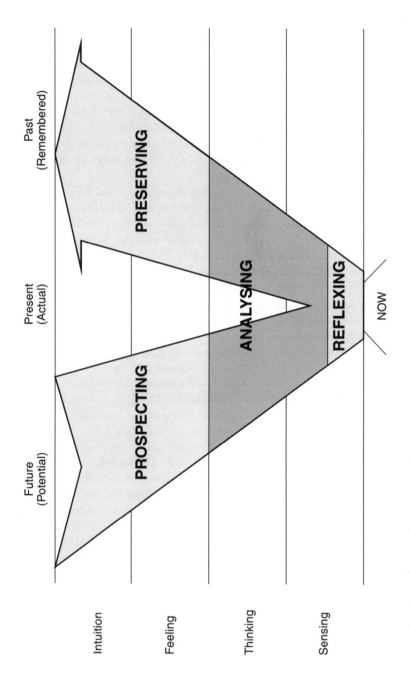

Figure 21.2 Strategy and the creative management model

Within the context of the CM model, the dominant coalition of an analysing organization can be seen as more oriented towards the present than either their preserving or prospecting counterparts. It also functions more at the thinking and sensing levels; less so at the intuition and feeling levels. As a consequence the management of an analysing organization is less accepting of radical, unproven ideas than the pure prospecting organization, but also less bound by tradition than a preserving organization. Accordingly, the analysing organization is less likely to be first with a radical innovation, although it may follow an initiative of a prospecting firm once it can be rationalized. It is not just the (subjective) time orientation of the management of an analysing organization that prevents it from pursuing radical innovations. This inability is also bound up in the interrelated issue of their preferred or dominant cognitive function: thinking and sensing. The management of an analysing organization functions more at the thinking and sensing levels, and therefore needs to develop a plausible logic before action. However, the actions they do take are well planned and a coherent extension of the established logic.

The remaining strategy orientation outlined in Figure 21.2 is the reflexing organization. Reflexing organizations (and their managers) exist only in the here and now. They have no view of their firm's future, nor sense of its past. Their behaviours are guided by instinctive or reflex responses to given stimuli. They do not attempt to understand their behaviours and actions, either before or after these actions occur. They function solely at the sensation level. Such organizations are highly responsive to a given set of environmental stimuli, but should the environment and the appropriate response pattern change these organizations are unable to adapt, to learn new behaviours.

Given the strategy types identified within the CM model – prospecting, analysing, reflexing and preserving – what are the corresponding organizational attributes? Consistent with Miles and Snow's original observation about the importance of the dominant coalition's perceptions, the CM model links perception and cognitive preferences, suggesting that the composition of the top management teams and their mix of cognitive and time orientations is the key to understanding this conception of organization strategy.

Prescriptively it would appear that organizations able to renew themselves need some of the attributes of each strategy orientation. The ideal management team needs both prospecting and preserving abilities; these combine a basis in its past with the ability to create its future. This is the problem of renewal: preserving the core of the business while allowing for the ongoing redefinition of that core. Like Janus, the Roman god of the threshold, truly adaptive organizations and their management teams simultaneously look forward, and create their future; and back, and appreciate their past. However, they also strive to understand their actions, and anticipate outcomes while being responsive to environmental stimuli. Even though a balance of all strategy orientations might be desirable, it seems likely that most organizations, like most individuals, will have a distinct preference.

Strategy and the composition of top management

The composition and interactions of the top management group affect behaviours which are ultimately reflected in the decisions and actions of the organization. Therefore, differences in composition of the management group should be manifested in patterns of action, that is in strategies (Mintzberg, 1978). The behaviours of the dominant coalition derived from the CM model can be related to the different cognitive types. Accordingly, relationships between the makeup of top management group and the strategic types of Preserving, Analysing, Reflexing and Prospecting can be hypothesized (see Table 21.4). The assertions made are largely descriptive. Prescriptive statements require a link to behaviours, patterns of actions and performance.

ON CAUSALITY

To this point the discussion has been largely conceptual, linking cognitive styles, behaviours, team composition and decisions and actions. However, it is recognized that other factors, like personal background and skills, influence managerial behaviours; as do organizational context factors, such as hierarchy, norms, rules, and decision-making style.

Table 21.4 **Hypothesized relationship between cognitive composition of the dominant coalition and business strategy**

	Dominant coalition's	
Cognitive composition	*Time orientation*	*Strategy orientation*
Mostly Intuitives with some Feelers	Future	Prospecting
Mostly Thinkers with some Sensors	Near Term Future and Past	Analysing
Mostly Sensors	Now	Reflexing
Mostly Feelers with some Intuitives	Past	Preserving
Mix of Intuitives, Feelers, Thinkers and Sensors	Future ↔ Past	Renewing

Empirical evidence

A complete review of the empirical work related to the CM model and top management team composition is beyond the scope of this chapter. However, this section will examine some of the existing work, much of which indirectly supports aspects of the CM framework.

Much research has focused on the relationship between background characteristics of managers and firm performance. After an extensive review of this literature Hambrick and Mason (1984: 203) observed: 'It is doubtful that this research stream can progress far without greater attention to relevant literature in related fields, especially psychology and social psychology.' This chapter attempts to progress from a psychological base while forging the link to decisions and patterns of action (i.e. strategy) for the enterprise. For the sake of simplicity and brevity, the discussion of empirical support for the model will focus on key relationships.

Team composition → decisions/actions/performance

Miles and Snow (1978) observed patterns in action, strategies, consistent with the CM process. Moreover, their strategy typology has been found to be reasonably descriptive of observed strategic attributes (Hambrick, 1983b). However, their observations about the composition of the dominant coalition are limited to functional backgrounds. For Defenders they note that the dominant coalition was typically composed of the general managers, the controller, and the heads of production and sales. They go on to state: 'the Prospector's dominant coalition centres around the marketing and research and development functions. Moreover, the Prospector's dominant coalition is also larger, more diverse and more transitory than the Defender's.' Their rationale is based upon the fit between managerial skills and the technical task requirements of the strategy. Although relationships have been observed between functional background and cognitive preference (McKenny and Keen, 1974; Macdaid *et al.*, 1986) no link was made by Miles and Snow to underlying psychological or cognitive attributes of the top management group.

Individual differences within top management teams such as age (Child, 1974), functional track record, education (Kimberley and Evanisko, 1981) and job tenure (Carlson, 1972) have been studied. These variables are usually recognized as proxy for some underlying psychological dimension (e.g. cognitive style, time orientation, tolerance for ambiguity), and used because they are more easily measured. In reviewing the literature on the relationship between background characteristics of top managers and organizational actions and performance, Hambrick and Mason (1984) developed a list of propositions based on demonstrated associations. However, this approach has several problems, First and foremost the propositions lack a consistent conceptual view of the top management group and its role in moving the organization forward. Second, the variables are not clearly related to broader theories of personality, or behaviour. Third, despite the observation that the group and group heterogeneity are significant factors, most of the work in this area seems to view the group as uniform. Most work employs either an average measure for attributes of the top management group, or selects one executive, usually the general manager, as singularly important.

A major empirical study associating underlying psychological variables and team performance was done by Belbin (1981). He administered a battery of psychological tests to executives taking part in a management training course. During this course, managers participated in business simulations. Team composition was varied and performance was measured. Evidence from this research suggests that:

1　The effectiveness of a team will be promoted by the extent to which members correctly recognize and adjust themselves to the relative strengths within the team, both in expertise and ability to engage in specific team-roles.
2　Personal qualities fit members for some team-roles while limiting the likelihood that they will succeed in others (Belbin, 1981: 132–133).

Belbin's work, although illuminating and highly descriptive, was not done in managerial settings. Neither was it a test, nor development of a theory of management team effectiveness.

Some work on team composition and effectiveness using Jungian types has been conducted. Blaylock (1983), employing a production simulation with business students, formed 17 groups, four mixed complementary types and 13 compatible or relatively uniform types. Three of the four mixed groups finished in the top five, a significant relationship.

The assertion that heterogeneous groups are more effective than homogeneous groups is not new. Filley et al. (1976) surveyed the literature on group dynamics and concluded that novel problems are best handled by a heterogeneous group and routing problems most efficiently dealt with by a homogeneous group. A concurring note was stated by Ziller (1972). Reviewing studies from further afield, he too found that performance is enhanced in groups with heterogeneity in membership. Rather than differentiate on problem types, he suggested that short-term groups ought to have homogeneous membership while long-standing groups have heterogeneous membership. He concluded that heterogeneity on a wide variety of variables including race, age, ability and personality and training in group dynamics, improved productivity.

Indeed, the outstanding question pertains not so much to the situational conditions favouring heterogeneity but rather to the appropriate dimensions for the heterogeneity, given the issues being considered. Addressing this question requires a conceptual perspective. The perspective of the CM model links the executive function of business renewal to cognitive preferences to managerial behaviours and organizational action.

Cognitive modes → behaviours

The empirical link between the group composition based upon differences or similarities in cognitive preferences and outcomes from group activity is sparse. Evidence associating individual behaviours and cognitive preference is more prevalent.

Several studies have indicated a link between MBTI (Myers–Briggs Type Indicator) and behavioural patterns. Mitroff and Kilmann (1975), Mitroff *et al.* (1977), and Hellriegel and Slocum (1980) have researched how different types view ideal organizations and their heroes. Most of these support the relationships posited by Myers (1962). They found that Sensing–Thinking managers concentrated on specific, factual details, preferring situations in which there is certainty, specificity and control. Their heroes used others to get things done; they were problem-solvers. Intuitive–Thinking managers focused on broad, global issues, general concepts and ill-defined macro-level goals. Their heroes were broad conceptualizers and problem-framers. Sensing–Feeling managers were more concerned with specific people issues, not tasks. Their heroes created personal, warm climates and made organizations like 'home'. Finally Intuitive–Feeling managers focused on broad global themes serving mankind. Their heroes were able to envision new goals and create organizations with a personal sense.

Reporting on the validity of MBTI, Carlyn (1977) states that Intuitives are more likely to participate in imagined events and engage in possibilities while Sensors prefer a command of reality. Although validity studies have been done relating MBTI scores to other personality measures, very little evidence is available linking MBTI directly to managerial behaviours. To the extent that profession and position correlate to behaviours, the data presented in Table 21.5 tend to inferentially support the relationships posited in Table 21.3.

As a group, management consultants and high-level executives have a predominant thinking preference for evaluating information; as one would expect, consultants prefer to gather their information more broadly and look for whole relationships (intuition preference). Practising managers, be they high-level executives, supervisors, accountants or small business managers, have a stronger preference for grounding their information gathering in the immediate representations of the world with which they must deal (sensation preference). Moreover, the proportions of cognitive

Table 21.5 **Cognitive style by profession and managerial position**

	Information gathering		Information evaluation		
	Intuition	*Sensing*	*Thinking*	*Feeling*	η
Managerial					
Management consultants	58%	42%	92%	8%	71
High-level executives	43%	57%	90%	10%	136
Supervisors and managers	42%	58%	64%	36%	3678
Accountants	38%	62%	59%	41%	427
Small-business managers	14%	86%	81%	19%	150
Other professions					
Artists	91%	9%	30%	70%	114
Architects	82%	18%	56%	44%	124
Steelworkers	14%	86%	74%	26%	105
Teachers (grades 1–12)	26%	74%	31%	69%	281

types do appear to differ by level in the hierarchy. Roach (1986) distinguishes between supervisors, managers and executives and reports that 'over half the executives were Intuition–Thinking' while for supervisors Sensation-Thinking was the largest category. Sensation–Feeling declined dramatically in relation to increasing organizational level.

While intuitive preference appears to increase modestly with level in hierarchy, it varies more dramatically among professions. As shown in Table 21.5, professions requiring a high degree of creativity (artists and architects) have a strong intuition preference. Architects, however, deal with a technical subject and tend towards the thinking preference for evaluating the content of their intuitive insights. Artists, unconstrained by many technical requirements, evaluate their insights based upon feelings. Teachers and steelworkers, by way of further example, whose professions require them to deal with and respond to direct stimuli, have a stronger sensation preference. Dealing with children, most teachers (grades 1 to 12) evaluate stimuli using feeling; while steelworkers working with a process technology prefer thinking.

While these data are provocative, they do not directly address the question of whether or not cognitive preferences are associated with the behaviours expected at the different levels of the CM model. These questions need to be addressed by empirical research.

TOWARDS RESEARCH

Empirical work from other areas tends to support the general relationships implied by the SM model for the composition of top management groups. However, many linkages in the framework need empirical testing. Our global proposition is that the composition of the top management group will affect firm strategy and performance. More specifically, it is proposed that the task variety implied by the CM model requires cognitive style difference within the top management group. However, diversity alone does not ensure effectiveness. The organization must transcend this diversity. We suspect that the patterns of interaction amongst the contributors to strategic actions – who interacts with whom and how they interact – will be a critical aspect of this transcendence.

Although conceptually appealing and with some empirical support, major questions remain to be resolved as the empirical study of top management groups proceeds. These include:

1 What is meant by top management teams? Is the team the management committee? Is membership determined by hierarchical position? Are they the psychometrically determined contributors to major decisions? Does membership vary by decision? Can a parsimonious classification of top management teams be determined?

2 Are effective top management teams composed of individuals exhibiting behaviour required by the CM model? Are these behaviours distributed among team members as would be predicted on the basis of their cognitive style, or are they distributed on some other basis? Are they integrative/facilitative behaviours exhibited by those with other substantive contributions the CM process or do they require specific individuals with different cognitive styles or personalities? Do behavioural patterns account for differences in firm performance or is it just sufficient to see the total set exhibited by the group?

Addressing these issues will require a variety of approaches and research methodologies.

Approaches to researching top management teams

There are two broad ways to approach answering the questions raised above. One is to take the theory to practice, the other is to bring practice to theory.

Theory to practice

This approach calls for the explicit statement of testable hypotheses, tight experimental designs and valid measuring tools. Because of the complexity of the phenomenon under study it is advisable first to conduct tests of these hypotheses under highly controlled conditions. We believe that well-developed behavioural simulations[1] provide many of the controls necessary, but recreate real life sufficiently well to be used as vehicles for such tests.

The following propositions could be tested through these simulations:

1 Individuals with certain cognitive styles exhibit specified behaviour, or a cluster of behaviours.
2 Exhibited behaviours cluster to reflect contributions to the levels of the CM process.
3 Certain patterns of interaction are better able to transcend these differences than others.
4 The behaviours and interaction patterns result in the expected patterns in action.

A simple research design would involve assigning individuals to top management teams (TMTs) on the basis of their MBTI types to create both homogeneous and heterogeneous groups. All groups then participate in a behavioural simulation. Following the simulation, participants are asked to complete a behavioural checklist (who did what) and asked to indicate who played what role. Linkages in the logic can be tested. Additional studies can test the effectiveness of different interventions prior to the simulation.

Practice to theory

Generalizability is limited with the designs mentioned above. Simulations, no matter how well developed, cannot completely replicate real life. They may unduly force individuals into roles and behaviours they would not otherwise exhibit, and they may impose norms on group behaviour that do not reflect the real-life behaviour of top management teams. Concurrent with highly controlled theory-to-practice design, real-life top management teams should be observed.

Initially this research should be descriptive. It is hoped that intensive clinical studies of a sample of top management teams would provide the basis for a parsimonious classification of teams. The stability of team membership, who contributes to key decisions and actions, could be examined both over time and over situations. Behaviours exhibited by individuals in different roles can be observed. With a taxonomy of teams and a more detailed behavioural checklist developed, larger-scale research could be conducted to test hypotheses emanating from the theoretical framework. Structured interviews and data collection could be conducted with members of a variety of top management teams. Administered instruments would include measures of cognitive preferences and other behavioural predispositions, checklists of behaviour to be completed of self and other top management team members. Performance of the teams could be measured, and effectiveness accounted for, on the basis of individual background and behavioural difference.

Although little has been said in this chapter about patterns of interaction among team members, it is clear that performance cannot be thought of strictly as a function of team composition. The case studies and survey research could also be useful for observing, documenting and understanding patterns of interaction. For example, do heterogeneous teams which operate with low status and power differentials outperform those that operate on the basis of hierarchical positions? Does job context suppress or extinguish intrinsic cognitive preferences?

Both types of research should proceed concurrently. Much can be learned from one that is useful to the other. Through studies of managers in simulated settings, reliable measures of behaviour could be developed. The validity of these measures could then be assessed in the field. Other intervening variables discovered in the field studies can be manipulated experimentally or statistically in subsequent laboratory studies.

TOWARDS PRACTICE

The ideas of teamwork at the top, cognitive style and innovation are not new to practising managers (Rowan, 1979; Sherman, 1984; Moore, 1987). Furthermore, Jungian concepts and MBTI types are to a limited extent already being used to help managers better understand their organizations (Mitroff and Kilmann, 1975; Mason and Mitroff, 1981; Moore, 1987). The CM model synthesizes many of these ideas as they relate to the executive function of business renewal. It infers roles, behaviours and differences in cognitive type for the top management group.

The conceptual insights can still be of use to practitioners even though as yet unsupported by detailed direct evidence. The CM model provides managers with an understanding that can make them more aware of their own behaviours and tolerant of others', especially when they appreciate the individual differences in cognitive preference which underlie those behaviours, and that such behaviours may play an important role in the CM process. In other words, it can be hoped that a conceptual understanding will result in behavioural awareness and modification.

If those responsible for the overall direction of the enterprise were aware of the behavioural requirement of its members as posited by the CM model they could use that understanding in several ways. First, an examination of the members of the TMT may reveal that they are inclined to exhibit the required behaviours, but feel, because of organizational factors, that they cannot do so. A further examination of the cultural norms, power relationships and the reward systems might reveal that those behaviours were discouraged or even punished. It might be a relatively easy step to legitimize those previously suppressed behaviours.

Often a change of context can help. The 'outward-bound' experience for managers, by providing a dramatic shift in context and in some respects tasks, presents an opportunity for latent preferences, suppressed in the normal organization context, to surface. It is well accepted that children learn through play. However, playful experiences for managers need not always occur outside the normal organizational context. It is now being suggested that certain organizational activities be conducted in a playful manner in order to facilitate institutional learning (Rutenberg, 1986; de Geus, 1988).

A second, and possibly a more controversial, use would be to employ the CM model for selection to, and development of, the TMT. With an understanding of the model those responsible for these activities might attend to, document and evaluate the behaviours of potential or current members of the TMT in terms of cognitive type. These behaviours, framed within the CM model, could be assessed and used as one criterion for selection. Development activities might also be suggested for some members who could most likely exhibit certain required behaviours. As a cautionary note, we do not believe that use of the MBTI as a cognitive indicator is warranted at this time. The test was not developed, nor has sufficient evidence of reliability and predictive validity been shown, for use in selection or promotion decisions. However, we do feel that Jung's conception of cognitive types does provide a useful way for managers to appreciate observable, individual behaviours and their contribution to the process of organizational renewal.

Throughout these brief suggestions for practice, the emphasis has been on behaviour. Managers attempting to employ the CM model should adopt a similar perspective. It is the insights into the behaviours of the TMT provided by the model that have the greatest utility.

SUMMARY/CONCLUSIONS

This chapter attempts to build a model of the behavioural requirements for the top management team from two perspectives. First, from the perspective of the individual, it is posited that the behaviours relevant to the renewal function of the executive which need to be exhibited by top managers are at least partly a function of their cognitive preferences. It is argued that the Jungian/Myers–Briggs typology is consistent with the model of renewal based upon the creative management (CM) model and an established framework for understanding and predicting these behaviours. Second, it has been asserted that organizations will evolve a pattern of actions, a strategy reflecting the cognitive composition of the top management team. As the cognitive preferences of the top management group vary so too will strategy.

It is suggested that research follow both a theory-to-practice and practice-to-theory approach, simultaneously developing theory and testing specific hypotheses about team composition and patterns of interaction.

This chapter makes a case for a management process that utilizes the full range of human potential. The need for a CM model to replace the conventional strategic management framework has been argued on the basis of the latter's inability to utilize the full range of cognitive functions and accordingly its failure to promote new and innovative strategies. The CM model, however, has implications for the dominant coalition. Since theory and evidence suggests individuals have superior or dominant functions, a mixture of cognitive types is implied. The CM process suggests that top management groups not only include the Thinkers and Sensors needed by the SM process but also embrace the Intuitives and Feelers needed to generate and infuse unconventional insights and new ideas. But difference without synthesis is anarchy. The organization and its members must also have the ability to achieve unity from diversity, the ability to transcend.

NOTE

1 Simulations developed by the Center for Creative Leadership, Greensbors, NC, and by the Management Simulations Project Group, New York University, are examples.

REFERENCES

Barnard, C.I. (1938) *The Functions of the Executive*, Harvard University Press, Cambridge, MA.
Belbin, R.M. (1981) *Management Teams: Why They Succeed or Fail*, Heinemann, London.
Blaylock, B.K. (1983) 'Teamwork in a simulated production environment', *Research in Psychological Type*, 6, pp. 58–67.
Bower, J.L. (1982) 'Solving the problems of business planning', *Journal of Business Strategy*, 2(3), Winter, pp. 32–44.
Carlson, R.O. (1972) *School Superintendents: Careers and Performance*, Merrill, Columbia, OH.
Carlyn, M. (1977) 'An assessment of the Myers–Briggs type indicator', *Journal of Personality Assessment*, 41, pp. 461–473.
Child, J. (1974) 'Managerial and organizational factors associated with company performance', *Journal of Management Studies*, 11, pp. 13–27.
Cyert, R.M. and J.G. March (1963) *A Behavioral Theory of the Firm*, Prentice-Hall, Englewood Cliffs, NJ.
De Geus, A.P. (1988) 'Planning as learning', *Harvard Business Review*, March–April, pp. 62–69.
Filley, A.C., R.J. House and S. Kerr (1976) *Managerial Process and Organizational Behavior*, Scott Foresman, Glenview, IL.
Follett, M.P. (1941) *Dynamic Administration: the Collected Papers of Mary Park Follett*, edited by H. Metcalf and L. Urwick, Harper & Bros, New York.

Friedlander, F. (1983) 'Patterns of individual and organizational learning'. In S. Srivesta and Associates, *The Executive Mind*, Jossey-Bass, San Francisco, CA.

Galbraith, J. (1973) *Designing Complex Organizations*, Addison-Wesley, Reading, MA.

Gardener, H. (1985) *The Mind's New Science: A History of the Cognitive Revolution*, Basic Books, New York.

Greenleaf, R.K. (1977) *Servant Leadership*, Paulist Press, New York.

Hambrick, D.C. (1983a) 'High profit strategies in mature capital goods industries: a contingency approach', *Academy of Management Journal*, **26**(4), pp. 687–707.

Hambrick, D.C. (1983b) 'Some tests of the effectiveness and functional attributes of Miles and Snow's strategic types', *Academy of Management Journal*, **26**(1), pp. 5–26.

Hambrick, D.C. (1987) 'The top management team: key to strategic success', *California Management Review*, Fall, pp. 88–108.

Hambrick, D.C. and P.A. Mason (1984) 'Upper echelons: the organization as a reflection of its top managers', *Academy of Management Review*, **9**(2), pp. 193–206.

Hampden-Turner, C. (1981) *Maps of the Mind*, Macmillan, New York.

Hellriegel, D. and J.W. Slocum (1980) 'Preferred organizational designs and problem solving styles: interesting companions', *Human Systems Management*, **1**, pp. 151–158.

Hurst, D.K. (1986) 'Why strategic management is bankrupt', *Organizational Dynamics*, Autumn, pp. 5–27.

Jaques, E. (1982) *The Form of Time*, Crane Russak, New York.

Jung, C.G. (1960) 'The structure and dynamics of the psyche'. In *Collected Works*, vol. 8, Princeton University Press, Princeton, NJ.

Keirsey, D.W. and M. Bates (1978) *Please Understand Me*, Prometheus Nemesis Books, Del Mar, CA.

Kimberley, J.R. and M.J. Evanisko (1981) 'Organizational innovation: the influence of individual, organizational and contextual factors on hospital adoption of technological and administrative innovations', *Academy of Management Journal*, **24**, pp. 689–713.

Koestler, A. (1976) *The Act of Creation*, Hutchinson, London.

Lawrence, P.R. and J.W. Lorsch (1969) *Organization and Environment*, R.D. Irwin, Homewood, IL.

Macdaid, G.P., M.H. McCaulley and R.I. Kainz (1986) *Atlas of Type Tables*, Center for Applications of Psychological Types, Gainesville, FL.

McKenny, J.L. and P.G.W Keen (1974) 'How managers' minds work', *Harvard Business Review*, May–June, pp. 79–90.

Mann, H., M. Siegler and H. Osmond (1971) 'The psychotypology of time'. In H. Yaker, H. Osmond and F. Cheek (eds) *The Future of Time: Man's Temporal Environment*, Doubleday, Garden City, NY, pp. 142–178.

Mason, R.O. and I.I. Mitroff (1981) *Challenging Strategic Planning Assumptions*, John Wiley & Sons, New York.

Miles, R.E. and C.C. Snow (1978) *Organizational Strategy, Structure and Process*, McGraw-Hill, New York.

Mintzberg, H. (1976) 'Planning on the left side and managing on the right', *Harvard Business Review*, July–August, pp. 49–58.

Mintzberg, H. (1978) 'Patterns in strategy formation', *Management Science*, **24**, pp. 934–948.

Mitroff, I.I. and R.H. Kilmann (1975) 'Stories managers tell: a new tool for organizational problem solving', *Management Review*, **64**(7), pp. 18–28.

Mitroff, I., V. Barabba and R. Kilmann (1977) 'The application of behavioral and philosophical technologies to strategic planning: a case study of a large federal agency', *Management Science*, **24**, pp. 44–58.

Moore, T. (1987) 'Personality tests are back', *Fortune*, 30 March, pp. 74–82.

Myers, I.B. (1962) *Introduction to Type*, Consulting Psychologists Press, Palo Alto, CA.

Myers, I.B. and M.H. McCaulley (1985) *Manual: A Guide to the Development and Use of the Myers–Briggs Type Indicator*, Consulting Psychologists Press, Palo Alto, CA.

Pascale, R.T. (1984) 'Perspectives on strategy: the real story behind Honda's success', *California Management Review*, Spring, pp. 47–72.

Peters, T.J. and R.H. Waterman (1983) 'Beyond the rational model', *The McKinsey Quarterly*, Spring, pp. 19–30.

Prahalad, C.K. and R.A. Bettis (1986) 'The dominant logic: a new linkage between diversity and performance', *Strategic Management Journal*, 7, pp. 485–501.

Roach, B. (1986) 'Organizational decision-makers: different types for different levels', *Journal of Psychological Type*, 12, pp. 16–24.

Rowan, R. (1979) 'Those business hunches are more than blind faith', *Fortune*, 23 April, pp. 110–114.

Rutenberg, D. (1986) 'Playful Plans', Working paper, Queens University, Canada.

Sherman, S.P. (1984) 'Eight big masters of innovation', *Fortune*, 15 October, pp. 66–78.

Simon, H.A. (1988) 'Understanding creativity and creative management'. In R.L. Kuhn (ed.) *Handbook for Creative and Innovative Managers*, McGraw-Hill, New York.

Taggart, W. and D. Robey (1981) 'Minds and managers: on the dual nature of human information processing and management', *Academy of Management Review*, 6(2), pp. 187–195.

Thompson, J.D. (1967) *Organizations in Action*, McGraw-Hill, New York.

Watson, J.D. (1969) *The Double Helix*, Mentor Books, New York.

Weick, K.E. (1979) *The Social Psychology of Organizing*, Addison-Wesley, Reading, MA.

Worthy, J.C. (1984) *Shaping an American Institution: Robert E. Wood and Sears, Roebuck*, University of Illinois Press, Chicago, IL.

Ziller, R.C. (1972) 'Homogeneity and heterogeneity of group membership'. In C.G. McClintoch (ed.) *Experimental Social Psychology*, Holt, Rinehart & Winston, New York.

Index

Entries shown in bold type are contributions to this volume.

of learning process 284–6;
management by wandering around
(MBWA) 40; paradigm shift in 9,
35, 49, 67; and performance 103–4,
382, 399–401; post-entrepreneurial
role 47; rational model 8–9, 32–41,
125, 381–2, 383, 384; strategy
formulation role 140; traditional
'top-down' 209–10, 214; *see also*
creative management; middle
management; participative
management; program
management; strategic
management; top management
management development 232–41,
247–53, 255–6, 311–12, 379; *see also*
training
management education 143, 277–86;
Crotonville Management
Development Institute (GE) 243–57
management information systems
(MIS) 186, 188, 328–30
management innovation 264, 316–33,
370; and systems thinking 318–20
market segmentation 34
Marketing Science Institute, PIMS
programme 102
Mason, P.A. *see* Hambrick, D.C. and
Mason, P.A.
Mason, R. and Mitroff, I. 294
Master of Business Administration
(MBA) 8
matching: idea generators and
sponsors 169; knowledge of needs
and means 170
matrix organization structure 36, 129,
185–6; Ford 218–19, 226–7
Matsushita Electric Company 18,
20–3, 31
Maytag 38
Mazda 131, 214, 289; product
development in 30, 214, 217–18,
224–6, 289
mental models: learning to change
14–15, 94–5, 97–9, 295; managing
313; and organizational culture
98–9; surfacing and testing 88–91,
264, 300–1, 308–10; transforming
individual into team 97–8;
unlearning 117–18; and views of
reality 296–7; *see also* dominant
logic; organizational culture;
schemas

mentors 152
Merck 136
mergers *see* acquisitions and mergers
Merrill Lynch 137
metaphors 19, 24–5, 28–9
Michael, D.N. 118
middle management 31, 162, 230,
401–2
Miles, R.E. and Snow, C.C. 10, 394–5,
397, 399
Miles, R.H. 104
Miller, L. 297
Minnesota Mining and
Manufacturing (3M) 38, 40, 112,
147; incentives and rewards 147,
174, 175–6; innovatory 127, 136,
143, 168, 169
Mintzberg, H. 1, 8, 10, 261–2, 294
mission: collateral design 188–9, 196;
Ford's changing 368, 369, 371, 373,
374; and program management
objectives 218–19; and role of
leadership 297–8
mistakes and failures 38–9, 151, 350
MIT New Management Style Project
264, 317, 318, 320, 330–2
Mitroff, I. 296; *see also* Mason, R. and
Mitroff, I.
Mitsubishi 93
modernity 125
Montgomery, C. 102, 103
motivation: in high-performing
systems 13, 63–4; and job design
148; and job rotation 148, 177
multinational companies: strategic
management 378–9; top
management as executive tourists
267, 374–8
Myers Briggs Type Indicator (MBTI)
379, 387, 401, 405–6
Myers, I.B. 387
myths: impact on innovation 153–4;
leadership 13, 69–70;
organizational 268

Nadler, D. *see* Tushman, M. and
Nadler, D.
Nathanson, D. and Cassano, J. 101
National Science Foundation,
Engineering Research Center (ERC)
330–2
NCR 145
NEC 18, 29, 225–6